D0179359

# White Men Challenging Racism:

## 35 Personal Stories

Cooper Thompson, Emmett Schaefer, and Harry Brod

With a Foreword by James W. Loewen

Duke University Press  Durham & London  2003

© 2003 Duke University Press

All rights reserved

Printed in the United States of

America on acid-free paper ∞

Designed by Amy Ruth Buchanan

Typeset in Dante and Clarendon

by Keystone Typesetting, Inc.

Library of Congress Cataloging-

in-Publication Data appear on the

last printed page of this book.

A stage version of *Just Living*,

adapted and directed by Jana

Gymer-Koch and Lucas Messer, was

first performed on October 24,

2002 at the Interpreters Theatre

of the University of Northern

Iowa, under the directorship of

Dr. Karen Mitchell and with the

technical assistance of Dr. Paul

Siddens.

White Men Challenging Racism

This book is dedicated

to the many people of color

who have been the conscience,

catalyst, and inspiration for

white men challenging racism.

They have made this book

possible.

As James Baldwin wrote, the white man here is trapped by his own history, a history that he himself cannot comprehend and therefore what can I do but love him?

Carroll O'Connor (on his Archie Bunker character from the TV show *All in the Family*). Quoted in the *Chicago Tribune*, June 22, 2001, after O'Connor's death.

# Contents

## Movement Elders

*You have to inform yourself of the realities of history, of what slavery was, of what Black people, especially Black women, went through. And you have to learn about the postslavery so-called freedom. . . . And knowing that we white people are responsible for the horror. Therefore, if we have some conscience, we should be very important in eliminating the horror. That's my life.*

*In the 1940s . . . I was infiltrating the Klan and feeding the minutes to both Drew Pearson and to the producers of the radio show* Superman *who were doing a series,* Superman versus the Grand Dragon. *As fast as the Klan would change its passwords for entrance to its meetings, I'd send 'em on up to the radio producers, and kids all over the country would all*

*have them the following week. In the minutes of the meetings I included the names of the businessmen and the politicians and the judges and lawmen who were in attendance. After their names were broadcast, they never showed up again at the meetings.*

*We had to make it possible for Blacks to live wherever they wanted to live, for Christ's sake. This was just a matter of ordinary humanity and justice and whatnot. That's what did it for me. That's what changed me from just another middle-class white guy trying to preserve property values into an increasingly militant housing integrationist.*

*The Sunday after Dr. King's assassination in 1968 . . . when I walked into the kitchen, Grandma Lushbough was ironing. I said to her, "I know what I must do with my life. I must work on the white problem." . . . You don't rush in, eager to help, eager to find the role—that wanting to rush in with the answer is sort of built into the psyche of a lot of us white men. You have to just let the relationship develop; you listen, and there comes a chance to say, "I can do that task." And you do it well, and eventually they'll begin to ask and trust you.*

51   Pat Cusick, 70, community organizer; Boston, MA
*The other two kids picked up rocks, threw them at the kid on the bicycle, and called him "nigger." . . . But this kid on the bike, who was smaller than us, he had guts. He stopped, got off his bike, and gave us a tongue lashing. . . . The actions of that Black kid certainly affected my life, piercing through my white privilege and the whole historical consciousness of growing up white in Alabama. . . . When I was sent to the chain gang in prison . . . I told the captain of the chain gang, using my best university manner, "Segregation is evil, and I can't participate in it. You have a segregated camp. I just want to inform you of this. I'm not going to work and I'm not going to eat while I'm here."*

60   Nat Yalowitz, 70, social worker and organizer; New York, NY
*Growing up meant living in hard poverty, being a witness to racial segregation, war, and social conflict. Fighting racial injustice and social class conflict became an essential part of my living. Being a left wing Jewish man meant participation in the movement to free oppressed people. Picket lines, marches on Washington— they were as essential as playing stickball as a kid.*

## Grassroots Organizing

73   Jesse Wimberley, 43, organizes working-class white men; West End, NC
*What fool would go up to a white male and say, "You ought to quit your good-paying job and try to do social change and ruin your family"? . . . Where are white men going to get support for change?*

82   Jim Hansen, 42, executive director, United Vision for Idaho; Boise, ID
*I joined the Chamber of Commerce in Boise. I have access to people in power because of my privilege. I wanted to exercise that privilege in a way that opens up greater opportunities for both learning and power for people of color and white women. . . . I'm in a rotary club, too. The question is whether and how you raise issues. . . . My role is to back up people of color and white women as they stick their necks out.*

90   Chip Berlet, 52, researches right wing groups; Cambridge, MA
*I learned two things from this experience. One, hate groups victimize communities that are in crisis and turn them toward white supremacy by building an identity among the young men. . . . Two, you can organize essentially prejudiced people to fight this hate, and that's a victory, even if on a very tiny level. You can't go in and eradicate white privilege overnight. If it means ten years to take a neighborhood from violence to peace, leaving unresolved lots of issues of prejudice, that's still worth it.*

## Art and Politics

152 Tim Wise, 33, writer, lecturer, social critic, and activist; Nashville, TN
*I'm not fighting racism for Black and Brown folks: they can and will, as always, save themselves. My role is in the white community. . . . I am beginning to think that whites are so dependent on people of color that we wouldn't know what to do without them. . . . If there were no Black and Brown folks around, then whites would have no one to blame but themselves for the crime that occurred; no one to blame but themselves when they didn't get the job they wanted; no one to blame but themselves when their lives turned out to be less than they expected.*

164 Billy Yalowitz, 42, community-based performance director and choreographer; Philadelphia, PA
*We know very little about humility, the loss of community, and how isolated we are from each other. That's a cost of whiteness and of being middle class, as we construct it—that you're special, that your knowledge separates you. You think you're smarter than other people. What a disability, to think that you're smarter.*

## Challenging the System from Within

175 John Allocca, 39, bilingual Spanish teacher; Boston, MA
*I say very honestly [to my students], "You have every right to have doubts about me and a lot of other white folks because we, as a people in general, have done you and your people wrong." . . . But there have been important allies.*

*Schools don't teach about John Brown to white kids or kids of color. . . . I tell my students that I grew up in a racist society and that I've changed because of my experiences living and working with people from different communities. When I was their age, I was a scared, confused young white boy who would never want to hang out with any of them.*

185 Bill Johnston, 60, former Boston police officer; Emerald Island, NC
*I have a vision that when we arrive at the Pearly Gates, we're going to find out that God is everything that we're not. If God made us all, then he is all of us. At my moment of death, the God who comes to judge me will be young, gay, Jewish, African American. And she is going to say, "How the hell did you treat me?"*

194 A. T. Miller, 43, teacher and director of multiculturalism at University of Michigan; Ann Arbor, MI
*When I was director of Africana Studies at Union, I took it as my responsibility to teach and lead in an African-centered style. . . . There is no ebony tower; this will always be community linked, always accessible; knowledge and research will always be shared. . . . I'm very uncomfortable in an all-white environment. . . . It makes me wonder if this is a hostile environment. Why would this be all white?*

203 Ken Kimerling, 56, lawyer for Puerto Rican and Asian American civil rights; New York, NY
*I do see myself as supportive; I'm more involved in supporting things that are*

happening than leading them. I've just sort of figured out what I can do and do well, and I'm not interested in leading something. I know what my strengths are, and that's not necessarily one of them. I feel I'm a better team player than the captain of the team. . . . I certainly live my job. Most of my waking hours, like everyone else's, are spent working. But this work is not something that I woke up one day and said, "I've got to go out and change the conditions of garment workers in Chinatown."

212 **Monte Piliawsky, 57, teacher and historian; Detroit, MI**
When I explain racism to a class and they begin to see for the first time that they have been victimized and how race is used to divide whites and Blacks for the benefit of capitalism and for their disadvantage, I feel alive. . . . I . . . think that whites want to be challenged. Deep down, many of us don't think we're very good people. But we want to be better. We want some redemption. So we like someone to confront us, and maybe in this way we will find a way to work through our insecurities.

222 **Lonnie Lusardo, 56, consultant and community organizer; Seattle, WA**
I don't go around singing "We are the world"; I get pissed off at people; I'm human. But I often think, "Wouldn't it be great if everybody at an organization felt as though they owned the company, truly owned the company, and enjoyed it?" If everybody who worked at an organization truly loved their job, what would the productivity be like? What would the profit be like?

228 **Lee Formwalt, 51, historian and dean at a historically black college; Albany, GA**
At that time I wasn't yet aware of my own racism and missed the obvious irony of changing my position because of what a young white Englishman said when I had been discounting the same thing when local Black people had been telling it to me. . . . As [my] kids got older . . . , I began to hear more about the fact that they were unhappy with my lack of sensitivity to their needs. They thought that I was more concerned with racial sensitivity than their particular concerns. That was a tough issue for me to deal with and still is today.

237 **Nibs Stroupe, 55, minister of a multiracial congregation; Decatur, GA**
This work is a calling for me on a theological level. . . . The people who taught me about God were strong, racist people. But they also taught me that God is the power of love. . . . My calling is to share that kind of love.

## Challenging the System from the Margins

249 **John Cole Vodicka, 53, founder of the Prison and Jail Project; Americus, GA**
Victories are few and far between, but sometimes we have a victory in the sense that something changes. A sheriff is run out of office, and for an instant, something is better for those who are in that jailhouse. . . . Even if those folks aren't run out of town or office, we can shake things up and get people asking questions. . . . This is a big part of what keeps me going.

258 Richard Lapchick, 56, advocate
for racial and gender justice
in sports and society;
Orlando, FL

*[My dad] had brought Nat "Sweetwater"
Clifton onto the New York Knicks
basketball team—that's what the
hanging and picketing and calls were all
about. Twenty-eight years later, in 1978,
my own son, who was five years old and
named after my dad, came to me one day.
He asked me, "Daddy, are you a nigger
lover?" I stepped back, paused for a few
seconds, and asked him, "Joey, what do
you think that is?" "I don't know, but
some mean man just called me on the
phone and told me you were one." . . .
They attacked me and caused liver
damage, kidney damage, a hernia, and
concussion. And they carved the word
"nigger" on my stomach with a pair of
office scissors.*

265 Chris Shuey, 46, environmental
health specialist; Albuquerque,
NM

*As a middle-aged guy looking back on
my life, I often wonder if it was a good
decision to leave Ohio as a young
man. . . . Whether it was good or not,
it's the choice I made and have lived with.
But sometimes I feel like maybe there's
part of my life that's now missing because
I'm not connected to the land where I was
raised. . . . As a result of living here and
being with the Navajo, I've been able to
understand and appreciate what it means
to be a land-based people.*

272 Terry Kupers, 58, psychiatrist,
prison activist, and author;
Oakland, CA

*Black people were saying, "You know,
we're not saying we don't want you.*

*We're just saying that we want you to
go organize white folks. We need you to
do that, and you need to listen to us."
I thought that was perfectly reasonable. . . . The Panthers asked me to set
up and work at their medical clinic. . . .
I taught a class to Movement activists
on health and how to handle any
emergency.*

280 Rick Whaley, 51, Native
American treaty rights
advocate; Milwaukee, WI

*I think about the skills I have from
raising a family and how that's connected
to building a political organization. Or
skills I learned in building a marriage
that are helpful when I'm facilitating a
meeting. . . . Being an interracial family
is connected to my getting involved up
north with the Witness for Nonviolence
for Treaty and Rural Rights in Northern
Wisconsin. It was a way to pay back
what I owed to the southern Civil Rights
Movement for making it possible for
interracial families like ours to live in
relative safety.*

289 Jim Murphy, 54, firefighter and
advocate for children's rights in
Southeast Asia; Boston, MA

*A firefighter presumed that I might be
gay. . . . It evolved into harassment. My
gear was sabotaged. . . . "One of the
reasons I'm sitting down with you
[Congressman Joe Moakley told East
Timor Action Network activists] is
because that firefighter over there has
been writing me and contacting my office
for several years about East Timor." I'm
very concerned about the tentacles of the
child sex trade. On my trips to East
Timor, I speak with religious activists,
NGO's, women activists, community
leaders.*

## The Next Generation

*The most important mission I have is challenging racism within the gay community. . . . I believe that race is a part of everything. It's part of the way we talk about "safety": is this a "good" neighborhood or a "bad" neighborhood? There's all sorts of code language. Race really permeates so much of the way we live, but it's this eight-hundred-pound gorilla that never gets addressed head on.*

*I can't talk about doing this work without talking about my spirituality. I don't know how other folks do this work without having a spiritual core. . . . My own journey in taking deliberate, proactive, public stances on antiracism in my own community has only been made possible out of my spiritual journey.*

*When I was seventeen, we were doing punk percussion protests against apartheid at the South African Embassy in Washington, D.C. It was a concrete way for those of us doing antiracism work to get in the streets and manifest how we felt. . . . The Zapatistas have always said, "Before you help me, go back to your own community, organize there, and do the work of liberation in your own community." If my liberation has been linked to my ability to "get real," my function with other white people is to help them achieve that, to "get real."*

*I'm proud about being a codirector who is always asking, "What are we doing about the racism in our own institution? What are we doing to challenge white privilege in this supposedly progressive organization?" . . . I don't like the way that whiteness has manifested itself in our society. I am profoundly displeased with what my culture has perpetuated in the United States. . . . And so I see my role as especially important in being what someone on a right wing talk show called me: a race traitor. . . . In some ways, I wear that as a badge of honor, that he thinks of me as a race traitor.*

*I'd never been face-to-face with Klan members like that. . . . They see themselves as fighting for the white race, but they don't speak for me, and I'm part of the white race. You carry everybody that you know with you when you're there. I speak for all these people when I go there—my mom, my dad, my family, my friends and their beliefs; I'm speaking for every organization I represent. . . . There's a rush to that because I know I have them behind me in spirit.*

# Foreword

## Challenging Racism, Challenging History

### James W. Loewen

Racist acts by white men in the Americas began on October 14, 1492, two days after the arrival of Christopher Columbus.[1] In his journal, Columbus tells about his actions that day: "These people are very unskilled in arms, as Your Highnesses will see from the seven whom I caused to be taken in order to carry them off."[2] Indeed he brought the seven Tainos back to Spain to show to his patrons, along with parrots and produce. Ferdinand and Isabella then provided Columbus with 1,200–1,500 men, 17 ships, cannons, cross-bows, guns, cavalry, and attack dogs for his return. This second voyage marks the real significance of Christopher Columbus, for in 1493 he under-took an enterprise altogether new in human history: the conquering of one land (Haiti, first) by another (Spain) an ocean away. At the same time he started the subjugation of one people ("Indians," as renamed by Columbus) by another ("Europeans," as they later came to be called, or "whites"), concomitantly introducing the ideology of racism. Soon enough a Catholic bishop in Spain was denying the basic humanity of Native Americans to rationalize enslaving them. We live with the consequences to this day.

Antiracist acts by white men in the Americas likely began shortly thereaf-ter, but the first such are lost to history. Perhaps some sailors on the first voyage argued against capturing the seven Tainos. As the Spanish conquered first Haiti, then Cuba, Puerto Rico, and Mexico, they started the practice of *encomiendas*—"commending" a whole village to one Spanish conquistador for his private governance, use, and enrichment. We do know that by 1511, some Spaniards were speaking out against the resulting enslavement and maltreatment of Native Americans. On Christmas Day of that year a Domin-ican friar, Antonio de Montesinos, thundered from a pulpit in Haiti: "Tell me, by what right or justice do you keep these Indians in such a cruel and horrible servitude? On what authority have you waged a detestable war against these people who dwelt quietly and peaceably on their own land? . . . With the excessive work you demand of them they fall ill or die, or rather you kill with your desire to extract and acquire gold every day. And what care do you take that they should be instructed in religion? Are these not men? Have they not rational souls?"[3]

And we know that his words had some effect: they fell on the ears of a young conquistador, Bartolomé de Las Casas, and convinced him he was wrong. Las Casas renounced "his" village, refusing to make money off the unrequited labor of others. He experimented with alternative ways to organize economic enterprises in the Americas, and eventually he got the king of Spain to appoint him "Defender of the Indians." He then spent most of his long life in the Caribbean, working for their better treatment.

Las Casas came to be the first great historian of the Americas (the Spanish having destroyed any works by Mayan historians). He was a fan of Columbus, and his excerpts and paraphrases of Columbus's journals are the best record we have of his first and third voyages, the originals having been lost. Nevertheless, Las Casas attacked the treatment of the Indians by Columbus and his successors. When other historians overlooked or defended the Indian slave trade, begun by Columbus, Las Casas said starkly: "What we committed in the Indies stands out among the most unpardonable offenses ever committed against God and mankind, and this trade as one of the most unjust, evil, and cruel among them."[4] Las Casas wrote of the encomiendas practice: "In this time, the greatest outrages and slaughterings of people were perpetrated, whole villages being depopulated. . . . The Indians saw that without any offence on their part they were despoiled of their kingdoms, their lands and liberties, and of their lives, their wives, and homes."[5]

At one point Las Casas suggested importing enslaved Africans, rather than continuing to enslave the Indians, who perished under the harsh regimen. But he recanted almost immediately and writing about himself in the third person, judged himself harshly for his lapse: "This advice to give a license for the bringing of Black slaves to those lands was first given by the priest Casas, who was unaware of the injustice with which the Portuguese take them and make slaves of them. Later, after falling into this snare, he regretted it, and would not have given that advice for all the world, for he always believed they were enslaved unjustly and tyrannically, because they have the same right to freedom as the Indians." Las Casas went on to write that he prayed to God to have mercy upon his soul for this error, "but he does not know if God will do so."[6]

Perhaps the high point of Las Casas's long life (1474–1566) came in 1542, when he took part in one of the most important trials ever to take place on the planet Earth. Held at Valladolid, Spain, the issue was: Are Indians human beings, or are they some subordinate species, appropriate for slavery? Las

Casas held for the affirmative, against Bishop Sepulveda and historians Oviedo, Cuneo, Gómara, and Garcilaso de la Vega, among others. "Indians are born lazy, idle, melancholy and cowardly, vile and ill-natured, liars, with a short memory and no perseverance," claimed Oviedo. Las Casas countered by emphasizing their many positive human attributes: "They used their leisure—which was considerable since their souls did not burn with greed for wealth and estates—in honest recreation such as certain strenuous ball games, dances, and songs that were recitations of their historical past. They also made very beautiful objects with their hands when they were not occupied with agricultural, fishing, or domestic chores." They were not conquered justly, he avowed, nor were they cowards: "Seeing themselves tyrannized and oppressed, dying every day from unjust labor and open war with Spaniards who disemboweled them with swords, trampled them with horses, and speared them from horseback, they fought back courageously."[7] Most important, Las Casas pointed out that Indians were thinking beings, like anyone else: "All the peoples of the world are men, and there is only one definition of each and every man, and that is that he is rational."[8]

Amazingly, Las Casas won, at least temporarily. For several years, Spain renounced slavery and published humane regulations, which almost led to colonial revolt. At length the regulations were forgotten, and Spain wound up among the last European powers to give up slavery. Nevertheless, centuries after his death Las Casas was still influencing history: Simón Bolívar used his writings to justify the revolutions between 1810 and 1830 that freed Latin America from Spanish domination. Even today, Las Casas lives. The ideological spark for the ongoing Zapatista rebellion in Chiapas was struck in the provincial capital, San Cristóbal, during a three-day indigenous Congress held in 1974 in conjunction with the dedication of a new monument to Las Casas at the entrance to the city, whose full name is San Cristóbal de Las Casas. "Brother Bartolomé is no longer alive," said one delegate. "Therefore, who will defend us? I believe that all of us organized together can have liberty and can work better. All of us together can be Bartolomé."[9]

Las Casas's life teaches at least four lessons. First, he exemplifies those courageous souls who in every age have stood for justice across racial lines. When Native Americans (and their allies) pointed out in 1992 that the Columbus Quincentenary honored their enslaver, opponents charged "anachronism." "You are judging Columbus by the standards of 1992, not by those of his own time." Bartolomé de Las Casas's words and deeds belie this assessment. Some white men in Columbus's time, even some who knew him personally, nevertheless condemned him and his associates for their racism.

Second, Las Casas teaches that among our tasks, as we work to eliminate white supremacy from our nation and our world, is to recover some of the white men who have preceded us in this struggle. Three centuries after he wrote, Las Casas's words helped mobilize a continent, but they do so no longer. The U.S. Capitol displays his portrait, but today not one citizen in one hundred knows his name. All know Columbus, whose name graces the district in which the Capitol stands. American history is full of antiracist white men who have been forgotten or whose antiracist words and deeds have been suppressed. Americans of all races and both sexes need to know about them.

Third, like most antiracists, Las Casas was imperfect. He began as a conquistador and at one important moment argued for the slave trade, only with a different racial group as victim. Other antiracist white men, including myself and many you will meet in this book, have their moments of weakness. At times, like Las Casas, they (we) did not see their bias toward one group—perhaps Chinese Americans, gays and lesbians, or women—while remaining splendidly broad-minded toward another. Some simply succumbed to the cultural racism around them as time passed. But their shortcomings do not give us license to dismiss the totality of their lives, even if on some occasions they slipped into racism. Examined closely, all past heroes have surely erred at one time or another. We must forgive their human failings, and our own, so we can learn from them—and from those episodes when they did the right thing. Unlike hero worship, such thoughtful assessment results in enduring role models.

Finally, the example of Las Casas, or rather Antonio de Montesinos, teaches us that we cannot know the value of our work. Probably de Montesinos never learned that his Christmas homily unleashed the tremendous force of Las Casas upon the world. We may feel it is not worthwhile to counter every little racist comment we encounter. But one white high school student did so in a small town in east Mississippi in 1955, and the incident was still remembered by novelist Lewis Nordan and still made its impact forty years later:

> I remember very clearly the day that I first heard the name of Emmett Till. I was in a football locker room. We were getting dressed out, and the body had just been found. There were terrible jokes being made, and . . . I was . . . sitting there in that locker room listening to this, probably smiling, I don't know, and some old boy, he said words I had never imagined a white boy saying before. He said, "It's not right to talk this way. He was just a kid who was killed, just like us. It don't matter what color he was." And that moment I measure as the moment that changed my life.[10]

Sometimes a tiny gesture makes an unknown difference.

High school textbooks in American history mystify the role of racism in our past, starting with Columbus. They therefore have no alternative but to mystify the role of *antiracism* in our past, starting with Las Casas. As a result, few Americans realize that throughout our past some whites have always worked for justice for all, without regard to race (or sex or social class). The history of American antiracism has been suppressed because antiracism has typically been on the losing side. Columbus set in motion global processes that continue to define our world today, including the seizure of land from native peoples and the Atlantic slave trade, first from west to east, and then from Africa, begun on Haiti by his son Ferdinand. Thousands of white men (and women, of course) grew rich off these processes; those who favored the just treatment of Native Americans and African Americans usually lost out. So it was that among the founders of the United States were huge slaveowners like George Washington, Thomas Jefferson, and James Madison. Indeed, eleven of our first fifteen presidents (before Lincoln) owned slaves or were members of the proslavery wing of the Democratic Party.

But again, there were dissenters. Among the most important and least known was Edward Coles, a Virginia planter who knew Thomas Jefferson and tried to enlist him in the antislavery cause. You have "great credibility," Coles wrote to Jefferson in 1814, asking his help "to eradicate this most degrading feature of British Colonial policy." In his own life Jefferson mirrored the dilemma on race that has afflicted our nation since its inception. "I have sworn upon the altar of God, eternal hostility against every form of tyranny over the mind of man," he wrote, meanwhile practicing tyranny over two hundred human beings, including their minds.[11] His reply to Coles shows him unwilling to risk his imported wines, ever-changing mansion, and ever-expanding library, all of which rested on the labor he wrested from the men, women, and children he forced to work his two large plantations. He advised Coles to leave slavery alone: "I hope, my dear sir, you will reconcile yourself to your country and its unfortunate condition."

Coles went it alone. He could not simply free his slaves, owing to a Virginia statute Thomas Jefferson had helped to pass requiring that they be sent out of state upon pain of reenslavement. So in 1819 he moved to southern Illinois with his slaves, freed them, and gave each family a quarter section of land.[12]

It is now that he played the key role for which he is forgotten in U.S. history. Although southern Illinois was originally part of the Northwest Territory, whose Northwest Ordinance forbade slavery, white residents there had made use of loopholes to hold hundreds of African Americans in bondage. In 1818 Illinois became a state and was no longer bound by the North-west Ordinance. In 1822 Coles ran for governor against Joseph Phillips, chief justice of Illinois. Phillips was for slavery, Coles against, and after an exciting campaign Coles was elected by a margin of just forty-six votes. Meanwhile, proslavery candidates won a majority of the legislature. In his inaugural address, December 5, 1822, Coles spoke for the repeal of Illinois's "Black Codes" and sought new legislation to prevent the kidnapping of free Ne-groes, who were being abducted from Illinois and sold into slavery in Ken-tucky. Instead, the legislature passed a call for a convention, the main pur-pose of which, it gradually became clear, would be to legalize slavery.

Imagine the United States that would have resulted! Slavery would have ruled from the Gulf of Mexico to Lake Michigan, hemming freedom into the Northeast and changing the fate of our nation. Illinois would have achieved in 1825 what Chief Justice Roger Taney tried to accomplish in 1857 in *Dred Scott*: to make slavery national, freedom local. "Believing slavery to be both injurious and impolitic," Coles wrote, "I believe myself bound, both as a citizen and an officer, to do all in my power to prevent its introduction into the state," and he did. Two events turned the tide. Four days after his inaugu-ral speech, a mob burned Coles in effigy at the State House in Vandalia, also setting the capitol on fire, which caused an antislavery backlash. And the next spring, the chief proslavery newspaper went bankrupt; Coles quickly bought it and turned it into the only antislavery organ in Illinois, deliberately sending it to all the old subscribers, even when they refused to pay for it. On August 2, 1824, by 4,972 to 6,640, the convention went down to defeat, and Illinois was saved from slavery.[13]

During the next decades, national policies went more and more proslav-ery, culminating in *Dred Scott*. Today our landscape is beset by statues cele-brating even people like Taney, Buchanan, and Franklin W. Pierce, tools of the slavocracy. But some antislavery warriors do get attention on the land-scape. Leaders of the Underground Railroad like Rowland Robinson, John Rankin, and Levi Coffin get remembered at their homes in Vermont, Ohio, and Indiana respectively. John Brown's home near Lake Placid, New York, tells his story, as does the National Park Service at Harpers Ferry. Charles Sumner, the senator from Massachusetts who was nearly beaten to death on the Senate floor in 1856 by Preston Brooks from South Carolina, gets remem-bered in Massachusetts and the District of Columbia.

During the Civil War, of course, antislavery finally became popular. The landscape of Washington, D.C., is replete with Union generals whose mili-tary ability and opposition to racism both grew as the war went on. Logan Circle, for instance, routes traffic around a statue of John A. Logan, who also gets impressive memorials in Chicago and Philadelphia, a statue at Vicksburg, and a peak named for him in the Rockies. Today, however, people remember Logan, if at all, not as an antiracist or even as the best volunteer general in the Union Army, but only as the person who established Memorial Day as a national holiday. Actually, John Logan made an extraordinary moral and intellectual journey during his lifetime, one that might be a role model for millions of white Americans—if they but knew of it. He grew up in southern Illinois, Democrat country, and the Democratic Party throughout the nineteenth century was the overt party of white supremacy, even calling itself "The White Man's Party."[14] In 1853, Logan was instrumental in pushing the "Exclusion Bill" through the Illinois legislature, making it a crime to bring African Americans into the state and subjecting violators to arrest and a fine. In 1860, when southern states broke with the Union, many whites in southern Illinois proposed to let them go or even to secede with them. Logan gave a famous speech from a farm wagon on the town square of Marion, arguing so eloquently for the Union that 110 men enlisted in the U.S. Army on the spot "and Southern Illinois was saved to the Union," in the words of his widow later. By then a U.S. Congressman, Logan resigned his seat to become colonel of the Thirty-First Illinois Infantry, participated in Sherman's March to the Sea, and rose gradually to the rank of general. In the process, events forcibly reeducated him and many other white Union soldiers in the area of race relations.[15]

The key year was 1864. In July, Logan used blatant racism to argue for equal treatment of Blacks in the military, shouting he "had rather six niggers . . . be killed than one of his brave [white] boys." For the rest of the year and into the next, marching through Georgia and South Carolina, Sherman's army encountered no one but African Americans for days on end. Soldiers saw firsthand the conditions under which slaves lived, touched the scars on their backs, and beheld and often burned the whipping posts standing in front of "the big house." Sometimes they met Union POWs who had escaped and been sheltered by the African American infrastructure. Everywhere Sherman's troops received the hurrahs of a newly liberated people, upon whom they relied for food, labor, and information as to nearby Confederates.

It was all heady stuff. Like many of his men, Logan grew convinced that Black people were just that—people—and deserved all the rights of other people, even of white people. As the war wound down and Lincoln was shot and President Andrew Johnson opposed every civil rights initiative coming from Congress or Lincoln's cabinet members, Logan played an important role in establishing what is now known as Congressional Reconstruction. When Johnson threatened to remove Secretary of War Edwin Stanton, the last hope of the freedmen, Logan told Johnson that he would mobilize the Grand Army of the Republic, an organization of veterans Logan had helped establish, to protect Stanton. This forestalled Johnson from forcibly removing Stanton, but Stanton and Logan slept in Stanton's office to make sure. Logan then campaigned for the Fifteenth Amendment, then the major controversy before the nation. Speaking in Ohio, he argued: "Now I want some Democrat to give a reason why the Negro should not vote. I have read their speeches, and all they say is, 'We don't want the nigger to vote,' and turn up their noses as they say it. A gentleman in Congress from your state says the Negro does not belong to the human species. But they are made the same as you and I; but they are Black—that is all the difference. If they were not made by the hand of God, I would like to know by whom they were made."

As Reconstruction lost favor, Logan remained in the "Stalwart" wing of the Republican Party, committed to Black rights. In 1884 the party nominated him for vice-president, with James G. Blaine for president, but Grover Cleveland, white supremacist Democrat, prevailed in a cliffhanger.

Emboldened by the Democratic resurgence and by Republicans' ideological retreat after failing to pass a voting rights bill in 1890, white Mississippi responded by passing its constitution of 1890, which used various mechanisms to disenfranchise African Americans "legally." During the next seventeen years, all other southern and border states copied Mississippi. This led to the notorious "Nadir of Race Relations," the period 1890–1925, when lynchings rose to their all-time high and segregation swept public accommodations even in the North.

Some white Mississippians were not racist in 1890, but their voices had already been stilled. John Prentiss Matthews, who made an intellectual journey much like Logan's but on the southern side, provides a heartbreaking example. Matthews was born in Copiah County in 1840. Although his family was wealthy and owned thirty-five slaves, John Prentiss—"Print" to his friends—was a Unionist during the Civil War. After the war, he ran a general store in Hazlehurst, the county seat. The interracial Republican coalition that governed Mississippi during Reconstruction elected him sheriff of the county.

White Democrats used violence and threats of violence to end Reconstruction in Mississippi in November 1875. Although the Democrats took over the state government, they did not capture every county, partly because of men like Print Matthews. Matthews organized a "Fusion" or "Independent Party" coalition of Black and white farmers in Copiah County. He maintained that African Americans were "entitled to all the rights, privileges, and immunities of American citizens." As a result, according to historian

William Ivy Hair, African Americans "were said to rank him alongside Abraham Lincoln."[16] He also won the loyalty of 600–700 small-scale white farmers. As a result, his interracial coalition could outpoll the Democrats by at least three hundred votes in any honest contest. Democrats responded with cannon shots at Independent Party rallies and threats before every election. Finally, as the 1883 elections loomed, Democrats resolved to do away with black political influence in Copiah County. They began night-riding—entering sharecroppers' cabins and threatening African Americans with death if they voted Independent. Many Blacks and some white Matthews supporters spent the last few days and nights before the election hiding in the woods.

The day before the election, the intimidation campaign reached Print Matthews personally. White leaders of Hazlehurst delivered a written ultimatum to him at his home, ordering him to "absent himself from the polls on election." Matthews knew his party could not win because many of his supporters were too terrified to come to the polls. "I have as much right to vote as any of you," he replied regardless. "I have never done any of you any harm. I have tried to be useful to society in every way that I could. You have got it in your power to murder me, I admit. But I am going to vote tomorrow, unless you kill me."

The next morning, he walked across the street to his polling place. Several Democrats carrying shotguns stood outside the door. Inside was Ras Wheeler, the precinct captain, a white farmer who had an account at Matthews's store. Hair tells what happened next: "Matthews looked around, saw Wheeler, and went over to sit beside him. The two men talked in low tones for a minute or so. Wheeler finally said, 'Print, I would not vote today if I were you.' Matthews then got up, walked over to an election official, and presented his ballot. He was asked to fold it. He was doing so when Ras Wheeler reached inside the wood box, lifted out a double-barreled shotgun, and taking quick aim, fired first one and then the other charge of buckshot. Print Matthews died instantly."

The day after the murder, white Democrats held a mass meeting in Hazlehurst and resolved "it is necessary to the safety of society and the welfare of all races and classes in the county that hereafter the Matthews family shall keep out of politics in Copiah county." According to the local newspaper, "The niggers met one mile South of here last Tuesday and passed resolutions of sorrow." A white-dominated jury found Wheeler innocent, whereupon Democrats appointed him city marshal of Hazlehurst. There was talk of running him for governor.

During the Nadir of Race Relations, historians derided men like Matthews as "scalawags," a term meaning "rascals," reserved for southern whites who believed in equal rights. Stalwarts like Logan were likewise besmirched as scandal-ridden and self-interested because historians between 1890 and 1925 could not believe that white men might be motivated by the sincere belief that Blacks should have all the rights of citizenship reserved to whites. Thus Logan and Matthews not only lost the struggle, and Matthews his life, but also ultimately their honor. But as John Logan's biographer has pointed out, "there was no political profit to be made from his advocacy of Black rights." And as Logan put it, at his best, "I don't care whether a man is black, red, blue, or white."

During the Nadir, some antiracist white men lost their idealism, or perhaps their nerve. General O. O. Howard, for example, had served alongside Logan during Sherman's march and was such a spokesperson for African Americans that he was called "the conscience of the army." During Reconstruction he headed the Freedman's Bureau and spoke so eloquently on behalf of the Fourteenth Amendment that some pundits labeled it "the Howard Amendment." But later in life Howard joined the "Mugwumps," the wing of the Republican Party that proposed giving up on "Negro rights." That faction came to dominate the Union League Club, an organization that was virtually synonymous with the leadership of the Republican Party in New York City and to a degree nationally.

The Union League Club had been founded during the Civil War to combat the prosecession sentiment that dominated New York City. The club raised and equipped a regiment of Negro troops and also forced streetcar companies to serve African Americans without segregation. During Reconstruction, the club helped found interracial Union League chapters across the South that helped African Americans to organize politically. By the 1880s, however, the ideas of the Stalwarts began to sound shopworn, particularly to new members of the Union League Club who had not fought in the Civil War. In 1894, Democrats repealed the remaining federal voting rights statutes. Union Leagues disintegrated across the South. In New York City, the Union League Club now began to stand for ideas antithetical to its founding ideals. Now members refused to admit upwardly mobile Jews, Italians, Catholics, and others of "incorrect background." Joseph Seligman had been a founder of the club; his son Jesse joined in 1868. In 1893, Jesse Seligman had to resign because members blackballed his own son Theodore because he was a Jew.

The management committee of the Union League Club went a step further: it proposed firing the club's Black servants and replacing them with an all-white staff. At this point, another long-time member, ex-Union General Wager Swayne, intervened. During Reconstruction, Swayne had headed the Freedman's Bureau in Alabama, helped found Talladega College, and was appointed military governor of Alabama. Now, just before his death, he fought one last battle "for his youthful principles," in the words of historian Michael W. Fitzgerald.[17] He got up a petition to bring the matter to a vote, spoke in favor of retaining the African Americans, and eventually got the membership to reverse the decision of its management committee.[18]

O. O. Howard teaches that the most committed antiracist white man can abandon the cause of racial justice.[19] But Wager Swayne shows that even in the worst of times, there have been those who *never* lost the faith. The larger panorama of the Nadir teaches more profound lessons. To this day, the biased history promulgated during the Nadir still distorts high school history textbooks and Civil War monuments across the nation. That there *was* a Nadir, or even that racism has played a continuing role in American life, North as well as South, goes unremarked in most American history textbooks. Thus we learn that when history was written and who did the writing make a profound difference. The most telling date on a granite memorial may not be on its face, telling of the event it celebrates, but around back—the date it went up.

During the first third of the twentieth century, white males elaborated their "blame the victim" ideology to justify keeping nonwhites in positions of inferiority with new "scientific" rationales. After all, slavery had been over for a generation and more. Therefore the continuing position of Blacks at the bottom of the social hierarchy could no longer be attributed to slavery. So biologists justified the Nadir with their eugenics, psychologists with their IQ tests, and sociologists with their Social Darwinism.

At the same time, a few white men developed understandings of the social world that helped people see how racism, rather than some presumed incapacity, explained racial stratification. Outstanding among them was Franz Boas, an immigrant from Germany who came to New York City in 1887. Partly owing to his Jewish background, which gave him firsthand experience with racism in Germany, Boas grew upset at the Nadir. Every culture had some merit, he held. In 1894 he told the American Association for the Advancement of Science that race did not determine intelligence. In 1906 he specifically attacked eugenic thinking, holding that slavery, not biology, had oppressed Blacks. The next year he blamed white racism for the lack of Black progress in the United States.

Boas never accomplished his dream of getting an African museum built in Washington, D.C., to prove to the nation that Blacks had produced culture and art. His testimony before Congress also failed to derail the 1924 Immigration Restriction Act, openly based on eugenics. But he did provide the basic anti-ethnocentric thinking that social science craved when Hitler's Germany finally succeeded in giving eugenics a bad name. His biographer tells how at his last public event in 1942, hosting a luncheon at the Columbia University Faculty Club honoring an anthropologist who had fled France after opposing Nazism, Boas "concluded by instructing the gathering to be vigilant and to fight race prejudice wherever it existed. He then fell back into his chair and died."[20]

Boas's students fanned out across the United States, seeding college campuses with professors who had evidence to support their belief that people of color were "rational," to return to Las Casas's phrase. Like those Jewish Americans who helped found the NAACP in 1909, Boas epitomizes the many "hyphenated Americans"—the term Woodrow Wilson used to disparage recent immigrants—who worked for justice for African, Asian, Mexican, and Native Americans in their new homeland. He also offers a lesson to ivory-towered professors everywhere: he acted in public and wrote for the public, not just in academic journals read only by scholars, because he knew that the issue was of paramount importance to the nation.

In most cities during the Nadir, in the North as well as in the South, white labor unions and management excluded Black workers. Not only were African Americans kept from practicing the skilled trades, they also could not be assembly line workers or even, in some plants, janitors. In Detroit, Ford and Dodge were exceptional; Ford even hired some Black foremen.[21] Except for the United Mine Workers, racially integrated labor unions were rare until about 1935. In that year, Detroit workers organized the United Auto Workers (UAW). Its president, R. J. Thomas, elected in 1939, acted to make the UAW an antiracist trailblazer.

During World War II, UAW locals protested promoting Black workers to assembly line and skilled jobs. Some whites fomented what came to be called "hate strikes"—wildcat walkouts to force management to reassign Black workers to janitorial and other menial jobs. At the Curtiss-Wright aircraft plant in Columbus, Ohio, the local UAW organizer led such a strike in 1941. Thomas responded by firing him and negotiating an agreement with Curtiss-Wright opening *all* departments to Black workers. In 1943, Packard Motor Company in Detroit faced similar strikes, sparked initially by the transfer of two Black workers to metal-polishing jobs. Ku Klux Klansmen dominated Packard's UAW local. The Packard manager was racist as well, insisting that metal polishing "was a white man's job"; he declared he would not make the transfers if white workers objected. When Thomas could not get either side to budge, he tried to get federal authorities to step in, but the feds equivocated. Historians August Meier and Elliott Rudwick tell how Packard employees then staged strike after strike when handfuls of African Americans were upgraded to drill press operators, aircraft assembly, and the like.[22] When Thomas faced Packard workers on May 30, 1943, he refused to back down: "This problem must be settled or it will wreck our union." Hundreds of white workers booed and marched out. Four days later, twenty-five thousand whites went out on strike, shutting down the plant. Thomas then secretly flew to Washington to seek intervention from the War Labor Board (WLB) and the Fair Employment Practices Commission—always a risky step for a labor leader. The WLB did send a strong telegram. Thomas vowed to end racial discrimination "even if it requires that large numbers of white workers out there lose their jobs." He threatened to expel any worker who stayed out on strike. Most whites returned to work, and an uneasy peace reigned at Packard.

Throughout the war, Thomas led the UAW to integrate workforces at Hudson, Dodge Truck, and other industrial plants. He also led the CIO to take a stand favoring integrated housing in Detroit. Today the alliance between unions and African Americans, symbolized by the role both play within the Democratic Party, is a fact of our political landscape, but it took work by steadfast pioneers like R. J. Thomas to get Blacks to see unions as an ally and white workers to accept Blacks as equal members.

Many of the men whom you will meet in the pages to come were spurred to work for racial justice by the Civil Rights Movement. But the struggle for civil rights is over. We are entering a "postracist" era. In times to come, it may grow harder to keep faith with Las Casas and Coles, with Print Matthews and R. J. Thomas. Few white Americans now announce, as did so many before World War II, "I am a white supremacist." Few admit to choosing where they live or where their children go to school on the basis of race. Yet we know that overwhelmingly white neighborhoods, even whole towns, not only still exist but are even regarded prestigious places to raise a family. We know that history as taught in grades 1–12 is largely a justification of our national past, which thus subtly reinforces white supremacy. And we know that without effort by white men, race will remain a problem even as our country grows more racially diverse.

In a way, the problem we face is similar to the ideological difficulty in the Nadir that so dispirited the Republicans. Around 1890, as we have seen, whites came to view the less-than-equal position of African Americans as their own fault; slavery had ended, after all. Today's continuing racial inequality can no longer be blamed on segregation, even though segregation endures in many places. Neo-eugenicists like the authors of *The Bell Curve* have again arisen to tell us that racial inequality derives from intellectual inferiority, whether innate or located deep within the cultures of the oppressed. Precisely because the causes of racial inequality are now less visible, those who combat them may appear less reasonable.

In this intellectual climate, there will be those like O. O. Howard who do not stay the course. No one wants to be marginalized. But examples like Wager Swayne and Franz Boas—and the thirty-five men in this volume—still exist to inspire us. Here is another reason why this book is so valuable. Its many mini-biographies persuade the reader that he is not alone and that other white men find the cause of antiracism worthwhile, even energizing.

One of the men whom you will meet in the pages that follow, John Allocca, wishes he "had activist ancestors." Probably he means "in my own family." But in a larger sense, *he does*. We all do. From Las Casas to Thomas, however, the history of antiracist white men has been lost or even suppressed. So we in the present have lost them as potential role models for our continuing struggle for equal rights across racial lines. Charles Pinckney Sumner, father of Charles Sumner, taught his children about Edward Coles as an example of a white man who opposed slavery. Years later Senator Sumner remembered Coles as a role model. In the same way, the men in this book will become activist ancestors for generations to follow. For unless our victory is swift and complete—which the past suggests is unlikely—those who come after us will need these stories, just as we need to know of Montesinos, Boas, and all the rest.

History is usually the tale of the winners and is usually told by the winners. Andrew Jackson is on our $20 bill, while the Whigs who opposed his forced removal of the Indians from the southeast lie forgotten. History is a process of deliberate omission, not just of the unimportant but also of the embarrassing, including those white men who have pointed out our failures to live up to our principles. History as handed down to us is part of the problem rather than our ally. One way to recover white men like Logan, Matthews, Howard, and Swayne is by enacting rituals at sites important to their memory.[23] We—and I include those who come after us—cannot rest until every American who knows of Columbus also knows of Las Casas. Until everyone who knows of Thomas Jefferson also knows of Edward Coles. Until Ross Barnett Reservoir in Mississippi, named for the governor who tried to keep Blacks out of Ole Miss, has been renamed for John Prentiss Matthews or someone like him. Until, in short, the library of volumes celebrating white men who became prominent partly through their skill at subordinating people of color is balanced by a collection of books celebrating, as this one does, white men who chose a different path, who worked for equal justice for all races.

Like my partial list from the past, what follows is only a beginning.

# Preface

*A Personal Preface from Cooper Thompson*

I used to think that this was "my book," but I can no longer do that. Since my first inklings of this project about twenty years ago, I've changed the way I think about this book. I came to realize that I didn't own this book, but that it was the work of many people and that ownership resided somewhere else, if at all.

The first step in that process was my making the decision that I didn't want to do this project by myself. As a traditional white man, I had had lots of practice working and living in isolation from other people. Although I had been a member of two families (one by birth and one by choice) and many organizations and teams, I still thought of myself as an individual rather than a member of communities. I didn't think I needed support. I thought I could "go it alone." I came to realize that that path was lonely and led to less effective outcomes. And so I asked for, and found, another white man to join me in this project. Estelle Disch, a professor at the University of Massachusetts at Boston, introduced me to Emmett Schaefer. In 1998, we began to meet weekly in a coffee shop to explore if we wanted to work together. Then, in 1999, on a trip to Pennsylvania, Maryland, and Virginia to interview several white men, Emmett and I asked an old friend of mine, Harry Brod, to join us. We are now three.

Although I continued to do most of the interviewing and development of the narratives and coordinated all the pieces leading to the completion of a manuscript, the three of us shared equally in all major decisions about content and style. Most important, we lifted each other's spirits when we were overwhelmed by the project or something else going on in our lives. I am so grateful to the support that Harry and Emmett gave me; without them, I doubt that this project would have been finished.

The second step in this process was the persistent voice of Gerald Jackson. Gerald is an African American friend and colleague of mine in VISIONS, Inc., an organization that provides training and consultation on multiculturalism.

It took a couple of years for me to hear what Gerald was telling me about the importance of sharing this material with other people. Initially, I thought of these interviews only as material that I was collecting for my own learning. Gerald repeatedly told me that I should publish the interviews, that other white men needed to hear what I was saying. Eventually, I also understood that he was telling me, in his Afrocentric way of being in the world, that I was obligated to share this material because it didn't belong to me. I was simply a vehicle for the voices of other white men.

A third step was the realization that there were literally hundreds of people who directly contributed in some way to this project. Although there are thirty-five white men profiled in this book, there are at least another fifty with whom I talked or interviewed and who have had an impact on how I think about this project. I have the names of at least one hundred other white men whom I didn't interview; the fact that they are out there inspired me to continue this project when I would lose the motivation to plug away. There are at least twenty-five people who gave me names of white men to interview. There are at least twenty people who gave me feedback on some aspect of the project. Colleagues supported my taking time to work on this project; many friends and acquaintances encouraged me and inspired me. Sometimes their voices came to me quite spontaneously. When I was transcribing Ken Kimerling's interview, I suddenly heard in my questions to Ken the voice of an old friend and colleague, Althea Smith. It was something about the way I was phrasing the question and pausing between my thoughts, and I knew that I had learned that from her. She would have asked the same questions in the same way. It was as if she were speaking through me.

Finally, a fourth step came late in the process from my friend Renae Gray. As she read some of the narratives of the white men we had interviewed, she saw that there were almost always people of color standing in front and behind and among and alongside these white men. Renae talked about this in both a literal and figurative way, as if it were impossible to bring these white men into a room without these people of color coming with them. She asked me, "How are you going to bring those people of color to the forefront?" Her question—and challenge—made me see that I had stepped one more time into the morass of white male arrogance in the ways that I was failing to recognize how people of color were the catalyst for white men challenging racism. And so this book is dedicated to the people of color who have been the conscience, catalyst, and inspiration for white men challenging racism. (In the introduction are examples of the people of color, and white people, who have been mentors, teachers, partners, and supporters of the white men profiled in the book.)

And so I have come to believe that this book belongs to a huge circle of friends, fellow travelers, writers, thinkers, beings, and doers, many of whom I've never met. It is our book, inspired by the voices and experiences of many. Consequently, from this point on in the book, whenever you are reading "our" comments, including the book's introduction, notes at the beginning of each narrative, occasional questions in the narratives, and the epilogue, you will see the pronoun "we," even though one of us probably put those particular words on the page.

*Authors' Preface*

This has been a labor of love. When we began this project six years ago, our primary interest was meeting other white men like ourselves. We wanted to reduce our own feelings of isolation and separation by being in the company of other antiracist white men and learning from them. But as we continued to conduct interviews and talked about the project to other white men and to people of color and white women, we were encouraged to publish the material. We were told again and again that the material we were collecting was unique and important. We came to realize that what we had learned could impact others' lives and have significant political impact.

We wrote this book for both personal and political reasons. We wanted to break the isolation we sometimes feel when we speak up and act against racism and inspire others to speak up and challenge racism. We wanted to find white men who could be mentors and teachers and supporters in our journey and others' journeys. We wanted to learn how other white men conceptualize and go about the task of challenging racism and then share that information so that others can benefit. There were so many questions we had: Where do other white men find the sustenance to continue challenging racism over the long haul? What's the role of spirituality in their lives and work? How do they manage their relationships with other white men? How do they build trust with people of color and navigate through the inevitable mistakes they make in those relationships? How do they make choices about what to do in the face of feeling overwhelmed by all that needs to be done?

We wanted to honor the white men who have come before us, the white men who are our peers, and the white men in the generations following us. Although some of the white men we interviewed had parents and grand-parents and aunts and uncles to inspire them to challenge racism, the three of us have for the most part not had the benefit of growing up in families where there were models for resisting racism. Nor have we, for the most part, known about the history of white men who have challenged racism in the United States. We saw this project as a way to address that void in our lives. We had a need to know that there were and are and will be white men challenging racism. James Loewen's foreword does a wonderful job of teaching us a little bit about the rich history of white male resistance to racism in the United States. A few of the white men whose narratives appear in the book are old enough to be our fathers; some are our contemporaries and even friends; some are young enough to be our sons.

Although we have had, and continue to have, women and men of color and white women in our lives who willingly and enthusiastically serve as mentors and teachers and supporters, we have realized that we need the support and mentorship of white men. So, in many ways, this book is for white men. But many people of color and white women have told us that they found value in these narratives. Our wish is that all readers use these stories for self-reflection, dialogue, and action.

We are pleased to be able to share this work with you.

*Harry Brod, Emmett Schaefer, and Cooper Thompson*

•  •  •

All authors' royalties from this book go directly to fund antiracist work through RESIST, which has been funding social change since 1967. RESIST helped us find several of the white men interviewed for this book and has provided funding to some of the organizations they represent. For further information contact RESIST at 259 Elm Street, Suite 201, Somerville, MA 02144 or www.resistinc.org.

# Acknowledgments

This project stands on the shoulders of many people. With apologies to those we have forgotten to mention, we'd like to thank the following people for helping to create this book.

Estelle Disch, Renae Gray, Rita Hardiman, Curdina Hill, Gerald Jackson, Jackson Katz, Jim Kilpatrick, Joycelyn Landrum-Brown, Jo Lewis, Afiya Madzimoyo, Wekesa Ojatunji Madzimoyo, Gordon Murray, Pam Newman, Michael Omi, and Michael Thornton, who encouraged us and inspired us.

Timothy Beneke (*Men on Rape*), Bob Blauner (*Black Lives, White Lives*), and Studs Terkel (*Race* and *Working*), who gave us book-length models of first-person narratives.

Valerie Batts, Christina Davis-McCoy, Patti DeRosa, Angela Giudice, Ted Glick, Renae Gray, Bob Hall, Lance Hill, Derrick Jackson, Stetson Kennedy, Tom Louie, Paul Marcus, James Mejia, Al Minor, Gloria Norlin-Wells, Joan Parker, Jennifer Phillips, Susan Rabinowitz, Mark Scanlon-Greene, Carol Schachet, Mab Segrest, Joe Steele, Becky Thompson, Jennifer Wexler, and Loretta Williams, who gave us names of potential interviewees.

Bob Allen and Ian Maher, who used high- and low-tech methods to find antiracist white men for us to interview.

Glenda Russell, who gave us a model for a cooperative consent form.

Catherine Lugar, who lent us her professional portable cassette recorder so that we could get high-quality audiotapes.

Don Snider, who encouraged us to share our questions with the interviewee prior to the interview, thereby making the process more cooperative.

Anne Bowie, Vendela Carlson, Sandra Knight, and Colette Perreault, who did literal transcriptions of some of the first interviews we did.

Elly Bulkin, who edited some of the first literal transcriptions into narratives and gave us invaluable feedback on the content of the interviews.

Angela Giudice, Renae Gray, Curdina Hill, Jo Lewis, and Raoul Ybarra, who read drafts of the narratives and gave us supportive and critical feedback.

David Attyah and Steve Bailey, who helped us see that developing the narratives was a creative endeavor in which the interviewees had shared their thoughts and then respected our process of shaping their words to fit our needs.

Inge Spiegel, who helped with the tedious process of typing handwritten edits.

Paul Kivel and Chip Berlet, for support and suggestions on finding a publisher.

Reynolds Smith, Executive Editor at Duke University Press, who believed in this project and encouraged us to give him a proposal so that Duke might consider publishing the book.

Sharon Parks Torian, Senior Editorial Assistant at Duke University Press, who answered our many questions about navigating the publishing process at Duke, always doing so with a smile.

Two anonymous reviewers who gave us very helpful feedback on drafts of the manuscript.

Rick Whaley, who gave us pages of insightful recommendations for editing the preface and introduction.

Bob Blauner, Doug Brugge, John Capitman, Matt Case, Mark Chesler, Jim Crowfoot, Tom Cummins, Peter Dougherty, Chuck Esser, Pat Farren, Todd Fry, Ted Glick, Paul Gorski, Bob Hall, Ralph Hergert, Jim Hussey, Joe Harvard, Nathan Henderson-James, Michael Jacobson-Hardy, Greg Jobin-Leeds, Jackson Katz, Paul Kivel, Arnold Langberg, Lester Langley, Ian Maher, Jerome Miller, Michael Novick, Tom O'Mara, Bob Paret, Ed Peeples, Dennis Poplin, Hyim Jacob Ross, Chuck Ruehle, Rob Sand, Joe Sexton, Barry Shapiro, Chris Smith, David Snider, Jim Wallis, Marc Weinblatt, and Larry Yates, who allowed us to interview them but whose narratives, unfortunately, we were not able to include in the book.

And last, the thirty-five white men in this book who have so willingly shared themselves with us, without whom this project would not exist.

# Introduction: Just Living

This is a book about the personal experiences of thirty-five white men who are trying to live a just life, sometimes successfully, sometimes not. To varying degrees, the white men in this book all think of what they do as simply what they must do, as if it is no longer a choice; they are just living their lives. And the task of challenging racism and other forms of oppression is integrated into their day-to-day existence in such a way that their lives are permeated with questions of justice, personally and politically. Challenging racism is, for these men, just living. This book is an attempt to provide some space for the reflections of a group of white men who we believe are living just lives in many different ways.

The narratives include incidents from and comments about complex and rich lives and reflections on antiracist activity. Some of the narratives speak about critical events that led to a life of activism; some of them speak about blind spots when it comes to racism or another form of oppression; some of them speak about offenses in relationships and mistakes in strategy; some of them speak about regrets of actions not taken. And there are expressions of pride in describing accomplishments and victories.

These narratives are like photographs. It is as if each of these white men were momentarily presenting himself to us and you. These narratives are not comprehensive life histories. The white men profiled in this book made decisions about what they wanted to reveal about themselves and what they didn't want to reveal. We encouraged them and sometimes challenged them to reveal more about their most favorite and least favorite sides of themselves.

*Why Another Book about White Men?*

Given the critical role that people of color have played in the lives of white men who challenge racism and given the fact that it is largely people of color (and to a lesser extent white women) who have given their lives to fight racism, you may wonder why we are writing a book exclusively about white men. In fact, we were occasionally asked, "Why are you focusing on white men? Aren't people of color the true heroes? Why are you ignoring them? Don't white men already get more attention than they deserve? And what about the work of white women in challenging racism?"

We spent many hours talking about these questions with people of color and other white people. Afiya Madzimoyo, a friend and colleague who lives in Atlanta, Georgia, and other women of color consistently told us that there is a desperate need at this point in history for white men to love themselves as white men; Wekesa Madzimoyo, her husband and another friend and colleague, supported us in our learning to love our white male brothers. Afiya and Wekesa emphasized the importance of our being with other white men, praising them for their accomplishments, and challenging them when they didn't "get it."

Wekesa is also emphatic that people of color need to break the centuries-old pattern of taking care of white people; we know from experience that we and other white men have fallen into patterns of looking to people of color—and white women—for encouragement and affirmation as we take on the task of challenging racism. In our worst moments, we have depended on people of color to acknowledge our good efforts, and if they didn't thank us profusely, we decided that they weren't grateful. Or we have avoided contact with other white men, believing that there is little chance of getting support from them. We believe that it is our responsibility as white men to give ourselves the "strokes" we want and need.

We are certainly not the first white people to decide that our work is with other white people. This is what Malcolm X and many other people of color said when asked by white people what their role might be in securing civil rights for African Americans. After reading many of these narratives and giving us feedback, Curdina Hill told us, "White people aren't really doing antiracism work unless they're working with other white people." In a variation on this theme, Winona LaDuke told Rick Whaley, one of the white men interviewed for this book, "You need to know prayers in your own people's language."

We believe that the narratives in this book do what Afiya and Wekesa and other people of color have encouraged us to do. By holding up these white men who challenge racism, we are celebrating their lives. By asking them to be vulnerable about their mistakes and shortcomings and by asking questions that push their understanding of themselves and oppression, we are challenging them. By supporting them and getting support from them, we are encouraging white men to use their white male privilege fully. It does nothing for racial justice if we are meek and shrink into a corner, abandoning people of color and white women to fight racism on their own. The struggle for racial justice needs all of us in the center of the room.

Just as we hoped our questions were challenging to the men we were interviewing, so we also hope that their answers prove challenging to our readers. In particular, we hope what they say challenges the images that usually arise when people begin to speak of men in connection with the issue of racism. All too often, in our view, introducing the topic "men and racism" into a conversation quickly narrows it down to a discussion solely of the problem of "angry white men." But there are other men, other white men, other than these "angry white men." These other white men have anger and many other feelings, as their words show, not toward people of color or women (against whom the anger of the "angry white men" is said to be directed), but against racism and sexism and injustice generally. And they act on those feelings not in hostile acts of rage against other, marginalized people, but in acts of solidarity with those other people and acts of compassionate confrontation toward other white men.

Why, then, yet another book on white men—and this time, irony of ironies, one that even claims to be in opposition to racism and sexism? Because the widely held gendered image of racism—it's "angry white *men*," not "angry white *people*"—needs an equally gendered counterimage of antiracism—antiracist white *men*, not antiracist white *people*. Because groups of people, even dominant groups of people, are not monolithic. And it's important to know this. To really know it, not just in the abstract, but in the concrete details of these people's lives, as they themselves speak about them. We need to have some personal knowledge of men who have crossed racial lines in pursuit of racial justice, against the dominant stand of their own dominant group. Such knowledge empowers all, whether dominant or subordinate, because it opens the horizon and raises the bar of the possible in pursuit of justice and may even help to empower and inspire others to do likewise.

It is not that we believe that white women don't have much to teach us. They have taught us much, and we hope to keep learning from them. In fact, our personal experience tells us that there are many more white women than white men who actively challenge racism, and we suspect that there is more contemporary antiracism literature written by white women than by white men. Given that, it seems particularly important to focus on white men, to fill in this gap.

Some of the white men we interviewed also had concerns about being part of this project. A few of them were surprised that we wanted to talk to them because they didn't think they had done enough. Others were reluctant because they didn't want to seem like heroes or be in the spotlight. For example, John Cole Vodicka is adamant that the real heroes in southwest Georgia, where he works, are the African Americans who are willing to stand up to overtly racist white sheriffs and judges in the face of threats and retaliation. Chip Berlet told us, "When you told me you were doing a book about white men who fight oppression, I thought, 'Oh great, this is gonna be another one of those bang the drum and howl about the burdens of fighting racism and sexism!' I see my personal battles as an inconvenience and nothing compared to the burdens of people who feel the sting of oppression." Even so, some of the white men we talked with admitted that some recognition is important to them and keeps them going.

We have chosen to primarily explore the experiences of white men who challenge racism and not their experiences challenging sexism or other forms of oppression. We don't believe that racism is more important than other oppressions. Indeed, we are committed to the proposition that there is no hierarchy of oppressions and no priority of one liberation struggle over another. But because of where we are in our personal lives and where we believe our nation at this moment stands in its political life, we have chosen in this book to highlight antiracist struggles. It seems to us that many white men have explored and taken seriously the personal and political impacts of sexism, while racism has been treated as if it were only a historical phenomenon or deemed too difficult to change. It seems critical, therefore, to hold up white men who are committed to challenging racism.

We are aware of the problems in using the word "white." Some argue that the very concept of "whiteness" is an oppressive fiction that falsifies a much more complicated social reality. For others, it is an all too real phenomenon but one that must be thoroughly rejected. For others, it is a simple biological fact to be accepted. For us, in the context of this book it is shorthand for people of European descent who have, for the most part, been whitewashed into losing or giving up their identities as European Americans with specific ethnic and national roots. "White" is, for us, primarily a historical and political, rather than biological, concept that has given these people unearned privileges that have had and continue to have tremendous impact on all of our lives. We use it merely to describe, not to endorse, certain identities and institutions, along with their racialized relations of power.

In addition to being asked why we were focusing exclusively on white men, we were also questioned about the fact that we are three white men. "Don't you run the risk of not knowing what you don't know? How can you objectively assess other white men? What is your accountability to people of color? Isn't this just another example of the use of your own white male privilege to enhance your own status as white men?" When we first contacted Tobin Miller-Shearer to see if he was interested in being interviewed, he asked us about the involvement of people of color in our project. Because we didn't have a formal structure for getting the advice of people of color and because he takes very seriously the creation of structures of accountability to people of color, Tobin was initially hesitant to be interviewed.

We did not create a formal structure of accountability. We did consult regularly with people of color and white women in our lives, and they have given us feedback. For example, Curdina Hill was struck by the ways that some of these white men seemed so wounded from incidents in their childhoods, so she wondered if we had asked them about their personal healing in the interviews. We realized that the question had not occurred to us. We had asked about isolation and the need for support but not the need to heal from past wounds. One of the things that Curdina persistently notices in white men is the residue of old pain and how this negatively impacts white men's relationships with people of color and therefore reduces the effectiveness of their efforts to challenge racism. We assume that there are other things we have "missed"; we assume that we have gotten some things wrong. In a sense, we are trying to do what we have asked the interviewees to do: we're sharing our work with you, knowing that you will see our strengths and shortcomings.

*Our Approach*

Early in this project, we knew that we didn't want to write a book that critiques the lives of other white men. The three of us have been socialized quite well to study others, find their flaws, point out those flaws in a patronizing way, and proceed to tell them what they need to do differently. We decided instead to let other white men speak for themselves and place ourselves in the role of listeners and learners. The methodology we chose for doing this was to find white men whom others describe, or who describe themselves, as challenging racism; interview them face to face; transcribe and edit parts of the interview so that it read as a first-person narrative, with an occasional question or comment from us; rewrite sections for clarity and arrange the material for dramatic emphasis; and last, review and edit the narrative with the interviewee so that it reflected what he wanted and was willing to say about himself. We were clear that we wanted this to be a collaborative process.

In looking for white men to interview, we wanted a diverse group in terms of age, place of residence, sexual orientation, class background and current class identity, spiritual tradition and practice, racial and ethnic identities of the people of color with whom they see themselves in alliance, and type of activities they do to challenge racism. We wanted "experts" who know that they are on a journey of learning about themselves and others and the world. We wanted white men who were willing to talk about their accomplishments and failures, who could be both proud and humble. We wanted white men who would be willing to be vulnerable in print. For the most part, we wanted to profile white men who were relatively unknown outside of their geographical communities or field of work. Notable exceptions are Herbert Aptheker, Stetson Kennedy, Si Kahn, and Richard Lapchick, although they are hardly household names.

We formally or informally interviewed about one hundred white men in the process of choosing these thirty-five. We know of or heard about well over one hundred white men challenging racism whom we didn't interview. Based on the number of white men we identified and the fact that our search was, at times, casual and never exhaustive, we know that there are many more white men in the United States who in some way challenge racism.

The interviews were both structured and spontaneous. We prepared for each interview by having a set of questions we wanted to ask, and the questions we actually asked depended on what happened in the interview. The broad questions we wanted to explore included the following: What do you do to challenge racism? How do you do what you do? Why? How did you come to be committed to doing what you do? What mistakes have you made? What are you proud of? What's the meaning for you of your various cultural identities? How would you describe your relationships with people of color? With other white people? How do you get support? Where is your community?

When we first started conducting interviews, we prepared a relatively long list of questions based on these themes and then kept those questions in front of us, on paper, as we conducted interviews. (This list is in the appendix.) We eventually realized that it would be a more cooperative strategy to share these questions with the interviewee prior to the interview and did so. At about the same time, we began to trust that we could keep the questions in the back of our minds as we gave the interviewee our full attention. We never asked all of these questions; we tailored our questions to the issues that we felt would be most salient in each interview and then modified them. Sometimes the person we were interviewing took the interview in directions that we hadn't anticipated; sometimes we took the interview in directions we hadn't anticipated; most of the time the interview seemed to have a life of its own.

Our decision to create first-person narratives from interviews was inspired by the work of Studs Terkel (*Race*); Bob Blauner (*Black Lives, White Lives*), and Timothy Beneke (*Men on Rape*). We liked the directness and intimacy of this approach. Using first-person narratives to explore complex and multidimensional material also appealed to our desire to use storytelling as a device for learning and teaching.

Creating the narratives from the transcriptions was challenging. When we created the first dozen or so, we didn't have a guide in our hands, nor had we articulated how we might develop the narratives. We were using our intuition and best guesses about how Terkel and others might have followed a similar process. After creating first and second (and third and fourth) drafts of about half of the narratives, we began to articulate what we were doing. At about the same time, Bob Blauner gave us a copy of "Problems of Editing 'First-Person' Sociology" (*Qualitative Sociology*, spring 1987), an article he had written in the process of writing *Black Lives, White Lives*. His essay affirmed what we were learning experientially and encouraged us to continue what we were doing. (Notes on the process of creating a narrative appear in the appendix.)

The final step in writing the narratives is one that we took very seriously. We worked collaboratively with the interviewee to assure that the narrative we had created from his interview was accurate and reflected what he wanted to say. In some cases, this meant hours on the phone, many e-mails, and detailed edits until we got it right. We are proud of our collaborative process and its results. We believe that it makes an additional statement about white men supporting each other in antiracist work. In doing this, we have been true to the spirit of what these white men want to say about themselves.

One aspect of our collaboration with them was to ask them to think carefully about the impact of the publication of their narratives. Some of the interviewees agonized about what to save and what to delete; in the end, a few of them decided to delete particular comments out of concern for their reputations or the potential impact on allies, colleagues, friends, and family. For example, after reading drafts of their narratives that included information about their affiliations with revolutionary groups in the 1960s and 1970s, a few of the white men asked that we remove any references to revolutionary groups out of a legitimate fear that they could be used by conservatives to damage their credibility and hurt the very important work that they were now doing. Clearly, the current political climate in the United States is having a chilling effect on some people's ability to claim a progressive political identity. We are saddened by this reality.

One pitfall in using first-person narratives is the implication that these white men are individual agents. When it comes to social change, we believe that the idea of individual agency is a myth. One of the challenges we face as white men is seeing ourselves as part of a movement, taking leadership from people of color and white women. In general, white men are socialized to see themselves as individuals, and often leaders, rather than as members of communities and followers; indeed, we began this project with that notion. By using the first-person narrative, we have unintentionally reinforced the myth of individual agency. We believe, however, that the content of the narratives challenges this myth: the narratives make visible the ways that these white men have accepted leadership from people of color and white women, are members of communities and organizations challenging racism, and are part of a movement for social change.

Another pitfall in using relatively short first-person narratives is that there is limited information about each person's life. Therefore, if a narrative contains no information about, say, the role of spirituality as an interviewee's inspiration for challenging racism, that does not mean that spirituality has played no role in his life. It simply means that we didn't ask about that and he didn't talk about that; or that we decided to delete that material from the narrative because it was repetitious of what was said in another interview; or that we felt there was other material that was more significant or interesting; or that he is not aware of the role that spirituality plays in his life.

There is no conscious attempt on our part to judge as good or bad what these white men do and think and feel. We have not analyzed them; we have not made distinctions about what are good and bad approaches to challenging racism. We have made no attempt to measure the frequency with which a particular theme is mentioned. We have not commented on how these white men resolve particular dilemmas in their lives. We didn't do any checking on their credentials to see if people of color and other white people thought they were "legitimate" in their attempts to challenge racism.

On the other hand, we did have to make many decisions about whom to interview, how to edit the interviews into narratives, what material we wanted to include in the narratives, and which narratives to include in the book. Our criteria for these decisions included the following questions: Have we included a wide range of white men in terms of who they are, where they live, with whom they work and live, and what they actually do to challenge racism? Is what they have to say compelling and engaging? Have they revealed themselves through the narratives? Do they acknowledge the existence of institutional and cultural racism? Do they account for their white male privilege? Are they aware of other forms of oppression?

Our responses to these questions have been highly subjective. In the end, we don't believe that we have judged these white men according to standards of what is right and wrong; we have judged their comments as being more or less what we found exciting and helpful in our own desire to learn from them and more or less what we believe will be useful and engaging to readers.

*People of Color and White People in the Lives of These White Men*

Almost all of the white men in this book have had and continue to have people of color and white people in their lives as teachers, mentors, partners, and supporters. People of color have been especially important to them. We want to spend some time here detailing the many ways that these white men speak about people of color in their lives, and then how white people play similar roles for them.

Herbert Aptheker, while writing his first book on Nat Turner, was befriended by Carter G. Woodson; while writing *A Documentary History of the Negro People,* he shared an office in New York City with W. E. B. Du Bois. And he considers as pivotal the time he spent as a young man with Dorothy and Louie Burnham, who were gentle and loving teachers. Pat Cusick was profoundly impacted by Mahatma Gandhi's concept of satyagraha (soul force) and a speech by Stokely Carmichael; he was personally encouraged to come out as gay by Bayard Rustin. Richard Lapchick credits Arthur Ashe with helping him see the importance of speaking out about being assaulted for his anti-apartheid activism. Billy Yalowitz recalls feeling lucky that he "grew up in a household where my dad's hero was Paul Robeson. . . . His voice was singing in the house all the time." Matt Reese describes how reading about the Black Panthers, Malcolm X, and Dr. Martin Luther King Jr. inspired him and helped him understand his role as an activist. Matt also considers Nailah Jumoke to be a mentor; she's the executive director of the Harriet Tubman Cultural Center in Louisville, Kentucky. In the introduction to his narrative, Sean Cahill talks about the importance of his relationship with Urvashi Vaid at the National Gay and Lesbian Task Force. In the narrative, he mentions his admiration for Massachusetts State Representative Byron Rushing.

Several of these white men mentioned to us during or after the interviews the importance of reading or hearing the words of bell hooks, Angela Davis, Marion Wright Edelman, Bernice Johnson Reagon, Audre Lorde, Barbara Smith, and James Baldwin. A. T. Miller credits lesbians of color and gay men of color for making connections between oppressions: "Stonewall was all people of color, and some of the earliest out people were the lesbian and bisexual blues women who later became part of the Harlem Renaissance. . . .

Women like Barbara Smith and Audre Lorde taught us all to think more clearly about the intersections of gender, race, and sexuality. They really developed intellectually the concept of multiple simultaneous identity."

Steve Bailey works with a multiracial staff. He praises the artistic director of Jump-Start, Sterling Houston, for pushing and advising him; one of the members of Jump-Start, S. T. Shimi, for teaching him about her South Asian background; and the director of the Esperanza Peace and Justice Center, Graciela Sanchez, for educating him about oppression. "My awareness of race issues has been really honed through collaborations with lesbians of color. . . . Graciela Sanchez is both a friend and mentor. Over the years, she has generously given her time and knowledge to help me deal with my place in the world as a white gay man."

Chris Shuey talks about the impact of his contact with Navajo people, giving him "a different theoretical, conceptual, and philosophical basis for what I do." For example, as an environmental health specialist, he has learned to incorporate a spiritual dimension in assessments of environmental impact, rather than relying solely on legalistic and scientific approaches. In his personal life, the emphasis in Navajo culture on family has helped him remember the importance of maintaining a connection between his children and his parents. Rick Whaley talks frequently about his mentor and Anishinabe friend Walter Bresette and being inspired by Winona LaDuke.

Nibs Stroupe, the pastor of Oakhurst Presbyterian, a multiracial church in Decatur, Georgia, with an explicit mission to challenge racism, talks about being challenged by a member of his church and a training colleague, Inez Fleming: "I remember a phone call; I don't remember what the issue was, but she had taken issue with something I'd done. I said, 'Why are you mad about this?' And she said, 'I'm not mad about this. Why do you think I'm mad?' I said, 'Well, you sound angry.' 'No, I don't sound angry,' she said, 'but if you want me to sound angry, I will. I think the problem is you're not used to getting this from a Black person.' . . . She is always pushing me and asking, 'What are you really thinking? I don't want this "preacher" stuff.' "

Bill Vandenberg, the co-executive director of the Colorado Progressive Coalition (CPC), describes his relationship with his former girlfriend and the other co-executive director, Soyun Park, in this way: "We have a great deal of respect for one another in the work we do. We know what we each do well and where we need a little support. And we give that support to one another." After going through a painful realization that CPC was dominated by older middle- and upper-class white people, Bill and Soyun and some of their colleagues pushed the organization into becoming more multicultural. By the end of the process, the staff was younger, and seventeen out of twenty were people of color. Bill says, "My life is enriched more than I can even quantify by working in a multiracial setting."

White people have also been the conscience, catalyst, and inspiration for these white men. Matt Reese told us about how much he respects and learns from Civil Rights Movement elders like Anne Braden, a longtime social justice activist in the South. David Attyah has such a strong artistic and personal partnership with S. A. Bachman that he prefers to identify their work as THINK AGAIN rather than his or her work. Steve Bailey and John Allocca have both used James Loewen's *Lies My Teacher Told Me* in their work. Herbert Aptheker's book, *Anti-Racism in U.S. History: The First Two Hundred Years,* includes hundreds of examples of actions by white people that challenged racism; he is currently working on a second volume because he believes that the material is so important. Nibs Stroupe talks about his friendship with David Billings, another white man challenging racism in New Orleans; John Cole Vodicka mentioned to us his respect for Nibs.

Rick Whaley has been deeply inspired by Wendell Berry's *The Hidden Wound.* For Rick, Berry's work is essential for exploring the impact of racism on white culture and the land. In 1990, as he was getting ready to join a dangerous witness against racism in northern Wisconsin, Rick told his son, "If anything happens to me, remember two things: take care of our family and read Wendell Berry when you get older." Interestingly, Rick told us that Berry was very influenced by the essays of James Baldwin.

In a conversation after the interview, Chip Berlet described his supervisor and colleague Jean Hardisty with deep respect, praise, and even joy at being able to work with her. "For me to be invited by her to be an employee to study the right wing is like somebody had just constructed the world's greatest job. I thought it was fabulous. In terms of the work environment, I've never questioned her leadership. I was mesmerized by her presentation the first time I heard her speak, and I'm still mesmerized by her speaking and thinking. She's quite astonishing."

In our interview with Art Branscombe, his wife Bea sat nearby, praising Art and sometimes adding details to his comments. At one point I asked Art about his experience accepting leadership from women. Bea responded, "He's had three daughters, all of whom are feminists." Art added, "Oh, boy, I've been surrounded here! Ye, gods. No way I could have avoided being somewhat of a feminist!"

Herbert Aptheker sings the praises of both his daughter, Bettina, and his wife, Fay. "I'm terrifically proud of Bettina. . . . She's a conscious antiracist, as well as a feminist. She's very militant about that, but she's very militant about the antiracism." As for Fay, who died in 1999, "I needed her, not only emotionally and physically, but in my work, where she did a lot of my research. . . . My first book is dedicated to her, and all of my books have something about her. She made it possible for me to produce so much writing. I could never have done it otherwise. It never occurred to me that Fay was anything but at least my equal. . . . She was basic to everything in my life."

*Doing Antiracist Work*

It is, after all, antiracist activity that distinguishes these white men from other white men, and the range of activity described in these narratives is impressive: organizing, protesting, engaging in civil disobedience, witnessing, writing, using power and position to raise issues, teaching, infiltrating racist organizations, rescuing people of color from oppressive conditions, getting involved in politics, building coalitions and supporting organizations of color, advocating, taking legal action, boycotting, lobbying, creating and building organizations to challenge racism, researching and spreading information, and making contact with and supporting white men. Here's a representative sampling from the narratives:

Some of these white men use their professional skills and position to challenge racism. Ken Kimerling is an attorney in New York City who works to protect the rights of Asian immigrants and other people of color. Lee Formwalt, as Executive Director of the Organization of American Historians, led the organization to cancel a six-figure contract to hold its annual meeting at a hotel that had been accused of racial discrimination. Bill Johnston, a former police officer in Boston and head of the Police Department's Community Disorders Unit, used his power to challenge his fellow officers about the racism, sexism, and homophobia he saw in the department and in the community.

Some of these white men use their art to challenge racism. Si Kahn writes and performs songs about racism and other forms of oppression; his narrative includes the lyrics to "Vann Plantation," a song about the incarceration of African American men in for-profit prisons. Billy Yalowitz directs community theater projects like *The Black Bottom,* a production based on the story of an African American community that was destroyed by urban renewal, and *Minstrel Shows,* a production about racism, becoming white, and the appropriation of Black culture. David Attyah creates postcards and posters that speak to oppression: "White Men Can't Count," a response to white male allegations that Affirmative Action has gone too far, and "Bash Bat," a response to the fatal beating of a gay man.

Some of these white men spend their days and nights observing racism and then speaking up. John Cole Vodicka sits in courtrooms and visits prisons in southwest Georgia, documenting racist acts by sheriffs, judges, and prison officials and advocating for justice. Rick Whaley was a coordinator of a multiweek vigil during nighttime attacks on Indian spear fishers in Wisconsin; he describes witnessing as the process of deflecting anger by receiving it. Sean Cahill has gone to Northern Ireland for many years as part of Peace Watch Ireland, a multiracial group of activists who maintain a nonviolent presence during the Protestant marching season and build solidarity between oppressed peoples in Ireland and the United States. Jim Murphy has repeatedly challenged Boston City Council members, Boston Fire Department officials, and his fellow firefighters to deal with the racism, sexism, and homophobia he has witnessed in the department, despite the fact that as the only openly gay man in the department he is at substantial risk for doing so.

Others have also put themselves at great personal risk in the service of challenging racism. Herbert Aptheker traveled to Georgia in the 1930s in a secretive mission to free African Americans from peonage, an economic system in which they were so indebted to white owners that they were essentially imprisoned. Stetson Kennedy infiltrated the Ku Klux Klan in the 1940s and 1950s and distributed the names of Klan members, the minutes of their meetings, and even their secret passwords; had he been caught, he believes he probably would have been tortured and killed. Terry Kupers worked with the Black Panthers at their request in the 1960s, using his training as a doctor to provide emergency medical care, even though there was a chance that he could be caught in shootouts between the police and the Panthers. Richard Lapchick was assaulted while organizing a boycott in the 1970s of the Davis Cup tennis matches and the Los Angeles Olympics because of South African participation. Two masked men broke into his office late one night, severely beat him, and carved the word "nigger" on his stomach.

Finally, there are white men in this book like Jesse Wimberley, who helps working-class white men in North Carolina explore the connections among capitalism, racism, sexism, and other forms of oppression. He believes that they have been exploited economically, cut off from a sense of community with one another, and therefore are vulnerable to being organized by right-wing groups. Jesse believes that working with these white men is healing for him and for them.

*A Final Comment about the Organization of the Narratives*

We decided to arrange the narratives into six sections: "Movement Elders,"

"Grassroots Organizing," "Art and Politics," "Challenging the System from Within," "Challenging the System from the Margins," and "The Next Generation." Our decisions about which narratives to place in which sections were somewhat arbitrary; some of the narratives could have been placed in more than one section. For example, Pat Cusick, because of his age and experience in the Civil Rights Movement, rightfully belongs with the elders. But he is very much a grassroots organizer and definitely fights the system from the margins. Although Tim Wise's narrative could have been placed in "The Next Generation" or either of the "challenging the system" sections, we chose to put him with the artists because he talks about his writing as a creative process.

We like the idea that the book begins with the elders and ends with the next generation. In fact, our final question to Herbert Aptheker, whose narrative appears first in the book, had to do with his advice to younger activists. Matt Reese, whose narrative appears last and who is the youngest of the white men profiled in the book, closes with these comments: "I wouldn't be where I am without the elders in the Movement. And they wouldn't have a future without us. Inevitably, everyone's going to die, and if we're not there to pick up the pieces, then the Movement is dead."

We believe that Matt's words bring the book full circle.

Movement Elders

# Herbert Aptheker

*We knew the name Herbert Aptheker because of his writing on the history of African Americans and racism. But we didn't know his whereabouts; a mutual friend wasn't sure if he was still living. Then we "accidentally" saw him at the grave of Mary Brown, John Brown's wife, during a memorial to John Brown in May 2000. We mentioned this project to him, Herbert agreed to be interviewed, and we subsequently met at his apartment in San Jose, California, on November 10, 2000. Herbert is eighty-six.*

*When we asked Herbert about the work he is doing now, he said, "I have tremendous work to do on the second volume of* Anti-racism in United States History. *I have thousands of pages of notes. I don't know whether I will be able to make a book of it under present circumstances." Herbert has had some problems with his health.*

*The interview began with a question about his early experiences with racism. He closed his eyes, paused, and then started to speak about his life.*

•  •  •

When I was quite young, probably in my early twenties, I got to know the Burnhams—Dorothy and Louie Burnham. Wonderful people, Black people. They lived not far from my family in Brooklyn. Louie asked me if I would be interested in joining him in an organizing effort in the South. I don't remember the exact year. It was probably about 1939. So I went with Louie.

We drove in a roadster with a rumble seat. Louie, who was a genius at organizing, put hundreds of copies of my pamphlets, "The Negro in the Civil War" and "Negro Slave Revolts in the United States"—one was a 10¢ pamphlet, the other one was 15¢; one was forty-eight pages, the other was seventy-two pages—in the rumble seat. And we started out.

I have a few clear memories. One was in Memphis, at a junior college, an all-Black school. I don't know how Louie did this, but the president of the college arranged to be absent when we were there. I was to speak at an assembly on some aspect of what we called "Negro history"—probably something on militancy, perhaps the rebellions. As you entered [the hall], there was a long table, and on the table were piles of my pamphlets. The students fell on these like locusts on a wheat field. And then I lectured, and then there were questions. And then we did organizing among tobacco workers in Tennessee, North Carolina, and Virginia. Then we came home.

We spent every day together on that trip to the South. It just occurred to me—I wonder where we slept? I must have slept in Black-owned motels, with him. I'm sure of that. I know we didn't separate. I'm sure that on that trip I developed a deep comfort being around Black people, so that it became second nature to me.

I later learned that Louie was a Communist Party member. He never mentioned this to me. He made no effort to recruit me. He didn't even talk about the party. The same was true of his marvelous wife, Dorothy, who had also struggled in the South against racism. That trip with Louie made a profound impression on me.

Personally important is the fact that I was the last of five and was sickly. My parents were very wealthy. We had a great big house and lived in Brooklyn, which at that time was rural. We had gas lights and very few neighbors and no Black people whatsoever. Mama hired a Black woman from Trinidad. Her name was Angelina Corbin. She was a big woman and very dark. She lived with us in the room next to mine. Mother had trouble pronouncing "Angelina," and with permission we called her "Annie." Annie was as important to me as was Mama, and I loved them both equally. I soon saw that Mama treated Annie as one of the family.

Annie raised me because Mother had four other children and was busy. Annie bathed me, dressed me, fed me. I don't know why she didn't allow me to kiss her. I remember trying to kiss her, but she never let me do it. She would push me aside and say, "Just be a good boy." She was absolutely decisive in my upbringing. I saw her every day.

The next thing that was of fundamental importance was that Papa was making a business trip in the summer to Alexander City, Alabama. I asked if I could join him, and he said, "Yes." I was about twelve or thirteen, which was about 1930. Depression had set in; it was very deep in the South. When we got to Washington, D.C., I saw Jim Crow for the first time in my life.[1] I was astonished.

In Georgia, Papa had some sort of car trouble. We were stopped by the side of the road. I got out with a bag of cookies that mother had baked. Alongside the road, there was a field. Deep in the field was a shack without a door. It had a cloth instead of a door. Standing at the threshold was a Black woman who looked just like Annie, with arms akimbo. In the field in front of her was a Negro child, perhaps my age, maybe a little younger, very thin, in rags. We saw each other. So I moved toward him, and I took out a cookie. I handed it to him, but he didn't take it. He bent forward, and he took a bite out of it and left it in my hand. I didn't know what to do. I was at a loss. So I turned around and ran back to the car. That scene is very vivid in my mind. I can see it now. My mind has been damaged from the stroke, but I can see that.

We went deeper into the South and ended up in Alabama. We saw the South in the deepest depression, with this kind of slavery that I later came to understand was peonage. I was astonished. Astonished. When I came home, I decided to look into this because I couldn't believe what I had seen. It was so contrary to what we had been taught about "God Bless America." I really studied it. I went to the census, I did research, and I had a column in the Erasmus Hall [high school] newspaper, a student paper. I wrote column after column on what I called "the dark side of the South," which I derived from what I read and what I saw. That was the beginning of my career. I was thirteen or fourteen years old.

When I was about nineteen, I wrote what I believe is the first extended study of slave rebellions in the South. I sent it for publication to the quarterly *Science and Society,* which was founded by the Communist Party. I got a letter from one of the editors that they were very impressed, but it was too long and could they cut it. I said, "No." I told them that the facts were very important, and they invited me to an editorial board meeting. I persuaded them to publish it in two installments. It was called "American Negro Slave Revolts." It was a good piece. Of course, I didn't know a great deal, but fundamentally, what I said in the article was true and was new. It created quite a stir.

. . .

I went to Columbia University. But at that time, Columbia did not allow Jews uptown. They had a ghetto school in Brooklyn. It was called Seth Low Junior College. It had two floors of a building that housed a law school, but the teachers and the books were the same as at Columbia. We were all Jewish or Italian. I became a leader of the student body in the struggle against Spain. I became known.

One day I was visited by a Black man who was an attorney in Chicago. His name has skipped my brain. This man was originally from Oglethorpe County, Georgia. He told me of the peonage that existed in Georgia and that it was really a form of slavery.[2] He wondered if anything could be done about it. I took him to William L. Patterson, who was also a lawyer, but he had given up the practice of law, become a leader of the Communist Party, and devoted himself to the struggle. So I took this fellow to see Patterson, and Patterson did what I thought he would do. He organized us, saying, "We now have the Abolish Peonage Committee. Herbert, you're the secretary" and told the other man that he was the chairman. So we now had an abolish peonage committee. We began to meet with famous people of the left.

We realized that we had to go down and get some of these people out of Georgia. You had to be white, and so I went. I was about twenty. I went as a traveling salesman, under the name of Beale. I don't know what I was selling. Of course the Black people knew I was coming—it was arranged ahead of time. I used to meet one or two, usually one, at night in a whorehouse above a saloon. Usually Black women serviced men in the whorehouse, so it was not unusual for me to be up there and have a Black woman come to me. The Black women I was meeting were not whores; they were slaves on plantations. There were thousands of them being exploited on the plantations.

In this way, I would be able to give a bus ticket to a woman each night so that she could go north. We had raised money through the Abolish Peonage Committee, including from the party. I would give them the ticket and some money and tell them that they'd be going to New Orleans—they couldn't go north from Georgia. In New Orleans, we had comrades who owned a bookstore. I would tell the Black woman, "They will know you're coming; they will meet you; you can trust them with your life. They will have a ticket for you to Nashville. In Nashville, there is a woman who is a piano teacher. She will take care of you and send you to Chicago, where you'll be free." That's what we did.

Well, I stayed in a different room every night, and in this way, we freed maybe fifteen people, maybe more. I used to shave about three times a week, and there was a separate washroom at this place. There was a mirror. I don't think it had a door. And there was a Black man who was sweeping, and he said, "Go home." I turned to him, and he didn't look up, and I asked him, "What did you say?" He said, louder, "Go home, now," which meant, of course, that I had been discovered. So I went home.

. . .

In my work in the South, I saw that Communist Party people were the most devoted and most heroic. When I came back north, I sought out V. J. Jerome, the editor of the journal *Political Affairs*. We had lunch together and then went to the party office in New York City. I had published—in either *Political Affairs* or *The Communist*—a very important essay called "The Labor Movement in the South, 1850 to 1860." It was a pioneering essay published under the name of Beale. So when we got to the party offices and went into the elevator to go to the ninth floor, where his office was, I said to him, "How does one join the party?" He said, with great surprise, "You're not in the party? Do you have 50¢?" I had two quarters. "Give those to me. Now you're in the party."

I ran for the Senate from New York on the Communist Party ticket in 1976, when Gus Hall was running for president. I got 25,360 votes in New York State, and he got 10,000 votes nationally. I remember apologizing to Gus. While I was campaigning, I was returning one night from my teaching job; a man came from behind a pillar and assaulted me. We lived in the ghetto. I thought it was just robbery, and so I took out some money and tried to give it to him. But he wasn't interested. He was interested in beating me, maybe killing me; I'm not sure. I defended myself with the boxing I had learned when I was younger. He was in his twenties and I was about sixty, and he was tall and strong. So he was getting the best of it. I was bleeding, and my clothing was torn. While I was on the ground, a Black woman neighbor who was walking her dog came near to us. The dog began to bark. And then she saw what was happening, and she started screaming, "Leave the doctor alone!" That's what they called me—the doctor. Well, he took his time, this professional; then he left. I had a letter in my pocket from Shirley Graham Du Bois, who was in Ghana at the time. He took the letter out of my pocket, probably to show his employer. He walked away.

I got up and didn't know how badly I was hurt. We lived across the street, but I didn't want to go home in that condition because Fay, my wife, would be terribly scared. But I didn't know what else to do. So I picked myself up and went home. It was very bad for her. The police came and wanted me to go to the hospital, but I didn't want to. I was campaigning and thought it would be bad publicity. I was not seriously hurt. I finished the campaign. I lost, although I got the most votes of all the minority candidates. Moynihan won.

I left the party in 1992, when the subservience of the party to Moscow became glaring. The activity of the party became useless. The party was destroyed, as was the Soviet Union.

. . .

*When your daughter Bettina was a child, did you and Fay explicitly teach her about racism?*

No. She just knew how we lived. She saw our friends; we frequently had Black people at our home. We went to their homes. Angela Davis was a childhood friend of Bettina's because Angela lived in Brooklyn.[3] After the girls were murdered in the church bombing in Birmingham, her parents sent her up to Brooklyn. Bettina and Angela formed a club when they were eleven or twelve, and they used to picket the grocery stores that had only white clerks but Black customers. That's the way it was. It was unbelievable. This was Bedford-Stuyvesant in Brooklyn. I used to take the kids to the stores to picket, with their signs, but they wouldn't want me to participate. So I would stay away for about an hour or an hour and a half, and then I'd go get them and bring them home.

I'm terrifically proud of Bettina. She was a leader in college. There was a fellow who got all the publicity in the protests where she got arrested, but she did much of the work. Which is what usually happens with women and men.

Now, she's a conscious antiracist, as well as a feminist. She's very militant about that, but she's very militant about the antiracism. And when I talk with her and she's telling me about some woman who's done a great thing, I will say to her, "Is she Black?" And she would respond in a way that said she hadn't thought about that. I've noticed that. She's aware of the racism, but it's not in her. She doesn't have that at all. The same was true of Fay. Fay was terrific in this. Fay was quite a woman.

I miss Fay terribly. She died June 15, 1999. She took care of everything. She insisted that I was hopeless, that I couldn't do anything. That was her belief. She was a very practical woman. Boy, was I lucky to have her. Over sixty years.

I needed her, not only emotionally and physically, but in my work, where she did a lot of my research. When I became notorious, there were certain libraries that would not welcome me. For instance, in Mississippi, I couldn't use the library in Jackson, so she would do the research for me. One time I asked her if I should sign both Herbert and Fay as the authors of a book, and she didn't want that. So my first book is dedicated to her, and all of my books have something about her. She made it possible for me to produce so much writing. I could never have done it otherwise.

It never occurred to me that Fay was anything but at least my equal. I raised the question of women in the Organization of American Historians and the American Historical Association. There were only men in those organizations. It was ridiculous that they didn't have women. I did that probably because of Fay.

When we would go to sleep, before I would put out the light, sometimes she would say, "Herbert"—she never called me Herbert, so when she did, I knew I was in trouble. So I would turn to her without putting out the light and ask her what I had done. Usually what I had done was that I was impolite to help—for instance I was abrupt to a waiter, or I didn't leave enough tip. She would explain to me, "You didn't treat the waitress right, baby." She was very sensitive to that because she was poor when she was growing up. She would do that regularly, and it would help me.

I had a certain sense of impatience with people who did not know enough, and Fay would let me know that, privately. "You have a ph.d., and they don't." She didn't graduate from college and was very aware of these things. So she would tell me about it. She would speak out when I was wrong. She was basic to everything in my life.

I'll tell you an interesting story. When Bettina was an infant, Fay wanted to give her a specific formula. I don't remember the exact name of it, but there was a number one and a number two. And Fay wanted number two. We were in North Carolina at the time; I was in the army; it was early in the war. So Fay told me to go get a supply of number two. I went to Fayetteville, and they only had number one. I went to Raleigh, and they had only number one. Well, I know Fay, so I better bring home number two. But North Carolina does not have number two. So after conscientiously searching, I went back home with number one. I knew she would say this: "Herbert, did you look for number two?" I said, "Baby, I went all over the state, and they have only number one, and Bettina will have to be raised on number one."

Now all this came vividly to my mind in Germany late in the war. I was in charge of displaced persons, slaves that we had freed. Most of them were Polish. Almost all of them were women, and so there were some babies. I had to find housing, and I did so. Well, there was a problem of getting milk. I finally did what I should have done sooner: I went to the mayor of Dusseldorf and told him I wanted milk. Whatever I asked for, he didn't have. Sometimes I would take my pistol out and put it on the table, and then he would have what I asked for. He got the milk. So the women would come and line up for the milk, and I thought of Fay and Bettina and the formula. In Dusseldorf, only one baby died and only one woman killed herself, out of several thousand women. I'm very proud of that.

I used to inspect the camps for displaced persons. There was a nurse in charge who wanted to tell me something, but she was too embarrassed. I said, "Look, if you don't tell me, I can't help you. What is it?" She says, "You know we are all women. We menstruate." I said, "Oh." And she said, "We have nothing. We're using rags." Well, you know, the artillery is not supplied with napkins. However, we were in Dusseldorf, and the Germans menstruate. They must have napkins. So I went to the mayor. And of course, "No. No." So I pulled out the pistol, and then my women had napkins. My babies had milk.

.  .  .

My first book is on Nat Turner.[4] I went to the Library of Congress in Washington in 1935 or 1936 to do my research. Carter G. Woodson met me.[5] I don't know how that began, but he met me. He was much older than I and very distinguished. At that first meeting, we could not eat together, except at a counter in the railroad station. So that's where we had lunch. He asked me what I was doing, and I told him. He encouraged me; I remember that. When I went down to Washington again, I let him know, and he met me. And this time he took me to the ghetto to a restaurant there that was below street level. I was about twenty. When we got there, there was a railing. It was dark. I was somewhat upset. I held onto the railing. He saw that, and he said, "Herbert, you may eat with us. We are civilized." I remember that vividly.

Now why all that occurred, why he treated me that way and helped me, I don't know. The same is true of Du Bois.[6] As a young man, I was sort of an editor and book reviewer of *New Masses*.[7] One of the books I reviewed was *Dusk of Dawn,* which was the first autobiography by Du Bois. I was about twenty-five years old, and therefore I thought I knew everything. And so I pointed out what Du Bois didn't know and didn't understand. I was not disrespectful, thank God, but I explained the world to Du Bois. Well, Du Bois wrote me a letter and told me it was the best review he had had. Now I was stupid, but not that stupid to let that opportunity go. We began a letter-writing relationship. And then the war came.

After the war, I got a Guggenheim Fellowship to write what became volume one of *A Documentary History of the Negro People.* Du Bois told me that I could share his office. He was then the research director of the NAACP. He had an office on Fortieth Street in Manhattan, across the street from the N.Y. Public Library. For a year and a half, every day, I had the unimaginable advantage of Du Bois on my left and the library on my right, doing my documentary history.

.  .  .

I never had any prejudice toward Blacks. I never thought about it. That's the fact. It's still true. In that sense, in a way, it's a limit on my part because I never really understood racial prejudice. I knew the history of it and wrote about it, but I never fully grasped the psychology of it. And I still don't.

There's a great paradox in this whole business. Many Southern people with the deepest prejudice have the profoundest love of Black people at the same time. People are complicated. But I never had that problem. Any idea that Blacks were inferior was just nonsense to me. It was ridiculous, just absurd, to think that they were inferior. Inferior to what?

*Did you have contempt for people who were bigoted?*

Oh, no, I understood it. I understood that racism wasn't personal. It was social. The person who's rich—you can't hate him because he has a lot of money. That's his misfortune to be rich, or to be born into it, like I was. I was born into a rich family. My mother was very rich. She's a bad person? It's ridiculous. She was a wonderful person. She was just rich. That was our misfortune in terms of character. If one was born into a slaveholding family, he couldn't help himself. And that was obvious to me. And if he broke from it, it was a great thing, a tremendous achievement. But if he didn't, it was understandable. Most people didn't.

We're all human. It means that we're subject to our environment. Some of us are fortunate in their environment and some are not. I've never blamed people for their prejudices. Personally, I've thought of prejudice as a kind of sickness. You're not angry with someone who's sick. You take care of them. It's just a misfortune, unless the person is physically vile; that's a different matter.

When we captured the head of the Gestapo in Dusseldorf and he was standing in front of me, I had to resist killing him. But I let him hear the Jewish in my German, so that he knew a Jew was in charge. I still see him in my dreams. God knows what he did to Jews.

Toward the end of the war, I was in charge of a sector. We had taken part of Dusseldorf. We occupied one-third; the other two-thirds were still held by the Nazis. One of my duties was to supervise the population. There was a very tall, thin man. His printer's apron was still on. He had a flyer he wanted to distribute for a meeting of the Communist Party and was asking me for permission to put it up. This leaflet said—I will never forget it—"Those who flutter with the breeze need not show up." I told him he could distribute it. When he left, I wept terribly. Imagine calling Hitlerism a breeze. This man was a survivor. One who didn't yield, apparently. He was asking me for permission. He didn't know me. I was a comrade. He didn't know that. A Jewish comrade; he didn't know that either. It was tremendously moving to me that I should give him permission to distribute such a thing. When he left, I wept. I can still weep thinking of it.

What's the alternative? There is none. The only choice is to believe that they cannot succeed in destroying us. Therefore, you have no choice if you want to live. If you don't want to live, then you kill yourself. Suicide is a sign of weakness, of completely giving up, capitulating. You must never do that. Believe me, I had moments of deepest challenge—physical, political, and mental challenge. But I never thought of giving up. On the contrary, those challenges invigorated me. How dare they do that!

*We think of you as an elder. What advice would you give to younger antiracist men?*

I've never thought about that, but I'd say that one of the important things is history. Of course the knowledge of the history and the reality is vital. To the best of your ability, you should spread it, let people know. That's what I've done. That's what I've tried to do. You have to inform yourself of the realities of history, of what slavery was, of what Black people, especially Black women, went through. And you have to learn about the postslavery so-called freedom. I think it helps to saturate your consciousness with that, so that you understand what you are dealing with—a horror that has to be overcome and how difficult it is. And knowing that we white people are responsible for the horror. Therefore, if we have some conscience, we should be very important in eliminating the horror. That's my life. That's the way I see it. I think that's logical, and a person should be persuaded of that.

I think it's important that people understand that it's not easy. If this is serious, if you're really committed to an egalitarian existence in life, it's not simple. Because the society is otherwise. You are a rebel. You have to be careful of your behavior, that you're not superior to others who are unfortunate enough to have the prejudice. And if you are superior, you'll never change them. You have to watch your own behavior. You mustn't be supercilious or a big shot. You mustn't think, "These poor, stupid people don't understand." Well, they don't understand. But they're not stupid, and they're not poor people. They just don't understand.

# Stetson Kennedy

*Stetson's lifelong campaign against racism and other forms of injustice began when he was a teenager at the University of Florida. Now eighty-five, he is still at it. A descendant of two signers of the Declaration of Independence with a grandfather who fought for the Confederacy and an uncle who was a great titan in the Ku Klux Klan (KKK), Stetson was disavowed by family and friends when he challenged racism.*

*When World War II came along, a childhood back injury prevented Stetson from taking part. But with the KKK in his back yard, he took it upon himself to infiltrate and expose it. Out of those experiences came books like* The Klan Unmasked, Jim Crow Guide, *and* Southern Exposure, *some of which were translated into other languages. Nowadays he is racing the clock, trying to finish his autobiography,* Dissident-at-Large, *and other works like* Hate No More *and* Naturalist Manifesto. *First Humphrey Bogart and then Mel Gibson took options for a movie on his life story but didn't like the scripts their writers turned in.*

*Stetson was born in Jacksonville, Florida, in 1916. He lives, with his wife of thirty years, Joyce Ann, in a simple cedar cabin he calls "Beluthahatchee," Seminole for Shangri-la. It sits on a lake he created by cutting trees and damming a stream when he was much younger. Both Stetson and the house seem like they belong to a different era: the cabin is down a quiet dirt road but now adjacent to strip malls and expensive housing tracts. Stetson is one of the last in the generations of the pre–Civil Rights Movement era white freedom fighters.*

*He takes great pleasure in catching fish and then feeding the egrets and herons who nest on the lake. On breaks during the interview, he patiently hooked fish onto a pulley system that allowed him to deliver meals to birds perched on a nearby cypress. Stetson speaks with passion about both racism and the environment; he believes that if we don't take environmental preservation seriously, there will be no need to deal with racism because there won't be anybody around to hate or be hated.*

. . .

I've always tried not to either credit or blame anyone for being the product of their upbringing. The surprising thing to me is that the white South isn't worse than it is and was. When I hear someone espousing what they were taught to espouse, I don't usually pay much attention. It's only when I hear someone talking the opposite of what they were brought up to believe that I prick up my ears.

I've had the benefit of seeing the same phenomenon around the world. That convinced me in short order of what I already suspected: that this thing we call racism and bigotry is universal. The earmarks are identical around the globe. In talking about white and Black America, I don't think we've got anything all that special. It's just a local manifestation of something that's global.

The South, and America, were one big training camp for bigots, and, with virtually every institution taking a hand, our indoctrination in intolerance was very thorough. But I have been convinced all along the way that every child is born with an innate sense of right and wrong—what's fair and what isn't. My wife Joyce Ann, who teaches a kindergarten class of refugee children from all over the world, once said it all. A Russian Jewish girl was late registering, and lo and behold, it was two Iraqi girls who took it upon themselves to show her the girls' room, bathroom, etc. Joyce remarked, "Nobody had taught them they were supposed to be enemies."

In America and wherever else you find racism, the institutions of the society, including the federal government, are all very much in the business of supporting and propagating the bigotry and racism and ethnic attitudes. So you've got an *institutionalized* phenomenon. Therefore, it's going to take the involvement of all institutions and the government if we're gong to have any hope of eradicating it.

This matter of looking to the individual to solve racism is in my opinion a naive way to look at the thing. It's about as hopeless to talk a bigot out of bigotry as it is to talk a Baptist out of preaching baptism. All the words in the world would have little or no impact on bigots. The history of our species on the planet has been such that there has been so much ethnic and racial and cultural and national strife that preachment alone is never going to provide a solution. Preachment may be all to the good—and we've had thousands of years of it—but it's not good enough.

• • •

In 1952, the United Nations established an ad hoc committee on forced labor and held extensive hearings all over Europe, focusing on refugees from the Soviet camps. Someone had the idea that the committee should come over to the Western Hemisphere—I suspect to make things here look good. They came as far as New York City, sat there a day or two, and then announced that no one had come forward with any evidence of forced labor in the Western Hemisphere.

I was here at my house, out in the mud, clearing water weeds, when I took a break to read the local newspaper and learned about the hearings in New York. I proceeded to send them a telegram, offering to fly a planeload of forced laborers up to New York to testify. They were all around here, in the turpentine camps and potato fields. I received a reply saying that they had already adjourned but that if I could get to Geneva, Switzerland, within ten days at my own expense, they'd be happy to hear me. I asked them if I should bring forced laborers with me, and they told me, "No, we'll just hear you as an expert witness." So I got a recorder and ran around in the woods here, getting interviews with these fellows. I took the recordings with me to Geneva. It put a stop to their investigations—they decided to drop the subject of forced labor.

I felt that this was something I was obliged to go through with. I had come in out of the mud, seen the article, sent the telegram, and had the invitation, so I felt there was nothing else to do but go. I hitchhiked to Miami and spoke to some Black Baptists down there and told 'em about the opportunity. I remember some Black minister raising his hand with a $5 bill in it and the chairman of the meeting saying, "Hell, we can't buy freedom for $5." They collected enough to get me to New York, where some labor union people got me a one-way ticket to Geneva, with $8 left over. It was winter, and I didn't have an overcoat, so a guy who was seeing me off at the airport gave me his. It was about five sizes too big. That's the way I arrived in Geneva, with a CIA reception committee standing around in the airport wanting to get a look at me. What they saw was this little guy in a great big overcoat, and they couldn't help laughing.

I was thirty-six and married at the time. My wife stayed here. I had no fare back to the United States and no job over there. I was eating hand to mouth. It was eight years before I got back to the United States. So that marriage didn't last.

Did I want to come back? Yes and no. Those were the Eisenhower and McCarthy years.[1] I suppose Richard Wright had the best answer to this question.[2] He was in Paris and in self-exile from the United States long before I got there. He had given up on America and moved to Paris. He once told me, "It took five years of getting lost in the grayness of Paris before I could stop thinking in black and white." He said on another occasion, "Once I got homesick enough that I got a ticket to go back for a visit, but when I got to the Canadian-U.S. border, I looked across and got back on the plane." I was pretty much in the same boat as Richard Wright. It was refreshing to see a mixed couple strolling in a Paris park, with children in the carts, and no one noticing that they were a mixed couple. I thought to myself, it will be a thousand years before America reaches that point.

While I was there, I wrote a thing called the *Jim Crow Guide*. It remains the one and only catalog or encyclopedia of the statutes, ordinances, regulations, etiquette, and mores governing the status at that time of African Americans and other minorities as second-class citizens in this country. I could not find a publisher in America, so Jean-Paul Sartre published it in Paris. It went on from there to being published in about twenty languages.

There were people who said, "You shouldn't be critical of your country. Patriotism dictates that criticism stop at the water's edge." But long before that, I had concluded that this thing we call racism was a universal struggle, that rights and oppression were universal issues and had to be opposed on that basis. So every time there was a new edition of the *Jim Crow Guide* in another language, I saw it as another bonfire on the horizon, giving Uncle Sam the hot foot. In fact, in Paris, a CIA agent came to me and said, "You know, this book hurts like hell! If you would just repudiate it and say that it was a put-up job, we'll see to it that you're financially independent for life." I said, "Well, if you can point to anything in it at all that is not true, I'll repudiate it for free." He couldn't point to anything. I called a press conference and told about the CIA's proposition.

I consider that everything I've ever done on the subject of race is patriotic. There's just enough language in the Declaration of Independence and the Constitution and the Bill of Rights to make it clear to me that the concept of this country was for an egalitarian, democratic republic. We have never yet fully qualified as such. Everything I've done, and a vast number of other people have done, has been with the view to do whatever we could to see to it that America lived up to that ideal. That's what I call patriotism.

While I was in Europe, I made a point of staying away from the tourist joints and, to some extent, Americans. I tried to immerse myself in whatever culture I was in. Eventually, I was all across Europe and North Africa and into the Soviet bloc countries and China. I found this thing called racism and ethnic cleansing where ever I went. It boiled down, in my mind, to a universal reality that says, "If you don't walk and talk and think and drink and dance and sing and cook and copulate like I do, then you've got to die." This leads to the further conclusion that every child is born a blank tape, and therein perhaps lies whatever hope there is for a solution. We must see to it that hatreds are not recorded on the tape and that cooperation and mutual esteem are recorded.

I don't think that "tolerance" is what we want. By definition, "tolerance" embodies a certain paternalism and patronage. Tolerance is not what we're after; it's mutual esteem. Whatever is conducive to mutual esteem is what we have to focus upon.

It seems to me that racial, cultural, and ethnic pride can be a good thing. There's nothing wrong with taking pride in one's culture. But such pride should always be a lift up and never a putdown. This kind of pride has almost always taken the other form: "I'm mighty, white, and destined to rule, and all the rest of you are no damn good." Our homegrown militia terrorists today are using the term "mud people." If you're not blond and blue eyed, you're mud people. The militia agenda goes so far as to call for depriving all mud people of citizenship, the repatriation of Blacks to Africa, and the staging of a global holocaust against Jews. So they're thinking of turning back the clock in a big way.

We can sit here and make tapes and talk about issues, but that's the reality that's lurking out there in the bushes. I recently saw a thousand or more militiamen just down the road here, training with machine guns, hiding in the palmettos. I had hoped that when I reached this age, there wouldn't be that sort of thing on the horizon. In my opinion, the militia poses as much of a racist threat to the world today as Hitler's handful of storm troopers did in the 1930s. They're similar in terms of the relative smallness of the groups, and the militia is actually ahead of the storm troopers in terms of numbers and armament. If bombings like the one in Oklahoma City don't prove that they mean business, I don't know what it's going to take. Suppose African Americans or Hispanic Americans or Jewish Americans put on camouflage and went into the woods to train with machine guns—they wouldn't last twenty-four hours. But the official attitude toward the militias is that these are good old boys and they're just having fun and are nothing to worry about.

• • •

When it comes to fighting racism, I'm pretty much for whatever works. In 1950, I campaigned as an independent, write-in candidate for the U.S. Senate from Florida, as a "color-blind candidate for total equality and right supremacy." Of course, I had no thought of winning. No one, South or North, had ever campaigned on such a platform. The big idea was to clear the air, break the ice, so that future candidates who might want to oppose racial discrimination, or even segregation, could do so as liberals rather than radicals. I was arrested inside the polling booth, and one of the deputies kept begging the other to let him do me in en route to jail. I had been endorsed by the Black Florida Progressive Voters' League (FPVL), which had just added 10,000 more Blacks to the voting rolls, but the state of Florida reported that I received only 817 votes. A year later, the FPVL leader, Harry T. Moore, was dynamited to death in his bed.

A few years earlier, in 1947, I was staying at Hull House in Chicago, on a speaking tour for the Anti-Defamation League (ADL), and I came up with the idea of creating a mock Klan dedicated to universal brotherhood. We held a press conference where I introduced an African American, a Jewish American, a Catholic American, a Japanese American, and an American Indian as charter members. By setting up an incorporated mock Klan, we could take legal action to preclude real Klansmen from using the name because at that moment there were no other Klan charters around. By working with the ADL, the NAACP, and other groups, we had succeeded in getting all the other Klan charters revoked in Georgia, Alabama, and Florida. I like to think it made an educational point, even though I almost got fired from the ADL— they didn't like the idea. After the news story broke, at the next meeting of the real Klan the Grand Dragon roared, "Only a pervert would come up with an idea like that!"

Another time I was able to use Superman to fight the Klan. When I couldn't get the FBI to listen to what I was telling them about the Klan's terrorist activities, I began to think in terms of the media. In the 1940s, Drew Pearson had a national, coast-to-coast Sunday afternoon radio program. I sold him on the idea of reading the "Minutes of the Klan's Last Meeting" every Sunday. I was infiltrating the Klan and feeding the minutes to both Drew Pearson and to the producers of the radio show *Superman* who were doing a series, *Superman versus the Grand Dragon.* As fast as the Klan would change its passwords for entrance to its meetings, I'd send 'em on up to the radio producers, and kids all over the country would all have them the following week.

In the minutes of the meetings I included the names of the businessmen and the politicians and the judges and lawmen who were in attendance. After their names were broadcast, they never showed up again at the meetings. This put a damper on attendance and recruitment and above all on Klan terrorism. They were afraid to make a move. After months and years went by, the Klansmen were saying, "We want action! We've been lying low long enough." The Grand Dragon would say, "Catch the rat, and I'll give you all the action you want."

*Were you scared?*

Yeah. Still am. When I got to Paris in 1952, I thought that I wouldn't have any more nightmares about the Klan. Lo and behold, in Paris, the French traffic cops wore white raincoats with white caps and hats. In the rain, they looked just like Klansmen going through all the Klan hand signals.

*You still have nightmares about it?*

Occasionally, yeah.

*How did you cope with that fear?*

I don't know. Some people said I was foolhardy. The investigating committee in the Atlanta Klan was composed of five members, and they were all city detectives. It was professional detecting I was up against. They were trying very hard to catch me, and I was trying very hard not to get caught.

At the time—it was the mid 1940s—I was Southeastern Editorial Director for the CIO. There were some Klansmen in the CIO, so I had to be very careful about what I was doing. I was working under one name in the Klan and my own name in the union. I stopped going to union meetings for fear of running into somebody I'd seen at a Klan meeting. The Klan was very busy beating up CIO organizers and doing drive-by dynamiting of union halls; the Klan beat some organizers almost to death. I remember one, a wonderful guy named Horace White, about three hundred pounds and a friend of mine. The Klan beat him to a pulp. He was in the hospital and told me, "Stetson, for God's sake, be careful! These sons-of-bitches are lowdown mean; they'll kill you." But he went right back out and organized, and I kept on going to Klan meetings.

At a Klan meeting, I once heard the Grand Dragon say, "For the life of me, I can't understand how any man would have the nerve, knowing the penalty, to rat on the Klan." They'd bring out all these weapons and put them out on the table to show how prepared they were.

I wore a Smith and Weston 32 automatic in a shoulder holster, which helped some. One time another Klansman felt the gun on me and said, "I thought so." I said something like, "Yeah, the streets are tough out there, and I have to take care of myself." When he found out about the gun, I thought that was the end of the line for me. But he accepted my explanation.

*So what kept you going? How did you keep the fire and passion to compensate for the fear?*

It's a long story. I believe that I came down on the side of what's right at a very early age, and without any debate with myself as to which way to go. For example, my playmates used to make my Black maid cry, calling her "nigger" and such. And I had refused to join in such "fun" as knocking Black grocery delivery boys off their bikes. By the time I matriculated at Robert E. Lee High School, some of my classmates were asking each other, "What got into Stet?" I had decided that I was going to do something about racism. My answer to your question, then and now, is: "Ask not what got into Stet; ask what got into America to enable it to embrace such evils as slavery, segregation, and racism for so many centuries." The very idea of any society asking one of its members why they are taking a stand for justice tells you a lot about that society.

Somewhere along the line, I think in college, some professor told me I should pursue a literary career. But I decided to write, not with a view to a literary career, but with a view toward the adage that was floating around at the time: "Know the truth, and the truth shall make you free." If I was going to cross swords with injustice, I decided I could do it with words: "the pen is mightier than the sword" sort of approach. It occurs to me that often in my life I've sort of prayed, "Oh Lord, give me a fang!"—not a pen, but a fang so that I could go for some jugular veins.

Especially during the 1940s, when I sometimes had a microphone in front of me and a national audience, I would tell myself, "Another quarter of a year is going by, and I haven't rattled the cages coast to coast. I'd better get busy." This was sort of a self-imposed goal—to make coast-to-coast waves at least once every quarter.

There has never been any question for me about keeping going. I get up at five o'clock and have most of my life. Being "self-employed" for most of my life, I've not only kept going, I've worked overtime, including high holidays, both Jewish and Christian. I did some of my best work on holidays. When everyone else is getting Christmas spirit, I'm up at my typewriter. Woody Guthrie spent quite a bit of time here with me. In one of his letters, he says something about me being up in my little room, grinding out ammo. That comes pretty close to what I've tried to do—looking for cracks in the Jim Crow wall and trying to soften up the South for righteousness.

. . .

One reason I came back from overseas was the passage of the early civil rights acts concerning the schools and segregation and so on. When Martin Luther King took to the streets, I decided I wanted to come back and get into the act. I decided for the first time that there was hope for America. I remember the morning after the decision to desegregate schools, seeing a Black guy on a bicycle and having the thought, "Okay, buddy, you're on your own now. I'm going to go fishing and do some other things I've always wanted to do. You're on an equal footing with other minorities. Before the law, you've got it made." I thought I was never going to write another word on the "Black problem"—which was always really a white problem.

But of course it didn't turn out like that. Some problems were resolved. Many were not. And new problems have arisen. I haven't gone fishing yet.

I think that the gains in race relations in America and South Africa and some other places have been appreciable. I guess that's the right word. It's true that we may no longer be Jim Crowed, but we're about as Black ghettoed as we ever were. And we may have a token Black middle class in place of the token Negro, but the Black masses in the inner city are just as jobless and skilless and hopeless as they ever were.

The issues, of course, have simply changed: for example, the attempts that have been made to put an end to Affirmative Action before it can finish its work. If David Duke or the Bushes or such people really believe that women and minorities are getting preferential treatment because of Affirmative Action, then they ought to get themselves a sex change and paint themselves Black and check it out.[3] There's many a move out there to turn back the clock—and with considerable chance of success if people don't take note and take action.

The trends are not good. Some of the trends that have a very direct bearing on my having hope or no hope are the polarization of money, the export of jobs, the abandonment of the public school system, the prospect of college education becoming a privilege of the wealthier classes. All of these things, I think, are problems just as serious as segregation, slavery, and racism ever were. The bottom line is that there has to be genuine equality of opportunity—not just under the law, but in society. We need to keep after government to do what it ought to do.

The United States of America has been a racist republic since its founding, all the way from the Declaration of Independence. In those days they didn't even think about women; when they said "All men . . . ," they meant "all *men*." They weren't even giving women a thought. So being responsible for the exclusion of women, I think that the federal responsibility extends now to helping to get rid of it. It breaks my heart, and doesn't do anything for my mood, when I see the Department of Justice and the White House line up in support of things I consider to be attempts to turn back the clock.

I have already said that I do not believe that preachment or individual or group soul searching will do. Intergroup antipathies and hatreds are so deeply rooted in our histories, traditions, societies, and institutions—often awash in oceans of reciprocal bloodletting—that we cannot just say, "Kiss and make up," and expect it to happen.

No amount of sweet talk about reconciliation and brotherly love will do any good. As believers in democracy, we must strive to maintain intergroup peace through democratically enacted and enforced laws.

Of course, we have to support the planet, or there won't be any theater for the struggle against bigotry to continue or succeed. The thing about "All the world's a stage" applies. If we burn up the stage, then it won't much matter whether we go down as racists or brothers. The stage comes first. If we don't protect it and preserve it and restore it, then the curtain comes down, and it won't matter that much anymore whether there was racism or not.

# Art Branscombe

*When we first contacted Art by phone, his wife, Bea, answered. She seemed to be running some interference for Art. After she checked us out, Art arranged a time for an interview. Art is eighty-one and uses a hearing aid, and yet it is his wife who is now in need of support: she has cancer, and Art is caring for her. They've been married for fifty-four years, known each other for fifty-seven. They are long-term community activists: the two of them fought for forty years to keep their neighborhood, the Park Hill section of Denver, racially integrated. They haven't dabbled in a variety of issues; they've more or less stayed focused on this one.*

*Art calls himself a "militant integrationist" and a patriot. He was on the governing board of the Park Hill Action Council for over thirty years, until 1999. "I pulled out of the governing board last year. I figured thirty-something years was enough. But then when Bea got sick and decided that she couldn't sit up long enough to get through these board meetings, why, just this last month I went back on the board to replace her." During some of the years that he was a volunteer community activist, Art worked at the* Denver Post *as an editorial writer.*

*We met at their home in the Park Hill section of Denver. Bea rested on the couch during the interview, occasionally adding her comments, especially when she seemed to believe that Art was minimizing or discounting the impact of his organizing.*

• • •

For a long time, Blacks were absolutely forbidden to live here in Park Hill. It was the same in other cities around the country because of the policy of the National Association of Real Estate Boards from about 1920 to about 1950. Starting about 1918 or 1919 in Chicago, the realtors asked the business leaders there to stop letting Blacks live wherever they wanted to live. They were getting spread around too much, and the Chicago Board of Realtors asked them to restrict Black residents to areas where they already were and fill up those areas with Blacks before they opened up any more blocks. That's where our big ghettos came from.

About 1955, after the area to the west of us filled up with Blacks, a developer bought a few blocks north of here and announced that he was going to sell to Blacks. The whispers and then panic started soon after that. In May of 1956, the ministers of seven of the big white churches here delivered a joint sermon, welcoming Blacks to the neighborhood, telling their parishioners that they should welcome Blacks to the neighborhood. All this did was increase the panic.

We moved here in 1959. We had trouble getting a loan for this place. The first two or three mortgage bankers we approached said, "No way. If you were Black, we'd give you a loan, but we're not giving loans to whites in that neighborhood anymore." Finally we got a loan from a banker who lived in Park Hill.

Soon after we moved in, we started hearing the rumors among our neighbors that the NAACP was going to move a welfare family into the middle of the block and scare the whites out. Flyers from realtors started landing on the front porch, saying, "Wouldn't you like to move out while you can still get a good price for this house?"[1] That's how the panic was being purposely spread by realtors to buy these houses up cheap and sell them dear to the Blacks—Negroes as they were called in those days. I had better things to worry about than that.

Eventually we got a flyer from Montview Presbyterian Church nearby, saying that they were going to have a meeting on the "changing character of the Park Hill neighborhood." The people at the meeting formed a laymen's committee to see what they could do. Out of that in due time came the Park Hill Action Council. The core of it was lay persons from seven churches; the agreement was that if the laymen would carry the flag and take the flak, the ministers and their churches would try to raise funds to support us. I guess either Bea or I were the first chair of the public relations committee. That committee rode off in all directions at once, trying to figure out what to do. Nobody knew what the hell was going on. So we had to find out what was going on and figure out what to do about it.

The goals of that initial group were to preserve property values. Part of the motivation was sheer fear—not so much us since we'd bought this house for only $13,500—but most of our neighbors thought they were going to lose their life's investment. There were also some people who believed that we had to do the right thing—welcome people. If white people fled, they weren't going to learn anything.

*(Bea chimes in): In my view, the person who put the real goals together was Art Branscombe. In my view—and I'm undoubtedly biased—I feel that in this little area of 25,000–30,000 people, he was the Thomas Jefferson; he articulated the goals.*

As we got to know more Black people and found out what they were going through—they kept telling us about various manifestations of racism in their lives—we saw things happening that we'd never noticed before. When we'd run across some of our Black neighbors downtown or on the street somewhere, they'd hurry by without saying hello. We asked them about this. They said, "Well, we're used to the white people not saying hello to us." So when I started saying hello to these people as I came on them, why, that made quite a difference. That really opened up things. Just a little thing like that, that never had occurred to me—I passed people on the street downtown, and so what?

There was one man in particular, a Black pediatrician who was moving into a house nearby, on Albion Street. I went to see him one day, and he was just furious because there were "For sale" signs on houses across the street and next to him. He said to me, "What are these clowns doing moving out of here? I've got a better education than any of them; I make more money than they do. How come they're moving out when I'm moving in?"

I started realizing that there was a lot more to this; it wasn't the NAACP putting welfare families into the middle of the blocks, the way the rumors had it. Somebody was telling these whites to move out. They weren't getting this idea all by themselves. Of course, they'd been telling us to move out, too. So that was changing my attitude on the whole business. I started out just believing that this was about preserving our property values, but pretty soon I started to realize what a tough row the Blacks were facing here, and this wasn't their doing; it was somebody directing this, making it happen.

I was reading these books about segregated neighborhoods, learning about what was happening in other cities. As I got more involved and realized what the heck was going on, why, I got madder and madder at the real estate people, except that the president of the Board of Realtors lived down on the next block and turned out to be a nice guy.

I think it only took me about three or four months to realize that preserving property values wasn't the real answer to this. We had to make it possible for Blacks to live wherever they wanted to live, for Christ's sake. This was just a matter of ordinary humanity and justice and whatnot. That's what did it for me. That's what changed me from just another middle-class white guy trying to preserve property values into an increasingly militant housing integrationist.

I realized what was happening to us: that this was white racism that I was fighting. I and some of the other leaders of Park Hill Action began to realize that we couldn't solve Park Hill's problems inside Park Hill. We had to open up the rest of the city to Black residents. That was why we supported strengthening the Fair Housing Act, and also we hatched a scheme of sending out what we called "missionaries" to the suburbs. We'd go in interracial teams to different suburban churches and urge those people out there to set up human relations councils to welcome any Blacks who were courageous enough to move out there. What really made it impressive to those people out there was that here was a real, live Black—well spoken and educated—with a white person, coming out to speak to them.

. . .

In the early years, we put in thousands of hours on this. We had at least one meeting a week and sometimes two or three. There was a cadre of fifty or sixty of us that did most of the work. Boy, we were really putting in the hours.

We thought we were doing something worthwhile, by gosh, if we could preserve integration here. If we could make Blacks welcome and at the same time keep the whites here, why, this was something my reading showed me that practically no other city had managed to do. So we wanted to make this a model for the nation of how you could stop that process and beat the realtors at their own game and create a racially and economically integrated community. We now have African American neighbors on either side of us and across the street; it's been that way for twenty-something years. And in the meantime our house value has gone from $13,500 to $300,000.

As I got into it and found out about the injustices and discrimination that were being committed against Blacks from left and right, that certainly offended my sense of what Americans should be doing. It offended my American civic faith, I guess you could say. But I don't know that I very often consciously thought of it in those terms. I was just mad at what the realtors were doing and sympathetic to what was happening to the Blacks. What was personal was my relationships with Black friends. I didn't want to see this kind of crap happen to them.

And of course some of them, like Jim Reynolds, put the finger on me. (Jim Reynolds was the head of the Civil Rights Commission in Denver.) My mother came out of deep Alabama, near Selma. She was the only role model I had as far as talking about Negroes was concerned, and she always said "nigra." She didn't say Negro. Once I talked that way to Jim Reynolds, and he poked me in the chest and said, "Pronounce it *Negro!*" He wasn't putting up with crap from any white person, including me. And I realized I needed to catch up to date on the pronunciation of things.

There was a lot of stuff I had to learn. I had never dealt with Blacks to any extent before then. I had to learn how they'd been kept out of places like Park

Hill, how they'd been told which blocks they could live in and which they couldn't. Crap like that. I just had to start learning from the bottom.

There was a hassle in the early days of Park Hill Action when the school board, which was going along with the realtors' segregation and stuff, wanted to build a new junior high in what was then a Black neighborhood. It was a way to keep Blacks out of Park Hill and keep all the Black people in that area, west of Colorado Boulevard. That was a revelation to me, and we had quite an argument in Park Hill Action about that. One of the assistant superintendents of the schools came out to a meeting near here and told us, "You're out of your mind. You don't want to be opposing the building of this junior high school. Why would you oppose keeping those Black people out of Park Hill?" He didn't understand it at all! He thought we were crazy. There were people in Park Hill Action in the early days who thought we were crazy, too.

*(Bea turns to Art): You were also the person who insisted that Fred Thomas be the first Black chairman of Park Hill Action Council.*

Yeah, that's one of the things I was proud of, all right, that I greased the railroad to elect our first Black chair.

*(Bea continues): Art's a fair man. He's just a fair person. And he's a patriot. His major in college at George Washington University was in American Thought and Civilization. He has a passion for American history and American ideas.*

**(We ask Art): Do you consider yourself a proud American?**

Yeah. Yeah. Of course we've done a lot of stupid and racist things in our history, but compared to almost any other place I can see, why, we've come off pretty well. Yeah, I'm proud of us.

. . .

**As you began to understand how racism was impacting your neighborhood, how did that impact your work as an editorial writer at the Denver Post?**

I had trouble trying to keep those things separate! Somewhere in there, for three or four years, I quit the board of the Park Hill Action Council so that nobody could tell that I was being impacted. I was writing editorials almost daily during the height of the civil rights revolution on one aspect or another of the thing, particularly schools. What was going on in the neighborhood was impacting me; at least it was educating me about stuff that I wouldn't have known if I hadn't been doing this.

In 1965, the question came up whether the *Post* was going to support a new, stronger Fair Housing Act in the State Legislature. Of course I was on the side, "Yup, let's go, let's do it." But the real estate classified advertising manager was under pressure from the realtors to stay away and not support it. So we had quite a session one day in the office of the publisher of the *Post*, with the real estate ad manager on one side and me on the other. The publisher was leaning back in his chair with his eyes closed, listening, not giving much indication which way he was going to go, and finally the ad manager and I each finished our pitch. My thing was that if we supported the strong Fair Housing Act, nothing much was going to happen for a while because Blacks would be too afraid to move out of the ghetto. And the ad manager was saying there was going to be chaos and they'd be marching down the street, and the *Post* would lose all its real estate ads. And finally, the publisher said, "Aw, the hell with it. We're going to support fair housing." I wrote a full-page commentary on it. That was one of the crucial battles, as far as I was concerned.

I had some guy call me down at the paper one day who said he was going to take his shotgun and come up there and get me. I kept my eye out for him, but he never showed up. He'd have to get through the security downstairs—I can't conceive of anybody bringing a shotgun in there and not being stopped before they got into my cubicle. And we got all sorts of anonymous phone calls here at home and a Molotov cocktail left on our front porch and a rock through our window. We didn't know who was doing that.

*(Art turns to Bea and asks her if she had been afraid and wanted to move. She answers, "No." Bea goes on to explain that their oldest daughter would walk home from a school that was 70 percent Black and had Black and white friends. "It wasn't that big a deal.")*

Two of our three daughters were teenagers then. I didn't fear for their safety. They were going to the public schools nearby. The third was in grade school. All went to integrated schools and were comfortable there. They had Black friends. Of course they were always seeing Black people coming in here for meetings and stuff, and so they were educated in that way, too.

What they picked up in their ordinary school day was the fact that there were Black kids in school with them; some of them they liked, some they didn't like, but they got to be good friends with some of them. Smiley Junior High in those days was, frankly, a little internally segregated. Our daughters went to the accelerated classes and stuff, and those were mostly white. East High School had a real pro-integration principal, and it's always been the elite high school around Denver. Except for a few years during the Black

Panthers' time, why, it's always been a real peaceful, integrated, and proud of being integrated place.[2]

. . .

Bea's been sort of working parallel with me most of the time and doing other parts of the job. I've been doing mostly public relations, I guess, and she's been doing some of that, but she's been doing more of the human relations, I guess you'd call it. She worked much more with the realtors and with the NAACP and other Black groups.

We were both interested in this problem and had a lot of fun working on it. Scared as hell for the first few years, afraid we were going to lose, but we worked like hell to prevent it. She was working parallel. I mean, God, she did a lot of the leadership of the statewide effort to get church people to support the Fair Housing Act. She was a ramrod for that stuff.

*(We ask Art about his experience taking direction and leadership from women.)*

*(Bea responds): He's had three daughters, all of whom are feminists.*

Oh, boy, I've been surrounded here! Ye, gods. No way I could have avoided being somewhat of a feminist!

*(Bea): He's been my prince and taken care of me on stuff I know he doesn't particularly like to do, but he's done it graciously. He's a gentleman.*

Ah, yeah, sometimes.

*(Bea): Yeah, sometimes, not always. But toward me, you're always a gentleman.*

. . .

**Two months after the interview, in the summer of 2000, Bea died. When he was editing this narrative, Art told us, "We were a team in this work. I miss her terribly."**

# Horace Seldon

*In the late 1960s, Horace founded and then was the executive director for twenty-eight years of Community Change, Inc. (CCI), an organization focusing on the "white problem" of racism. This focus went through a series of shifts of emphasis. The first period focused on where white people lived; CCI worked in suburban neighborhoods, training and building groups in several Massachusetts communities. Then the focus shifted to places where people worked in mostly white settings. CCI provided training and consultation, mostly in nonprofit organizations such as the National YWCA. Another phase focused on every level of public and private education, including CCI's cofounding of the Society Organized against Racism in Higher Education (SOAR). Working with artists led to the creation of a photography collective with the theme "Struggles against Racism." Finally came a gradual shift toward working with and in nonprofit groups controlled by people of color and working against racism.*

*At seventy-seven, Horace is technically retired, but on the day of the interview, his "to do" list included working on projects for the Rainbow Coalition Party, Affirmative Action Voices, Citizens against the Death Penalty (an anti–hate crime group), the Immigrant Solidarity Action Alliance, and editing a newsletter on white privilege. And his class on the history of racism in the United States, which he's been teaching for eighteen years at Boston College, began that afternoon. He says, "I don't spend much time in activities not connected to racism because everything for me is connected. I almost can't imagine what isn't connected to racism."*

• • •

The Sunday after Dr. King's assassination in 1968 I was scheduled to preach at a sunrise Easter morning service in Westfield, Massachusetts. I had already announced my resignation from my position with the Massachusetts Conference of the United Church of Christ, which was to be effective in June of 1968. Some job offers had come to me, two from national offices of the church, but none appealed to me, each simply beckoning me into higher echelons of a bureaucracy that had less and less appeal to me. My restless heart somehow knew that I was to be led into whatever the future direction should be.

The Easter Sunday would be the last while I was in my state position, and my friend Tuck Gilbert, a minister in Westfield, had invited me to speak. I stayed overnight on Saturday with Tuck and his wife, Bobbie, arising very early for the sunrise service. That Easter Sunday was an absolutely gorgeous day—bright, warm sun with no clouds in the sky. Part of my sermon reflected on the life of Dr. King, and in it I drew some parallels between his life and the last days of Jesus' life, enough to annoy a couple who stalked away in obvious dismay. I said some very nice "preacherlike" things, calling for us all to match our convictions with our actions.

The service ended, and we all went to the church for a fine breakfast, where there were probably a couple hundred people. Breakfast over, farewells completed, I headed for the Massachusetts Turnpike, eastbound for home. The warm air circulated through the open windows, and I gloried in the day.

At about the Chicopee marker on the turnpike my life was changed for good. I heard no words, I saw no vision, but suddenly, instantly, I knew that I was to use the next years of my life to work on the "white problem." Remember that the Kerner Commission report of early 1968 had clearly placed the causes of our divided, unequal nation(s) in white communities and people. I had no idea what it meant to work on the "white problem" or how to proceed. I only knew that I *must* do that. There was no question to be asked. There was no option to decline. There was only to do.

The rest of the journey home was punctuated with loud singing of hymns and weeping. I was no longer a restless heart. Direction was clear; the way was not. While there was no option, I wanted no option. The command that came found a heart that experience had prepared for the moment. What a wonderful congruence of "have to" and "want to"!

I arrived home in Wakefield. When I walked into the kitchen, Grandma Lushbough was ironing. I said to her, "I know what I must do with my life. I must work on the white problem." There was little response, no discussion. In later years, Grandma told me that as I came into the kitchen that noon there was a "glow" about me, which she knew was not to be penetrated, and she stood back in silence. That was the major epiphany of my life. The next day I began to talk with people about what to do.

. . .

Before I started Community Change with my friends in 1968, for nine years I was on the denominational staff of the United Church of Christ. I was a minister of education; my primary job was to direct a statewide youth group. It was called Pilgrim Fellowship. Eventually, some Black kids from

Roxbury joined the leadership of the youth group. As trust was developed, they began to question the do-gooder things I was doing, like taking white kids from the suburbs to "see Roxbury" and paint buildings. And they began to say, "We feel like animals in a zoo. People are coming here to look at us. We really don't like this." I didn't quite understand what they meant, but I clearly understood that they didn't appreciate what I was doing.

And so when suburban churches would call and say that they wanted to set up some kind of way to help in Roxbury, I began to suggest, "Let's find out how we can get some of those kids to come out to your church and fix up something." And they would think I was crazy. In that process, I was learning something about how the relationship of the white suburban church to the predominantly Black section of the city had to significantly change.

Because I was having contact with those Black kids, the United Church of Christ appointed me to be the liaison to the Blue Hill Christian Center and work with the director, Virgil Wood, who eventually became a good friend. As the liaison, I was asked to attend annual budget meetings, where the denominational staff of white guys would sit around and decide how the mission budget for the United Church of Christ would be spent. Part of the budget would go to the Blue Hill Christian Center. I began to see the stupidity of the institutional arrangement because these white guys would all turn to me and ask me what the budget should be—I knew more than they did, and they would take my word for it, but no one from the center was there. I suddenly realized that it was pretty stupid that I should have the power to decide the budget. I asked myself, "What the fuck am I doing here? What gives me the right to make a decision that will have a real effect out there?"

I was recognizing that my role as a white man had to be different. That really got articulated when Virgil Wood kicked Louise Day Hicks, the chair of the Boston School Committee, out of a school graduation ceremony. The community had said clearly to her that they didn't want her in their community because she was leading the School Committee in policies that segregated the schools. But she attended anyway. Virgil grabbed the microphone and told her to get the hell out. He was arrested. I was out speaking that night and heard about this on the radio while I was driving home. My first comment was, "Oh Virgil, why did you do that?" and then I heard myself saying, "Oh Virgil, why didn't you do that a long time ago?" That was a very clear signal to me: "You white folks come into our community only when we ask you, and you come on our terms."

Valerie Russell was Virgil Wood's program director; she had been one of those kids in the youth group, and we were close. I called her right away and asked her, "Valerie, what do I do now? Do I make contact with Virgil?" She said, "No, don't do anything right now. Come to his trial and sit with me. He'll see you." So that's what I did.

You don't rush in, eager to help, eager to find the role—that wanting to rush in with the answer is sort of built into the psyche of a lot of us white men. You have to just let the relationship develop; you listen, and there comes a chance to say, "I can do that task." And you do it well, and eventually they'll begin to ask and trust you. Now I don't have to worry as much about that anymore; I have a track record, and I can call a lot of folks and get attention. The younger folks don't know me, and I have to go slower.

The principle on which I'm operating now is that as a white male, I am not going to take leadership from people of color until they give it to me. I'm willing to do lots of work. But I'm not willing to coordinate a project until I'm asked. I've become very, very careful about that. In the immigrant group I'm working with, I presented an idea about conducting focus groups of immigrants. They loved it. When it came to facilitation of those focus groups, I suggested a woman from Portugal. But the people of color in the Immigrant Action Alliance suggested I do it, and I agreed.

Let me use the example of Peter Kiang, who started the Asian American Resource Workshop. I read about him in the *Boston Globe* and said to myself, "Gee, this sounds interesting." So I called him up and said, "Can I come down and see you?" I went to his office two or three times, and he came to visit me, and we talked about what was going on in the city. At that time, he had begun to organize around the Huang case—where a Chinese gentleman named Huang had been falsely arrested by a big, strapping Irish cop named Kelly for solicitation and then resisting arrest. I would go to the meetings and the trial and just show up.

The pattern has been one of my going and listening and being there. And then waiting and waiting and waiting and finding a place where there's something I can do. If there's some small task that needs to be done, I say, "I can do that." And it may be a tiny task—make one or two phone calls—but I do it promptly and well. It's a small task that relieves someone else from having to do it. Confidence goes up, trust builds. Pretty soon there's another thing I can do. And so on.

At Community Change it was different because I had the authority from the board of directors. That gave me a certain kind of authority to act. When we first started, I used to get very upset at how we were building an organization centered in a large way on my personality. I used to get very worried about that. This was in the days when the board was really an advisory group, and I wanted it to be a strong board of directors. I struggled to build it as a board of directors. We finally moved in that direction, very slowly over the years. I didn't want to be the big cheese. But they finally said to me, years ago, "Look, we don't have time to be the board of directors you want us to be. We're advisors. Let's face it. Don't worry that it's built around you. You've got charisma. Use it as long as you can do something good with it." That might be different today, but it worked then.

We had Black and white board members, and that changed to include Asian, Latino, and Native Americans so that the board was predominantly women and of color. We didn't talk about accountability—that wasn't the language we used. But it was clearly built in. I used to consciously and deliberately ask the people of color on the board, "As the white male director of this organization, I'd like to know, are we dealing with the real issues as you see them?" Now, other white people need to find their way of dealing with accountability. Times change, the needs change, the issues are a little different. Some are the same. At the same time, I hope that they will be willing to hear about my experience.

The fact that I accepted the role of executive director of Community Change and used my personality to get things done indicates to me that it wasn't as difficult to be a recognized leader as I may think, or I wouldn't have accepted it. There's a certain amount that is personally gratifying, obviously. You know, I go to meetings—it happens so often, it's almost embarrassing, but I love it—and State Representative Byron Rushing is speaking, and he starts by saying, "I didn't know that Horace was going to be here, but I was going to start by quoting him." Or *Boston Globe* columnist Derrick Jackson stands up and says something about me. Or Mickey Roache, the Boston police commissioner, refers to me three times in a speech to the Dorchester Task Force, and I hardly know the guy. There's a whole lot of that kind of stuff. It certainly is gratifying and wonderful. But I don't want to be so enamored with it that it gets in the way of the work that has to be done. Do I get off on it? Sure, but the ultimate question is, "Can I use that successfully for social change?" It's what the board said to me: "Don't worry about it, if you can accomplish something with it, use it." And they said that very clearly to me.

*Did you ever think you weren't doing enough?*

I'm never doing enough.

*(We notice all the awards hanging on his living room wall and ask him to tell us about them.)*

I had a real problem putting these up. Whenever I've gone into someone's office and they've had awards hanging on the walls, I've thought, "What a terribly egotistical thing to do!" I really had to struggle with this, but then I said to myself, "No, damn it, these are my friends." [*Horace starts to walk around to each of the awards and begins to cry.*] Now this is an award from Political Research Associates. When I received this award, Jean Hardisty, the director, told this wonderful story about me. When they moved their office from Chicago to Cambridge, one of the first people that Jean wanted to meet was me. So she asked me to have lunch with her. Her sole purpose was to assure me that she was not interested in competing with Community Change. Within five minutes after talking with me, she realized that competition was not even on my screen.

Here's an award from CPPAX—Citizens for Participation in Political Action. I was really active with them years ago but finally left them because I didn't feel that they were doing enough about racism. I still have a high regard for their political analysis, but it was a very white group and I felt increasingly alienated from them.

This is a Boston Police Special Citation, given to me by Joe Carter. When I got that one, I thought, "Oh, my reputation is ruined forever!" Joe was the superintendent in charge of their internal hearings. I got that award because of my work during the Huang case—the Chinese man who was falsely arrested. The charges against Mr. Huang were dropped, and there was an internal hearing in the police department. The hearing was dreadful. Mr. Huang was treated very disrespectfully by the hearing officer. I learned that there were no rules for the hearing. Then I did some research into administrative law and talked to two or three judges. They agreed to train a hearing officer if the Police Department asked them, so that the hearing process would at least be fairer. I proposed all of this to the police commissioner, he established a training process, and Joe Carter became the head of it. It's a long way from a civilian review board, which they don't have, but at least there are some constraints on the hearing process. As a result of my work, Joe engineered the award for me.

And this is from the National YWCA—I worked with them on developing their "Imperative to Eliminate Racism." Here's a photograph of me speaking at a demonstration on the Boston City Plaza during the first Rodney King trial. This is an award from the Society Organized against Racism in Higher Education; I helped start that, and there are now chapters on about thirty campuses in New England. This is a certificate from the City Mission Society. And that's from Beyond War: "To Horace Seldon for demonstrating a model of commitment to solving critical issues of our time, thereby helping to build our common future."

And finally I have this huge picture that Don West took of me at the African American Meeting House last year. He gave it to me a few months ago at my seventy-fifth birthday celebration at the Old South Church in Boston. When Don gave that to me, I said, "What am I supposed to do with that?"

# Pat Cusick

Pat was born in Alabama, was active in the 1960s Civil Rights Movement in North Carolina, and has lived in Boston since 1964. He considers himself a community organizer. He's been the executive director of the South End Neighborhood Action Program (SNAP) in Boston since 1982. He is seventy.

Pat is proud of the fact that he has successfully avoided jury duty in Massachusetts because of his long record of arrests, including his favorite, "criminal insurrection against the state." He considers himself such a mild-mannered guy committed to nonviolence that he always chuckles when he remembers that particular arrest. In the Civil Rights Movement, Pat and some other activists in Chapel Hill, North Carolina, were trying to put as many people in jail as possible. When the police chief decided not to arrest them as a shift in tactics, they forced his hand by blocking access to the town hall. He is also proud of his work in the 1980s in the South End of Boston to secure affordable housing and in the 1990s successfully forcing Northeastern University to build affordable housing as it was expanding its campus into poor and working-class Black and Latino residential neighborhoods.

One of Pat's crowning moments was in 1970, when he and some other activists held the Harvard commencement ceremony hostage and seized the stage over housing issues. They were trying to negotiate with Harvard to build housing for poor and working-class people instead of student housing. They had been unsuccessful and so decided that they might get some attention if they seized the stage at the Harvard commencement, a very high-profile event. They did and then proceeded to tell everyone in attendance what a racist institution Harvard was. Harvard officials cut the power off, but the activists had an auxiliary power supply. Behind the stage, the officials agreed to negotiate. Pat says, "I've been a bad ass at times."

In April 2001, Pat had a severe stroke. Eight months later, he was still in rehabilitation at Benjamin Health Care Center in Roxbury, Massachusetts. In his own inimitable, stubborn way, Pat intends to return to his job as executive director of SNAP and continue the good fight, organizing against racism and classism in the South End of Boston, as soon as he leaves the health center.

. . .

My great grandfather, William Perry Hollingsworth, was the largest slave-owner in North Alabama, an officer in the Confederate Army, and the founder of the first Klan unit in Alabama after the War between the States, as it's called down there. That's the tradition that I was raised in. My other grandparents were abolitionists. It took a lot of guts for them to be abolitionists in Alabama. That grandfather—Lemuel Standifer—was also a socialist and a close associate and supporter of Eugene V. Debs.[1] I only found that out a few years ago. Growing up in Alabama, I had to learn the poems of the "Poet Priest of the Confederacy," Father Abram J. Ryan. That's what I was raised with. Luckily, my mother sent me away to boarding school, St. Bernard's, a Benedictine monastery in northern Alabama.

In high school, I was very much a Confederate. In 1948, when I was seventeen years old, I avidly supported the Dixiecrats and J. Strom Thurmond.[2] The chink came that same year, when Henry Wallace, who was running on the Progressive Party ticket, came through my town.[3] He had a racially integrated entourage. I was part of the scene at the courthouse, curious to see an integrated group. Wallace and his entourage were pummeled with rocks; the crowd was absolutely vicious—that's actually an understatement. I was very ashamed of the people in my hometown.

A few years before then, some whites had lynched a Black World War II soldier, and that was also something that impacted me. It was the usual story—he supposedly raped a white woman, and when they were transferring him to another town for his own safety, he supposedly jumped out of the car, and the deputies had to shoot him. I knew that was bogus. That impacted me at a very fundamental level.

At school, I had been writing papers defending segregation. The priests were very clear about their opposition to segregation, and they gave me a hard time about what I was writing. It was difficult to find sources in the library to back up my prejudice. By the time I finished high school, I knew that segregation was wrong, but that was only a theoretical type of thing.

Luckily the Korean War came along a couple of years later, and I joined the air force rather than be drafted. I was an air traffic controller in Berlin. This was 1951; Truman had desegregated the armed forces in 1948. Several of my colleagues and even my supervisor—the head of the control tower—were Black. That was a new cultural experience. I had grown up with Black people, but it was the paternalistic imbalance.

I think the key event, the decisive moment for me, was when I was about ten. Our little town, Gadsden, Alabama, was like the one in *To Kill a Mockingbird*. Behind the big houses was an alley called St. John's Alley, and there were these shacks where Black people lived. Many of them worked for the white people who lived in the big houses. One of my friends, Willie, was the son of the washerwoman. I would go to their house and eat a meal or take a nap. All the kids in the neighborhood, regardless of race, played together until we were about eleven years old, and then the parents on both sides pulled us apart.

This is a very vivid event in my memory. I was with two of my white friends, standing on the sidewalk, talking. It's a summer day. Down the alley comes a Black kid riding a bicycle. The other two kids picked up rocks, threw them at the kid on the bicycle, and called him "nigger." I was pissed at them. I thought it was wrong, and I didn't want to be a part of that. But this kid on the bike, who was smaller than us, he had guts. He stopped, got off his bike, and gave us a tongue lashing. He rode off, we went home, and I was extremely upset about that for days. That event is etched in my memory. For me, it's an example of how if you stand up and do the right thing, it will affect things. The actions of that Black kid certainly affected my life, piercing through my white privilege and the whole historical conscious-ness of growing up white in Alabama. I believe that was the beginning of my changing.

. . .

In 1963, when I was in prison, I fasted for almost thirty days. Several times, I had to make up my mind whether I was going to live or die. In the Move-ment, we got caught up with Gandhi and his concept of soul force, sat-yagraha. The first step of satyagraha is where you decide that your life is over, that you are giving your life to the cause. I've seen this soul force at work. We all participated in the development of this soul force. It wasn't just a tactic; it was a philosophy. It saved my life on the chain gang.

When I was sent to the chain gang in prison, there were only a few white people, and we could see the apartheid rules. I was about thirty at the time, and I thought, "I can't deal with this." I told the captain of the chain gang, using my best university manner, "Segregation is evil, and I can't participate in it. You have a segregated camp. I just want to inform you of this. I'm not going to work and I'm not going to eat while I'm here." He looked at me wide-eyed. I went over to the bunkhouse where the other white inmates were hanging out. The guard there said to them, "This here is one of them nigger-lovin' demonstrators from Chapel Hill, and he just told the captain that he'd rather eat and sleep with niggers than you people." With that, he closed the door behind him.

I was petrified, scared shitless. But I knew I shouldn't show that I was scared or it would be worse. So I went over and lay on my bunk. The guard came back, and I didn't get up. "Look," he said, "I don't know what you told the captain, but nobody in this camp eats till you get off your ass and go to the mess hall." I thought, "There's nothing wrong if I postpone my decision for a few minutes," so I went to the mess hall but decided I wouldn't eat.

I got my food, threw it out, and turned my back to show that I was finished eating. That's what you were supposed to do when you were finished. But it aroused people's curiosity. That night, I was scared to death. I pulled the blanket up to my nose. This guy came up to me, and he said, "I know why you're in here, and actually I admire you. I'm a socialist. They're going to try to kill you tonight, and I can't help you because I'm not going to get into this. But I think you should at least know what they're planning to do. The guards are talking it up so that the inmates will do it." That night, I got roughed up quite a bit, but they didn't kill me.

After a couple of days, I was still refusing to eat, and some inmates saw that I was bucking the system. They wanted to know why I was fasting. I told them truthfully, in terms of the Movement and what we whites had done. It got their curiosity up. The captain got worried over the publicity I was getting; he didn't want this shit going on in his camp, so he sent me to the penitentiary in Raleigh, where I finished my fast. That's where I had all these conversations with the prison commissioner, Charles Randall. He tried to get me to come off of my fast, telling me that I would have bodily damage if I kept fasting. He said, "I like you, and I agree with what you are trying to do, but you're not going to accomplish much if you hurt yourself." He offered me the chance to go to the one racially integrated prison camp in North Carolina if I would end my fast. I went.

When we first started participating in the sit-ins at restaurants, we naively thought that if we just talked to the restaurant owners, they would open up their doors. At that time, I did not believe in marching. By the time we were marching, I didn't believe in civil disobedience. By the time we were arrested, I didn't believe in more radical forms of nonviolence and action. The thing I got a year in prison for—and I'm real proud of this—we recruited 150 college students, mostly Black, who were willing to die. We sealed off all five highways coming into town with bodies. Then, since the basketball game of the week was between Chapel Hill and Wake Forest, we got onto the floor and seized the basketball. That was my idea. I was in charge of tactics. I think that was the real reason I got arrested—for trying to stop the basketball game. We lost the support of the Quakers and religious pacifists in Chapel Hill. They thought we were way beyond the bounds of nonviolence as they knew it.

I wasn't a courageous person, but I did have a sense of justice and injustice. I so admired Dr. King and others like him, and I really admired those young Black people who were at the forefront. The Movement was led by Black teenagers. That was a very strong influence on me.

The idea of laying our life down came from a group I helped form, the Student Peace Union (SPU). We were one of many chapters of SPU around the United States. SPU was the predecessor of Students for a Democratic Society.[4] Through SPU, I met radical pacifists like David McReynolds, now head of the War Resisters' League, and Dorothy Day.[5] They were too radical for me, but since no one would sponsor them to come to Chapel Hill, our chapter of SPU brought them to town. I met people like that who introduced me to Gandhi and satyagraha.

• • •

I came to Massachusetts in 1964 and soon started working with teenagers in Roxbury. I was very involved in getting them into the Movement. Stokely Carmichael came to town to talk about Black Power.[6] He had a rally about two blocks from where I worked on Intervale Street. I knew what he was going to say, and I knew that I would be uncomfortable if I went, but how could I not go? He was going to be talking about me as one of the white folks. Hopefully not one of *those* white folks, but nonetheless I felt I had to hear him. So I went, and sure enough, I was the only white person there. Stokely said that white people were irrelevant and shouldn't be working in Black communities—they didn't need us and we should get out. I was really hurt, oh, I was really hurt.

I went home, which was about two blocks in the other direction from my office. I dealt with what Stokely had said for about three weeks. Without defining it intellectually, I knew I had to grapple with it. And so I decided that I would never organize in the Black community again. I got a job in Cambridge, working with white teenagers in a housing project.

The incident with Stokely motivated me to make a change. I'd like to think I wouldn't have needed it, but maybe I did. By leaving Roxbury at that time, I didn't get to the point of feeling so hurt and rejected by the Black Power Movement that I decided to give up challenging racism altogether. It is distressing to me that many white people did feel hurt and rejected in such a way that they decided to give up. I can understand the hurt, but their leaving distresses me greatly. It was a matter of putting it in context.

• • •

I have only two white friends. I don't hang out with white people. I really don't associate with white people.

*Why?*

I haven't thought about that until recently. There was a big shift for me in my willingness to hang out with white people that's related to my sexual orientation. In the early 1960s, I had not come out of the closet. I knew I was gay, but I hadn't come out. In 1963, my mental sexual object choice shifted from white men to Black men. Up to that time, my ideal sexual object choice was blond-haired and blue-eyed. That totally shifted in a month. Looking back on that, I can figure that out. There were two things. White men were a danger to me—white people were beating me, kicking my teeth out. And my heroes were the Black high school students. At every step of the way, white meant danger to me.

Here in the neighborhood where I live now, the people I fight with every day are white. The whole white privilege thing is pervasive in their lives. The greatest example was last Thursday. There are two Black guys from Roxbury who want to develop a shopping complex down the street. The city tried to slow them down, and yet at the same planning meeting, the city is pushing Best Western to move more quickly on developing a site just up the street.

Now the NAACP ranks hotels in terms of what it's like for Black folks to work there. Best Western is in the worst category. At the planning meeting, we asked the representative from Best Western about this, and he said that he didn't know anything about that. This was a very patrician-looking guy with silver hair. I knew that this guy owned several Best Westerns, and so I asked him, "In the hotels you own, how many people of color work there?" He said, "I'm a liberal. I don't know. I don't keep track of those things in my business." I was outraged. I said, "You know, if you're going to build here, you will report weekly on the race of the construction crew"—because these were Boston requirements—"and you will do that if you want this hotel." I felt like I had been thrown back into the '50s and '60s. He got very angry, and he didn't understand it. His white privilege was all over the place. Unfortunately, he got the hotel he wanted.

*Do you care if white people like you?*

No. If you look at all the pictures hanging up on the walls of my apartment, other than my socialist grandfather, there are not many pictures of white people. Almost all of them are people of color.

There are no white people in this neighborhood. Well, actually, that's not true. There's the white gentry. This is one of the most poverty-stricken neighborhoods in Boston and one of the most affluent at the same time. This is a neighborhood of haves and have-nots, and I'm not interested in identifying with the haves, especially not the gay white gentry in this neighborhood. I got over being ashamed of being gay and came out of the closet. And I've also been ashamed of being gay because of the way they act and the racism in that community. It's very much a kind of trench warfare here between the haves and the have-nots.

*Do you have a disdain for white people?*

I have a disdain for the white gentry in this neighborhood and their racism. But no, I'm not disdainful of white people who are antiracist. I believed in the Rainbow Coalition for the time that it was in existence here—I coordinated eastern Massachusetts for Jesse Jackson's presidential campaign. In the Rainbow Coalition, I met progressive whites I considered not flaky but really, really with it. So it all depends on what white people are doing.

*Do you feel any sense of loss in not hanging out with white people?*

None whatsoever. It's not hostility. It's just that they don't matter to me. They matter because they're doing a lot of damage. Now this sounds really crazy. I don't think of myself as a white person that much—I don't ponder it. On the other hand, people are always telling me, "You're Black." I'm not trying to be Black. I've never tried to be Black. In fact, it's insulting to me if someone says that to me because it's saying that to be humanistic, you have to be Black. If a white person is sensitive and progressive, people will say that you're trying to be Black, when you're just trying to be a white person who is a human being who has certain values.

The phrase I use with my Black friends is "my white cousins," as in, "My white cousins are embarrassing me again." I won't call them my white brothers. That's how I feel most of the time. I'm aggressive toward my white cousins, and I'll also try to make peace with them. If we kick somebody's ass, I'll try to make peace, but until that point I'll be aggressive in terms of the stuff we do around here.

. . .

I'm an unusual white gay man. I just got an award from the Massachusetts Lesbian and Gay Political Alliance. I was shocked when I got the award because I have never been an activist or organizer in the gay community. I've been an activist who is openly gay, which I think is toughter than being openly gay in the gay community. It's more difficult sometimes to be openly gay in a Black community, but there's a great value in it, too, because it helps break down the stereotypes that my white gay cousins in the South End— whom I despise so much—don't care about racism. I guess that's why they gave me the award. The gay community needs more organizers and activists who are openly gay. I was pleased to get the award because it may encourage other people.

Lord, it took me a long time to come out. But around Black folks now, I never hesitate to come out. It's easy to slip back into the closet, so I will intentionally go out of my way to come out. I'll casually say something like, "As a gay person, . . . " That helps me not go back into the closet. I don't think I could, but nevertheless, it's insurance that I don't go back in.

I worked in the Movement for Bayard Rustin for about a year.[7] I knew he was gay, and he told me I should come out. He and some peace groups in New York City hired me to work in the South with Dr. King's staff to help make the connections between the Civil Rights Movement and the antiwar movement. That connection wasn't apparent in the early '60s. In that context, I was one of the coordinators of the 1963 March on Washington.[8]

Bayard came up here one time in the late '60s, and we went to supper and then to a jazz club called Lenny's on the Turnpike. Bayard asked me, "Are you still in the closet?" I said, "Yes, but." In this impeccable, put-on British accent, he said, "Don't hand me the 'but.' I want you to come out of the closet. Don't let happen to you what happened to me. All my life, I ran from being exposed. I didn't want to be exposed in the Montgomery bus boycott." He'd been arrested in California on a morals charge, and he thought it would hurt the Movement if he were out as a gay man. But then Senator J. Strom Thurmond dragged him out of the closet, saying that Rustin was a "notorious pervert" in charge of the March on Washington.

After reminding me of this, Bayard said to me, "Pat, the next day after Thurmond did that, what else was new? That which I had run from for decades was over in about twenty-four hours. So don't let that happen to you." I didn't take his advice immediately, but I've never forgotten what he told me.

In 1984, when [Michael] Dukakis was running for president, I was head of the Second Suffolk Ward Committee, which was predominantly Black. At the Democratic Convention, there were 13 openly gay delegates out of 2,500. We wanted a change in the charter [to the effect] that the Democratic Party would do outreach to Blacks, Latinos, women, the handicapped—the whole laundry list—and we wanted to add lesbians and gay men. I've never seen such a big fight over nothing—there was an uproar. This was a touchy issue with Dukakis. He pulled out his whole machinery at the convention and organized a roll call vote against us. Given my whole life, I had to declare myself a gay delegate. We actually picked up a thousand votes but not enough to win; eventually our proposal got into the platform.

My colleagues in the gay delegation came to me to ask me to speak. Bruce Bolling [an African American state representative] was supposed to speak in support of the proposal, but they couldn't find him, so they asked me to speak in front of the convention. I thought, if I'm going to come out in front of 2,500 people, I might as well do it with flair. So I'm on my way up to the dais, and here comes Bruce. I say to him, "Bruce, I'm glad to see you." He ends up speaking so that I don't have to. I went back to the Second Suffolk delegation and told them why I supported the proposal and that I was gay.

*Did you ever question your commitment to challenging racism?*

After I had been roughed up in prison, I thought, "What the hell am I doing here? This is more than I bargained for." And then I thought about it a lot and realized that I had to do this. That's the only time I've questioned it. I've been fortunate to have been thrown into a lot of situations where I could have gone ahead or backed out. I've had to make an awful lot of choices over the last thirty years in this whole area. I haven't copped out yet. The more that happens, the stronger I get. I was certainly not that strong when I joined the Civil Rights Movement.

I'm an organizer. There are consequences when we challenge the people in power. I was part of a coalition with Mel King, Dianne Wilkerson, Byron Rushing, and others to stop Northeastern University from expanding into Black neighborhoods.[9] Because of my involvement in that, my agency, SNAP, will never get funding from the city. And I have a reputation of being a bulldog. I have to watch that, too. The local HUD office then characterized our coalition, which is all people of color except me, as "Cusick's gang."[10] That's a racist statement.

The question about being a white person and having the option to leave a movement led by people of color is rhetorical for me. This may sound elitist, but I can't conceive of leaving this work. My life as I know it would die if I did. I'm delighted with my life. I should have been more judicious in terms of saving money, I think about that, but I wouldn't swap this life for another. No way! I look at myself in the morning and I like what I see.

# Nat Yalowitz

When we interviewed Billy Yalowitz, he suggested that we also interview his father. Billy wanted us to include in this book someone like Nat who was a part of the New York City left-wing Jewish movement of the 1930s and 1940s. Billy felt that this was important for both the history of antiracism in the United States—the impact of the left wing and the prominent roles of Jews in the movement are largely invisible—and because Billy appreciates having had the opportunity to grow up in a radical environment.

Nat is seventy. He and his wife Wendy have lived for the last forty years in the International Ladies' Garment Workers' Union (ILGWU) housing co-op on the Lower West Side of Manhattan with 2,800 other families. Nat describes it as a big community and a little city. When they first moved in, it was low to moderate income, about 95 percent white and Jewish. Today it's about 90 percent white, 80 percent Jewish, and 70 percent seniors: a Naturally Occurring Retirement Community (NORC), where a group of people are "aging in place." Nat has come out of retirement and become very involved with NORCs across the United States: promoting them, organizing them, and consulting with them as they set up social services for their residents. He founded the NORC Supportive Service Center, Inc., a nonprofit cooperative to develop NORC programs all over the United States. In particular, Nat is working with two NORCs: Rochdale (the second largest housing cooperative in the United States and overwhelmingly Black, in Queens) and Esplanade Gardens (an all-Black housing cooperative in Harlem).

The interview took place in Wendy and Nat's apartment on a Sunday afternoon. Billy came up from Philadelphia to sit in on the interview. This is the apartment where he grew up; his family moved here when he was three years old. The interview began with Nat making some brief comments about the history of radical immigrant Jews and then talking about his own experiences as a young Jewish man in New York City. As the interview unfolded, Billy began to make comments to us and his parents about his experiences as a boy growing up in New York in a left wing Jewish family. Toward the end of the interview, Billy talked directly to his dad about a couple of formative experiences with him, and Nat talked about having influenced Billy.

· · ·

Many Jews who came over here from Eastern Europe were liberal to radical. Many were not political. But when they got here, they took jobs in industries where they were very exploited, like a lot of other immigrants. Unions added a certain flavor to Jews' lives, in terms of radicalizing them to fight back against the bosses. Added to that were the progressive political parties of the early twentieth century like the Wobblies and the Socialist Party.[1] If you lived in a big city like New York, it was a big stew that was being stirred.

The religious aspect had nothing to do with it. Many Jews were religious, from Orthodox to Reform and everything in between, and many Jews were not religious. I would say that those who were more religious were less political, at least in terms of American politics.

I'm a second-generation Jewish American. My dad was born in Russia; my mother was born in Romania. I was born in the Bronx and have lived my whole life in New York City (NYC), except for the time I was in the army, stationed in Europe and other parts of the U.S. I've lived in Manhattan for the last forty years.

New York politics are fast and furious, whether you're conservative or radical or in between; it's not slow. That has to do with big city politics and the drama of living in a city with everything that goes on. And the last 60–70 years have been very dramatic in American politics. So if you have any politics at all, and you live in NYC, you still know what's going on. And you have a position or a point of view about everything. That includes me.

I was a "young man" by the age of seven, because if you grew up in the Depression and you knew what poverty was, you were a young man. I think that's almost a definition of being a man. You know what poverty is. You're a man. If you don't know where breakfast is coming from, you become a man. At that age, I knew intimately what was going on in NYC, from my point of view. What was going on was politics of survival, politics of struggle, politics of a life of the poor against the rich. I was living in a working-class Jewish community that was also Italian and Irish. There wasn't a Black face in my community.

At the same time, I was aware of Black people because I went to a radical children's camp in New Jersey. Maybe it wasn't the first, but it was one of the first interracial children's camps in the country. It was called Camp Wochica. It's not an Indian name—it stands for "workers' children's camp." It was sponsored by some left groups and unions. Summer was very very special for me. That's where I learned about the Scottsboro boys and the fact that there were Black men getting lynched.[2]

*(Billy interrupts: "I've got to go get the photo, Pop." He brings us a camp photograph, points out his dad, and also points out that Paul Robeson is in the picture.)*

My memories of Camp Wochica are very vivid and mostly positive. There was a lot of fun and a lot of what you would call left wing proselytizing. You sang all of the leftist songs, and you believed in all the good things in life: brotherhood and internationalism. During the 1930s, there was a little war going on in Spain, and we knew about that because some of the counselors went there and fought and died there.[3] It was pretty rich stuff.

The impact of going to that camp was profound, very profound. It's like the title of the book, *Bred in the Bone,* by the Canadian writer Robert Davies. That's the way it was, like bred in the bone. The camp had a deep socializing effect, a deep intellectualizing effect, a deep emotional effect, a deep political effect. It really grabbed my heart and held me. For most of the people who went there, I'd say that's true. The same is probably true for many children's camps, but this more so because it was an all-engulfing kind of thing. You had a lot of fun and nourishment from elders and a lot of encouragement and support. The whole combination was wonderful.

Back in NYC, I was involved in some left wing political clubs for kids. One of them was American Youth for Democracy (AYD). In AYD, we did what had to be done in politics at the time. In World War II, AYD was very active in supporting the home front by collecting money or whatever we had to do to support the war effort. During the war, there was some discussion of integrating the army. It didn't go very far. The army wasn't integrated until after the war. But we talked about that in AYD, the need for equality of men in the army. Women in the armed forces weren't an issue at that point. And we talked about internationalism. If your politics moved you to understand and celebrate people in other parts of the world, the war emphasized that. So I was very much aware of people in Europe and people in Asia. And of course, I was still very aware of people in the South, especially Blacks, and how they were being treated.

There was a sense of the unity of all people that developed during the war and the possibility of a friendly relationship between the Soviet Union and the United States. In AYD, we wanted to maintain that kind of internationalism. But as soon as Roosevelt died in 1945, Truman became anti–Soviet Union. We were aware of this shift and talked about it in AYD, and we said that bad times were ahead. We said, "We were allies during the war and we should continue that. The enemy isn't Russia; it's poverty." The enemy became Russia.

In 1946–1948, I was in high school and still very active in politics. We had all kinds of clubs. I was vice-president of the Frederick Douglass Society; the president was a Black student. And I was the president of the American-Soviet Friendship Club. Both clubs had faculty advisers, and we were encouraged in those clubs. Each club promoted the cause: interracial and international brotherhood, understanding, values. Something that they supported that at that time I was opposed to was "tolerance." I always looked down my nose at "tolerance." I thought "tolerance" was patronizing. You have to tolerate me? Whites have to tolerate Blacks? Oddly enough, some of the Black students said, "We want to have tolerance." And I said, "Oh, my, are they limited in their understanding. Forgive them, oh Lord!" I wanted to promote more than tolerance. Now, I would accept tolerance as very important because so many people are still intolerant.

*Were you ever at risk?*

Yeah. You were at risk because you were poor. You were at risk for having ideas that were not supported by the government and the newspapers. So you were at double risk. And you were at risk for being Jewish in terms of what was going on During World War II. So there's a triple risk. The biggest thing creating risk was being poor.

I felt protected and nourished by being with radical people. These were achieving young people. They were not outside the system. They worked hard to achieve within the system. We were involved in protesting bad things in the society. We had May Day parades in NYC, where I would march with all the unions, and progressive and radical groups would march down Eighth Avenue. Picketing was a big part of my life. When it first came out, we picketed *Gone with the Wind* because it was full of racist images. We felt part of a bigger movement. We felt very identified with FDR and big things in the society. And of course, I got a real deep sense of all that when I went to Camp Wochica. That gave me a tremendous surge. Whatever we were doing, I could feel a real strong level of confidence that I wouldn't be hurt. That wasn't altogether true. That came apart. Everything has its little crevices, its limitations, its contradictions. But for the most part, I felt safe.

In the 1930s and '40s, as far as I was concerned, issues of oppression were mostly related to racism. Jews seemed to get by, even if they weren't doing well. There were quotas in terms of where they might live and work and go to college. Medicine was closed. Certain businesses were closed—banking and real estate, forget about it. Some Jews who became leaders in their field actually converted—they were no longer Jews. Robert Moses, who became big in the field of public works, became Episcopalian. Even though he was a left winger and a model for me, my brother changed his name from Yalowitz to Yale, and he maintained that name until he died.

I knew all of that by the time I was sixteen, but it didn't personally affect me. I wasn't aware of anti-Semitism in any real sense of the word, even during World War II. We were aware that Hitler was anti-Semitic; we weren't aware of how many people he had killed and the crematoriums and the concentration camps until after the war, when all that emerged.

So growing up meant living in hard poverty, being a witness to racial segregation, war, and social conflict. Fighting racial injustice and social class conflict became an essential part of my living. Being a left wing Jewish man meant participation in the movement to free oppressed people. Picket lines, marches on Washington—they were as essential as playing stickball as a kid.

*(Billy makes a comment): I grew up at the tail end of that radical Jewish world. I was lucky to have some tastes of it. By the time I came along, it had really come apart for many reasons. But there was a sense of protection. I lived here in the ILGWU housing co-op. A lot of our neighbors were old union folks. In those decades before the '60s, the Jewish ethos was so pervasive. And the Jewish ethos was part of a radical ethos that could exist before McCarthy. The sense was that you could be out in the street as a radical Jew. You might get beat back, you might get excluded from many walks of life, but you could be public in a certain way, and there were vehicles for that that don't really exist any more. By the '60s, the Jewish radical world had been so beaten back. McCarthyism took an enormous toll. Pre-McCarthy, you could be out in the street. Post-McCarthy, you had to hide as a left wing Jew. All the progressive movements in this country were affected by McCarthyism. Jewish, non-Jewish, Black. It has so limited the discourse that is allowed in the country, so that "liberal" is a dirty word now. Before McCarthy, progressives thought of a liberal as a right winger.*

It almost felt like—from a political point of view and almost literally from a physical point of view—the U.S. was covered by a gigantic iceberg. It was like we were back to the Ice Age. Now, the iceberg is receding, but there's still not a comfortable feeling in this country for radicals.

*(Billy again): Jews get scapegoated. If the economy gets bad enough, then you blame the Jews. Part of what gets said there is that the Jews control everything. So to stand up for yourself as a Jew, you run the risk of becoming a direct target of anti-Semitism. So for a left wing Jew, it has been easier to stand up for someone other than for yourself. That is still true for me. I have to remind myself in the work I do with people of color to be out in the open as a Jew. I trace that back to the history of the political movement that I grew up in.*

When you get involved in radical causes and organizations where you're really striking at the source of oppression of people in this society—which is the economic system—then you feel that it's going to help you, too, as a Jew. That was always part of my feeling, and I was very conscious of that as a young person. If I spoke, as I did many times, on street corners about issues like racism, I was speaking (in my mind consciously) as a left wing Jew who was poor at one point. While at college, I joined and became active in Hillel, a campus organization for Jewish students. This was soon after Israel became a state. I was a proud, open, radical Jew in a Jewish organization and enjoying it very much, even though some other Jewish radicals criticized me.

As radical people, Wendy and I supported our kids in being radical. Our life was radical. Our life was interracial. That's what we believed in. We took them to concerts to hear Pete Seeger, and he sang certain kind of songs. We took them down to Washington, D.C., where we paraded against the Vietnam War. We took them to peace parades over at the United Nations. We sent them to radical camps. We bought a country house in Goldens Bridge, N.Y.; there was a small community there founded by people who were left wingers in the 1920s for working-class people who wanted a place to go in the summer. It was a progressive place, mostly Jewish. It was like a kibbutz. We organized many, many speakers on topics like racial justice and anti-lynching; we had representatives from SNCC come and talk to us.[4] We raised money. In 1963, we had a couple of buses that drove all night to Washington, D.C., to participate in the March on Washington.

*(Billy): I grew up in an urban environment where there were lots of different kinds of folks around, and I appreciate that my parents decided to stay in NYC at a time when there was white flight to the suburbs. It was courageous for them to do that. I went to public schools in Manhattan. P.S. 33 was one-third Black, one-third Puerto Rican, and one-third white when I went there. It wasn't easy, but it still informs what I do in my life around racism and ending oppression of all kinds. I was lucky enough to have this left wing Jewish background and to live here in the city. And I was lucky to inherit the work that my mom and other feminists have done: how does oppression psychologically affect each person growing up in an oppressive society? How does structural oppression get internalized into individuals?*

My family came first, my work came second, and my politics came third. I had children and a wife, and it was very important to me that that came first. I was a social worker, and that was very important for me to master. If, in between, I had something else I could do and wanted to do politically, I did it. Other folks I knew whose politics always came first had unhappy family lives and unhappy professional lives.

*(Billy): I should say, as a product of this union, that this was a very child-centered family. My parents were excellent parents. You did good by me. So then the questions are, "How did I come out with a Jewish identity, a political identity, and a white antiracist identity? And how do you build a life of integrity when you're standing*

*pretty far outside of the mainstream because you're living values of ending oppres-*
*sion? To what degree does one conform? How do you live in the society?" The old left*
*took a correct stand around racism but didn't understand other things about people's*
*lives, including, for example, their identities as Jews and their personal lives. On the*
*other hand, it's very tough to live a radical life in a nuclear family. I had communal*
*experiences, like camp and being at our place in Goldens Bridge, that were ex-*
*ceptions to that. I think the questions I just asked are tough questions, and I in-*
*herited the contradictions in those questions, and I'm continuing to live those*
*contradictions.*

• • •

Twenty years ago, I directed a settlement house in a Black and Hispanic
community, but the board of directors was all white, Protestant women.
They were conservative, mostly Republican. I was the first male they hired. I
was the first Jew they hired. I was the first radical progressive they hired. I
was really all too much for them.

The people who made use of the facility were not from the community.
We had very few Puerto Rican and Black kids using it. The first thing I
decided was to open it up to people who lived there. A group of kids
approached me and said that they'd like to come in. I said, "Fine. We'll be the
W. E. B. Du Bois Club." So I announced to the board that we were going to
have a new club in here and that there were going to be many more young
people and a group called the W. E. B. Du Bois Club. They said, "Fine." Well,
they thought I had said "the boys' club." They woke up about two years later
and asked me if this was a radical group. I didn't last too long in that place.
But I did integrate the board, and the membership became more integrated
with Blacks and Puerto Ricans.

*Was there any conflict you experienced, internally or externally,*
*between your having a graduate degree in social work and your*
*organizing working-class people?*

Good question. At one point, I became very much involved in union activities. Unions have benefit funds for the workers, and the fund is a separate
organization. It works with both the union and the employer. I was executive director of a benefit fund for a radical union. Ninety-nine percent of the
workers were Black and Hispanic, low paid, and new to unions. Here I was,
the executive director, probably one of the few professionals in the whole
building, much less in the benefits fund and the union.

I was supportive of everything the union did, even though I sometimes had questions about what they were doing. I never voiced my criticism of the union. When it came to singing the old radical union songs, I sang the songs with them. But I knew I was the odd man out. I did the job as well as I could and lasted as long as I could. My fallout was with the employer, not the union. The representative of the employer didn't particularly like me—I was too radical for them.

*(Billy): Dad, as you talk about your experience with the union, it makes me think about my experience at the university. I basically work for a large, white, Protestant corporation, the University of Pennsylvania. It represents an enormous concentration of resources, and I am in the position of trying to distribute those resources to working-class and poor people of color. It's a classic Jewish position: the tax collector, the moneylender. Now, as Jews have become middle class, we are in positions of being social workers and teachers. It's a tricky thing. I have the pseudo-privileges of being white and having a good education, and I can get myself in the door in certain ways. I have access to resources and have to figure out how to distribute them. It's uncomfortable. More and more, I have to figure out how to get out of the middle person position or to figure out how to use that position to build relationships and trust.*

In the early '90s, there was some anti-Semitism going on in parts of the Black community. There was this guy, Khalid Mohammed, a leader in the Nation of Islam, who was pretty vicious in what he said about Jews. It set off a lot of reaction in the Jewish community and the Black community. I decided that we would have a meeting here at the co-op on Black-Jewish relations. I got some good people, Blacks and Jews, who live here to speak about the issue. We had an overflowing audience, I chaired the meeting.

Some of the members of the audience pointed the finger, saying, "Why don't you talk about Black anti-Semitism instead of Black-Jewish brotherhood and unity?" People in the audience had a right to say anything they wanted to say, and there were some pretty mean statements made about all the speakers. We had boos and catcalls and applause. We knew that was going to happen. But then we had some Blacks and Jews in the audience who said, "We'll talk about what we have to talk about. If you want to talk about Black anti-Semitism, you can talk about anything you damn well please, even if it's anti-Jewish or anti-Black. This is an open meeting."

We wanted to say that being anti-Jewish is as bad as being anti-Black. Khalid Mohammed doesn't represent all Black people any more than a Jewish person who is anti-Black represents all Jewish people. I organized the thing, and I was not going to have a meeting at that time in history that would focus only on how terrible it was for Blacks to be anti-Semitic because while there is anti-Semitism among some Blacks, there is also racism among some Jews. It was important for this community not to have that anti-Black feeling because of some loudmouthed Black in New Jersey.

What we wanted to represent was a move toward some common ground and toward some unity and toward some understanding of each other. We were trying to focus on how we could work together. We didn't want to criticize anyone. I believe that most of us are trying to lead the best lives we can. The society places limits on people who don't have power, including Jews and Blacks. We wanted to get some understanding about how those limitations can be overcome, in the mind and in the heart. We said what we wanted to in an affirmative way. I think that's what came out of the meeting.

• • •

*(Billy): There are two memories I have of you, Dad, that I think are significant for me. The first is that we would go to the Lower East Side on Sundays to buy halvah and pickles. I remember watching you interact with everybody. I was amazed. I thought, "He knows everybody." You addressed everyone as if you knew them—the gas station attendant, the guy who was selling us the pickles, the woman who was selling the halvah—even though you didn't know them. The main thing about that for me was your valuing of working people. I function like that more and more in my life. People around me will ask, "How do you know everybody?" "Well, I just made friends with them." I learned that from you. I think that that is a New York, working-class, Jewish perspective.*

*The second is that I grew up in a household where my dad's hero was Paul Robeson. I had an African American role model. It was very personal for you. We sang the songs. His voice was singing in the house all the time. And when our family was driving someplace, we sang civil rights and union songs. In a self-deprecating way, my dad calls that proselytizing. But you don't call it proselytizing when it's Christian religious training. You call it learning the liturgy or learning a tradition. And in fact, that's what it was. There was a learning of a tradition that included songs from all over the world and the songs of peoples of color. That's what I was lucky enough to sing.*

*As a result, there's a way that African American culture was close to me. It wasn't removed. It's probably why I can pull off some of the things that I pull off around race and working with African Americans. In a certain way, I've had to fight against leading a segregated life the way that any white person does. But I think I was lucky enough to not have a sense of separation from African Americans. Early on, I didn't feel that separation. So, because of that, maybe I had a head start on building relationships with African Americans and other people of color.*

*(We ask): Nat, was it intentional to give Billy that tradition?*

Oh, yeah. Very much.

*And was it okay for Billy to form his own ideas about race and being a Jew, and even challenge you about your ideas?*

Sure it was okay. What informs him is very different from what informs me. He's acting on current experiences and some history that he's learned and heard about from me. The history is my life and the times I've lived through. Today, what he's doing, I'm only hearing from him, and I'm not part of it. He's doing his stuff in Pennsylvania; I can only see it through his eyes.

Billy has a lot of experience in life. I can relate to some of it. As he tells me more about his life and as I get to understand it, then pretty soon, we're talking about things that we're both interested in. We don't talk about everything, but we do talk about things that we feel deeply about. Our conversations raise all kinds of issues that are interesting to me and that I learn from. All you can do is hope that your kids' values are good values. A kid is a work of art.

# Grassroots Organizing

# Jesse Wimberley

*Jesse is forty-three. He's a single parent; his children are seven and eight. They live on a fifty-acre farm in West End, North Carolina, in a house that was built in 1870 by his Scotch-Irish great grandfather, Gonsolvo Speight.*

*Jesse worked at the Piedmont Peace Project (PPP) as an organizer from 1988 to 2000. Before that, he worked on projects in Africa and Central America. Now, he wears three hats: consulting and training for nonprofit organizations, carpentry, and what is called locally "raking straw"—collecting and selling the pine needles that fall from over twenty thousand trees he's planted on his farm. "I hope that one day I'll be able to live off of that." But at present, he struggles to make enough money to get by.*

*He's interested in exploring sustainable models for living. One of his long-term goals is to set up an environmental education center for young people at the farm. The ecosystem at the farm is diverse; he hopes to teach kids that "diversity is a key to making life interesting" and that water, plants, and soil are dependent on one another, just like human beings are.*

*If he had the funding, he'd spend his time working with low-income men. "I hear the pain in their voices when they make angry comments at people of color. Their fear is poking through the costume they're wearing. I just want to go up and hug them, and of course if I did that, I'd get hit. If I could, I'd stand out on some newly plowed ground with some seeds and say to them, 'I wonder what we can grow here.'"*

*The interview took place at the farm. It's at the end of a sandy road that winds through the pine trees. The house feels warm and used, like an old, favorite sweater.*

. . .

I grew up here in Moore County and spent time on this farm as a child. As early as nine, I knew that I'd live in this house. In 1986, I moved to the farm and began to restore it as a family farm, so that it would look like it did in 1870. I knew that the farm was a place that was important to a lot of people. I wanted to see what meaning it held for me. I was very involved with Central America at the time but realized that that was not where I needed to be. I needed to go home. Home represented both a physical place and a spiritual place. I knew it would be the closest I would get to doing what I had learned was important in both Africa and Central America—that is, people coming back and reclaiming a heritage that was defined by them and not by capitalism. There are places on the floor carved out by the feet of my ancestors. When I run my hand over those places, I remember that I am part of a continuum.

My mom and grandfather were born on the farm, but the poverty gave them a real negative feeling about the place. And my heritage has a lot of negative stuff: low income, southern white guy. The energy that people feel when they come out here has gone from one of shame to being honored. This is where we hold all our family gatherings now. They don't feel the poverty that they once felt.

Being on the farm has given me a chance to be more intimate with my children and the land. The farm also gives me time to be still and listen to my own self instead of information coming in from the outside. I remember my grandfather telling me, "If you are still, all the answers you need will come to you." I know it's a privilege to be able to do that. There are a lot of guys around here who don't have the opportunity each day to be still in the woods. I've done enough work to know that it's not an option for most people.

. . .

I joined PPP in 1988. I had come back from Africa and Central America and was doing some speaking around North Carolina on the parallels between what was happening to low-income people in this country and what was happening in Africa and Central America. Linda Stout, who founded PPP, heard about me and said, "I hear you're interested in the same things I am. How would you like to be an organizer?" I said, "Sure, that sounds good. What's an organizer?"

At PPP, we look at connecting issues of national and international economics: GATT [General Agreement on Tariffs and Trade], NAFTA [North American Free Trade Agreement], the whole restructuring of the economy and how it plays out in local economics. How barriers of race and class and sexual preference are used as wedges to keep that patriarchal economic system in place.

In the early organizing, we learned that if you are going to do community organizing and community building, you're going to keep running into barriers of oppression. When you cannot grasp what the larger oppression looks like, the matrix of it, you fight against those closest to you. The same thing happens to my wife and me when we don't have food; instead of being able to sit down and be rational and go, "It's not your fault or my fault," we turn on each other. So a big part of the organizing in each community is just helping low-income people of color to not blame each other for the living conditions but to realize that poverty is a political, not a personal, failure. That is a huge undertaking in any community. Moving from personal shaming to the larger context of economics and politics is a day-in, day-out challenge. We spend the largest part of our energy right there. We don't try to get as many large showcase victories as we do people saying, "I get it. We need to work together."

In the early days, when we did organizing with Blacks and whites, Black folks would be talking, but as soon as white folks said something, the Black folks in the room would shut down. What the white people said had more weight. Do you know what I mean? No matter how you set it up, you couldn't overcome that dynamic. The white folks could not let go of that because if you are a low-income white person, carrying that sense of being better is one of the few things you have. The local people of color have to be clear enough in their voice so that the white folks won't be able to take up space. I take up space in a room because that has been given to me as a birthright. It is a challenge, day in and day out, not to use it. I have to pay attention to myself all the time when I am with women and people of color. I have to say to myself, "I need to listen."

As a white man working with a Black group, I don't get treated as just Jesse. It is normal, and I have learned it as an organizer. I had a wonderful mentor, Ron Charity, a Black man, who used to watch me do training. He would tell me, "If you are going to do work in a Black community, you have got to know your voice. Because people are going to be smelling you; they're going to be watching you; they're going to say, 'What's up with this white guy?' You can't understand a situation until you've had to stand under it. Women know a lot about men, Black folks know a lot about white folks, gay folks know a lot about straight folks, but it doesn't go the opposite direction. So they are going to be watching you very carefully."

We're also working now in an all-white community. The lack of community in the low-income white community is astounding! At least in the Black community, there's still a sense of community, something that bonds, a history, a legacy of oppression that has helped keep people together.

. . .

I grew up down here. As a child, I used to go down to the railroad tracks on Saturday night and watch what was going on in the Black community on the other side of the tracks from where we lived. You could just see a sense of community over there. Everyone was out having fun. When I looked back at where I lived, no one was on their porches talking; everyone was closed up in their stone houses. I remember trying to figure out what had happened to the white people on my side of the tracks.

I've had the luxury of talking to elderly people in lots of different places who saw what community looked like before it was taken from us in a very deliberate, economic set of occurrences. I've talked with my mom and my grandfather about what life used to be like. They've told me that it used to function as a community all the time. When your tobacco was done, you would move with all your neighbors to the next farm. There would be square dancing, corn shucking, all kind of community building.

At the end of the day, you knew who you were. You knew where your value came from and could go to bed at night with a sense of self that was healthy. I am one of the last folks who knew people who lived that way. My family was completely self-sufficient on their farm. They produced everything from their clothing to their food to their own entertainment. It is all gone now.

I believe that the demise of subsistence farming in this culture happened when the multinationals decided it wasn't good for them. If people are providing their own food, then corporations can't make a profit off the people. That's the problem with capitalism, right? If someone is self-sufficient, then they are not producing money for the capitalist good. I think that really did a slam on my family. All that farming community went into factories. Now, most of my family works in factories. And the factories are closing up and moving to Mexico.

It goes back to the old saying, "If you put a frog in boiling water, it will jump around, but if you put a frog in nice, cool water and sit it on the stove and slowly heat it up, he won't ever know what happened." It's not that one day this new world government came in and set up shop. It's been a slow, steady eroding of the old system. It keeps going on because most folks believe that if they support the new system, one day they will get to be a part of the system. It's like my grandfather believing that if he supported slavery, he'd be a part of the economic system. The myth says, "If you are white, this is what you can have; if you work hard enough, you will get to have your part of it." My cousins have busted their asses for generations and still don't have a pot to piss in, and guess what? They are pissed off because they have been lied to. That is where the rage comes in.

. . .

When I think of what is going on for low-income white men, I think that their backs are up against the wall. It is a very sad place. The more life gets economically squeezed, the less space there is to do personal work. That is what brings us all into the same boat. I don't care if you are Black, white, gay, straight, whatever. You are being squeezed by the system, and it's going to get tighter and tighter. That is where I have tried to bridge the gaps. It is helping people see.

One day, my cousin Bob, who works in a panty hose factory here, had tears in his eyes talking about [his family] living on the farm and growing their own food. I said, "We could work together and do it again." And he said, "Yeah, but let's not hire any damn Mexicans." So I said, "Okay. What does that mean to you that you don't want any Mexicans working for you?" And he said, "They're taking our jobs. It used to be all white. Now, I'm one of the few white people there. The owners are thinking about moving to Mexico, where all these people come from." He was translating it [to mean] that they were taking his job. I said, "Well, I hadn't thought about it that way. I thought the Mexicans were coming here because they haven't been able to make any money. They've been thrown off their farms, too. They're paid 50¢ an hour for the same work you get $12 an hour for." He said, "Well, that makes sense." He can't stay with that thought all the time, but he could hear that.

The rub I always have with the progressive community is about their thinking they should always call low-income white folks on racism and sexism. I don't see it as my job to always be correcting people. Bob is not at a place where he can hear that he is a privileged young man. He makes panty hose seven days a week, twelve hours a day to put food on the table. For me to teach Bob that he carries privilege is like teaching a pig to sing. It's a waste of time, and it irritates the piss out of him. There's a time to share information and a way to share it so that it doesn't come off as preaching or blaming. Every once in a while Bob will say, "They are shortshifting us at the factory." I know he's telling me that because he knows I do something around organizing, but he doesn't know quite what it is, and he can't come right out and say it.

What I really see here with low-income white men is a group looking for community. Presently, their form of community is not "what we are for" because I don't think low-income white men know "what we are for" anymore. All of our identities have been removed from us, if we ever had any. Our identity used to be agrarian, but now—making panty hose in a factory? That doesn't feel good. So what you have left is what you are against: gays, Blacks, Jews.

Of course, I wouldn't dare ask a person of color, like my coworkers, to even try to make sense of it. But that's my work as a low-income white man who has had the luxury to have access to other information. I'm hoping I will meet somebody who will say, "You know, I'm thinking the same thing." I see men looking for community in a desperate way. I see the men in the militias looking for community.

A couple of summers ago, I was interviewing some farmers to learn how farming had changed and what effect it had had politically and on communities. I asked a woman who admitted she was a member of the Klan, "What did you get from the Klan?" She said, "I was so tired of being kicked and spit on and abused by people; when a hand was offered to me, it didn't matter what that hand represented. Any hand was a hand." That just named it. My cousins are looking for anyone to say, "I hear you. Your life sucks, and I have an answer for you as to *why* it sucks." I can't give as clear and simplistic a reason as the far right for the pain that the low-income white male is experiencing right now. It's much easier when the right just says, "It is the damn niggers."

. . .

The South sees organizing as a very communist type of idea. I get called a communist all the time. I get threats. I get phone calls from the Klan at home. The mailbox gets destroyed all the time. We were doing a program in Cabarrus County a number of years ago. We were just talking about taking money out of the military budget and putting it into the domestic economy. And fifteen robed Klansmen were out front of our meeting. My ex-wife even got fired from her job because of some organizing I was doing to stop a four-lane, 250-foot-wide bypass through the remaining farm area left in the southern part of this county.

Finding balance between my work and family is difficult. I'm at a real tough place with that. Where do you draw the line between your family and your work? I can come off with a real cool political saying, "If we change the economic system, we'll all be better off." Well, if one of my kids gets killed by the extreme right, I don't know how to balance that one.

I have had family members say, "It's a luxury for you to work out of your belief system because it's causing us an economic nightmare." I don't get paid much money as an organizer. I'm making a choice to do the work that makes me feel good. I can come home at the end of the day and feel good about the work that I'm doing, but then I got two kids who are dependent on me economically. I made a choice not to take a job that could be bringing in big bucks. That impacts them. I thought I was doing the right thing, and now I wonder. I'm not using my privilege to provide for my family. What does that mean?

If we want to start making change as white males, it's up to us to do a lot of this work. But if we can't get support and end up impacting negatively our own family members, it ain't working! What fool would go up to a white male and say, "You ought to quit your good-paying job and try to do social change and ruin your family"?

. . .

My dad died when I was eighteen months old. He never saw his daddy, who was an alcoholic. On my mom's side of the family, the men rarely talked. The male voice has never been available to me. That piece is missing.

I was raised by women. I am much more unclear about what a healthy male model looks like than what a healthy female model looks like. That is very scary for me. I am much more in touch with my feminine stuff than I am with my male stuff. My mom was the caregiver, along with my grandmother and my two older sisters. I was getting a lot of female teaching. I wasn't getting any "this is what a healthy man looks like" teaching.

I was raised that men don't cry. I haven't cried since I was about four years old. That is unhealthy! Whatever the messages are that you get when you are growing up will ride with you for the rest of your life unless you do some deliberate work. Those messages don't simply drop like leaves in the fall.

My mom did the best she could. She would say things like, "Men don't cry; men are strong; men provide." She used to call me the man of the house when I was four years old. My grandmother said, "You're in charge." The women literally put me in charge of the house on some emotional level when I was five years old. Now, that's a problem. That goes on for a lot of men.

I know now—and this is getting really personal—I know that because of my ex-wife's training, she would look to me and say, "You don't provide enough for the family." Now who set it up that that's *my* role? We would get real stuck there. When we were relaxed, we could name that as "traditional sexism." But when you put us into stress, the kids are crying, and we can't buy food, that stuff is out the window. We go back to early teachings, and we start dancing the most incredible dance. I don't know how to pull out of it.

. . .

I just have to accept my white male friends for where they are. But I do tell them that they can't use racist or homophobic statements when they are here on the farm. Now they will do that. Some of them will say, "Oops! Can't say that; we're at Jesse's." That's weird, but it's the only place I know where to draw the line. Now if I'm in your space, you do whatever you have to do. If

I can handle it! My ex-wife Kissy used to ask me, "How can you hang out with these men? They are so unhealthy. What is it that bonds you?"

That's the beautiful part. There's something that's much deeper. The racism, sexism, and homophobia is thick, but it's not nearly as thick as the human connection. We'll go out in the woods and talk about historical stuff. I had some friends who helped me put together the house and who just love history. We're looking at an old piece of wood, a male thing, and just getting into a really intimate place. That's where I try to go. I don't try to make a connection in this other place, where I know men aren't going to be able to go.

It is much easier to be intimate with gay men than with straight men because the boundaries are set up and you know what they are, so you don't have to wonder about them. And doesn't that suck? There are a few gay men down here. One guy is very out with his sexuality, and he and I get along very well. But I want that type of community with straight men.

If I start talking with some of my male friends and I start bringing up the stuff about how we are part of the change that needs to happen, it doesn't ring true. From where they sit in the struggle to survive, there isn't space to see that place. It's like me saying, "You need to walk off this cliff." There isn't an example for men to look at and say, "This is the man I would like to be." I don't know if women have that; I don't know if people of color have it. I imagine there are role models for both the women and Black people that are healthier than anything I'm going to find among low-income white people. Now *there* is a problem. So if we start asking men to make changes, where can we show them what the change looks like? The men's movement probably has some value when it comes to this change, but that movement is basically only for men of privilege.

And even if there were a model, where are they going to get support for changing? If they go back to the panty hose line, they are going to be laughed out of the place. It is certainly more acceptable for women to look at women's issues, for people of color to organize. There are some real clear reasons to do that. I don't see clear reasons for low-income white men to organize and make changes internally that would be manifested in our culture. Until we find those reasons, we are the wall. *We* are keeping the movement from happening, and the system knows that. As long as the militia movement is the broker between people of color getting organized and making alliances with the majority of low-income white folks, there's a barrier keeping things agitated.

. . .

For seven years at PPP, I was the only white male. I don't think I will ever get over the damage that that has done to me personally. The women at PPP were really trying to get by their own woundedness from being in a society with men. Which is a real thing. Yet at the same time, because of that woundedness and the work that they were doing—especially the women of color—they did not see me as a person who needed support. I represented everyone who has power. So they couldn't separate that out and say, "Wow, this must be hard for Jesse, to be a male on staff by himself with seven women."

Some stuff has changed because of the mere fact that we now have another man on staff. But I don't think that group of women would have figured it out. Maybe it isn't their responsibility. I might never know how that could have worked out better. It was very difficult for me to try and be in community with women who were trying to rebuild community with other women. There really wasn't a space. Don't know that there *should* have been.

So I need to look for my support elsewhere, and that might be fine, but I just haven't run into too many other white men that could be a support for me. And this movement isn't going to make a path for other men. Let me tell you that. If other white men have to go through what I went through, it's fucked. But until low-income, working-class white men are part of the movement, it isn't going to go anywhere anyway because we are the voting majority right now. These are the folks who are voting for Jesse Helms, Pat Buchanan, David Duke.[1] There has to be work done with low-income white men. You cannot bring in white men who use racism, homophobia, and sexism for building their community and then expect them to build community with women or with people of color. Their attitudes and behavior have to be dealt with first. That's where I come in.

One of my coworkers told me yesterday that he just doesn't know if he can stay in the movement. He's just tired. We're trying to present a new model where white men consciously try to take a back seat in the organizing, to create space for women and people of color. It takes strength on a daily basis to hold that in your head and not hear a coworker say, "You're doing a good job of holding your privilege in check."

What I really long for is to be whole, so that I don't have to leave part of me behind. What I've learned about working with women and people of color is that normally, when they enter, they leave something at the door. That becomes a way of life. Now I'm learning about that, and it feels like shit to have to leave part of myself at the door. I'm hoping one day that that experience will bring us together instead of keeping us separate.

# Jim Hansen

*Jim Hansen is the executive director of United Vision of Idaho (UVI). UVI is a permanent, multi-issue progressive coalition based in Boise. Jim describes it as a relationship-building process to build a progressive movement. UVI has worked to identify constituencies and voices in the progressive movement that are absent. For example, UVI has built an interfaith alliance, so that the faith community can have a relationship with progressive organizations, and an organization for youth, so that progressive organizations have a way to reach high school and college campuses. UVI grew out of discussions with many grassroots groups in Idaho that were doing good work on a shoestring. Sometimes they were even working against each other—labor unions and environmental groups being the most visible. Recent projects have included tracking money in politics and being a counterpoint to corporate efforts to influence budgets and taxes where there was no organized voice challenging corporate positions.*

*Jim was born in eastern Idaho, then lived in suburban Washington, D.C. He grew up in a political family; his father was a congressional representative. He moved back to Idaho to go to law school and start what he thought at the time was a "normal professional career." Jim served in the Idaho legislature as a state representative for six years, from 1988 to 1994, returned to law practice, quit, and started UVI. He's forty-two.*

. . .

Two years ago, I joined the Chamber of Commerce in Boise. I have access to people in power because of my privilege. I wanted to exercise that privilege in a way that opens up greater opportunities for both learning and power for people of color and white women. And I wanted our presence to challenge and provide learning opportunities for the other members of the chamber. It's given United Vision entrée to go into the meetings, get information, and build relationships with leaders in the Chamber of Commerce. I mean, they're not evil people, but they are certainly operating from perspectives that can be really oppressive, largely without knowing it, without having experience to tell them otherwise.

Every experience we've had at chamber meetings has been a learning experience for me and the staff members, board members, and interns of United Vision who go with me. Typically, people of color and women, even people with disabilities and low-income people, have never experienced testifying in a committee, whether that's a chamber committee or a legislative committee. And there are dynamics and reactions I don't anticipate. I still process stuff up in my head—it's almost like I don't feel it to the extent that my colleagues do. Their first reaction is oftentimes a feeling of pain, a feeling of oppression. Being at the chamber or the legislature is another reminder of something painful in their lives. That's not the case with me. I easily intellectualize it. So the challenge for me and the other white men in United Vision is to make the connection and learn how to "be" with the dissonance between your head and your heart. We have to learn how to put our hearts and our heads together.

We men have to do things! We see something, and we intellectualize it. If we feel something, then we really have to do something about it. It's very tough to just "be," to just sit with it. It's a challenge to convey that to men who haven't had the experience of working with people of color and understanding their privilege.

I'm in a rotary club, too. The question is whether and how you raise issues. For the eleven years that I've been a member, I've been pushing for more women to join the club. There have been more women joining, and I believe it's helping to transform the club. But I understand that if the club were mostly women, men in this community would not value the club as much as one of the other three rotary clubs. That's a reality we have.

We had a speaker last week on domestic violence. She gave a very powerful presentation on violence and the impact on children that really touched people's hearts. She played a tape of an actual emergency call; you could hear the screams in the background, and the child, who was probably six or eight years old, was reporting the violence. People were close to tears listening to this, feeling the pain. But the speaker didn't challenge the audience as deeply as I wanted her to, to make them feel a little more uncomfortable and see their own role. And I didn't know how to raise that issue in a way that would push them a little more. One of the things that I was thinking about saying was, "All men benefit from a society in which violence against women is tolerated." Of course, if I had said that, every man in that room would have said, "No, we don't." That would require a much deeper discussion about what it's like to be a man walking at night or working at a university and what it's like to be a woman doing the same thing. All the obstacles and challenges that she must face.

So all I did was to talk about a survey taken of some elementary school children, probably the same age as the kid on the emergency call. The girls were asked, "If you woke up tomorrow as a boy, how would you feel?," and the boys were asked, "If you woke up tomorrow as a girl, how would you feel?" And of course the responses were that the girls would feel much better and the boys would feel much worse; in fact, some of them said that they would kill themselves. That's how the meeting ended. I hope that that sunk into some minds. I wanted them to take what they were hearing and instead of saying, "That's about those other people who are being violent to their spouses and hurting their kids," to think about how we're raising our own kids and the messages we're sending about who's valuable and who's not. If girls and women are not being valued, then the logical consequence of that is some people will believe that they can treat girls and women as less, commit crimes against them, be violent; you can kill them.

I don't know what impact it had. I think I have some credibility with them. I automatically have credibility as a white guy. I have less credibility because I'm known as the resident liberal in the club.

There's no doubt that there are people at the rotary club who just shut me out as soon as I start to speak because their perception of me is that I'm way too aggressive. Perhaps there are others who think I am being inauthentic in letting people off the hook, but I doubt that's the case. There are activist allies of mine who aren't in the room who are thinking that. But it's about relationships, you know, and the members of the club are all basically good people. I think my role is to try and walk with them to help them understand how privilege is operating, that we're in this club enjoying the benefits of this community to a far greater extent than the people we're supposedly helping because we do a whole lot of charity work. We can either feel defensive and guilty about it, or we can actually think about it and "be" with it and start making changes in the way we think.

. . .

UVI's financial success is built on my ability to access money because I can communicate what the white-run foundations and sources of money want to hear. They automatically assume a level of credibility and stability when they see a white guy at the helm who has a law degree and experience as an Idaho state representative and all the other things on my résumé. They are much more likely to trust us financially. I use my white male privilege, educated background, and skills to make reports look good. In order to live up to the demands and expectations of our principal funders, you have to keep them happy. Latino organizations or organizations run by women are far more likely to say, "Here's a little bit of money, enough for starvation; we'll see how you do. We don't want to trust you with big bucks yet. And we can pat ourselves on the back that we've funded an organization for minorities."

I can pass in the establishment. This project I'm working on now, a six-month hiatus from United Vision to set up a network on campaign finance reform, has required me to get into lots and lots of geographical communities in Idaho, to find out who the key opinion leaders are. I have entrée immediately as a white, educated man. Then, of course, having been born in Idaho Falls, I have the credential of being a native Idahoan. At the same time, the white people who sort of know me best, here in Boise, feel like I'm way too liberal, taking positions on progressive issues, and that I should be careful as I pass in and out of different contexts.

I know that I'm going to screw up and do things wrong. I need to constantly check in and not think that I've got the solution. It means having a process in which I can receive, and people of color can give me, feedback and information to help me grow in a way that's not patronizing, that's meaningful, that they can see how the feedback is used in the organization.

At the heart of this process is our organizational change team, and within that we encourage the use of caucuses—a men's caucus, a women's caucus, a people of color caucus, and a white people caucus. It is incumbent upon the men and the white people to meet often and to raise issues and challenge each other and not wait for women and people of color to raise issues. Of those four caucuses, the men's caucus has the hardest time meeting. The white caucus, largely because of the women leading it, meets regularly.

The men don't meet very often, and there's usually just a few of us. It's tougher for us to get together. I think a lot has to do with the fact that we don't form relationships with each other very well, so it's just another meeting. When I call up somebody on the board or staff and say, "I think we should have a men's caucus meeting," I'm approaching them from an intellectual position; there's something around sexism or gender justice that we really need to discuss. But there are all these other work commitments that we have, and this doesn't reach a high priority. I think when the women say, "Let's do a women's caucus," it's a whole lot about, "Let's check in with our relationships with each other. We have good relationships, and we want to invest time and energy in strengthening those relationships and get to an issue that's making one or more women in the organization feel some pain."

I don't know many executive directors, even those who are progressive and working on social justice issues, who have been through the kind of experiences and training I've had in understanding and dealing with oppression. The ones who have had to grapple with oppression, putting their organization's reputation and strategies on the line, are women. So I have better relationships with executive directors who are women. I think they come to this more naturally. They see oppression operating from a gender perspective and so are more open to working on issues of race and class.

It can be pretty lonely. There are not many folks, especially white men, in the same position I'm in.

. . .

Idaho has a much richer tradition with our Latino and Native American communities than 90 percent of the white people in this state would even acknowledge exists. There's sort of a cultural nod to that part of our tradition, mostly the Native American part of Idaho's history. But by and large, the Latinos and Native Americans here are invisible. Demographically, they are slightly less than 10 percent of the population. The rest are white, mostly of northern European ancestry, who moved out here in the last 100–150 years.

The Latino population here is largely of Mexican origin, dating back to as long as the white folks have been here. We have a large migrant farm population, folks who have come up here for generations. Many of them have stayed, and so there are second- and third-generation Latinos, but they are still perceived as being lumped together with the migrant farm workers.

We have an organizer on staff, a person of color who's really helped us understand how, in Idaho, many facets of oppression have played out in the Latino community. One of those facets is the struggle among Latinos to deal with internalized oppression in such an overwhelmingly white state. There are white people in political institutions and businesses who serve as gatekeepers, making decisions about who are the "worthy" Latinos and who aren't. Another facet is that many of the organizations that serve Latinos are run by men, and issues of gender overlay issues of race. And there are issues of class among Latinos.

It's been painful for me to observe and experience some of those struggles. There are struggles between Latino organizations, just as there are between environmental organizations. They're constantly working out the turf, who's got a good relationship with this funder or that funder. It makes our role challenging because there's a risk that if we pick one organization over another or emphasize one more than another in our projects, then we, a white organization, have decided who's best. Not that we aren't asked—and asked a lot.

Sometimes I just have to sit with it. Sometimes it's an invitation in a more circumspect way to raise the issue with allies of color, not in a way that says,

"Boy, do you have a problem; let me try to help you." But more like saying, "Not all but some of the lights are on in my head, and I'm aware of what you are struggling with." That's part of building that trust. It allows me to learn about how they're struggling with internalized racist oppression.

. . .

The First Nations, the Native American or Indian tribes in Idaho—they refer to themselves in a variety of ways—their culture is a stark contrast, organizationally and spiritually, to what we're used to. It's something that's always been difficult for white people to really understand. Native people may be affiliated with a Christian denomination, but the cultural context is very different. The Tribes themselves are very different communities. For example, the Coeur d'Alene tribe, the Nez Perce tribe, and the Shoshone Bannok tribe are all different. They're getting resources now because gaming has been permitted under federal law, much to the chagrin of the establishment, and they are asserting some political power in the state.

Our strategy at UVI is not to come and say, "What is it you want, what can we do for you," but just to build a relationship. A lot of organizations would probably feel frustrated that after five years, what we've basically done is just built relationships with individual Native American leaders and groups of leaders in the Tribes. A person of color on our staff has been the key to that because she has a deeper sense of just going and being, not saying, "Here's all the great things we're doing, you should hook up with us." And she's helped us to understand that it's a new and different kind of relationship than what we have with, say, a conservation group.

My role is to back up people of color and white women as they stick their necks out. I try to make sure that there are resources for them to do this work. I don't have a compass to say, "This is how we're going to do it," but it feels right. We have a tight budget, and because we're successful, we have more requests than we can handle. So prioritizing relationship building with the Tribes is one of my responsibilities. When the executive committee of UVI sits down and asks, "What concrete thing can we measure from this investment of money and time with the Tribes?," there's nothing tangible that we have. I tell them that we're spending time building relationships. We're not sure where that's going to go, what it's going to look like, how we're going to measure it. I can exert my power as the executive director, saying that I feel that this is a strengthening experience for us and trusting that others will lead us toward the next steps.

What has also helped me understand the necessity of building relationships is the framework of oppression. Understanding how oppression operates, understanding how leaders of organizations can play a role in transforming a community over a long period of time, through building relationships. Most racist, oppressive societies continue to operate because they choose not to prioritize building relationships. White leaders choose not to build relationships with people of color. They don't view them as valuable or equal. And so they give people of color one seat on the board, one seat on the city council, a few tokens here and there.

And there are also folks who come into a community, work on an issue, and then move on. But the people in the community are still there and are still struggling. It all ties in with how we measure success. It's self-fulfilling. If we measure success by the accumulation of financial resources or the number of people at a given meeting, then we simply reinforce racist systems. Among the social justice organizations that I've been exposed to, the successful ones have deep commitments in communities.

*We want to ask a cynical question. What if someone looked at your career and said, "Well, he was an attorney, and that didn't suit him. Then he did the legislature thing for six years. Why should anyone believe that he won't leave this in two years and decide that what he really wants to do is consulting for Weyerhauser?" What would lead someone to know that you're in this for the long run?*

Good question. Why would I come back to a conservative state and act like a progressive? Something has to feed your soul. The fact that I left the law firm—my soul was not being fed. In fact, it was starving. I made more money the last year I was at the law firm, in 1991, than I've made since.

But there's something in my work about being righteous. I'm able to look myself in the mirror. A number of people, including friends who went to law school with me, have come to me and asked, "How did you leave law and start uvi?" Some of my attorney friends, by all the standard measurements—a nice home, a good legal practice—have all the trappings of success. But they don't like it; something's wrong. And so they're coming to me, someone whose career path looks pretty chaotic, and I don't have a 401k waiting for me when I retire. A good friend who has done uvi's legal work and who obviously has been exposed to lots of other nonprofit organizations is leaving his practice to run a nonprofit.

My dad was a congressional representative. He once told me, "When you're in a role of leadership, you have to constantly reach out beyond your inner circle." It's very easy to surround yourself with people that you're comfortable with. They'll just reinforce what a great guy you are all the time, and you'll start to believe it. But you've got to break through that and constantly be building new relationships with people who will question that leadership and will challenge the perspective of that inner circle and make you feel uncomfortable. Mostly you have to struggle with that inner circle, who doesn't want that to happen.

I'm on this journey that's constantly unfolding. On this journey, I can go down blind paths, come back and go down another path, or make mistakes along the way without having the dire consequences that a woman or someone without my educational background or a person of color might have. And it's not just because of the work I've done; it's because this society has said that the things about me—my maleness, my whiteness, my class and education—mean that I'm that much more valuable. I have to constantly remind myself that this is a journey I can go on because of the privileges I enjoy.

# Chip Berlet

*Chip identifies himself as a straight, white, Christian male. His paid work is as an analyst with Political Research Associates (PRA), an organization founded by Jean Hardisty to study the intellectual and strategic operation of the American political right wing. PRA focuses primarily on four forms of oppression—racism, sexism, homophobia, and anti-Semitism—and provides information to progressive activists, researchers, and journalists. Chip describes himself as the "gumshoe" in the organization. He's the editor of* Eyes Right! Challenging the Right Wing Backlash *and coauthor of* Right Wing Populism in America. *He's fifty-two.*

*He's put a lot of time into thinking about the right wing, organizing, and the history of social change. He thinks in terms of what is both ethical and practical. "It's immoral to demonize people on the right. I don't want to live in a society where we progressives win by crushing the opposition. Strategically, progressives are cutting their own throats if they demonize the right; it will make it difficult, if not impossible, for organizing a broader movement down the road."*

. . .

I live a kind of dual life. We live in a predominantly white suburb of Boston. Where we live, a lot of people look at my wife and me as extremely unusual. We'll be in casual conversations with neighbors where we're constantly raising our eyebrows and saying, "I don't quite see things that way." But I'm comfortable doing that, and I think people now expect it of Karen and me. They know that we're always going to be taking some positions that are way out there in left field.

But because we are part of the neighborhood and our kids are in the same schools and I'm on television a lot and I have celebrity status, I think we're acceptable. Anybody on TV has to be okay by definition, and so I think for all of this people give us a free pass on our ideas. I have my persona as a person who is an activist in progressive circles and research, and then I go home at night, and on weekends I'm a soccer dad. It's a little strange, but it fits in my own strange way.

The hardest issue has been raising a child. When our son Bobby was little, we lived in Chicago. He went to a predominantly Black day care center and then attended a very integrated school for a while. When we moved here, it was harder to find integrated schools. There's much more segregation in the Boston area than a lot of people would like to admit. It was easier to have diverse relationships in Chicago.

So when we moved here, he was old enough to be aware of racial differences and racism. You can't pretend that those differences don't exist when you're raising a son in the modern American milieu. There are a lot of his friends who were not raised that way, and so that becomes something he has to deal with. He's going to stand out if he's been raised in an egalitarian way. There are days where he wishes he had parents that were "a little more normal," but he's seventeen now, and he's pretty clear that what we've done is the right thing to do. So it's not really an issue for him anymore.

That's part of breaking the chain. He was brought up with the expectation that men and women are equal, that we share tasks at home. That was very intentional; Karen and I talked about it when he was growing up. I do some things that are traditionally female, and my wife does some things that are traditionally male. He's grown up assuming that these are all choices that you make based on interest, not identity. For example, Karen is very good with cars; she used to build them, and I know nothing about cars.

We'd role-play sometimes. We'd go see a film and then we'd say, "What would you do if they came to round up all the Jews or all the gays? Where would we hide them? Could we hide them in our house? How would we do it? How would we get food?" I know that's trivializing it to make it almost like a game, but it got him thinking about how he would resist that form of oppression on a dramatic scale. If you're actually thinking about how you would hide someone in your home if people were being rounded up, then you can imagine saying to somebody at a party, "That kind of racism is really yucky." I don't think he could respond to stuff unless we actually gave him a language and talked about an appropriate response.

When he'd come home and tell us that somebody had done something and he hadn't responded and he felt bad about that, we'd tell him, "It's really great that you feel bad about it, and let's talk about what you might do next time so you don't feel so bad." It's wonderful that he's willing to bring that to us.

We also had to worry about his safety when he was growing up. Because of the work Karen and I were involved with in Marquette Park in Chicago, we were both at risk for our safety. I had a somewhat higher profile because I was speaking in public about the Klan, but we were both at risk in some of our work. And so he had to learn, in an age-appropriate way, to have security consciousness.

That's a real burden. I had a colleague in Wisconsin whose kids were stopped on the way home from school and threatened by a white suprema-cist group. Some people stopped his kids and told them to take a message home that "We're gonna kill your dad unless he shuts up." My colleague had to get out of the work because there was no way we could protect him and his family twenty-four hours a day. It was a horrible experience.

So Karen and I were always worried about that. When Bobby was very young, we would talk about it as a cartoon kind of thing: there are these bad people, and they might try to trick you. As he got older, it became clearer to him, but you know it's a burden to have to teach your kids about hiding in the bathtub if you hear gunshots. That's a whole different level from raising your kid in feminist principles or egalitarian principles. I wish that hadn't been this way, but he turned out okay. He's a good kid.

. . .

I work in a great place, but it can be disturbing at times. Every day we open the mail, and there are jokes about the ovens and the gas chambers in Germany, or cartoons of lynchings, or the most vicious kind of language about gay men and lesbians. A day doesn't arrive without some horrible anecdote, some artifact of hate. There is a fair amount of inappropriate humor around the office, like in an emergency room. I don't think that either Jean or I could have done this work for this many years if it weren't done in this collegial manner, in an atmosphere of not wanting to exploit people in service of fighting exploitation. We're in this for the long haul. We don't want to burn out.

I can always walk out of here and get a good job in some TV station doing stupid, trite news stories about some government worker who took an hour off. I wouldn't do that, but the point is that I have access based on that privilege. That exit can look very attractive. Why am I putting up with this? And the reason you are is because you want to be part of this change, and to be part of this change, you have to put up with it because that's the price of admission for any coalition building. Bernice Johnson Reagon says, in an essay that I quote a lot when I do public speaking, that if you're doing coalition work and you don't feel like you're just about to have a heart attack, then it's not real coalition work.[1] And I thought that's exactly right, exactly right. I describe it as bungee cord jumping without a safety rope.

There are people who say, "I'm gonna do this for a few years, and we'll eradicate racism, sexism, homophobia." Well, it ain't gonna happen. There's always gonna be oppression. There will be oppressions we haven't even imagined. It's a process that never ends. The metaphor I use is canoeing upstream. If you stop paddling, you go backward. But if you build into a day-to-day kind of reality that you are paddling upstream, after a while you don't notice it. It's what you have to do. It's part of getting up in the morning. And if you do that, it becomes relatively unconscious—not that you don't have those interior monologues and dialogues going on all the time about what's going on; you do, but you're used to it.

If you're gonna do this work, you're gonna get criticized. When my colleagues criticize something I've done, I say to myself, "She's saying some very profound things, and I'd better listen really carefully." And there's another voice saying, "I can't believe this is happening. I feel like I'm just going to die, and I want to crawl under the rug." That's the voice of my privilege. And then there's a third voice that's processing the criticism: "Oh wow, she's right. This is actually pretty good criticism." And, of course, emotionally, it's the second voice that's the most powerful: "I'd like to crawl away now." You have to learn to live with all of those voices.

There are other times when I've had little pissing matches with other white men on analytical issues. They criticize me, and I argue with them about their criticism. My response at some point is pretty universal: I apologize to them. I apologize even if I think I'm right because I believe that it is better to apologize and keep the lines of communication open. That form of response is not typical in this culture. Sometimes I don't like doing it, but I think it's the right thing to do.

. . .

In the late 1970s we were living in Washington, D.C., and my wife wanted to do a different type of political organizing in Chicago, and I agreed to go. It was my turn to follow her to Chicago. We decided to live in the Marquette Park area. There's a famous scene of Martin Luther King leading a housing march into Marquette Park, and there are bottles and stones being hurled at his head. That's the neighborhood we moved into.

Many white people didn't want more Blacks living in the neighborhood. White people thought that the neighborhood would go downhill. What was really happening was that a coalition of real estate agents would get together and bust a neighborhood and turn houses over two or three times and make a lot of money.[2] When you break it down, part of this is an economic analysis, and the other is a race analysis. And the part that's an economic analysis is tough because you can't guarantee that if Marquette Park gets blockbusted, it won't economically collapse because it might, and if you're white working class, your pension is your mortgage. You might have a decent pension from where you're working if you're in a union, but if you're not in a union, then your pension is your mortgage. You put a lot of your money into that house; if your house loses half of its value, you have no retirement. People were scared to death that that was gonna happen. So there were people who were absolutely dead set against integration.

There was a coalition that was being built between the Klan, the neo-Nazis, racist skinheads, and white supremacist youth gangs to keep Blacks out. Quite a coalition. Lovely. And they were starting to hold rallies in the neighborhood. The fact that the neo-Nazis were there didn't imply that everybody in the neighborhood liked them. In fact most people in the neighborhood despised the neo-Nazis. This was an ethnic, East European neighborhood. They didn't despise the neo-Nazis because they were white supremacists; they despised them because of the history of Nazi oppression and invasion. Elderly Polish women would go by and spit on the uniformed neo-Nazis handing out leaflets in a shopping area. So, okay, they're obviously not welcome, but on the other hand, no one was really standing up to them.

We formed a neighborhood block group with a couple of Latino families who were progressive. We discussed strategies on how to bring up these issues in a way that wouldn't force our neighbors out the door and yet would make it clear what we think. And we would have these meetings with our neighbors, listen to what they have to say, and then tell them what we thought. We didn't tell them how much we disliked what they said, and we didn't say that we're here to discuss racist segregation. They would have just gone out the door. How are they ever going to change? How are you gonna move them if that happens? Suddenly the whole vocabulary that you used to use to deal with white racism changes. And a lot of progressive people will call you a sellout and ask what you did to confront the racism. Where would you like me to start? If I'm going to start with my neighbors on the block, I can't just tell everybody who disagrees with me to go get fucked. It ain't a strategy, folks; it's not gonna work.

And while this was happening, there were Black residents in the neighborhood whose houses were getting firebombed. Later on there were race riots—five hundred primarily young white men storming through the streets chasing Black people after a Klan / neo-Nazi rally. I mean it was tense. And we were getting death threats from the neo-Nazis. It got very interesting.

We knew that the five hundred kids running around after the Klan / neo-Nazi rally were our kids; they were neighborhood kids. Many of them looked like they were on the football team. Young, white teenage boys who think they're doing the right thing. They think that this is what's expected of them. They don't hear another narrative. The narrative is "Blacks are coming into our neighborhood, and it will collapse." Therefore, to defend the neighborhood you keep the Blacks out; very simple equation. You're the hero by doing that.

So we went to some Black community leaders and asked them, "What is our role? What are we supposed to do in this neighborhood?" We were trying to deal with these issues, but they had obviously gotten out of hand. And the Black leaders were absolutely clear. They wanted people to be able to go to bed at night and not worry about being killed. Firebombing happens at night, and you can't keep your job if you're up all night; and if you can't keep your job, you can't keep your house. It's a very simple equation. They told us, "Fight racism, fight white supremacy, deal with all these issues, but what this neighborhood needs is for kids to sleep through the night." So we lowered our expectations a lot. Our job was to stop the firebombing and stop the attacks. Now how do you do that?

We went back into the neighborhood, working with a multiracial neighborhood group called the Southwest Community Congress. We began to develop a strategy that was much simpler, basically deciding that at that point in time it was important to get people who were relatively prejudiced to stand up against violence. And we began to build a campaign around that issue. We kept building and building, meeting with labor unions, going to churches, doing organizing, just talking to people.

At the beginning we got no help from the mainstream political and religious community downtown. None! Zero! No help from the biggest institutional human relations groups. The Anti-Defamation League's position was the white supremacists are troublemakers, and you can't even give them publicity because it only builds up their organization. We kept saying, "Excuse me, they're taking over the neighborhood; it's not a question of giving them publicity. You can pretend they're not there, but they're handing out flyers at the high school. They're having rallies where five hundred people show up."

Little by little, things began to change. You come up with a line and you pursue it, and eventually more people see something changing. One of our goals was to get respected community leaders across the board to stand up and extremely clearly and publicly speak out against this stuff. It was exactly the opposite of the advice that groups like ADL were giving. We believed this was a neighborhood of people who looked to certain people for leadership, whether it's the shop floor leader in the plant or leaders in their religious communities. There were people in the community who were respected, and if they spoke up in a dramatic, loud, public way, people would listen.

The real break for us came with a Catholic priest, a really good-hearted guy who wasn't even a main priest in his parish. He just decided he had to speak against this, and so he gave a wonderful homily on what Christ's Sermon on the Mount would be if he gave it in Marquette Park today. He talked about the shame of living in a neighborhood where kids couldn't go to sleep at night for fear of being firebombed. He asked, "If those were your kids, how would you feel? If you feel bad like I know you do, then you need to do something about it."

Really simple stuff. After the service people came up to him and said, "Father, thank God somebody is talking about this. This neighborhood is going to hell in a hand basket, we all feel like shit about it, and we don't know what to do. What should we do?" They were desperate for people to say something about it. They were desperate for someone they respected as a leader to say, "My God, look around. This is chaos. We have to stop it."

Out of that grew a button campaign called "Rise Above It," and all these kids in the local Catholic high school started to wear "Rise Above It" buttons. It meant that the violence is beneath us; it is contemptuous; it is absolutely unacceptable behavior. We actually had patrols of folks walking the streets at two in the morning with flashlights, spotlighting cars full of young white men looking for trouble and then speaking to them. "Hi, Harry. What are you doing here this time of night? Does your mother know where you are? Get your butt outta here." The kids know that once they've been spotted, they're in trouble. The parents find out and the priest finds out, and they're in big trouble.

Eventually, the Klan would have a rally, and no one would show up. Ten kids would show up, and little by little folks began to change their perspective on what was acceptable behavior and keep track of their kids.

I learned two things from this experience. One, hate groups victimize communities that are in crisis and turn them toward white supremacy by building an identity among the young men. White supremacist hate groups don't bring prejudice or hate or racism or discrimination into a neighborhood. They smell it. They sense that something has gone awry in a neighborhood, and they swoop down like vultures to pick at it, to inflame it, to make it worse. Two, you can organize essentially prejudiced people to fight this hate, and that's a victory, even if on a very tiny level. You can't go in and eradicate white privilege overnight. If it means ten years to take a neighborhood from violence to peace, leaving unresolved lots of issues of prejudice, that's still worth it.

It was clear to us that people committing the acts of violence were white young men, and we needed to reconstruct their identity such that being manly meant something other than violence. Our narrative was based primarily on young white men because they were the actors; they were the ones carrying out the violence. But the narrative that we presented was that all people of good conscience should resist the violence. So what we tried to do is have a strategic line that people of good conscience stand up against violence. But then we had a subtext in the campaign specifically aimed at young white men, to hold them to that larger standard.

Creating an alternative discourse is what was key to changing that neighborhood. And yet some people might question that because the alternative discourse wasn't "fight white supremacy" or "be a race traitor." In academic discussion or among a lot of people who fight white supremacy, what we did would have been seen as a complete sellout, a ridiculously pathetic enterprise. But you're not gonna go into a white, working-class neighborhood and say that you need to abandon white identity. It ain't gonna fly. Intellectually it might be valid, but if you're an organizer, it's not the narrative.

And the other thing is: what was a white male supposed to do in this neighborhood? And the answer was stand up against violence. We wanted to construct a white male identity in that neighborhood that saw violence against people because of their race as something that would make you less of a man. So to be a real man in the neighborhood meant to stand up against the bullies and the violence and to stop the race hate from leading to injury or possible death.

We didn't change the nature of the neighborhood fundamentally except in that one area. The Klan and the neo-Nazis went away. It [support] just collapsed. They were not welcome anymore; nobody was listening to them.

It was absolutely imperative that we live in the neighborhood to do this work. I don't think that white folks who want to fight racism have any idea how irrelevant it is to drop into a community after some crisis or event and decide that they're going to do something about racism. It is so misguided. I hate to tell people that because I know their hearts are in the right place, but nine times out of ten it makes things worse. Having been inside a neighborhood, I can tell you if you want to fight racism in a white community, live in it. That gives you a stake; you have a place at the table. You have neighbors, and no matter how much they hate your ideas, they'll still give you coffee and pie when you talk to them about what's going on because you're a neighbor.

We lived in the neighborhood ten years, and it took ten years, working with hundreds of people, to turn this around. If we could have thought of something better to do, we would have done it. We broke our butts. It was a tough, wearing experience. You couldn't call it a huge success historically because there's still racism in the neighborhood, but there's not that level of violence. And that has made other things possible.

# Joe Fahey

*Joe is president of Teamsters' Local 912 in Watsonville, California. Before being elected a union official, he was a rank-and-file Teamster and an activist in the union. Local 912 represents a broad range of workers; from package deliverers to pallet makers to maids, but most of the workers are in the food-processing industry, working in canneries. Most are poor women, immigrants from Mexico.*

*Joe's proud of the victories he's had as an organizer, what he has learned in the process, and what he knows about working-class people. He also notices where his racism limits him. Joe still is more comfortable around people of color, even though he knows that they are not "better" than white people fundamentally. In the end, his experiences tell him that his preferences for one racial group over another and choices about racism are largely an accident of birth: "I didn't exactly choose racism. It was thrust upon me in a unique way as a little white boy. I responded. I'm proud of my decisions and my life. But like everybody else, I just played the cards I was dealt the best I could."*

*Like many of the white men in this book, as a child, Joe witnessed racism and its impact on his family. "From the age of six, I saw racism tearing my family apart. I knew it wasn't their fault and that I had to change the world to get my family back." Joe realizes that he is still carrying that hurt with him; now, at forty-four, he is trying to figure out how to create a sense of family and home around him as he continues working for a better world. One of the tools he uses for his own healing is reevaulation counseling: "It's made it possible for me to face my difficulties, past and present. It's helped me prevent burnout and think more clearly about undoing the emotional damage caused by racism and capitalism."*

*The interview began with Joe talking about an experience he had as an organizer at Gatorade.*

. . .

In contract negotiations, Gatorade wanted the right to use more subcontractors and temporary employees; three of their six plants nationwide were run by temporary agencies; there every single worker was a "temp," even though they had worked at Gatorade every day for years. Basically, the company wanted to turn good union jobs with high wages into lower-paying junk jobs with no benefits. My local took over this plant from another local that hadn't backed the workers, who were mostly Black. People were bitter. They felt sold out. They were really pissed off at each other and at the union.

This was my first experience as a union leader working with a mostly African American group. At my first meeting with them, they were running their shit against each other bad. They were shutting each other off, yelling at each other, blaming each other, and blaming me. People were drinking in the parking lot. It was a mess. I wasn't at all sure what to do.

Eventually, I said, "Look, we need more unity than we've got. I'm not sure what we need to do, but I *am* sure that what you've been doing ain't working. I'm going to propose something, and I want you to try it. If it improves things at all, then you take it over and make it better." I suggested that we leaflet sporting events as a way to try to win public support for our fight against Gatorade. And so we decided to leaflet Candlestick Park, where the San Francisco Forty-Niners play football. Our leaflet had a roster with the names and the numbers of the players of each of the teams and our message explaining that the whole community loses when big companies like Gatorade turn good jobs into junk jobs.

The first couple of games we leafleted, I ran everything. I told the workers where and how to leaflet. After the second game, back in the union hall, Janice, one of the workers, told me, "Joe, next time we're doing a tailgate party after the game starts, and so-and-so is cooking, and so-and-so is bringing this, and so-and-so is bringing the beverages." They talked with each other and figured out how to have fun and do the leafleting at the same time. They had it all arranged. I didn't have anything to do with it. I wouldn't have even thought of doing it that way.

So they continued leafleting, and luckily the Forty-Niners survived until the final playoff game to determine who would go to the Super Bowl. For that game, we'd rented a plane to fly over the stadium with the same message as the headline from our leaflet: "Gatorade Wants San Francisco to Lose." Some fans had given us extra tickets to the game, and so we took turns watching the game inside the stadium.

There had been planes flying over the stadium all day, but ours didn't come until the first five minutes of the fourth quarter. San Francisco was getting its ass kicked, and people were bored. Zillions of planes had already flown over with advertisements, and I didn't think people would even look up when ours came over. When it did, people not only looked up, but also pointed at our banner with expressions on their faces like, "What the hell does *that* mean?" Then other fans started pulling out our flyers from their pockets, and I could hear the fans near me explaining our issues to each other. I was cracking up! Yeah, we really scored that day!

When workers realize that it is all in their hands, that's the best. That's when beautiful things happen that exceed what any union organizer could come up with. That's when workers use the tactics and good ideas that come from their own experience and culture. This happened when I was involved with a strike in 1987 at a cannery in Watsonville that involved 2,000 workers, lasted for eighteen months, and devastated the town.

Before the strike began, there was no real leadership in the union. Like at Gatorade, the officials were basically doing nothing, and the workers were kind of throwing rocks at them, calling them names for doing nothing. I changed my work schedule so that I could be available and provide some leadership. I would get together with the workers before the official union meetings so that we could agree upon a plan to take to the meeting.

The strike happened, and people got behind it. After eighteen months on strike, not a single striker had crossed the picket line. The workers had bankrupted the company, gotten a new owner for the cannery, and a contract that offered them their jobs back. At the vote, I told the workers that it wasn't time to go back yet—I believed that they hadn't gotten the health benefits they deserved. The workers voted not to take the contract.

They set up headquarters in a striker's home across the street from the cannery. Monday morning was tense. It wasn't clear whether people were going across the picket line or not. Several hundred strikers and supporters were there, physically blocking all entrances. Managers at the cannery were trying to hold onto their jobs, and one way to do so was to provoke a riot. So they had scabs and applicants for replacement workers at phony higher wages standing in the parking lot for hours, like sitting ducks. They were surrounded by hundreds of angry strikers.

At our strategy meeting the night before, a Mexican woman had suggested that they march on their knees, like they do for the Virgen de Guadalupe. So as the cannery bosses were trying to start a riot, these women were lining up on their knees, ready to march. The national press was there. And then the women started walking down the street on their knees to go to church and pray for justice and health benefits. Other workers were laying blankets out in front of them on the asphalt.

The closest church was the rich church where the managers and growers went. It was not clear until fifty feet before the women got there whether they would be allowed in. If they kept the doors locked, it was a mile across the bridge over the river to the poor people's Catholic church, and there was no question that they would've gone there, even if some of them passed out along the way. The doors of the rich church opened, and the workers went in with the network television cameras rolling. That was a good day. The women won their medical insurance three days later.

. . .

As an organizer, I try to get workers to move from complaining to working together to solve a problem. Sometimes I get tough with them when they complain or expect me to fix their problems *for* them. But I want to help fix problems *with* them. I want them to know and remember they have the power. My ultimate goal isn't running the show but creating the conditions to increase worker initiative. Being a union leader often requires that I do run the show, at least to get started. I have experience. I usually do have a clearer picture of where things need to go. Although I keep asking workers what they think needs to happen, they ask me, "What do you think we should do?" That's always the dance. How can I lead and still check things with people? How can I lead with respect but not take over?

I was trying to organize the workforce at this big frozen vegetable plant in Watsonville. This was the worst place in Watsonville, union or nonunion, to work at. Many of the workers who stayed there year after year were very timid, and for good reason. The plant owner was nuts. His brothers and sons ran the place, and they were nuts. When the owner got pissed off, he'd scream. Sometimes, he'd even fling his toupee to the ground and stomp up and down on it, right there on the floor of this food factory. Every week he was firing or demoting one of his sons or brothers and promoting another one. There were seven hundred workers, but this food factory ran like this huge, dysfunctional family.

The first time I went into the lunchroom, people were too scared to even make eye contact with me. But every day I'd hang out at lunch with different workers at these small round tables where a few workers would be sitting. We'd hang out and talk. I was trying to figure out who the leaders were. It was a typical, textbook organizing technique. It wasn't working. No one could agree to do anything differently.

Then one day, workers got pissed off. The owner's brother had just been promoted to vice-president for production. He had the bright idea to increase production by making it harder for the women to use the toilet. And so he puts a floor lady (like a foreman) full time in front of the women's bathroom. She's behind a podium with a clipboard and stopwatch. You had to check in with her if you wanted to go, and she would time you. I tried talking him out of it, but he wouldn't budge an inch. To him, this was a brilliant idea.

At the end of the shift, about fifty workers were gathered in the hall, near the time clock, pissed off and complaining to me about him. They asked me, in Spanish, what I was going to do about it. I said, "What am *I* gonna do about it? By *myself*? What can *I* do to try and make this stop?" I told them that I had already talked to him, that there was no way I was going to talk him out of it, but that I could write a grievance. Then I told them, "Maybe we'll win, maybe they'll abide by the decision, and maybe, two or three weeks from now, they'll remove this woman from the toilets. But you know what? They will already have won because the shy people will have stopped using the bathroom when they need to go. And less people will have gone to the bathroom than before, so they will already have won. If that's what you want me to do, I'll do it." Then I walked away and said, "I'll go write up your grievance."

As I'm walking away, someone says, "Wait a minute. Isn't there something else we can do?" I asked, "What is it they are telling you?"

"We can only use the toilet during our breaks."

I asked, "How long are the breaks?"

"Ten minutes."

"Well, how many women are on the broccoli line?"

"Two hundred."

"How many toilets are in the women's bathroom?"

"Six."

They came up with the idea of all going to the bathroom at the same time. I told them, "If you try that, let me know, so I can be here." So after we talked some more, they told me to be there the next day at 10 A.M., on the first break. I thought, "Well, maybe they will do it, maybe they won't. Who knows?"

The next day, I'm driving to work like usual through the industrial district at around 7:30 A.M. I see women walking to work. On an average day we nod and smile at each other. This day, when I nod at them, they start smiling and waving at me big time. I think, "Fuckin' A, they're actually gonna do it. They're scared shitless, but they're still gonna do it."

So I get to the plant, and the vice-president of production is also wondering if this is going to happen. His snitches have told him. But neither one of us knows if it's for real. So he and I are hanging out there together, close to the bathroom, just talking about the weather and shit, because neither one of us will cop to what we know, and neither of us is sure what, if anything, will happen.

The line shuts down for break at 10 A.M. You know in school, when there's recess and the kids are supposed to walk but they're trying to run, so they're kind of stiff-legged? Two hundred women were doing that walk! With smiles ear to ear! They're all lining up at the same bathroom to use one of the six toilets, and the bosses are going crazy—screaming at me, but they are pleading with the women in line, begging them to go back to work. The women are talking back to them saying, "Nope. You told us to wait for break to use the bathroom, and we waited. Now you have to wait for us." That was the end of the stopwatches and the podium in front of the women's bathroom.

It was great. Again, that was one of those moments where people just took it. They just took something good and ran with it. And what I learned that day was that there's a critical mass. I learned that the minimum number necessary to make that decision in that plant on that day was about fifty angry women.

Lately, I've been trying to organize another way, to organize less on the guy model—strategic campaigns, blitzes, class warfare, and other military models. I want to build organizations that are based more on relationships. Some would call this a more female model. Right now, for example, I'm working in San Jose with about fifteen hundred workers at a cannery that's about to close. I've helped build a team of people that is a leadership group for the workers. We have trained sixteen peer counselors from the factory floor, and there are eight interns backing them up administratively—all young people, mostly Latina university students from working-class families. Everybody on the team is doing great.

It's exciting and difficult to work with people who are trying to succeed in doing something new and different. It means challenging the racism in the community, so they can have more options to get jobs. And it means challenging their internalized racism, where they believe and act out the racist lies on themselves and each other.

Capitalism keeps people feeling scared they won't make it. It keeps everyone feeling alone and believing that anything bad that happens is their fault. Good organizing creates the conditions where people can tell they are not alone. It reminds them that the bad things that happen to them aren't their fault but problems that they can solve by working together.

Our job is not to stop this plant closure. It will close anyway. The issue is how we organize the people who worked in these plants. How can unions put workers in control of the process instead of just government and social workers with a "taking care of" model? How can we keep these people together? What can a union do to increase the likelihood that people will stay in touch when the time clock is no longer the basis for their relationships to each other? In preparing workers for this closure, we are trying to preserve the sense of family that the workers have created. We're helping the workers figure out what they want. The most revolutionary thing you can ask working-class people is what they want, instead of their having to choose from a menu that's offered to them.

. . .

I know that there are times when I act racist and am perceived as racist. But it doesn't work for me to second-guess myself. It paralyzes me. So I just throw myself at things, sometimes without thinking about it much, sometimes without much planning. Sometimes it works; sometimes it's a mistake. I guess I've always trusted that if my mistakes are big enough, then somebody will see them and stop me, or I'll realize it myself. And I try not to blame myself too much for my own racism. I try just noticing it more.

At one plant where I was working, I noticed that some new Chicano workers initially liked me and trusted me. But as soon as they began hearing other workers blame the union and me for their plant closing, they looked at me differently, and I suddenly felt very, very white. It surprised me. I realized how often I forget I'm white. That's who people see, and that's who I am. I'm embarrassed by how stupid this is, but I know I am not stupid. When I remember how I experienced racism as a kid, I can give myself a break. I remember all the harsh racist comments that I heard from my dad. And I remember the racist looks I saw on the faces of white strangers when I would walk down the street with my Black stepfather and white mother.

I started out "normal" enough, living in a house outside L.A. with my white mom, white dad, and white younger brother. When I was five, she went to a mental hospital for several months. For the next couple of years, I lived with our mom when she was out of the hospital and my dad when she was in. Living with her wasn't easy. Whenever she felt alone, I felt like it was up to me to save her. At six, I moved in with Dad for good. I know he loved us a lot, but he struggled. Nothing in his life had prepared him to raise two boys alone.

For most of my childhood, Dad and my brother and I lived in an apartment complex near Los Angeles with poor families. They were mostly southern refugees from Arkansas, Alabama, and Texas—single moms with kids who came to Los Angeles looking for work or welfare. My dad made enough money to not live there, but he grew up in the Depression and was really tight about money. I was bused to a school where there were middle- and upper-class kids. I lived in two different worlds. I felt like the only person who crossed between those two worlds every day.

My mom met my future stepfather while they were patients in the mental ward of Los Angeles County General Hospital. He was Black, a returning

POW from Korea who'd been tortured a lot. My dad didn't take it too well. He was not happy about being dumped for a Black mental patient. I remember him driving around with me in the passenger seat of his vw as he ranted and raved and pounded the steering wheel, all the time spewing racism. His girlfriend and her family were racist, too. I was at their house in April 1963, when Bull Connor was doing his thing in Montgomery, Alabama, turning fire hoses and dogs on Black people. They were out of their chairs, yelling ugly things, pounding their fists in the air, rooting for the dogs.

My response was stoic and angry. My dad noticed this, and it bothered him. He didn't like it. I remember him taking me to a Catholic church for a pancake breakfast the morning after he'd seen the movie *In the Heat of the Night*. He never liked going to the movies, and he hated the church, so I knew this could be trouble. At breakfast, for over an hour, he acted out every scene where Rod Steiger called Sidney Poitier a "nigger." He repeated each line with such hatred and venom. That was the worst thing he'd ever done to me. At least when he would go nuts and beat the shit out of us with fists, shoes, and curtain rods, I could forgive him. There was a way that I knew that it wasn't really him. But this was different. The day at the church was worse than any beating because it was calm and calculated. It felt like he was trying to break my spirit. I still remember exactly where I was, walking back from the church, the first time he said "nigger" and I was no longer furious. I'd gone completely numb. I felt so defeated. I've cried a lot about that moment.

And so I grew up serious. We'd go camping a lot with my dad. Dozens of other kids would be playing together, and I would sit by myself and think. I was trying to figure this world out, trying to figure out what had gone wrong with my family and how to fix it. And I was trying to hold on to myself in some way.

I became very interested in the Civil Rights Movement. I would read the caption of every newspaper photo showing a march or a protest. My heroes were men who combined great athletics and courage: Muhammad Ali, Sandy Koufax, John Carlos, and Tommy Smith.[1] They seemed to stand up for themselves and for what was right. When I was in second grade, I organized my first picket line at the day care center. We wanted to be able to play outside before school.

Being with my other family was easier than living with my dad. Although I never lived with them or even slept over for a single night, for months at a time we saw each other every day. I was always welcomed. They were always happy to see me. My stepfather was hopeful and fun. He sang, danced, and taught me to twirl a baton. When my mom was depressed, he'd dance her around in circles and get her laughing. He gave me rides on the back of his motorcycle. He told stories of being a boy in Jamaica and about great things we would all do together. My baby brother was born when I was ten. He was a joy. And for those few years I didn't have to handle my mom. Then a bunch of bad things happened, and that family fell apart. I lost my stepdad at fourteen. Mom committed herself again. After a series of foster homes and a difficult adoption, my half brother disappeared.

Today, I don't know where my stepfather and brother are or even if they are alive. I miss them both so much. They were my hope and my connection. Until my mid-thirties I thought of myself as an orphan. Then I realized that I *did* have a family, and they were it. And because of them, I know I move easier around people of color than white people.

. . .

For the past year I have been trying to go home. It's a challenge. I never figured out a home situation. I do have a home, a family—a wife and a daughter—but still I feel like an orphan. So home is where I do the worst. In sports, there's always the home field advantage. I don't have that. I've always done better in the street or on the road.

So going home has been hard. Watsonville's a mess. More plants have closed, and thousands more workers have lost their jobs over the last five years while I've been running around the country, doing this national job. People feel abandoned, and I feel guilty. There were a lot of things I couldn't figure out: my family, my town, my boss, the members of my local, and the day-to-day stuff. And I took this interesting and exciting job, flying all over the country. So now I'm trying to figure out how to come back.

I want to be less isolated. I have close friends and comrades all over the U.S. and Mexico. I don't have close friends where I live. I work a lot. I understand work and working together with people and getting to know people through work. It's harder to just hang out with people. I want that. I want to be able to talk more openly about things that I don't know, things that I don't understand. Not just about race—about anything that I don't quite get, when it looks to me like someone else understands it better than I do.

I need to deal more with the people that I am most afraid of. For me, that means dealing with white people. I didn't identify as a white person growing up. I was angry at white people, the strangers on the street with their hateful looks, people on television, my father. They all looked so mean. I believed they were bad people. I couldn't tell that they'd been hurt. In many ways I still can't see that. But when I see another white person confronting racism in themselves or in white people they love, it moves me to tears.

I'm realizing that I need to be closer to white people. I need to be a better friend and ally to other whites. I need to love them in their hard places. Mostly I'm realizing, for what feels like the first time, that I need to do this for myself. A very special woman of color has helped me more than anyone else to open up to, and like, white and middle-class folks.

As a working-class guy who grew up poor, I've fought a feeling of being "lesser than." To push myself out of that, I flipped it over and told myself I was "better than" or morally superior to other whites, especially middle-class whites. I'm tired of that. I don't want to feel better or worse than anybody else. You know, we are all in this together. Under all the conditioning and the oppression, we are all lovely human beings who want the same things out of life. I want to build a team that I feel a part of, not to figure out things by myself. I want to contribute what I know and learn from others and form teams that include every kind of person. I want us all to work together to create the kind of world we all want, the one we all deserve. That's what I want to do—I want to have one life with everyone I love in it.

# Mike McMahon

*Mike is currently the director of programs at* GANO / CARECEN *(Gulfton Area Neighborhood Organization and Central American Refugee Center), a community organization in the Gulfton neighborhood of Houston. Gulfton is the most densely populated and fastest growing neighborhood in Houston. Its residents are primarily immigrants and refugees from Mexico, El Salvador, Guatemala, and Honduras. Mike was the first executive director of* GANO / CARECEN *and was replaced by his friend and colleague, Nelson Reyes, to fulfill an organizational commitment to having leadership from people of color. Nelson is an immigrant from El Salvador and a graduate of the local high school. Mike says, "Nelson has become an important leader and spokesperson for the Central American immigrant community."*

*Mike describes himself as an entrepreneur and problem solver; he was a small businessman for about twenty-five years before getting involved in community organizing in the late 1980s. He gave up his business completely in 1995. Mike's the first one to admit that he doesn't know what he doesn't know. He often starts out with little or no understanding of a situation but sees a problem, contacts some people, learns about the situation, and then puts together something to address the problem. He's received several awards, including Public Citizen of the Year from the Houston Chapter of the National Association of Social Workers for his work in establishing the health clinic that serves the residents of Gulfton.*

*Mike is sixty. Looking back on his life, he regrets that he didn't get involved in the Civil Rights Movement of the 1960s. "I had a very conservative background. My father was always in management; he worked for some paper mills when I was growing up. At one place he worked in Louisiana, there was a really bad strike that lasted for two years. There were people shot at and cars blown up and people died. We moved in the middle of that strike. I voted for Barry Goldwater when I was in college, and I voted for Ronald Reagan. But I've changed some of my values. When I had my business, I wanted the employees to find a way to feel some ownership in the organization, so I had some sort of leanings that way.*

. . .

Ten years ago, we had no social service agencies here in Gulfton, no programs, no clinics. As I look back, that's primarily what I did—put together coalitions and brought people together and created an atmosphere of collaboration so that agencies would participate. And we did attract some large grants that allowed for a lot of programs here. I just worked on the obvious things that we needed here.

When I first moved into this community, I didn't go out and say, "I want to help a certain group." This was the community where I lived, and I wanted to make it better. Probably people think that I have some affinity for Hispanics or immigrants. I definitely have developed that, but it wasn't something that motivated me to get involved. It was just that this was my community. I have lived in apartments in Gulfton since 1990. I think it is necessary to live in the community in order to build trust. The social service model that we practice is patronizing; we treat people like we are the doctor and they are the patients. We need to receive help in our needs from the people we are working with, as they receive help from us.

The Gulfton community is 3.4 square miles in size. There are about twenty thousand apartments and some industry and warehouses. In the late '50s, this area was basically a cow pasture. When the freeway system came out here in the '60s, the developers started building apartment complexes. We didn't have zoning, and the developers just came out here and built all these apartments. In 1969, I moved into one of the larger apartment complexes here, a new complex with almost eighteen hundred units in it. During the oil bust of 1981, apartments emptied out. When they started filling back up, they filled up with people from the inner city. The apartments were nicer than where they had been living. And the apartments also filled up with immigrants and refugees from the wars in Central America and from Mexico.

I operated a business here from 1970 to 1995. We sold cleaning supplies—janitor's supplies, paper towels, that kind of thing—primarily to offices. It started as a coffee service, got into the restaurant repair business. My business had been here for years, and I didn't realize the change that had come to the community. I drove through it, and I knew that there were more Latinos here, but I didn't realize how much it had changed in the '80s.

Half a block from the GANO / CARECEN offices, on a vacant lot was where the day laborers gathered. There were like 150 men who would gather there every day. If you drove by too slow, you'd get 5 or 6 men in the back of your pickup truck. They whistled at the women; they urinated on the ground because there were no facilities there; there was trash everywhere because there were no trash receptacles. For several years, this was the number one complaint of the homeowners and business people. They talked about this even more than crime or drugs. We were able to develop consensus from all groups in the community around the concept of having an organized, supervised site. GANO / CARECEN has been operating the Gulfton Day Labor Center since 1994, with funding from the city of Houston.

In 1989, the city council called a meeting about the crime and drug problem. My business had been broken into a couple of times in a six-month period, and so I went to the meeting. In May of 1989 we formed a community association called the Gulfton Area Action Council (GAAC). I was elected the first chair of that. The focus of that organization was to reduce crime and increase property values.

Shortly after that, I read an article in the local paper that talked about how the low-income families in this part of Houston didn't have any place to go for health care. We had a public hospital about five or six miles away. I just assumed that it took care of all their health needs. I never gave it much thought. So I started looking into what the needs were in the community, and it made sense to me, even though I didn't know much about public health clinics. The particular one we advocated was preventative—it helped pregnant women and did "well child" things, but it wasn't for sick people. I didn't know the difference at the time. I just started calling people that I thought ought to be involved in solving this problem. Within eighteen months, in June of 1991, the clinic opened.

GAAC's mission statement said that we were there to improve property values and reduce crime and drugs. My concept was that we needed a community organization and that it needed to address all the sectors of the community. I had studied about health care and education and crime and was trying to figure out all these different components. When I got involved with the health clinic, some of the board members called me to a private meeting and said, "Look, if you're going to work on getting services for these people, you need to do that on your own. That's just going to serve as a magnet to bring more immigrants here. So don't do that under our name."

But I continued working with GAAC in hope that they would change. After a couple of years, I asked them if they would be willing to change their mission and broaden their base and be more inclusive of the people who participated. They said, "Well, we haven't solved the property values and crime and drug problem, so we don't want to take on anything else." To be honest, there were very few minorities in GAAC, and most of this community is Hispanic. There was a Hispanic principal of an elementary school and from time to time one or two others, but it was embarrassing to sit in a meeting and listen to some of the comments that the white people had to say about the immigrants.

Finally, I gave up on them when they declined to be more inclusive. That's when we formed the Gulfton Area Neighborhood Organization (GANO). A couple of years later we merged with the Central American Refugee Center (CARECEN), which was organized in 1985, primarily by Salvadorans. I asked the board if I could be the executive director of GANO / CARECEN, and they said, "Fine."

I never actually sold my business. I had a friend who had started a similar business. We talked about him taking over my business and worked together for a couple of months, and then I said to him, "We'll just work out the arrangements on how to sell it." But I never got around to it. I just walked away from it and let him take it over. I think he took the assets and converted it into another business.

*You walked away from your business? Do you regret that decision?*

No, I've never looked back. I'm just doing something different now. I very seldom ever think about it, and when I do, it's just a memory. I was never a great businessman because I wasn't motivated by profit. I never have been that interested in money. I was in business because I enjoyed putting it together. I was always adding new things—vending, retail packaging, printed grocery bags—we were always getting into something new. To be successful, you need to focus a little bit. In my heart, I was never really into the operation end of it. I didn't do a very good job of it, I guess.

. . .

When we first started this organization, we were confrontational. Some Anglo homeowners wanted to close off the streets around a subdivision here, so we marched in the streets. That's very popular with people from Central America because that was the style that they brought with them from their countries, where things were very confrontational. There wasn't another avenue, I guess, because the government and military were repressive and not going to support their policies. So they had to build power.

The Anglo homeowners blamed me for the neighborhood changing, for their property values going down and all that, because I was the visible leader. They blamed me for opposing them, for being on the opposite side. They wanted to close their streets to protect their property values, to protect themselves from criminals, and so forth. I didn't see it that way at all. The crime in their neighborhood wasn't that bad. They wanted not only to close off the streets to traffic, but they wanted to close the neighborhood off to pedestrians. That was something that just wasn't right.

It didn't bother me that the Anglo homeowners hated me because I didn't think they were right! And there wasn't anything that I could do about it. When I was growing up, it used to really bother me when someone didn't like me, but when I got to be an adult, I realized that even if you're a nice guy, not everybody's going to like you.

I don't think that confrontation is the most effective method to use now because Anglos have begun to accept the community more as it is. Not that they don't still have prejudices. But they have accepted the fact that these people aren't going to go back home. The Anglos aren't going to get rid of the immigrants and make the community back like it was in the '60s and '70s. This community is not going to go back to what it was. So confrontation is not a basic approach that I would use, even though I believe it's necessary sometimes.

But I was interested in getting white people to confront their racism. For a while, I was the chair of the Interethnic Forum in Houston. The purpose of that was to create dialogue and to build bridges between people of different races and cultures. Unfortunately, we had too many United Way people involved in the forum. They wanted to process things for two years. It killed the project. They just wanted to process everything, like this intricate way of selecting board members and the bylaws. They spent so much time on this organizational stuff. After a year of this, I lost all my enthusiasm. I was more interested in getting into the issue and not spending all our time organizing the organization. I've seen that happen a couple of times; it kills all the interest in the good things.

I thought we could start groups all over the city where people would do dialogue and confront their racism and that there could be healing in that. I think that can happen, but so many people move to the suburbs to get away from the cities. There's so much segregation that I don't know how it's going to eventually work out. People are not serious about confronting their racism. It's kind of like the churches. There are a lot of superficial things, a lot of fluff that goes on. How do you find people that are serious about dealing with racism?

I think that the Christian church should be playing a role in this. I'm ashamed that the Christian church is so segregated. I know that there are different styles of worship, but there is absolutely no reason for the segregation. And I'm ashamed that the evangelical part of the Christian church has neglected the poor and the social ministry. They've left that up to the Catholics and the Episcopals and some other churches. I can't agree with that at all. That's one reason it took me two years to find a group that I could identify with and work with religiously. The spiritual group that I'm involved in now is very multiracial. I can't go into a situation where it's all Anglo, middle class. That's not my kind of Christianity.

. . .

When I was the executive director of GANO / CARECEN, I wasn't about empowering people. I was putting programs together and getting resources into the community. I wasn't working individually with people's needs. So some of the programs we have at GANO / CARECEN are probably inappropriate. Somebody else ought to be doing them. We need to be more about empowering people, accompanying them in solving their needs and problems, and developing community leadership.

So a couple of years ago, I decided that I had to make a commitment to turning power over to the community. It's not going to happen by itself. If you just say, "Well, we invited them, but they didn't show up," it will never happen. I was replaced as the executive director and became the director of programs. Nelson became the executive director.

Since I'm no longer the executive director, one thing that has developed—and it's a healthy part of the process—is that I'm not included in some of the meetings, and a lot of them are now conducted in Spanish. Overall, that's good. But sometimes I'm asked to participate, and since I haven't been involved in developing a program, I really don't know exactly where the other staff are on that program. I understand that, and I'm glad that we have leadership from the community.

I've learned to respect the leadership abilities of the people in the community. We have a health promoters' program where we're training women in the apartment complexes to assist and educate their neighbors around their health care needs. Those women are great. You give them a task, and they get it organized, and they do it. Maybe not everything is going to work out perfectly, and maybe I know the ropes better than they do, but they know the needs of the apartment residents better than I do.

We helped organize a holiday festival in the apartments through a fiscal agent. The residents of the apartments wanted to invite some of the consulates from Central American countries. It was only two weeks before the event. Well, the word came back from the fiscal agent of the event that their public relations department requires at least two months' notice to invite consulates. They might not have come, but that's ridiculous to tell the people that they can't invite them!

GANO / CARECEN dropped out of a collaboration that we helped initiate— Bridge / El Puente—because they didn't like our style of empowerment. It was funded by all the major foundations in Houston. They committed $5 million—something like that—over a five-year period. Bridge / El Puente was one of the two programs they funded. Ours was community-based, the other one was countywide. Our program was based in the apartments, and it focused on empowering preschool children to be ready for school, making sure that they're ready to learn. We were the organizer component, working with the parents and the other apartment residents. The collaborative was always complaining about the way we were organizing. And we made some mistakes, but they wanted to run it like a service provider. So we withdrew at the end of the year. That was $50,000 a year out of our budget.

Most of the service providers, Anglo homeowners, and Anglo business leaders are perfectly happy with the power structure—the people from the social service agencies and city government who don't live here but who run a lot of the programs here. The Anglo business people and homeowners are in charge of the advisory committees. That hasn't changed. It's still here. So I really have very little to do with them.

I'm now working with Nelson to put together a Community Development Corporation (CDC). He and I have been talking about that for a couple of years. We both have become involved in Christianity the last couple of years, so we're setting up the CDC as a faith-based organization. Nelson's heart is in having a community center that would meet all the needs of the people of the community—not just for charity and to give help or to provide programs, but to get to know them, build relationships with them, and get rid of the oppressive spirit. Poverty kind of beats your spirit down. We want to deal with the total person—not just their physical needs, but their emotional needs and their spiritual needs.

I won't have any regrets when I move on to the next project. I realize my limitations. That's just the way I am. I was focused on what needed to be done, on problem solving. When I started working with this community, I didn't know anything about community organizing. I had a lot to learn. I guess I had some common sense from my business experience. I don't have any baggage around ego or building a base of power for myself.

• • •

I feel uncomfortable around Anglos. The union meeting I was at today had a lot of Anglos, but they were social workers and union members. That's different. But being around a group of middle-class Anglos—I don't enjoy that. The things that they talk about are not of interest to me. If it's friends, we talk about old times and family and that sort of thing. But middle-class Anglo's perceptions of issues are different from what I've developed from being in the community. I don't miss that connection with other Anglos. It's not something I think about. It's just that when I'm there, I feel strange because I'm around Hispanics all day long.

I think I have some very strong friendships with Hispanics. Nelson and I can speak to each other's hearts, and we pray together. Because of my age, I'm not going to fit in with some of the younger folks in my neighborhood—they're not going to be as interested in hanging out with me. And this is a very young community. I don't think about it very often, but I have realized in the last couple of years that I'm not middle-aged any more! I finally realized that twenty-five-year-olds aren't interested in me. The older Hispanics here, for the most part, are not likely to speak English.

I'm treated really nicely and friendly and with respect from the people that I work with and the people that are involved in the organization, but it would be a lot more if I spoke the language. Why didn't I learn the language? It is hard when you're over fifty to learn another language. I ask myself that sometimes: "Why didn't you make the commitment to learn Spanish?" I think that speaks somewhat to my affinity for the culture.

Obviously, if I was more in love with the culture, I would have made a greater commitment to that because it is important. But I think part of it is that I'm working on problem solving, and most of the people I work with can speak English. I can't answer the phone here, and that's irritating sometimes when I have to watch it ringing. But I know that when I pick it up, more than likely I'm not going to be able to communicate. That's sort of an enigma for me. I will learn Spanish eventually.

The people I know here are good people. If the people I work with were Asian or African American, I would feel the same way. I haven't gone out and chosen a culture. The people around me, who I work with—this is my community. It's just not an issue with me, I guess.

It's a conscious decision to do what I'm doing in this community, but it's also a natural process. It's just what I want to do. I don't put a label on myself, but I identify with the issues of working-class people. That's where my life is. I don't think of myself as being poor. I definitely don't think of myself as being middle class. But I identify with the people and their problems. I guess I want to make things better for people. I have an added incentive now that I've introduced my faith into it. I want to try to build a world the way God intended it. That's my overriding motivation now. This needs to be a better world for everybody.

Because I've stayed single, I never have been concerned about making a living. And I never have cared about having things. I live very meagerly. I don't know if you would say I'm a risk taker, but I'm not worried about making changes. I just move to what I think I want to do or what I think I should be doing and don't look back. I have no fear of trying something new. I think in terms of the solution and not worrying about "what if."

Last fall, I offered my niece—my brother's only daughter—and her children to come live with me. She had separated from her husband, and she was the only Anglo living in a housing project in Jasper, Texas. That's where I was born. I just felt, "She's my family." We've never been close. She's twenty-one, started having children as a teen, has four of her five children living with her. They've lived with me for six months now.

I've never even been engaged, so I've never raised children. This is a real blessing for me because I'm learning how to teach people, how to be patient, sit down and work out people's problems. Kids bring a lot of 'em. I'm definitely still learning a lot. Sometimes I get irritated with some of my niece's faults, and then I realize that instead of getting irritated, I need to do some education here. We went to a parenting and grandparenting class together. She's young; she doesn't know how to do everything the right way, so I need to kind of help her be a little more organized. She's reverted back to her old ways of shouting at the kids. We've got to sit down and work on that.

I have to learn to relate to her and the kids, to share love, to relate to people's hearts and needs. These are young ones that are unprogrammed in a lot of ways. They're already programmed wrong in some ways. So it's a challenge, but it's a learning experience for me. It's a blessing because I now have this family that I'm learning to love. And I'm learning how to teach, which is something I've never been good at. I just accepted people as they are. I get upset and aggravated with 'em and hold it inside instead of teaching, instead of saying, "Why don't you do it this way?"

It had never entered my mind to have kids. I'm fifty-nine; I'll be sixty in November. I had thought that maybe, eventually, I might get married. But I never thought about raising kids. So it wasn't anything that I was prepared for; it just happened. It's easy. I mean, it takes a lot of your time, but I guess I'm old enough now that I can adjust and realize that that's the reality. If you're going to do this, then that's the way it's going to work.

# Art and Politics

# David Attyah

*We wanted to include white men working in the arts: musicians, actors, poets, and visual artists. Early on, we had interviewed musicians and actors, and several men shared their poetry with us. But we hadn't found any white men working in the visual arts as painters, muralists, or graphic designers. Then we remembered some material we had seen in a newsletter published by* RESIST, *an organization funding progressive groups. One of their grantees was* THINK AGAIN, *a collective of artists whose work has appeared as billboards, posters, and postcards. We contacted* THINK AGAIN *through its web site, asked if there were any white men involved, and got David's name. Although David lives in San Francisco, the interview took place in a coffee shop in Brookline, Massachusetts, during Gay Pride Weekend. David is thirty-four.*

THINK AGAIN *uses visual art to stimulate political conversation. In fact, Cooper had used one of their pieces to accompany an article on white male backlash he had written for a journal called* The Diversity Factor; *the illustration showed a group of white men in suits sitting around a table, complaining that all the good jobs were being taken by women and minorities. It was entitled, "White Men Can't Count." The editors of* The Diversity Factor *at first thought that the illustration was too radical for their readership, which included corporate white men, but Cooper encouraged them to use it, and they eventually agreed. Little did he know at the time that David, along with artist and educator S. A. Bachman, were the cofounders of* THINK AGAIN.

*David identifies as queer. "For me, queer is a political identity, not just a label for my sexual orientation. It is a frame for critiquing mainstream, homophobic, and racist culture and a commitment to building alliances. 'Queer' goes beyond 'gay,' linking my experiences to others who live outside of mainstream culture—single mothers, immigrants, and people of color, for example. It might take us some work to understand how the issues faced by these people relate to white gay men in the city. But they're linked. 'Queer' is one of those words that has been reappropriated by those of us who don't want an apolitical category like 'gay.' "*

•  •  •

My politics didn't start as queer politics. I was political and interested in race, gender, and class long before I came out of the closet. If you look at my age— I'm thirty-four—I should be able to remember the political climate of the late '70s. But I'm definitely a child of the '80s, which is terrifying because those were Reagan's years. In a lot of ways, I became political, as did my friends and colleagues, against the conservatism of the '80s. We were going against the grain, as opposed to people who came of age in the '60s and '70s and felt that they were really part of a movement. When I was in college, I never felt like we were part of a movement. I thought that we were a bunch of renegade political science students who couldn't get on board with supply-side economics. It was definitely an oppositional birth into politics.

I actually didn't come out of the closet until after AIDS activism had been at its height. If AIDS activism really flowered from 1985 to 1990, I didn't get out of the closet until 1993 or 1994. I was even doing AIDS work before I came out.

I think I'm somebody for whom the political has always preceded the personal. I've been able to enter the political world first and then a little later do the math about how my identity gets formed. My political sensibilities matured well before my emotional sensibilities or even my sexual sensibil-ities. It was easier for me to go to protests against the Israeli occupation of Palestine or go to AIDS rallies as a political act long before it was easy for me to have sex or to be comfortable having sex with a man—or to see my having sex with a man as a political act. It certainly is a sex act that aggravates politicians, isn't it?

I would argue that my work with race and gender made it much easier to come out of the closet. And in a lot of ways, I'm personally thankful for that work. Many young gay and bisexual women come out of the closet into the language of feminism, so their sexual orientation is seated inside of a political awareness about what our culture wants us to do and not do and how it punishes us or rewards us for conforming. I think that many gay, bisexual, and straight women have always had a better sense of how their identity as sexual beings is political.

I think that for a lot of gay and bisexual men, AIDS became a defining political reality, and AIDS activism provided a political stage to come out into. Now that AIDS activism is waning and gay men have the incorrect perception that they are now a part of the mainstream, there is a decided apolitical backlash that disturbs me. To come out of the closet and not have a language to understand society and social norms or to understand what's normal and not normal—the absence of a political language is amazingly difficult. I'm very thankful that I had a political and social analysis that could help me through that.

. . .

Sexuality and sex are these issues that rest close to our bodies. Sex is either literally in your body, or between you and your hand, or between you and your lover. Or it's about how you're going to create intimacy or how you think about pleasure. It's personal, internal.

When it comes to race and gender, I think it's very easy for most white Americans to focus on structural issues like welfare or the Supreme Court or hate crimes. Being a queer man has really helped me to understand the "near to our bodies" effects of oppression and to imagine how people of color or women feel oppression rub against their skin. I would like to learn more about how close homophobia is to my body and to connect that to how close sexism is to an immigrant woman's body, for example. These are not abstract propositions. It's about who's following you through grocery stores, how you look at yourself in the mirror in the morning, and whether you believe there's any hope for your surviving in your life. I would never be one to say that the experiences of queers and the experiences of Blacks, or people of color generally, are comparable, in that horrible and unproductive way where people want to compare who's worse off or who's better off. But there are a lot of resonances in these experiences—differences and similarities that are productive to explore if we want to develop a better racial and sexual analysis of social life.

Given this, I feel it's really important that white queers start talking more to heterosexual people of color. In my experience, the role and meaning of homosexuality in communities of color is different and complex and in many cases can really inform white ideas around sexual identity and family. White gay people generally presume that people of color are going to be hostile to them. That is part of the widespread lack of knowledge that white society has of people of color. What a waste that we don't have much conversation about that.

One of the questions we need to ask is, "How is it serving mainstream racist society to get white queers to think that Black people hate them and vice versa?" For example, I have a number of Black associates who feel that the strongly homophobic language emerging among Black musicians and Black politicians is new. It feels alien to them. I'm certainly no expert on it, and I can't explain the public perception that Blackness is essentially homophobic and that gayness is essentially white racist.

But it's certainly occurred to me that racist and homophobic society has an investment in making sure that queers and African Americans hate each other, just as the society has an investment in making sure that Asians and Black people hate each other. I think it's really convenient that white gay people walk around with this presumption that communities of color hate them, and vice versa, because there would be a hell of a whole social movement if we could all get it together. So when queers refuse to take on race as something that's relevant to them, they're also refusing to look at the possibility of coalition building with people of color. And they refuse to honor the experiences of queers of color, who have such an intimate knowledge of how race and sex intersect.

. . .

Many political artists go to a community, spend time there, work closely with the people, get kids involved. S. A. Bachman and I have made the choice not to do that work. THINK AGAIN has focused on printed matter, political posters, and billboards. The work makes strong, declarative political statements and speaks to a broad array of progressive issues—from race justice to queer liberation to economic justice to gender parity. We make the work visually provocative and craft messages that are accessible to the public. We focus on ways of thinking and kinds of analysis that can help people take apart a lot of the racist, homophobic, sexist blather that saturates mainstream culture.

THINK AGAIN distributes its work in face-to-face encounters. We try to represent something political that people think but won't necessarily say, and we connect it to the big picture. To me, that is what the work is about, that middle place where you can go up to someone in the street, show them a postcard, and have a conversation. We try to create a moment where people feel not offended but empowered. That's the goal of our work—to be in the middle place between the personal and the political.

Because THINK AGAIN does art work, sometimes we're taken less seriously than the people who do outreach work or policy work. That concerns me. I understand that the practice I have chosen might not be the practice that changes policy. Personally, I feel like I'm out on a limb. I'm doing the kind of work that I never thought I'd be doing, that I'm not really sure is relevant, that feels a lot like the creative process, not the political process. Sometimes you run it up the flagpole and it flies, and sometimes it drops like a lead balloon.

In the work we do, we don't have to be polite. That's part of the reason I really love it. When people tell us that our work is way too confrontational, I think about their privilege. If I didn't censor myself, I might say, "If you think this is confrontational, try being on welfare and getting it cut off. If you think this is offensive, imagine getting followed around in an airport or being told that you're incapable of achieving because you're a big failure or that there's a bell curve." Or when people get personally upset by our work, I feel like saying, "Get over it! This isn't about you!" Isn't that quintessentially white? To privilege feeling "offended"? To form opinions or make policy based on your fears?

I am not afraid of the idea that people are challenged or alienated by our work. I'm not somebody who gets really disturbed by confrontation. Confrontation means that we're having a conversation. That feels better than silence. And I'm somebody who believes that the step after confrontation is resolution, or at least understanding. I'm a big believer that under the offense and under the guilt, there really are noble impulses.

My wish is that our work makes political conversations okay. When people tell us that they find our work confrontational, that's really a way of saying, "We don't even want to have this conversation." It's a way of saying, "We don't want to have a conversation about what it means to live in America or what it means to live in a society where racism is active." I believe that art can be the provocateur in people developing a political imagination. There's a lot of room for play in art. There's a lot of room in art to say things and experiment with ideas.

That I prefer confrontation to silence is so embedded in my personality. And in a way it comes from a place of anger and fear. I'm a queer boy in a straight world, and it sucks. And I am pissed off. I'm not interested in comparing that to anyone else's oppression. I simply feel the stress of being a queer boy in a straight world.

Because of that experience, I can't keep quiet. I have so many friends who have exactly the same experience and say the same thing and many friends who are organizers and activists that say the same thing. If you don't speak up, you get squashed or abused. It's a survival strategy. Even though it's also a source of criticism from people who think that speaking up is counterproductive, I do it as a way to make sense of my own experience. This is a defining feature of my invaluable collaboration with S. A., something that bonded us from the beginning and something that I relearn from her every day—that there is nothing more politically toxic, more personally debilitating, than agreeing to silence.

• • •

"White Men Can't Count" is one of the very first pieces that S. A. and I worked on. The title is a joke on the movie *White Men Can't Jump*, and we're certainly not the first to use the line. THINK AGAIN's piece came out in postcard form about 1998, when people were debating Affirmative Action. We wanted to respond to the anti–Affirmative Action rhetoric of the moment. We wanted to talk back to the racist and ridiculous idea that African Americans thrive easily in our economy, do even better than their white counterparts, and steal jobs from innocent white guys. That card is about taking false things that people say about race, stating those myths directly, and then blasting those myths with the facts.

The process of creating a card begins with S. A. and me agreeing that we need to do work on a particular issue. Then we start talking to a lot of people, and we try to figure out how an issue is getting spun in the mainstream cultural imagination. We do the hard research, and we often adapt material from other sources. In this case, we distilled the statistics and phrasing that appear on the card from a book by Patricia Williams.[1]

The problem for us as artists was how to make the card really intelligible to a lot of people. So S. A. and I put what we thought many white people were really thinking, and some had the nerve to actually say, "If I were Black, I'd have gotten the job" or "I'm sick of minorities getting all the breaks." On the back of the card, we state the rebuttal: "There is no evidence that Blacks have overtaken whites in any sector of the economy, except at the very lowest levels."

The visual image for that card came from a piece that S. A. had done about a decade earlier. We collect images all the time, and then there's a really long process of experimenting to see what will work. One of our artistic values is that the image always contributes to the analysis so that the image is not just compelling to look at. In this case, we flipped the image over on itself so that the business men are talking to and agreeing with one another. The image questions who is included in the conversation about job fairness.

The visual and textual are equally important in our work. It's easy to write text that's compelling, and it's easy to make pictures that are compelling. But it's hard to get the pictures and text talking to each other in a way that enhances both.

"Bash Bat" was also released in 1999, right after the murder of Matthew Shepard in Wyoming. That was also around the time of the terrible truck dragging of James Bird in Jasper, Texas. Hate crimes were on the table, for both people of color and queers.

As a visual device, we chose an image that was completely understated, almost invisible, and not at all about the horrible violence the card refers to. It's not an image of Matthew Shepard hanging from a tree or the Klan

Figure 1. "White Men Can't Count" (1999). THINK AGAIN, www.agitart.org.

sticking a rifle down James Bird's throat. Most people don't know what it really is until they pull in close. The card was designed so that you figure out it's a baseball bat—a surrogate for acts of violence—at about the same time that you're able to read the text: "What if a straight man got bashed every time queers felt threatened by heterosexuals?" And on the reverse, "And what if a white man got lynched every time Blacks felt threatened by whites?"

There's the irony, of course. Most queers and most Blacks move through the world feeling in danger all the time. It's a fact of public life. The card tries to create a sense of danger—only rhetorical, not actual, danger—for those who enjoy the privileges of heterosexuality and whiteness.

A lot of our aesthetic and content decisions get driven by the questions, "In what context is this going to appear? And what do people need to see and hear in that context?" These two cards dramatize that decision. The "White Men Can't Count" card didn't come out after an event. It came during a debate that was going on largely in the white-owned, white-controlled, white press. Whereas the "Bash Bat" card came out at a time when people were reacting emotionally to an act of violence. Those two different contexts require two different artistic strategies.

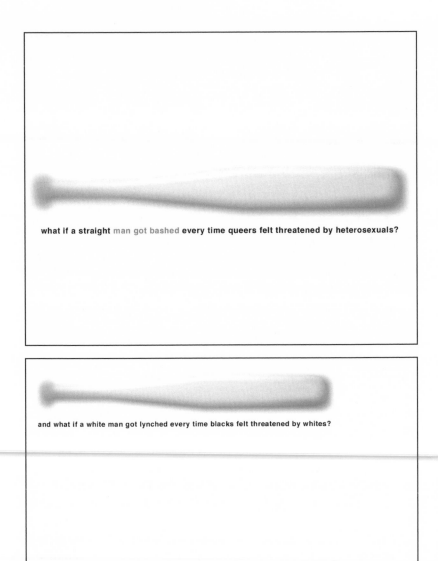

what if a straight man got bashed every time queers felt threatened by heterosexuals?

and what if a white man got lynched every time blacks felt threatened by whites?

**THINK AGAIN**

THINK AGAIN are artists who strike back at mainstream ideas that perpetuate injustice. We believe that xerox machines and wheat-paste can still incite people to THINK AGAIN. AgitArt@aol.com or http://members.aol.com/agitart/

Figures 2 and 3. "Bash Bat" (1999). THINK AGAIN, www.agitart.org.

S. A. and I are often asked about the didactic quality of our work—it's parochial, some say. There's a stigma, especially among artists, about being so direct, as if ambiguity were in itself a laudable artistic value. THINK AGAIN strongly disagrees.

Sometimes we can be elliptical and poetic and give the reader a lot of credit and allow the reader to fill in the blanks. The "Bash Bat" card is an example of that. But on many political issues, I worry about whether people have enough information to fill in the blanks. For example, African Americans as a group are not doing better in the economy than whites as a group. Period, no question, no ambiguity, no artifice. Especially when whiteness is operational, whom can we trust to fill in the blanks correctly, humanely, justly? If we leave it up to people's imaginations, they might imagine the wrong things. Certainly queers and people of color know that if you leave it up to the imagination, mainstream Americans will only imagine gay discos, jailed rappers, lesbo prison guards, ghettos and drug dealers, terrorists, and AIDS. So THINK AGAIN is not going to leave it up to their imagination.

. . .

I'm uncomfortable identifying myself as an antiracist white man for a number of reasons. First, it sounds like I'm taking credit as a white man, that I should be credited somehow for not believing lies propagated about Blackness. That's basic, required; no awards for that. Part of the problem of maleness and whiteness is that white men take credit for everything. I mean, George W. Bush is even taking credit for saving the environment and loving Islam. So taking credit is loaded for me. As far as I'm concerned, we can put Angela Davis's name on everything.

Another reason I'm uncomfortable identifying myself as an antiracist white man is that I identify both as white and nonwhite. I have white privilege because I can walk around and get served first, and when I'm in public and there's a fight, no one thinks that I started it. I'm the beneficiary of white privilege based on the way I look. The bottom line is that I have a certain kind of income potential and a certain kind of education and a certain kind of privilege bestowed by whiteness that allows me to do this work.

I'm an Arab American. Culturally and ethnically and personally, I feel very alienated from white culture. Arab Americans are simultaneously raced and not raced. We're invisible and present in this culture at the same time. So in most contexts, I would not identify as white.

And now the context for Arabs in America has deteriorated. In order to wage Bush's infinite war on terrorism, Arabs must finally be rendered visible in American culture—as thieves, fanatics, and terrorists. What a disappointment that Arabs would finally be revealed in keeping with a classic pattern of racism.

Sadly, I find my own identity and my work interpreted differently now. When I'm white, it's political critique. When I'm Arab, it's evidence of disloyalty to the nationalist project of America. White: it's commentary. Nonwhite: it's subversion. Another classic pattern of racism.

The last piece of it is this. I'm uncomfortable proclaiming that I'm antiracist. I would be more inclined to say that I am someone for whom race justice is an important commitment. The difference for me is that I get tired of left-leaning white people saying that they're antiracist.

I put away a lot of the angst and guilt that liberal whites have about race. I've stopped asking whether I'm doing enough, or whether I need to do more or do less, or whether my work is really important, or whether it's meaningful or not meaningful. The question "Do I do enough work on race justice?" doesn't make sense to me. All I know is that in one capacity or another, over the course of my life, to a greater or lesser extent, I will be interested in and engaged in this work. I'll have to do it, and I'll want to do it. I think race work is one of life's mandatory practices.

A question I do ask myself is, "How much of my time am I spending on social justice work versus making art?" In a certain regard, it's an easy question to answer, given that I've chosen an artistic practice that is unambiguous in its political agenda and effect. But as a draftsperson, colorist, designer, I do have purely aesthetic and formalist interests, and it's a choice to spend more time on, for example, making a beautiful drawing and less time on politics.

There is a part of me that wants to be a painter and paint red paintings and meditate on red all day and think about red minimalism. Sometimes I'm thinking, "Why am I busting my butt to do a damned postcard when I could be in my studio meditating on water lilies and naked bodies? Especially when George W. stole the election and there's not a damn thing anyone can do about it." That feeling usually passes in under a minute.

So for me, there is always this calculation of how much time I'm spending doing social justice work and how much time I'm spending doing (for lack of a better word) the art work. And then how much time I'm spending reflecting, observing, and relaxing. Let's put that on the docket. I think I'm somebody who does a lot of internal work. I spend a lot of time meditating, trying to get a grip, trying to manage my emotions, trying to work on something like a spiritual life. I also spend a lot of time watching our culture, observing social life. I can't necessarily see how these activities directly impact social justice work.

One way or another, for better or for worse, I'm always pulled back to social justice work. I think it's partly because those concerns are just part of my coding. Certainly, I like the people and I enjoy the interactions, and I find the work nourishing. And certainly, it's important for me to be in places where my values feel affirmed and that I am affirming values. But a good part of it is existential. I'm reminded of our mission statement: "THINK AGAIN are angry atists with a good offset printer. We also have a sense of humor."

Like everyone on the planet, I've come to realize that I'll always struggle with trying to get internal questions to balance with the external ones. Nothing grandiose or special about that. The problem is art making tends to be this place where the internal and external collide with often cataclysmic effects. It's true what they say: the personal is political and the political is personal, and it's all an art problem. So the grassroots street work is tempered by a good dose of self-reflection.

I'm going to be honest with you. When a white guy says—when I say—I need to go inside and reflect, part of me says, "Great. We need way more self-reflective white guys in the world. Let's get every white person in the world self-reflecting a little bit. Maybe things will improve." And part of me is going. "Uh oh. More emphasis on how white people feel. Or worse, more emphasis on how white people feel about themselves. Whiteness at its worst." This is where you and I and all the men in the book have to be smart and have to be willing to call ourselves on our own shit and have to be willing to get called on our shit. We have to invite our allies of color to keep us real, to check our whiteness. Because whiteness—even liberal, antiracist whiteness—is a problem.

# Si Kahn

*Si Kahn is an organizer, folk singer, and songwriter. He's fifty-seven. He began his political work with the Student Nonviolent Coordinating Committee (SNCC) during the southern Civil Rights Movement of the 1960s. He has worked with the United Mine Workers of America and with the Amalgamated Clothing and Textile Workers' Union. He's the founder and (since 1980) executive director of Grassroots Leadership, a multiracial team of organizers who do civil rights, labor, and community organizing in the South. Grassroots Leadership is currently coordinating a national campaign to abolish for-profit private prisons. All of the income from his concerts goes to Grassroots Leadership.*

*We met in Si's home in Charlotte, North Carolina. We began the interview by asking him to sing a song about racism. In a soft, unaccompanied voice, Si sang a song he's written about for-profit prisons, "Vann Plantation."*

. . .

I was hiding in the brush
By the Ohio River
Sarah by my side
The baby in my arms
When the slavecatchers found us
With our backs against the water
Winter come late
And the ice not formed

And they sold me back South
To the old Vann Plantation
Two hundred miles
From my home and kin
To be buried in a grave
With no marker on it

*Right on the spot*
*Where the new prison stands*
*Right on the spot*
*Where the new prison stands*

*I was walking the streets*
*By the Anacostia River*
*But no one was hiring*
*A young Black man*
*When the district police*
*Picked me up for no reason*
*Gave me fifteen years*
*For less than ten grams*

*And they sent me down South*
*To the old Vann Plantation*
*Two hundred miles*
*From my home and kin*
*To be buried in a cell*
*In a for-profit prison*
*To make some men rich*
*From the trouble I'm in*
*To make some men rich*
*From the trouble I'm in*

*There were 4 million slaves*
*From the African nation*
*Now there's 2 million prisoners*
*In the land of the free*
*It might be right on this spot*
*That my great-great-grandmother*
*Had done to her*
*What they're doing to me*

*I can feel her spirit*
*On the old Vann Plantation*
*Beneath the towers*
*And the razor wire*
*All for the profit*
*Of some prison corporation*
*If you say that's not slavery*

*You're a goddamn liar*
*If you say that's not slavery*
*You're a goddamn liar*

*(copyright 2000, Joe Hill Music [ASCAP]; all rights reserved)*

In "Vann Plantation," I'm trying to figure out how to create a sense of power, passion, and emotion without being too didactic. I had to sneak in the lines about "4 million slaves from the African nation"—that's the estimated number of slaves at Emancipation—and that there are 2 million prisoners now. But I don't want a song to have a lot of statistics. I'm trying to connect with people emotionally but not necessarily to connect them to me as the songwriter. I am not in the song. I am not there as a character, a commentator, or even an observer. The person who's telling the story is this young guy who's gotten picked up in Washington, D.C. Either he had ten grams or he didn't have ten grams, but he's going down. He's the narrator.

Now, of course, I'm making up his comments. But I would be very disappointed if people heard that song and said, "Wow, Si really has a righteous attitude about prisoners." This song is not supposed to be about me. They're supposed to feel the situation of this young guy and his great-great-grandmother. That's who I want the audience to imagine; that's who I want them to remember.

So partly what I think you do as a songwriter or as an organizer is you tell stories, rather than present people with facts. You don't overdramatize the stories; you understate them as much as you can. I tend to write and organize in a fairly unadorned narrative style, without telling people what they should think or do.

I really hate it when at the end of the song, the narrator says, "So now we've heard the story, let's all get together and fight the injustice of the prison system." I think, "Oh, for God's sake, give the listener some credit for being intelligent." I assume that people will figure out the lesson. But I also don't want to shift them out of an empathetic mood into an intellectual mode. I want people to sit with the emotion. If there's a question, if they want to come up afterward and ask me what they can do about the issue, then we can talk. But I don't want to allow them an easy intellectual escape. It's kind of a guy thing to get the emotion over with. We don't want to let it sit there. It's uncomfortable. It creates tension. We want to resolve that and say, "You know, I do emotion okay, but now let's get down to business."

•  •  •

To me, what's happening in prisons is a counterattack on the gains of the Civil Rights Movement. Look at who is in prison: it's not guys like you and me, and if so, we're at one of those country club prisons. If you take African American men between the ages of twenty and twenty-nine in this country, one out of three is either on probation, on parole, or in prison. African American women are approximately 12 percent of the women in this country, but they make up half of all the female prisoners. You tell me that this is not about race? The great majority of drug use is by white people. The great majority of people who are in prison for drug use are people of color. Prisons are about race; they are about racial control.

I'm very, very hesitant as a white person about drawing parallels to slavery. But I will certainly say that what is going on in for-profit private prisons shares some of the characteristics of a slave system in terms of the transportation of inmates away from their families across state lines, the buying and selling of prisoners, the profiteering from prisoners. It's tragic enough that people are in prison. And to make profit from that—I find that beyond the pale. So for me personally, the campaign against private prisons is about my sense of justice.

The private prisons didn't start what's wrong with prisons. Private prisons are a relatively recent phenomenon. In the South, there are historical connections to the convict lease system, which operated in the years after the Civil War. Prisoners were hired out for a dollar a day to the railroads, steel mills, and coal mines. Conditions were so awful that one out of three prisoners died every single year. The connections between that and the current system are too clear and profound to be ignored.

Private prisons also offend my sense of democracy. My partner and spouse, the feminist philosopher Elizabeth Kamarch Minnich, teases me about this. She says, "For all of your radical politics, you're the most patriotic American I've ever met." I'm a big fan of the Constitution, despite all of the exclusions that were built into it. We should always remind ourselves of those exclusions. Slaves were counted as three-fifths of a person; neither slaves nor women were allowed to vote. These are serious defects. But the Constitution contains some fundamental ideas of the potential for building a remarkable society. Someone once asked me, "Just what is it that you want?" I said, "I'll take the Constitution with a grievance procedure and binding arbitration." If we could enforce the Constitution, we'd be in pretty good shape.

The current struggle in the United States is very much one between the corporations and the ideal of democratic processes. I find the idea that corporations should run our schools, hospitals, libraries, and parks completely and totally unappealing. The idea that corporations will run our prisons for profit I find appalling. I cannot see how you can sustain a democratic structure if that is one of the ways that corporations make money.

The people of this country have shown an extraordinary capacity for justice and for injustice. You see that in the history of the South. One of the reasons that I continue to love living in the South is that I am always surprised. Sometimes, I can't believe that such a high level of racism is still here. It is. And here in Charlotte we're not far from many Klan strongholds. Probably tonight, someone's burning a cross. And then there are acts of resistance, of love, of care, of sisterhood, of brotherhood that are amazing and powerful and moving. I see them every day. We are struggling to learn how to live with each other.

. . .

I'm an organizer, and as an organizer, I believe there needs to be a call to action. But the question is, who issues the call? The organizer actually shouldn't be the one to issue the call. People should issue their own call. I set the stage to the extent that I need to. If I were an artist, I'd be a minimalist. It's a question of what you believe about people. I believe that people have extraordinary common sense, great intelligence, and a lot of experience. By and large, they have pretty good ideas about what they need to do. As an organizer, I just need to create the space.

There's a parallel in twelve-step programs. I haven't been a long-term participant in any programs; I've been to maybe three or four meetings with friends and read descriptions of programs. It seems to me that what you get is a very basic structure and a couple of common sense rules. Everyone has to take some responsibility for making sure that the meeting goes well, for teaching as well as for learning. There's an assumption that the process will bring out the knowledge that people feel they and others have to have and that out of that, people will figure out what to do and where to go.

That's an organizing process. You get people in a room; people tell their stories; they do some analysis; they help each other figure out why they're in this situation. "What has happened to us? What has made us this way? Is there a way to be different? What would that be?"

Here's an example. People call up and say, "We have this terrible problem. Could you come and help us figure out what to do?" And I say, "I'd be happy to do that." So I go, and they say, "Thank God you're here because now you're going to solve our problem for us." I say, "Well, I'm glad to be here. What's the problem?" People tell me. I tell them it sounds like they really have a problem, that they have a reasonable sense of what it is and where it came from. Then I ask them, "What have you thought about doing?" People talk to me about options they've considered, things they've heard other people have done. Then I ask them, "If you balance all these out, which seem to make the most sense? What do you think people would actually do? What do you think people would get out of doing this, beyond the victory? How would they grow, how would they feel differently?" After people respond to those questions, I ask them, based on all of that, what they think is the way to go. They tell me, and I say, "Sounds good to me."

Now it's not always that simple. As an organizer, I do have knowledge about what has and hasn't worked elsewhere. I can say to people, "Are you aware of when people tried this, or are you aware that this is an option?" I can help people sort things out or tell them that a strategy has been tried and hasn't worked very well. In my belief about how you organize, a great deal of it is a process whereby people discover each other and learn to know each other, to work collectively, to strengthen community.

. . .

I am so fortunate because I find a sense of community and connection in many different places. I find it especially in this really amazing family that I'm a part of. This is a family that actually functions within reasonable limits. In the extended family, I have twelve first cousins. I stay in touch with about ten of them.

Last weekend, I was in Miami, Florida, at my first cousin Jack's oldest child's bat mitzvah. Jack had asked me to bring my guitar so that we could do a little singing before everyone left at the end of the ceremony. I brought some songbooks and thought we'd sing a couple of songs together. It turns out that this is not what he has in mind. He got a little stage set up in the backyard, and he wants me to do a concert.

Over the years, I've written lots of songs about family, including many songs about the close relatives of people who are there at Jack's. There's a song about Gabriel Kahn, my grandfather and Jack's grandfather, who was the first to come to this country and who with my grandmother, Celia Leibowitz Kahn, started the U.S. branch of the Kahn family. There's a song for my great-aunt Nellie Israel and for her husband Al and a story about my aunt Shirley Kahn. Although there have been times when individual members of the family were in the audience, I've never actually performed these songs to a gathering that includes three U.S. generations of this family. Furthermore, I haven't sung some of these songs to the people that the stories are about. I wonder what level of exaggeration I've built into these stories?

This was one of the most important concerts I'd ever given. I feel, unlike so many people that I know, really centered in family. I know my place in the world because I know my place in this extended family.

Second, I'm centered in what I think of as "the Movement," as in the southern Civil Rights Movement, what John Lewis, the former president of SNCC and now a member of the U.S. Congress, used to call "the Beloved Community." I feel a connection with the Movement. In contrast to my family, my sense of connection is not so much about people—I don't actually run into many people I know from that time and place—but to the Movement as a phenomenon. It is a political community that continues today and has a set of principles and values. As a member of the Movement, I feel like I have continuity in my organizing work.

I would say that family centers me, in some ways, in emotion. The Movement centers me in work and time. And being Jewish centers me in history. I claim a white identity because, functionally, I enjoy white privilege. But in conversations with white men who do not have an ethnic self-identification, I find a difference in being Jewish. I believe it would be irresponsible for me to sidestep the question of the privilege and access I get as a white man and say, "I'm not really white; I'm Jewish." I don't think that's a responsible act for most Jews in this country, although there are also many Jews here and elsewhere who are people of color.

I function with a sense of Jewish history and identity. It has to do with expectations more than anything else, expectations from history and values. The piece of Jewish tradition that I carry with me, that was given to me very strongly by my parents, is that you are not in this world for yourself alone. If you think so, then you are being selfish and irresponsible. For my father, this was a religious meaning; for my mother it was much more social and cultural. Just because you are here, you have a responsibility. That responsibility includes trying to leave the world, or your little part of it, a slightly better place than you found it. It includes a responsibility to stand with people who are being pushed around, to speak up, to try to be useful. It's not high drama. It's not about, "You should be a leader of the Movement."

Those are by no means exclusively Jewish values. Every religion teaches those values. But my container is Jewishness. I think my experience has a lot in common with people in the Catholic Worker Movement, folks who come out of the Friends or the Methodist Youth Fellowship, which produced numbers of white civil rights activists. Religion can be the carrier wave for a set of useful values.

I don't suffer from existential angst. I don't have the question, "What am I here for?" I know what I'm here for. I can be in relative harmony with most of this set of history and values. I don't have to create something new. I may have questions about whether I'm living up to my values. And I can have an overactive conscience. My struggle is to be less responsible. But I definitely still feel rooted and in the midst of something that matters.

I'm secure about my place in history. It's not that I will be written up in certain ways. It's that the work I do has a secure future. It will be continued. I am sure that it will be done quite capably. That gives me great peace of mind. I don't have the modern disease of feeling that if I don't do this in the next two years, then it will all be for nothing.

I used to work for the Amalgamated Clothing and Textile Workers' Union. Where we are now in Charlotte was the epicenter of the textile industry. The houses in this neighborhood used to house the mill workers; the brick buildings up the street housed the mills. Within one hundred miles from here, you had 75 percent of all the textile mills in the United States that were operating about thirty years ago. In those days, the mills ran twenty-four hours a day, seven days a week, fifty-one weeks a year. They even ran on Christmas.

Working in a textile mill is basically keeping an eye on machines that are doing the different operations that together produce the finished cloth. In a twenty-four-hour operation, when you go to work, the job is already running. You start your shift, and the first thing you do is check with the person on the previous shift to see what you have to do to keep the job running. At a certain point, a whistle blows; they step away from the machine, you step in, and you take over from them. You want to keep the job running as smoothly as you can. If you're a responsible worker—and most workers are—you want to leave the job in a little bit better shape for the next person so that you can say, "It was a little off when I got in here, but I got it straightened out. You should have a good evening." You do your eight hours, and at the end somebody steps in beside you, and then you leave. Your job is to pull your shift as well as you can.

That's how I see my work. This Movement was running long before I got to work. I have a defined shift. I have a period of time in which to run my piece of the overall job. What I need to do is run that job as well as I can. And, hopefully, I can make it run a little bit better during the time that I'm here. But I do that work in the absolute assurance that the job doesn't end when I stop working. The job continues. Somebody else steps in and takes over that work from me. It's not just an individual; it's a collective of people.

My sense of history teaches me that these are very complicated problems. We're not going to resolve racism in our lifetimes. We're not going to figure out how to redistribute wealth and power and build a just society unless they figure out a way to make our lives last for thousands of years, which I hope they don't. We may come up with theories and make pieces of programs, but a just society will not be created in our lifetime. Ever since history has been recorded—and we assume before that—people have been struggling for justice. It's documented in a thousand ways. I have the assurance that the responsibility for straightening out the world is not just on my back or even on the backs of this generation. We should do our best. We should do conscientious work as well as we can. But I do not feel the pressure that either you solve poverty or you've failed. If we make any kind of dent at all in the span of history, that's a success.

Lastly, history teaches me about backsliding. History is not steady progress in the right direction, nor steady progress in the wrong direction. There are revolutions and counterrevolutions. There's progress and reversion. I am not disheartened, although I may be angry, when, for example, racism, which has been somewhat suppressed for a while, rises up again. I'm sorry it is that way, but I expect that to happen. I also believe that with each round, we improve a little bit. That's how I interpret the Christian hymn "Jacob's Ladder." Every round goes higher, higher.

I've tried to build these values into Grassroots Leadership. One of the things about Grassroots Leadership that I'm proud of is that we've been leaders in paying staff a decent salary and providing good benefits. To my knowledge, we were the first southern social justice organization to get a serious pension plan and to provide sabbaticals to the staff. Organizing should be the kind of a job where someone who doesn't have a high school diploma or college degree can go and get the kind of job that they deserve. To me, the political principle is not subsistence but that we should be paid fairly. We're workers, too. Just because we work for justice doesn't mean that we should be exploited, even by ourselves.

I get occasional whiffs of the myth that organizers are some kind of martyrs. I am the furthest thing from a martyr. I have no desire to be one in any physical or emotional sense. I believe that organizing is skilled, honorable work, and it ought to be reimbursed. At Grassroots Leadership, the people who have been there twenty years, like me, should make what an autoworker with a good union contract makes. We should have that level of job security, of income, and of benefits. If we don't do that in our nonprofit organizations, we discriminate. We say that the only people who can afford to work here are people with privilege.

I have an extended family that is pretty much middle class. That means that if I were seriously ill, family members would pitch in. If I need to borrow money, I can go to any number of family members who would lend it to me, particularly if I had a catastrophic need. Collectively, the financial resources are there. That is not true of most of the people I want to see working at Grassroots Leadership. They didn't go to Harvard; they don't have extended, middle-class families with a level of security. They have far larger numbers of people dependent on them, many of whom are not working.

So if you structure an organization at subsistence wages, you're basically saying to most people of color, to women who are heads of households, to people who have medical needs, "This is not the place for you." If we're going to build a movement and have diversity within a movement, we have to have some justice in terms of what people are paid.

. . .

I want to be a good boy. This is what my parents told me to do. My mother was passionate about this. She died when I was twenty-four years old. I want my mom to be proud of me. It is at an emotional level for me. I have other self-interests. But that's the heart of the matter. That's the truth of the matter: I want to be remembered as a good guy.

There are different Jewish views on mortality. The view from much of the non-Orthodox part of Judaism is that there is no afterlife. This is it, buddy. This is what you get. But there is remembrance. This is what Rosh Hashannah and Yom Kippur are about. You will be remembered for good or evil; you are written down for good or evil. My father used to quote the Torah: "A good name is more precious than oil." I hope that many different kinds of people will say, "Si was somebody that you could pretty well count on most of the time. Every once in a while he messed up, but by and large, he really worked hard to be a reliable ally." That would make me feel good.

That's at an emotional level. At a practical level, the question of self-interest has to do with being Jewish. In this country, by and large, in the year 2000, anti-Semitism is at a fairly low level. Anti-Semitism in this country is nowhere near the level of racism that is experienced by African Americans and other people of color. But it's not absent. It's under the surface here, and you never know when it's going to hit.

I was in Tampa last week to visit my aunt and uncle. I grabbed a taxi at the airport and gave the driver directions to the assisted living center where they live. He claimed that he knew where it was. He goes about three or four miles, turns around, and goes in a different direction. I ask him, "Do you know how to get there? Should we stop at a gas station and ask?" He said he thought he knew how to get there. A few minutes later, when he still seemed unsure, I suggested he call the dispatcher, but he said, "No, I know it's up this road." After a few more minutes of wandering around, I said for the third or fourth time, "Look, I want to stop at a gas station if you're going to keep that meter running." And he blew up and said, "You Jews just drive me crazy. You give me a pain in the gut. Always with the money." With all due respect, I don't think this ever happens to Lutherans or Baptists or Episcopalians. Well, I basically screamed at him, told him it had nothing to do with being Jewish, and don't you dare talk to me like that. He calmed down and later, to his credit, apologized to me, saying, "I'm really sorry. I lost my temper, and I know better than that. I shouldn't have said what I did." I told him, "You're right."

In a country that exploits and oppresses African Americans, that uses violence against gays and lesbians, that uses violence against women every day, Jews, who are not people of color, lesbians, gay men, or women—which is to say white male Jews—are pretty safe. We're not anywhere near the top of the list. But we're on the list somewhere. I'm profoundly convinced that if you let hatred and fascism and racism and homophobia and sexism get out of hand in this country, my kids are on the list, and I'm on the list. So I have a serious self-interest in making sure that we beat racism down as far as we can because the permission to hate spreads like wildfire.

I'm very cautious in how I frame this and talk about it. I want to make it absolutely clear that when I walk out my door as a Jew, I do not believe that I run anything like the risk of someone who is a woman, evidently gay or lesbian, who is African American, who is Asian. I run nothing like that risk. But I'm aware of the historical context. I'm aware of what happened in the past century. I'm aware of the history of anti-Semitism in this country. And I'm aware of my taxi driver. At that level, which is both intellectual and emotional, I'd better be fighting for a democratic, antiracist country. Otherwise, as Malcolm said, "Those chickens come home to roost."

# Steve Bailey

*Steve is a founder and currently the executive director of Jump-Start Performance Company in San Antonio, Texas. Jump-Start is now in its sixteenth year. There are twenty members who collectively create and perform work as well as manage the company. Steve's artistic role is as a director and lighting designer. He's forty-three.*

*Jump-Start is a multidisciplinary theater company doing all original work. It's often experimental or different. And it's usually—although not always—political or about social justice. Steve says, "Challenging oppression is integrated in our work; it's in everything we do. That doesn't mean we're always good at it; that doesn't mean we always succeed at it."*

*Jump-Start also does programs in the community with youth. One is called "Historias y Cuentos," which in Spanish means stories and tales; the underlying theme is identifying who you are in the world in relation to your community. The vast majority of the students in that program are of Mexican origin. Another program is called "Healing Arts," a consortium of social service and counseling agencies and arts organizations. It's designed to help youth who have been sexually abused.*

*Steve has been very involved with the Esperanza Center, a local progressive organization founded by lesbians of color. In the mid-1990s, Esperanza and its executive director, Graciela Sanchez, were attacked politically for being pro-lesbian, pro-women, and pro-people of color. Steve and a few other gay white men took public positions in support of the center and directly challenged white people who were hostile to the executive director. "We didn't create the racial tension, but we had to do something about it. Graciela and the other lesbians of color get set up. They are the ones who really get threatened. And Graciela is a dear friend, and I've learned so much from her. She's done so much for this community. I had to speak up."*

*The interview took place in the office of the theater at the Blue Star Arts Complex in San Antonio. That evening, Steve and other members of the company performed an original piece called* Illusions, *a dance/theater piece using "sleight of hand and perception, magic tricks and deception to investigate unexplored aspects of U.S. history."*

. . .

Sandy Dunn and I were two of the original founders of Jump-Start; as a celebration of our fifteenth season, we wanted to do a piece together, and *Illusions* was the result. We started talking about the meaning of elections and democracy, with the 2000 election really cementing the idea: an illusion of inclusion, the hypocrisy of democracy. It came from a sense that many people in the United States believe we live in a democracy. But there are voices that really aren't heard. For the text of the play, we decided to use common and uncommon documents of U.S. history. We looked at reams and reams of material: Jim Crow laws, Civil War documents, anything we could find that dealt with hidden exclusions. One of the books we used to research the show was [James Loewen's] *Lies My Teacher Told Me.*

Instead of us pontificating about how we feel about the issue, we wanted to let some of these historical words speak for themselves. We particularly wanted to use some obscure quotes by Abraham Lincoln and Thomas Jefferson that reveal some of the beliefs they had about the inferiority of people of color. For example, Lincoln said at some points in his life that the "Black race" was inferior to the "white race." He really believed that. I wasn't taught that in school. It's not like he didn't do some good things—nothing is one way or the other. But many people in the U.S. revere Lincoln and Jefferson and other "forefathers" as the personifications of democracy, and this kind of deification seems hollow when you hear some of the things they said.

We took the source material and used some experimental theater techniques to develop vignettes and scenes. And then Sterling Houston, artistic director and playwright in residence at Jump-Start, got really interested in what we were doing, even though he wasn't actually involved in the play. After watching a rehearsal, he wrote a speech about Thomas Jefferson's children and gave it to us, saying, "Here, do with this what you want. Use it if you can, or don't use it if it doesn't fit." What he wrote inspired each of us in the play to write a speech. Each was very personal, very fierce, a hard-line contemporary view, and from our own point of view as a Chicana, a gay man, a Black person, a European immigrant, a woman. These became interludes in the play to get our own voices in there.

Sandy and I tried to make the development of this piece a really democratic process. Different sections of it were created by different cast members, so it's not just Sandy and I saying, "You do this." The cast was an integral part of the creation process.

We called *Illusions* a "postapocalyptic vaudeville show." We wanted the piece to be visually interesting, experimental, and "in your face." We tried not to be didactic. We tried not to make conclusions about the material but let it rest on its own. I'm not sure we were successful all the time, but sometimes I think we were.

Another piece I directed was *Le Griffon*. Sterling had this idea to rewrite the Frankenstein story, setting it in New Orleans in the early 1800s, where a crazy white scientist creates a living man out of the pieces of Black men who are different colors. It's both a literal and metaphorical symbol for the construction of race. Sterling adapted the play from a novel he had written. I think the piece turned out really well. Directing it was a lovely experience because Sterling and I had a history together and a common language, both artistically and in our political views.

Initially, I wasn't very knowledgeable about the history and the construction of race in New Orleans. To prepare for the production, we did a field trip to New Orleans, shot videotape of the streets and the swamps to use in the production, and delved into the history. We stayed at a bed-and-breakfast where the owner lives in the main house and guests stay in the old slave quarters. In it are historical pictures of freed and enslaved Black folks. So we were immersed in it.

There were eight people in the piece: four African Americans and four whites. I may be wrong on this, but in the production, it seemed like the Black folks were strong—they knew this history—and the white folks were a little more subordinate and deferring to the African Americans in the cast.

*Did you find yourself doing the typically liberal white male thing of trying to prove what you already knew about Black history? And to what extent were you open to asking questions and just learning?*

I would say both. I would say I'm better at it now, and I'm trying to get better at it all the time. On the trip to New Orleans, I would admit that I didn't know things and ask Sterling, "Oh, what is that?" But I also find myself pretending sometimes, nodding my head like I already knew this. I think we white men do that all the time. And what's wonderful for me as a white man is that I learn through experiences like *Illusions* and *Le Griffon*.

. . .

In some ways, San Antonio is a northern Mexican town in the United States. The majority population is Chicano or of Mexican descent—about 55 or 60 percent. This is a unique city. There are both established Mexican families and recent immigrants from Mexico. This was Mexican territory, and we are a Mexican community with close ties to Mexico. San Antonio is really poor— nowhere near as poor as a lot of cities in Mexico, but it's closer to the poverty of Mexico than any other city in the United States. A lot of the issues that come with poverty—lack of affordable housing, high dropout rates, poor children's health—are here.

We have a lot of Chicanos who work at Jump-Start, people whose parents might be from Mexico or their families may have been in the U.S. for generations—"Chicano" meaning those born here in the United States, of Mexican descent here, and people in Mexico. There's a local arts organization that was trying to do all collaborative work between people of Mexican descent who live here and people who live in Mexico. You should see the racial conflicts in that, the class issues—who define themselves as Chicano, who define themselves as Hispanic, who define themselves as Latino, who define themselves as Mexican American. All those words are really charged in San Antonio.

In the last five or six years, we've consciously increased the work we do that specifically speaks to the Chicano community. And you know what? Those are our moneymakers. For example, we've collaborated with Burras Finas, another Chicano group, which does a Christmas play called *Las Nuevas Tamaleras,* which means the new tamale makers. In San Antonio, it's not *The Christmas Carol* that's the big hit Christmas show because it's not the culture. It's this Chicano play about grandmothers passing down the art of tamale making during the holiday season.

Language is one of the challenges I face in working with the Chicanos here. I speak some Spanish, more than most white people, but I feel nervous using it. I'm not Chicano, so I don't want someone to think that I'm trying to usurp a cultural thing, although people I'm around really like it that I use my Spanish. I don't think they mind it at all. It just makes me a little nervous sometimes, particularly when I use it around people I don't know real well.

We do a festival with contemporary Mexican and Chicano artists every other year. Around that time, we're speaking a lot of Spanish. There's a lot of Spanish flying. With day-to-day communication that's not a problem, but I can't sit down with an artist from Mexico and have a philosophical or a deep political conversation. I can't have an in-depth conversation about art with that person, which is really sad to me. There are a couple of artists that we just love and have a long-term collaboration with, and I know I can't have the same kind of conversation we're having right now. That makes me sad.

. . .

My political activism didn't start with queer activism but with late '70s and early '80s feminism. After that, it was AIDS, queer stuff, the cultural wars. I was very influenced by feminism. I think there is a certain kind of consciousness about race that is relatively new to me. I know I'm not there yet.

My awareness of race issues has been really shaped through collaborations with lesbians of color. Since about 1990, Jump-Start and I have been working in close alliance with the Esperanza Peace and Justice Center, which is led by an incredible group of lesbians of color. Esperanza has worked since its inception to educate the community about the intersection of oppressions—the connections between racism, sexism, homophobia, ageism, classism, etc. Esperanza's director, Graciela Sanchez, is both a friend and a mentor. Over the years, she has generously given her time and knowledge to help me deal with my place in the world as a white gay man. She and the other folks around Esperanza have included progressive white people in their organizing efforts and made the effort to challenge our racial shit. For me, their contributions have been invaluable.

Sometimes people of color see me as one of the few "good white men," even though I do things that are racist. And even though I want to be accepted as a good white man, I don't like the dichotomy that gets set up about who is the better white person. That whole dynamic is very complex. Sometimes they introduce me to other people of color by saying something like, "This is Steve Bailey; he's white, but he's my friend. He's really good." It's like they're saying to me, "This is a good white guy." And I feel like saying, "You don't have to explain me. If there's doubt about me, let me prove myself." I think it's actually good for white people to prove themselves.

It could be that this is internalized stuff for me. As a white person, it's like you're only okay if the people of color frame you in a certain way. I just want the chance to prove myself. You do not need to make excuses for me or frame me ahead of time. It's a vulnerability issue—I can fuck up, too. Then do I have to be perfect to be acceptable?

And I do fuck up, and people of color do call me on my racism. When that happens, it upsets me. I'd be lying if I said, "Oh, I have no problem with that." I'd be lying. I think most white people would be lying. Because (a) you're defensive, which I think almost all white people are; (b) if you really care about this work and you're trying to be better and really work on it and someone calls you on it, it's like a little bit of a slap in the face, a little bit of a reality check; you still carry that with you, thinking you're better than other white people. I might get upset. I try not to be horribly defensive about it. But I will get over it.

I think we would be deluding ourselves if we didn't recognize that there is a social wall between any of our identities and others' identities. I would say that there's a social wall between queer and straight. Period. It doesn't mean we can't become really close, that we can't become even best of friends, that we can't discuss things. But there's always going to be a curtain, particularly in this culture, right at this time, that separates us because of our different identities. It's always there between women and men, between whites and people of color. There's a separation, and there's nothing you can do about it.

And there's a separation between white people. Sometimes I think to myself, "There are a few good white people I happen to know in this town, and the rest are bad." Even though I know that is really dangerous thinking, I do it. So I don't hang out with white gay men, and there are only a few straight white men I hang out with.

I hate demonizing straight white men, and I still do it! I think it's a really bad thing to stereotype them and assume their motivations and predict their actions. Certainly, they have some responsibility for oppression, but it's not like they're the whole problem. I believe in institutional racism. It's not the individual that is at fault but a larger system that continues the cycle of oppression. It's not like we only have to deal with them and everything would be okay. It's too late for that. It's not going to help to blame them, thinking that oppression is all their fault.

***Do you demonize white gay men?***

Way more than straight white men. That's the thing! White gay men are my people, and I just think that their behavior is appalling! The misogyny and the racism! They drive me crazy! And I am being dramatic when I say I don't like white gay men. I like some, and there's a lot of gay men of color who drive me nuts.

I expect white gay men to be better than straight white men. They understand what it means to be afraid of who you are, to fear for your safety, to not have job security, to not be able to assert legal rights. So you'd think that they could translate that to other forms of oppression, and that's not always the case. I have higher expectations of them, and I've learned that those expectations aren't realistic.

I think this whole thing is probably not very different from the issue of straight white men not wanting to be around other straight white men. And there is a gender issue that drives me a little crazy. I think gay men are sexist in a really different way than straight men are. There's a whole thing about the language that gay men use, and I do it too—calling people "missy," "hon," "girl," "baby," all that kind of stuff. There's a layer underneath that. Part of it's about the homophobia and trying to claim those gender issues, but part of it is about how we portray women. There are really complex issues there. I would say that gay men emulate the very things that feminists are trying to get rid of as stereotypes for women.

I am all for transgender power and drag queens. I think that's a really important thing, particularly for young queers of color. It's been a way out from poverty and isolation, in addition to breaking gender boundaries. But there's misogyny and sexism wrapped up in that, what they're emulating, and how they're emulating women—the makeup, the hair, the attitude— these are things that women have fought against for a long time. We need to deal with those issues. Not throw them all out because I think it's too complex, but deal with them.

· · ·

*Are you ever ever ambivalent or fearful about being the white male executive director of Jump-Start?*

All the time. All the time. Sterling always pushes me, saying, "Take your leadership role; don't be afraid of it. It's important; you have good vision. You're a progressive man." He's very helpful. I think he's a wise person. He's a good adviser. Bell hooks says, "I'd rather be in a room with progressive people than simply in a room of Black people who don't share progressive politics."[1] Sterling pushes that idea.

When he says that to me, I say to myself, "Well, that's all well and good, but there are still issues around a white man leading an organization that has a lot of people of color and women." There are power dynamics. This organization is run by two men. I think we're better than most when it comes to inclusion, but that doesn't mean there aren't problems. Trust is long term and hard won and rightfully so. There's a long history of distrust.

I think people of color here would also say—I know they would say this because they tell me sometimes—that I still function as a white male. I've grown up in that culture. I'm sometimes bossy and don't listen to ideas and believe my opinion is right. The caveat is that I think I'm better than most white men about recognizing power issues, but I know I still carry that with me all the time, and sometimes they call me on it. That's a good thing, and I keep trying to work on it.

I get it from both ends. I hear, "Don't be wishy-washy. Don't back down. Take some leadership. Take some control sometimes." And then other times, other people complain, "You're too hard; you're too white; you're too male."

I have been known as a kind of person who says "No" when people come to me with an idea. My negativity usually comes because I think their ideas are going to mean more work for me. Now, I'm getting better at saying, "Great idea; make it happen. I'll help you in whatever way I can. But I'm not going to do it." We did this series last year called "Young Tongues," works by artists under thirty. When the idea was first suggested, I said, "Great." Jump-Start found them a little money; they got a steering committee together—it was all done by people under thirty. They programmed it, did the brochure; they did everything. But the older Jump-Start staff provided support. I really hate to leave people dangling and lead them down a short trail for failure. We were there for advice but really let them control what was going on. I like that approach now.

One of the things that I think I do well as executive director is inclusion. Jump-Start started as a primarily white theater company and has transformed itself. Now, there is no racial majority on our staff, on our board, or in our company. There's not even a Latino majority. It's Latino, Black, Asian, and white. So we're not actually a culturally specific organization.

Sterling and others readily admit that because I had a leadership role in forming this organization, because I was white, because I was pushing an agenda of racial equity, it happened in a way it probably couldn't have happened if people of color pushed it. Early on, we had a big fight over Jump-Start becoming a multiracial organization, and it made a difference that I, as a white person, was doing the pushing. This has been an agenda for me for a long time because of the city we live in, because of the times we live in, because of the country we live in, because of the way things are going.

What's hard about being a multiracial organization is that Jump-Start doesn't fit in anywhere as a group. People don't see us as a certain thing. We get criticized from white people and from people of color. We get it from the white people who don't like us because we do too much work around race. I heard this just yesterday. A white person who gives us some financial support went off on the "Hispanic" work we do—that's the term she used. I said to myself, "Uh huh." Because we're an opportunity for local talent and the larger arts institutions are not really geared for trying the smaller stuff, we do a lot of Chicano work here. It's very popular. Over the past five or six years, we've really done a lot of work on that. At the same time, we get criticized by the Chicano arts organizations that we're taking all their artists away. And we're not thought of as a Chicano company, even though we have plenty of Chicano representation in our company, on our board, on our staff.

I think it's really interesting in this country, right now, to try to figure out how you deal with multiracial issues in a day-to-day way. Not at a once-a-month meeting. Not a support group. We deal with this every day. If you walk into our office, you're going to see a multiracial group, and some of us are Jewish, some are gay and straight; we're different ages. There's a lot going on there. I don't think we're the best at it; we don't do a lot of therapeutic retreats—like we don't go off and spend five days talking about race, stuff like that. Maybe that's because sometimes we don't deal with race, or sometimes we just do deal with it on a daily basis.

I feel like our conversations are different from other conversations in most arts organizations. We're not afraid to talk about race and gender in our day-to-day lives. If you dropped in here next week, you'd hear us talking about "white people" as a group. You'd hear people talking about race. You'd hear us talking about gender. You'd hear someone say, "Oh, he's got some issues with sexism." That's just in the air, all the time. You wouldn't hear that in most arts organizations. Period.

It's not just in our office that we deal with racial dynamics; it's in our artistic work. I direct Shimi's shows—she's one of the members of the company and a performance artist. I've learned more about her history and her background through the artistic work than I have through doing administrative work or educational programs with her. Shimi is of Tamil descent, from Singapore, where the Tamils are a minority. She's an atheist who was originally Hindu, whose mother converted to Evangelical Christianity—I mean, like the issues are just enormous. I've learned so much about those kinds of dynamics. I had no idea of the situation because I'm not usually around South Asians. Not that I didn't know some, but I had only scratched the surface. Being around company members like her and doing this artistic work at Jump-Start has made me a lot more sensitive. You know, it's a cliché, but you learn about this from being around folks who are open about who they are. There's no other way.

# Tim Wise

*Timothy Jacob Wise is a thirty-three-year-old social critic, writer, and speaker currently living in Nashville, Tennessee. He has been a social justice activist since age fourteen. From 1990 to 1992, he was the assistant director of the Louisiana Coalition against Racism and Nazism, the group credited by many with the political defeat of David Duke. He is the author of* Little White Lies: The Truth about Affirmative Action *and* "Reverse Discrimination," *and his frequent essays on racism have traveled far and wide on the Internet. We have included in this narrative one of his essays,* "Breaking the Cycle of White Dependence" *because we believe it is a great example of how he challenges racism.*

*Tim has spoken to over seventy-five thousand people in forty-five states, defending Affirmative Action; challenging institutional racism in education, housing, and the criminal justice system; and responding to political assaults on poor and working-class people of all races. He has spoken on over two hundred college and high school campuses, to dozens of community organizations and labor unions, to corporate leaders, and to federal and state officials. He has appeared on hundreds of radio and television programs, debating Nazis, representatives of the religious right, and prominent conservatives such as Dinesh D'Souza, Nathan Glazer, Armstrong Williams, and Ward Connerly.*

• • •

Like many white folks who do work against racism, when I started speaking out, there was a sense of missionary zeal. There is no question that I felt the need to "help" people of color without feeling any real connection to them. That feeling was there when I was doing anti-apartheid word at Tulane University as a student. It was there still, though to a lesser degree, when I was doing the anti-Duke work, as if I was thinking, "I'm going to rush in and save this community from this Nazi." It was only after I'd had the opportunity to read the works of people of color and to listen to antiracist leaders of color in New Orleans that I learned what my role really needed to be.

I probably learned more from and have been saved more by the people of color in New Orleans I worked with than I ever could have saved them. Reading James Baldwin was very instrumental to me. Probably more than any writer, artist, or political figure, Baldwin speaks to me and a lot of other whites about what it means to be a white person.

I also learned a lot from people like Bob Zellner, who was the first white field secretary for SNCC. Lots of whites in SNCC, including Bob, his ex-wife Dorothy, and numerous others, came to realize that it was important for white people to work with white people and save ourselves from the system that was destroying everyone.

It's not about trying to save others. I'm really trying to save and redeem the community that I live in so that that community can join with communities of color in a real sense of equity and not a paternalistic arrangement. That is such a critical precursor before we can link hands and sing "Kumbaya." We have to be able to clean up the crap among whites. That's not something that liberals usually talk about or want to hear.

Lots of whites resist doing this work because they aren't sure how people of color are going to receive them. Although I used to think about that too, I have since learned to let go of that concern. I'm not fighting racism for Black and Brown folks: they can and will, as always, save themselves. My role is in the white community.

One of the ways I play that role is by participating in debates on college campuses, especially about issues like Affirmative Action. Debates on campuses are usually well attended, sometimes for the wrong reasons—people just want to come see a fight. But there have also been many occasions where the people who come really have learned something because the format is well structured enough and audience members have had the opportunity to participate and there's a moderator that keeps things under control.

Every time I've done a debate, folks have come up to me afterward and really wanted to engage in some good dialogue. They'll tell me, "I've never heard these points made about Affirmative Action. I've only heard the other side. I've only heard a very weak liberal defense of Affirmative Action. I've never really heard this spirited, militant defense. Although I don't necessarily buy everything you've said"—this is something I hear frequently—"I really appreciate having heard it said so forcefully and so confidently by you without apology."

Most peope who support Affirmative Action are apologetic in their defense; pretty much just stressing the need for "diversity" without really mentioning the ongoing problem of institutional racism, which makes Affirmative Action so critical. So when I make a forceful presentation about why Affirmative Action is a good thing and really discuss the ongoing barriers to equity—like the "old boys' network" that tends to exclude people of color and also women of all colors—I have people say to me, "That's the first time I've ever heard anybody say so strongly, 'This is a good thing.' " So I think that there's real value to my doing these debates.

And if I don't debate conservatives like Dinesh D'Souza or if someone else doesn't, he will be brought onto campus by himself and get to speak unimpeded. I think it's important if he's coming to a campus that someone be there who has really analyzed his arguments and can do a decent job debating him. I believe that's valuable.

. . .

When I was eleven, I played on a baseball team here in Nashville. Only four of us on the team were white. We would play games outside of the area and had gone to Joelton, a rural community about thirty miles from Nashville. There were hardly any Black folks living there. The Black kids on our team were city kids that the folks in Joelton were not at all fond of. After the game, the team we had played—all white of course—surrounded our vehicle. They were pounding on the vehicle with their baseball gloves and making threatening gestures with their bats. Their white coaches and parents were right there—they could see what the kids were doing. The kids were yelling at us in the van, calling the Black kids "niggers" and calling the white kids and our coach "nigger lovers."

We had never seen anything like this. I'm sure this was terrifying for the Black kids; it was certainly terrifying for me. There were two or three of the guys who were focusing their anger at me and a couple of the other white folks in the van. It was the first time I'd ever been called a "nigger lover" and seen hatred like that. In their mind I had crossed over. I was, to them, on the other side of humanity.

I had made what was maybe the ultimate mistake in the eyes of these white kids and their parents: I had transgressed against my group; I had transgressed against whiteness, even though I didn't know what whiteness was at age eleven. It was compounded by the fact that at this very same time, I was getting the same kind of crap from other folks. It wasn't just the kids with the baseball bats—that was the most obvious physical manifestation of it. I was getting looks and comments from teachers about the fact that I was hanging out mostly with Black kids during the school day, the fact that for about six or seven months I had developed a Black affect in my voice and sounded "Black."

A lot of authority figures didn't take to that very well. My own grandmother on my mother's side found it very disconcerting and disturbing. So all at once in the course of a year or two, there were attempts by various white people to push me, and the other white kids who hung out with Black kids, back into whiteness and the role that we were supposed to assume. It was very clear to me that I was being targeted because of those close friendships. What that did to me was to make me question how close I would ultimately be able to get to my Black friends. By the time I got to high school, the system had begun to track us so dramatically and separate us out that no matter what I might have wanted or what they had wanted, separation was imposed on us.

I still get attacked of course. I remember getting a call at the anti–David Duke coalition office. I picked up the phone and some guy said, "You're a damn race traitor!" And, of course, I've been called that by neo-Nazis and Klansmen and skinheads for years. Of course, once they find out that I'm Jewish, then they think that I'm not white. Then I'm just a damn Jew or a son of Satan and no longer a race traitor. In fact, they've written me out of whiteness.

. . .

When I became an activist and leader at Tulane, I knew that it was important for other people to be involved in a collective effort. I knew that it was bad for me to be the one on television every night, doing the interview with the news people about divestment from South Africa or whatever. I understood this intellectually at the level of movement politics. But at the same time, there's that aspect—part of it's being male, part of it's being white, part of it's being nineteen—that says it's so cool being on television and getting all this notoriety. It's very intoxicating.

Even though I knew it was poison for the movement that I was trying to be a part of, there was part of me that could not, or at least did not, resist. So by the time I had graduated and hadn't done enough of the movement-building work to get other people to feel confident in their ability to lead once I was gone, it started to fall apart. I knew it wasn't because they couldn't have done it. I knew it wasn't because I was this person who was inherently more capable. I knew this. But I had screwed up and hadn't done the collective work that I needed to do.

Now I try to surround myself with people who support and love me and aren't that impressed with me. My wife, for example; she's a very smart, beautiful, and funny woman; I love her dearly, but she's not really into this stuff. She respects it and appreciates what I do, and she agrees with me politically, but she's just not a political person. The few friends that I have in Nashville and the few I had in New Orleans are not very political people. And so it's hard to get a real big head when you're surrounded by people who aren't impressed, who say to you, "Yeah, whatever, great, great; you went out and spoke to one thousand people. Fine. Let me tell you about my day."

You get humbled by the fact that there are people who really don't give a damn, or at least don't place the same emphasis on the things that you do. My wife's proud of me, but she doesn't sit there and say, "How wonderful." My wife will watch a video of me speaking, and she'll say, "That's a really good speech, honey. That's excellent, very powerful." Then we're playing with our new daughter and not thinking about that kind of thing at all.

It's nice to be able to get some down time from my political work so that I don't get eaten up by it, and it keeps me from getting too caught up in my own bullshit. I know that there are people who love me and care about me, but they're not my "fans." They want to talk about other things.

I read constantly, sometimes a book a day. The more I read, the more I realize how much I don't know. That also helps to keep my ego in check. Because as much as I think I know, as long as I'm constantly reading what other people have written, I end up seeing things I had never thought of at all.

I remember five years ago, when I started lecturing, thinking to myself that because this is a small field and there are very few white folks doing it, that there was some potential for me to get recognized if I stuck with it. So, when I was about twenty-five, I thought to myself, "When I'm thirty-five, I want to be"—whatever this means—"the leading white antiracist theorist and activist in the country." And I used to think that.

But over the last few years, as I got closer to thirty-five—I'm now thirty-three—I started to realize that (a) I wouldn't know what it would mean to actually be that person—I mean, how would one know? and (b) it's not really desirable. I just want to make whatever kind of difference I can make. I want to do the work I do with a sense of integrity, knowing that I'm doing what I'm supposed to be doing and making whatever contribution I can make.

If I get notoriety for that, great. I love it, of course. I love it when someone e-mails me and says, "I saw you speak—it changed my life." I've had people say that, and it's very rewarding. But the idea that I have to be the leading person is something that I'm trying to get away from.

But yeah, there's still some part of me that wants my name to be one of the names that people are thinking of when they think of white antiracists. It's hard to get totally away from that.

. . .

While I was living in New Orleans, I had always wanted to go to one of these plantation tours they do along the river as a way to see how these places handled the history of slavery, or rather mishandled it. Unfortunately I never got a chance to go. But a couple of years ago, my wife and I were down there visiting, and we took a tour of this plantation called Nottaway.

And of course the tour guides were essentially apologists for the chattel system, as expected. But what I found interesting and what I hadn't expected was that in trying to downplay the depravity of slavery, the guides actually ended up making a point that they probably hadn't considered. By talking about the servants—and that's what they call them of course—and discussing all they did to keep the house operating smoothly—which is probably their way of paying homage to their hard work or something—they ended up making it painfully clear just how utterly dependent the white folks were on Black people. Everything was done by slaves, from the building of the levee that kept the river from destroying the house to the cooking and cleaning and heating of the fireplace—everything.

In one room they showed us this very elaborate bell system. It had twelve different rings so that when the house slaves heard the ring, they knew exactly what it was they were supposed to do before they even came to talk to the mistress or master of the house. It was a symbol of how utterly helpless these very wealthy white people were. I tried in vain to even come up with twelve different things to ask someone to do for me in my home, and I couldn't do it. I mean, we are talking about every little minor task to be sure. The whites were paralyzed without Blacks.

On the way back home, I got to thinking about the ways that white people were, and are still, dependent on people of color. Around the same time, I had been getting a lot of e-mails from white people about how dependent Black people are on programs like welfare and Affirmative Action. That really crystallized for me the need to write about white people's dependence on people of color. It was the combination of the personal, visceral experience on the plantation tour and the constant repetition of what I was hearing from white people. And so I wrote the following essay.

## BREAKING THE CYCLE OF WHITE DEPENDENCE

I think it's called "projection." When someone subconsciously realizes that a particular trait applies to them, and then attempts to locate that trait in others, so as to alleviate the stigma or self-doubt engendered by the trait in question.

It's a well-understood concept of modern psychology, and explains much: like why men who are struggling with their own sexuality are often the most outwardly homophobic. Or the way whites during slavery typified Black men as rapists, even though the primary rapists were the white slaveowners themselves, taking liberties with their female property, or white men generally, raping their wives with impunity.

I got to thinking about projection recently, after receiving many an angry e-mail from folks who had read one or another of my previous commentaries, and felt the need to inform me that people of color are "looking for a handout," and are "dependent" on government, and of course, whites.

Such claims are making the rounds these days, especially as debate heats up about such issues as reparations for enslavement, or affirmative action. And this critique is a prime example of projection, for in truth, no people have been as dependent on others throughout history as white folks.

We depended on laws to defend slavery and segregation so as to elevate us, politically, socially and economically. We depended on the Naturalization Act of 1790, to make all European immigrants eligible for nearly automatic citizenship, with rights above all persons of color. We depended on land giveaways like the Homestead Act, and housing subsidies that were essentially white-only for many years, like FHA and VA loans. Even the GI bill was largely for whites only, and all of these government-sponsored efforts were instrumental in creating the white middle class. But it goes deeper than that.

From the earliest days, "whites" were dependent on the land and natural resources of the Americas, Africa, and Asia. Since Europe offered no substantial natural riches from its soil, European economic advance and expansion was entirely reliant on the taking of other people's land by force, trickery or coercion. That, my friends, is dependence.

Then these same Europeans relied on slave labor to build a new nation and to create wealth for whites; wealth that was instrumental to financing the American Revolution, as well as allowing the textile and tobacco industries to emerge as international powerhouses. From 1790 to 1860 alone, whites and the overall economy reaped the benefits of as much as $40 billion in unpaid Black labor. That, my friends, is dependence.

Then whites were dependent on Native peoples to teach us farming skills, as our complete ineptitude in this realm left the earliest colonists starving to death and turning to cannibalism when the winters came in order to survive. That, my friends, is dependence.

We were dependent on Mexicans to teach us how to extract gold from riverbeds and quartz—critical to the growth of the national economy in the mid to late 1800s—and had we not taken over half their nation in an unprovoked war, the emerging Pacific ports so vital to the modern U.S. economy would not have been ours, but Mexico's. That, my friends, is dependence.

Then we were dependent on their labor in the midtwentieth century under the *bracero* program, through which over five million Mexicans were brought into the country for cheap agricultural work, and then sent back across the border.

And we were dependent on Asian labor to build the railroads that made transcontinental travel and commerce possible. Ninety percent of the labor used to build the Central Pacific Railroad in the 1860s were Chinese, imported for the purpose, and exploited because the railroad bosses felt they could better control them than white workers. That, my friends, is dependence.

In fact, all throughout U.S. labor history, whites have depended on the subordination of workers of color; by the marking of Black and Brown peoples as the bottom rung on the ladder—a rung below which they would not be allowed to fall. By virtue of this racialized class system whites could receive the "psychological wage" of whiteness, even if their real wages left them destitute. That too is dependence, and a kind that has marked even the poorest whites.

And northern industrial capitalism relied on Black labor too—especially to break the labor militance of white ethnics by playing off one group of workers against the other. That also is dependence.

During the Civil War, the armies of the Confederacy relied on Blacks to cook for the troops and to make the implements of war they would use in battle; and likewise, the Union relied on Black soldiers—around 200,000 of them—to ultimately win the war. That, too, is most assuredly dependence.

And white dependence on people of color continues to this day. Each year, African Americans spend over $500 billion with white-owned companies: money that goes mostly into the pockets of the white owners, white employees, white stockholders, and white communities in which they live. And yet we say *Black people* need *us?* We think *they* are the dependent ones, relying as we assume they do on the paltry scraps of an eviscerated welfare state?

But who would be hurt more: Black folks if all welfare programs were shut down tomorrow, or white folks, if Blacks decided they were through transferring half-a-trillion dollars each year to white people and were going to keep their money in their own communities?

Or what about the ongoing dependence of white businesses on the exploitation of labor of color? Each year, according to estimates from the Urban Institute, over $120 billion in wages are lost to African Americans thanks to discrimination in the labor market. And millions more are siphoned away from Asian laborers working in makeshift sweatshops, or migrant laborers from Latin America, getting paid only about a fourth of the value of the wealth they generate for agribusiness and state economies. That's money that doesn't end up in the hands of the folks who earned it, but rather remains in the bank accounts of owners. That, my friends, is dependence.

Indeed, I am beginning to think that whites are so dependent on people of color that we wouldn't know what to do without them. Oh sure, some neo-Nazis say they would love to try, but in reality I doubt they could make it. If there were no Black and Brown folks around, then whites would have no one to blame but themselves for the crime that occurred; no one to blame but themselves when they didn't get the job they wanted; no one to blame but themselves when their lives turned out to be less than they expected. In short, we need people of color—especially in a subordinate role—as a way to build ourselves up, and provide a sense of self-worth we otherwise lack.

To be sure, our very existence as white people is dependent on a negative: to be white has meaning only in terms of what it *doesn't* mean. To be white only has meaning in so far as it means *not* to be Black or Brown. Whiteness has no intrinsic meaning culturally: can anyone even articulate what "white culture" means? Not our various European cultures mind you—which do have meaning but have been largely lost to us in the mad dash to accept whiteness and the perks that come with it—but white culture itself.

In workshops I have asked white folks and people of color what they like about being Black, white, or whatever they in fact may be. For African Americans the answers always have to do with the pride they feel, coming from families who have struggled against the odds, fought injustice, persevered, and maintained dignity in the face of great obstacles. In other words, to be Black has internal meaning, derived from the positive actions and experiences of Black people themselves. Variations on the same theme tend to be expressed by Latinos, Asians, and Indigenous peoples as well.

But for whites, if they can come up with anything, it is typically something about how nice it is *not* to have to worry about being racially profiled by police, or how nice it is *not* to be presumed less competent by employers, or discriminated against when applying for a loan, or looking for a home. In other words, for whites, our self-definition is wrapped up entirely in terms of what and who we aren't. What it means to be white is merely to not be "the other." And for that to have any meaning whatsoever there first must be an "other" against which to contrast oneself.

And that is the most significant dependence of all.

A friend of mine once described my writing by saying that I was "a master at the rebuttal mode." I take what someone has said and critique it and deconstruct it point by point. That probably comes from my background as a competitive debater in high school and college, which was such a formative experience growing up. That part of my personality definitely comes through in my writing.

I also write like I speak. I write the way that I would probably give the same argument in a speech. As a result, my writing has a flow to it that's good on the ear. When I was writing "Breaking the Cycle of White Dependence," I remember thinking, "How would this sound if I was giving this as a speech?" I liked the line, "That, my friends, is dependence." So I repeated it at the end of almost every paragraph. That style of repetition makes the most sense in an oral tradition.

I write because I feel that I have to write. I have a burning need to say some things. There are things that I can only express, at least initially, on paper. My mom was a dancer and a painter. For her, dancing and painting was a way to let go of things that she needed to express that were pent up in her. For me, it's similar. There's a lot of stuff bouncing around in my head. Sometimes I wake up in the middle of the night, get out of bed, go up to my office, and start typing.

I think I also write for somewhat therapeutic reasons. Writing is a pressure valve to keep me from becoming a much more bitter and angry person. When I'm done venting on a page, I feel much better. If I don't get my anger out, it will only build. Then when I do let it out—none of us can keep our anger in forever—I'm going to end up venting on someone and being cruel. I don't want to do that.

Writing is a way to forgive people who anger me about racism, like the white guys who think that people of color are dependent on whites. I don't want to hate those guys. That's not constructive. I really want to be able to forgive them because I realize that they've been tricked and played for suckers by a system. So by writing, I don't have to resent them, I don't have to hate them, and I certainly don't have to unload on them if they e-mail me.

*In his book on Affirmative Action, Tim credits Olympic diver Greg Louganis for teaching him to believe in himself.*

I wrote the book about two months after I met Greg at Kansas University [KU]. The gay and lesbian student association at KU invited Greg and me and several other folks to speak. I was asked to speak about the connection between racism and hate crimes against gays and lesbians. It was a wonderful experience for me. I had read Greg's book and talked to him that evening. He recounted his journey, particularly since he had contracted HIV, his personal journey of coming to believe in himself, not only as a diver, but as a person who was able to have good relationships in the aftermath of the abuse he had gotten from other guys and in the face of his fears about coming out as a gay man and then a person with HIV.

This was at a period in my life when I was just beginning to forge my way professionally. I had gone through a number of years where I was having a horrible time making a living and getting anything accomplished. I couldn't get anything published. I had a relationship that had fallen apart. It was just a really bad time for me.

Even though my situation was so different from Greg's and not at all to be compared to his—I hadn't been subjected to physical abuse, I didn't have to face coming out in a homophobic society, I didn't have HIV. In terms of the drama that was in his life and the drama that was in mine, I still had this sense that here was a person who had every reason to give up, yet he had this unbelievable faith in himself that came from somewhere. And so reading his book and talking to him was really important to me at that particular moment in my life. I went away from that evening thinking, "I really *can* do the work that I'm doing, and I really *can* impact people's lives."

I mean, here's a gay man with AIDS. He's having to wake up every three hours so that he can take twenty pills to keep living, and I'm worrying about the fact that I might be a week late paying my phone bill. It really put my worries into perspective. I said to myself, "For me to give up, for me to question my ability to make it, for me to give up this dream of making a difference in the world and doing important social justice work would be unthinkable."

The fact that I felt pumped up by the gay and lesbian community at KU was important, too. That invested me with a sense of accountability to another community. And it made me realize that there are people who are now counting on me, who want me to do this, who believe in me. If they're going to believe in me—people who hardly know me—then who the hell am I not to believe in myself?

So I just kept telling myself, this is going to work. I'm going to do the things I need to do to make this happen. I'm going to take the chances that I need to take. I'm going to seek out the support I need. And I'm going to learn what I can from other people about how to maintain my self-respect and confidence when things get bad.

# Billy Yalowitz

*Billy's background is as a performing artist in dance and theater. He teaches community-based arts at the Tyler School of Art at Temple University in Philadelphia and has been a teacher of Re-evaluation Counseling for many years. In the summer of 2001, he was a delegate to the U.N. World Conference on Racism in Durban, South Africa. He's forty-two.*

*He grew up in a neighborhood of New York City called Chelsea in Lower Manhattan where there was a rich mix of cultures: African American, Puerto Rican, Jewish, Greek, and Irish Catholic. Billy moved to Philadelphia in 1990 to the neighborhood of Mt. Airy. Intrigued by its racial diversity, he developed Joshua's Wall, a theatrical production based on interviews with residents that was performed in June 1995. At the time, he described Joshua's Wall as an opportunity to learn the story of the neighborhood. "People took very courageous stands in building an integrated community. To inherit such a community is a gift, but it needs to be rebuilt continually in terms of building relationships. Once relationships are built, you can use that as a base to tackle the ongoing struggles. There is a quote from the Passover Haggadah that 'in every generation we ought to regard ourselves as though we had personally been liberated from slavery.' We have a chance to build that kind of life for ourselves. Each new generation has the chance to take that on."*

• • •

The University of Pennsylvania hired me to teach a course about theater and community. I knew I wanted to create a performance like I'd done in other Philadelphia neighborhoods that would be based on oral histories. A faculty member at the university told me about a neighborhood called the Black Bottom that used to be adjacent to the university, just north of the campus. It was a thriving, working-class African American neighborhood, like many neighborhoods in northern cities, that really began to take shape in the 1920s and '30s with the migration from the South. By 1969 the neighborhood was flattened, demolished by urban renewal. Some of my African American friends from the Black Bottom have sardonically called that process "Negro removal."

The Black Bottom is now a community in exile. As a Jew, I know about exile. My background is left wing Jewish from New York City—that's also a community that had, in a sense, gone into exile. The story of my antiracism work begins there. Some of the really important antiracist work in the United States was pioneered by left wing Jews in the 1920s and '30s as part of the labor movement and an early wave of the Civil Rights Movement. I was born in 1959 and grew up with this legacy of antiracism work. I inherited that.

Folks who lived in the Black Bottom now live all over the Philadelphia area and beyond. After thirty or forty years, they're still in close contact with each other, elders now, in their sixties and seventies and eighties. They've wanted their story told for a long time. They're remarkably generous while trying to figure out what restitution might mean for them.

So I decided to create a performance about the Black Bottom. The project is a three-way partnership between the university, the Black Bottom community, and a local high school—University City High School, which was built on the ground where the Black Bottom used to be. The goal has been to give voice to that story and in doing that, to create a vehicle where Penn students could learn about building relationships and listening to people and then creating a performance that's based on the people's stories. This project has transformed the students' lives. It's very clear to me and to them that this has been a very powerful part of their education. I think we've done well with the project. I mean, here they are, paying my salary, raising money for me to tell a story about how the university has been perpetuating institutional racism in the neighborhoods around it.

Penn students and faculty and the students and teachers at the high school were for the most part entirely unaware of what happened to the Black Bottom. The Penn students are primarily middle- and owning-class white, some students of color, but they've been actively taught to fear the neighborhood that they live in. The university has acted like many urban universities act, as a kind of colonial power in that neighborhood.

My advisers on the project are always cautioning me when I speak about this. Stanley Edwards, one of the men from the Black Bottom, once said to me, "Now don't go getting yourself in trouble over us, Billy." He told me about being in the Korean War and how some Black soldiers wanted to challenge decisions about not getting to go on leave and other privileges that white soldiers had. A guy who wanted to advocate for them was a Jewish sergeant. Stanley's telling me this story as a cautionary tale. He said, "We told the sergeant, 'Let us fight this battle.'" Stanley understood that a Jew sticking his neck out in that way in a gentile military institution would put him in a tough position.

So here I am. I'm adjunct faculty in the arts at Penn, one of the most marginal characters on the faculty. When I walk over to the University City High School to introduce this project, I'm a Penn professor. I have this "great idea" about the Black Bottom. I've come to work with the African American teachers. They come on board, almost in spite of themselves, because the work is driven by a story that's very familiar to them.

But, boy, I'm this professor "expert," coming in with an agenda instead of coming in to ask, "What do you want to have happen around here? What have you been hoping for? What are some of your ideas?" I don't come in with that at all! I come with a full-blown project that is accurate enough so that I can repair some of the damage that I've already caused, but some of the Black teachers won't even look at me.

What I think I understand now on a deeper level is that we come in with some kind of resource; there has to be an exchange of expertise and knowledge. I know how to get a theater performance up on its feet, and you know firsthand the history of your neighborhood and how institutional racism has made your life so difficult. We have an exchange to make there. At that point, if the agendas are compatible in some way, then it's workable.

In my case, doing antiracism work through the arts has been very effective. It's a cultural resource that I have access to and training in. There I am at Penn, and I can get grant money so that people in the community, without any specialized academic training in theater, can have their voices heard through the arts. I'm interested in a lot of different levels of people who have formal academic or conservatory training working with people who have another kind of training, where there is another kind of virtuosity and aesthetic or skill. For example, in my productions there's often double Dutch or drill team, which are African American street games and dance forms respectively. Or the night before the opening performance of *Black Bottom*, a man who grew up in the Black Bottom and became a city planner gave me a poem he'd written for the performance. He hadn't been involved at all in the performance up until then but told me, "I heard that there's this performance and wrote a poem." It was called "Round the Way." And we included it in the performance that night.

In general, my feeling about working on racism with people of color is that it makes no sense to work directly at it, especially at first. If you can find a project to do together, the issues come up. Race can be talked about very comfortably once you prepare the white people, including myself, to build relationships. I had a seder here, and I invited many of the people from the Black Bottom. That was lovely. They came to my house because they know me. It wasn't, "Let's do a Black-Jewish thing." I don't want to disparage that too much, but finding another way to build the relationship has been much more effective for me.

. . .

There are some scary things about doing this as a white male leader. I still don't like having Black people angry at me. At the opening night of the Black Bottom performance, everyone was nervous and really wanted it to go well. I was tense, I wanted it to go well, and people were getting pissed at me. Boy, that was hard. And now I look back on it and say to myself, "That was all right, even though it scared the shit out of me to do that." Any time that you're working hard to produce something like that and when there is something at stake, people are going to have all sorts of feelings come up. You're the leader, and it comes out at you.

I had one high school guy, Darnell [a pseudonym], who had missed the rehearsal and come to the performance late. So we had assigned the understudy role to one of his classmates, who got on stage. The other guy was up there, doing his lines, and Darnell was cursing in the audience, "He's fucking up my lines." So the whole audience is hearing this. So I go over to him, say, "Darnell, we'll get you in tomorrow night, when we have another performance." This is probably the one thing he's cared about in his high school year. So I tried to get him out of the auditorium, put my hand on his back. And he just about swung at me. "Take your hand off my back, Billy." Stanley saw that this was happening, came over to us, and took Darnell outside and talked to him for about forty-five minutes. Darnell came back into the auditorium with Stanley to watch the performance.

Stanley wanted to tell me afterward what had happened. He told me, "You know what I did is I explained to him that you're a good man, that you were not trying to fuck him over. I told him, 'If you blow this thing, the police will come, and you don't want that kind of scene. Or the other thing that's going to happen is if you keep wanting to make this kind of scene here, there's plenty of guys from the Black Bottom neighborhood whose story is being told right now who don't want your little ass interrupting it.' Billy, when you see Darnell tomorrow, I want you to talk with him and put your arms around him." I talked it through with Darnell. The next night, Darnell performed and was pleased with himself.

Where that circles back to is the importance of building relationships, and then something happens that transcends the racial divide. The elder in that case was helping keep that relationship going and helping Darnell under-stand that I wasn't being this oppressive white guy in this case.

*You've mentioned how Stanley has twice intervened on your behalf, once by giving you the cautionary tale and now by protecting you. What do you make of that?*

We've become friends; it's nothing more than that. I'm part of his crew now. I've listened to him, and I've gained his trust. We have each other's respect. He would do that for anybody. They understand that in his neighborhood. They understand loyalty—that when you go out on a limb, you need people backing you.

I think part of the damage of being white and middle class, and the individualism of your career track, is that you don't stand with other people. You don't have a union and that kind of solidarity with anybody, really. I've crafted this unique career; I've kind of figured out this unique little niche as a director. But it's really led me back into working in communities where I become part of the group and share the resources I have.

That's a lot of what I try to communicate with my students from Penn—that we know very little about humility, the loss of community, and how isolated we are from each other. That's a cost of whiteness and of being middle class, as we construct it—that you're special, that your knowledge separates you. You think you're smarter than other people. What a disability, to think that you're smarter.

I think that for many of us white people, the kind of learning we usually get in school is backward. You theorize and then you try to get out and do something with it. It's not very useful. Maybe it's male, maybe it's white, maybe it's U.S. and middle class. I think it is probably some of all those things. It's a disadvantage. It's a kind of cultural deprivation.

I was lucky. My dad was a working-class Jewish guy. I walked around the streets of New York with him. He would talk with everybody. He talked to the hot dog vendors; he talked to the guys who were pumping gas. I'd ask him, "Do you know that guy?" I think I learned a sense of community from my dad, that you belong to the world.

• • •

One of my African American high school students in the performance, Dawn, was doing well. She's very talented. She wanted to be in a scene. And I said, "No!" I don't do that much, but I snapped at her. She had been coming to all the rehearsals. One of my white students, Maggie, who has a nice relationship with Dawn, came up to me afterward and said to me, "You lost

Dawn on that one." What I did was, within Maggie's earshot, I went over to Dawn and I said, "Dawn, that was my mistake. I'm sorry; I was worried about getting the work done. There isn't really a reason for you not to be in that scene." Making mistakes and copping to them is really important.

I can get defensive and tense about being correct. But I'm learning that I can have a life where I get to make mistakes, and that's expected, and people will back me. That's a tough one, learning that people will back you if you make mistakes.

Getting criticized when you do this work is inevitable. What equips us to go out and take these risks is that we have a place where we can go and recover from the mistakes we make. I have a support base in Re-evaluation Counseling. I have a network of people who are doing this work all over the world in different ways. So I go to these rehearsals, and I make these mistakes, and I do these things that I'm pleased with. I have a place I can go several times a week and be scared about it, or cry about it, or be very proud about it. As a result, I can actually think better about my work.

In terms of being a white male, having the capacity to notice and be able to heal from when you're terrified, that's a big deal. That's a big deal! I don't think we're going to be able to do this work very well until part of the practice of doing it is to notice how scared we are. Otherwise, I don't think you can make mistakes and really recover from them and learn from them.

Walter Palmer has been another of my advisers. He's very different from Stanley. He teaches courses in racism at the School of Social Work at the University of Pennsylvania. He grew up in the Black Bottom. At first, he didn't trust me, but we continued to work together. He performed in the Black Bottom piece, ending the show with a stream-of-consciousness monologue and tap dance about the neighborhood. It was very powerful.

He's about sixty-five, a huge guy, tap dancing, saying, "Billy Yalowitz, a white guy, he came into my office two years ago." All this anger was pouring out of his legs, and I'm thinking, "What's he going to say about me?" He's tapping and saying, "He came into my office, I don't trust white people, I want to see what he wanted." And then there's more anger pouring out of his legs. He left it with an ellipsis. He didn't close it at all.

He told me later that some of the Black students came up to him after the performance and told him how important it was for them that he talked about not trusting white people. He said to me, "It's a defense mechanism because you don't know when you're going to get burned." For these young Black college students, it was important to have that acknowledged, that you get to figure out how to trust white people and figure out what agenda is coming at you.

I was surprisingly fairly relaxed about whatever he was going to say about me. He could say whatever he wanted to, and it would be okay with me. To that extent, I knew that I had done pretty well with this agenda that I had.

***Does it bother you to know that Walter doesn't trust you?***

Yeah. I did feel a little hurt. With some of the other folks from the Black Bottom, I really have their heart, and they have my heart. I don't have Walter's heart. I'd like him to say to an audience of white and Black people, "Billy Yalowitz is a good white man."

We can't go to people of color with the hope that they will tell us that we're good. It's a kind of racism to look for that reassurance. I need to know that I'm good as a white person regardless of what people of color tell me.

. . .

I played the saxophone when I was a kid. One of the ways that I learned how to play jazz was to play transcriptions of Miles Davis's solos. So I have the headphones on and I'm reading the transcriptions and playing my saxophone. I'm being Miles Davis.

Many years later, when I was at Temple University studying the history of Black performance in the United States, I learned about black-face minstrelsy.[1] I asked myself, "What's the difference between my trying to be Miles Davis and putting on black face?" I noticed that the minstrels were white men, primarily Irish immigrants, the "black Irish," the "Irish need not apply" guys. This is in the 1840s and '50s and all the way up to the middle part of this century. The Irish figured that the burnt cork they put on their face was their passport to America. They put on the burnt cork and became white because they weren't really Black.

I did a performance about this called *Minstrel Shows*. The piece looked dead center at what we as whites take from Black culture. The performance started with me playing a Miles Davis solo, and then there was a journey back in time to my becoming a minstrel. The cast was me and a white woman traveling back in time and three African American performers witnessing and commenting on our journey. The piece ended with white bluegrass guys who learned their picking style from Black bluesmen and never acknowledged them. Boy, that was a scary one, too. I'm putting this black face on and thinking, "Why am I putting myself through this?"

One thing I learned from *Minstrel Shows* is that mainstream U.S. white culture is fed richly by African American culture. The ways that we relax, express ourselves, play sports, and the dances we do—all of those things come from African American culture. We enjoy it. We appropriate it. We profit from it. New Kids on the Block and Elvis Presley and Mick Jagger are modern-day minstrels who have taken Black cultural styles and profited from them and not acknowledged that. Now, it's a very complex mix, but it's a little like you go out to dance to Black music on Saturday night, and then you go to your very white corporate office on Monday morning. In a very separate part of our minds, the racism we carry stays intact.

Another thing I learned from *Minstrel Shows* is that the things I love and value about Black people have separated me from white people. My heroes growing up were primarily Black musicians, Black basketball players, and the Black Panthers. I styled myself as cool because I had some facility as a basketball player, I could play some jazz, and I was interested in left wing politics. What sense do you make of that and not have it be that I'm different from the other whites? Many of us whites who are interested in eliminating racism feel that we're the only white person who "gets it." It separates us from whites because we're ashamed of the other whites who don't "get it." We end up feeling better—even cooler—than the other whites.

There was one last thing I learned from doing *Minstrel Shows:* the minstrels in this century were primarily Jewish—Al Jolsen and Eddie Cantor and others. That's one way that Jews became white in the twentieth century in the U.S. The irony in that. I think there is some connection with my being a Jew and trying to assimilate and become included. That's the experience of many urban Jewish boys of my generation. I went out into the street and really wanted to be accepted by the gentile boys in the neighborhood.

*Toni Morrison's book* Sula *starts, "There was once a neighborhood called 'the Bottoms.'" It's about a neighborhood that's not there anymore. So here you're doing this project about the Black Bottom and helping people reclaim their home. And, in effect, you're also saying about your own background, "Once there was a left wing Jewish community, and it's not there anymore." You live in Mt. Airy, a neighborhood that defines itself as a community that's very rare in this contemporary United States. In all the work you do, is there a sense of coming home and redemption from exile?*

Yeah, it's got to be that. In a very real sense, it's what we all had—not only my particular Jewish left wing background, but you want to be friends with everybody. It's just ridiculous not to. So home, in the biggest sense, is the way that I watched my dad make friends with everyone.

That's what's really in it for me as a white person—to get everybody back. That's the biggest reason to do this work. The most trustworthy motivation is that you just want to be friends with the people that you haven't been able to be close to.

Challenging the System from Within

# John Allocca

*For the last nine years, John has worked in the Boston area as a Spanish bilingual teacher, mostly with people from Dominican and Puerto Rican communities. He is thirty-nine.*

*Politically, John identifies himself as a socialist. He's a member of the* Freedom Road Socialist Organization. *"I was attracted to it because it's nondogmatic and very firmly grounded in a commitment—not just on a moral and spiritual level—to antiracism and to an understanding that the whole system of capitalism, as it developed in this country, is predicated on white supremacy."*

. . .

One of my mother's parents was born here, and the other was born in Poland. My father's grandparents came here from Italy. They were in the early wave of southern Italian immigrants. My last name is not very common among Italians in either Italy or the Italian diaspora. It's problematic in Spanish because it means "crazy."

I see myself as being different from and somewhat hostile toward the white Anglo-Saxon Protestant dominant culture in this country. And I see myself more than anything as in a state of confusion and mourning over how many people from both of my European ethnic backgrounds, after a generation or two in this country, stopped being who they were and stopped identifying as working-class people and identified more as white. You hear all these immigrant family stories, "My father was this great trade unionist, labor leader, anarchist socialist, whatever"; there's very little, if any, tradition of that in my family. I supposedly have one Polish great-uncle who was some sort of a socialist. But in general, my ancestors were either reactionary or pretty nonexistent in terms of progressive or antiracist politics.

I wish I had activist ancestors. When I hear about people from my background and other European immigrant backgrounds who fought against racism and for social justice in this country, I always feel inspired. But I also feel a longing. I wish there was someone I knew who was part of my family. I wish I got to know my great-uncle before he died.

My mother and father have their own, home-grown social justice, and I think it has positively influenced my brother and me. I think they're in the right ballpark. They are not radical types. I wouldn't consider them activist, but both of them in little ways have done things that make me really proud of them.

I have to give my parents credit. Although I can be critical of them on the fine points of their belief and practice and judgmental toward them, they both in different ways tried to push me in a positive direction. They didn't know that they were creating a Frankenstein's monster, inspiring me to think critically, question authority, and serve the people—that I would take it several steps further than they might have imagined or hoped for. When I was growing up, my parents conveyed to me directly and indirectly that racism was wrong. There would be more than the occasional joke in my neighborhood and extended family that I would consider racist, but the basic impulse in the immediate nuclear family was that racism is not cool. It wasn't like this really elaborate theory or anything like that. It was that racism is wrong, and you have to treat everyone with respect and fairness.

When I would experience basic injustice on the street—like bullying—I felt a deep anger well up in me. Over time, I learned that it's not just about the individual bullying on the street; it's that the system we live in is a system based on bullying. The system even gets oppressed people to bully each other. Making that connection and feeling anger helped spur me toward a certain level of activism.

I went to a Jesuit Catholic high school. I'll never forget junior year in Father DiGiacomo's theology class. He wasn't one of the cool teachers; we made fun of the way he looked and all kinds of stupid things like that. But he brought out issues in the class around ethics and theology, using issues of the time like Affirmative Action and the My Lai massacre in the Vietnam War. I found myself being viscerally moved by that in a way that I couldn't admit at the time. When one of my classmates—a kid of Italian immigrant parents who identified strongly as Italian and spoke Italian at home—tried to compare his family's experience as hard-working European immigrants with that of African Americans, I told him, "Wait a second. There's a big difference between our people and African Americans. We were never enslaved and dragged over here in chains." The discussion ended there, but those are the kind of discussions that came up in class.

1980 was a pivotal year for me. I turned eighteen. In El Salvador, Archbishop Romero was assassinated, and four nuns—including the aunt of a student at my high school—were murdered. I'm making connections. I'm Catholic—I haven't rebelled against it yet—and I'm feeling the currents of social justice and antiracism flowing through my veins. I'm thinking that something is wrong with all this. Jimmy Carter reinstates registration for the draft that year, and I'm the only one I know among my friends and acquaintances who said, "Screw that. I'm not even going to sign my name on the piece of paper." I started seeing that the government I was taught to love and trust and respect was supporting people who are killing people of the cloth. From an early age, I was taught to love and trust and respect people of the cloth, no matter what. So that was a contradiction for me. And the victims of the injustice in El Salvador were primarily Latino people.

I went away to college—Georgetown in Washington, D.C.—a school that I really hated. It was politically very conservative. I went there to study Middle Eastern politics because in the seventh grade, I had gotten interested in that and written a paper about it. Something had told me that things weren't right in the Middle East. My mother, who was teaching high school then, had gotten some pamphlets for me that gave me a radically different perspective. I remember thinking, "You mean, the people that our government backs tooth and nail actually massacred civilians? And this never came out?" That was one of the first issues around which I got radicalized and felt isolated about. I thought I'd go to college, study Arabic, and somehow help the Palestinian cause.

Well, at college, I became a multi-issue activist. I moved quickly from being a pacifist to believing that people who are being gunned down have the right to use any means necessary to defend themselves and fight back. In Washington, D.C., at the time, the Latino community was mostly Central American. After studying and doing well, I realized that I needed something that's more practical than learning Arabic. I liked languages but realized it would take me forever to learn Arabic to the level I could use it. So by the beginning of my sophomore year, I started studying Spanish. And it was at least partly because I wanted to work in solidarity with the struggles in Central America and with the Central American immigrant community in D.C.

I was totally clueless about what I wanted to do with my life. I drove a cab in D.C. for two years. My dream was to go to Nicaragua, learn about the situation up close, and serve the people in some vague way. The only thing I could afford to do was to go on a coffee harvest brigade. That was a formative experience. I didn't learn much about the struggle that I didn't know already; I didn't learn much more Spanish because I was mostly surrounded by other gringos. What I learned is that it's hard to build a revolution. It's really hard. It's not just all the stuff from the outside that's trying to keep you down, but it's your people's fears and insecurities and all the contradictions in a society.

I came back to the states with the idea that people with my skills and talents need to work more closely with regular, everyday, working-class people in this country and not just go back to grad school and work with other academics and college students. I had this vague idea that I would be more involved with working people in an internationalist fashion.

Eventually, I got a job as a bilingual teacher in Lynn, Massachusetts. I wasn't very outspoken. I was a first-year teacher and could barely do my job. I didn't know what the hell I was doing in terms of the day-to-day formality of teaching. But I listened to the students and their concerns about racism in the community and the school. And I tried to help them use that to develop their language skills in English and Spanish, and I tried to help them develop their organizing skills in subtle ways.

My second year of teaching, in 1993, was at Boston English High School. During that year, I was involved in a bitter struggle over school-based management. Forty percent of the student body was Latino and Latina, and there were many other linguistic minorities: Somali, Polish, Ethiopian and Eritrean, Armenian, Lebanese, Palestinian, you name it. There were one hundred staff and twelve hundred students. When the elections were held for the school-based management team (the School Site Council), there was almost no chance that any Latino or other linguistic minority staff, students, or parents would be elected without some form of affirmative action or proportional representation.

One of my colleagues confronted the headmaster during a staff meeting about the lack of representation on the council: "This isn't South Africa. We have to have somebody representing all the different groups here!" My colleague and another guy then began circulating a petition, saying that we should have guaranteed representation on the council of all groups at the school, and I signed the petition. The petition was passed into the headmaster with only six signatures on it. I was really angry and resentful that not more people had signed this simple petition; I was just beginning to realize how isolated I and the other signers were.

One thing leads to the next, and a small group of us began organizing around the issue. I thought to myself, "I know who I am. There's no way I can take a back seat on this. I just can't back down." Little did I know how heated this would get and what the consequences would be. We thought we'd have some easy battles. Boy, were we naive.

A lot of the Latino and Latina students were feeling like they were second-class citizens at the school. An ad hoc coalition developed between a few of us on the faculty and some students—later on, we were accused of manipulating the students. A good chunk of the Latino students declared a strike on the day before February vacation. It was, "Which side are you on?" I did not want to be seen in any way as agitating for the students, but I also didn't want to be seen as undercutting them. Their demands were not just for more representation on the council, but for more social activities at the school and communication in their languages. I had a ninth grade bilingual social studies class; they were young and unsure about the strike, and they asked me, "What should we do?" I told them, "You have to make a decision. I can't tell you what to do. These are the issues as I understand them."

There was a network of students who put out the call to walk out of classes at 10:30 A.M. My students asked me again, "What should we do?" "You heard what I said." They walked out. The headmaster comes bellowing through the hallways, "Get back in your classes!" They ran back into the classroom, terrified. The headmaster then announced that he would meet with students in the auditorium. I told my students, "I don't know what you should do, but if you do go to the meeting, go with dignity, with respect, with courage, but organize. You should have a delegation, not just everybody going there and shouting."

In the weeks after that, the struggle really heated up. There was a lot of controversy within the staff, a lot of people really hating us, to the point of threats, some not so subtle. By the end of the year, we were going up against the administration of the school, our own union, and 96 percent of the faculty in the school. Our allies were a good chunk of the students, a good chunk of Latino and Latina community activists, and one or two people on the Boston School Committee. In a sense, we won the war—if you call the "war" getting representation written into the contract for the School Site Council—but several of the core staff involved in the struggle lost our jobs. One decided he was sick and tired of this and retired early; two of us were unceremoniously not rehired for other pretenses.

That summer of 1994, I was still in my world of naiveté, thinking that there were people in the system who would support me and help me get a job. Because I was certified as a bilingual teacher, had a couple of years experience, and was flexible about where I worked, I should have been able to get a job somewhere in the system, certainly by September. I had some interviews, but by the start of school, I didn't have a job. It seemed pretty clear that the word got out, "Don't hire this jerk." I got a gig as a long-term sub at one high school in another town, and then, totally by luck, I got a job where I work now, at El Centro de Cardenal.

. . .

*A few days prior to the interview, John took his students to New York City for a field trip—in Spanish,* paseo. *They visited the Museo del Barrio in Spanish Harlem, met with community activists at the Community Center in Hunts Point in the South Bronx, and attended a play put on by members of the community. John felt moved to write a poem after the trip and wanted to share it with us.*

I think it's important for teachers to put themselves out there and on the line and write with the students. Doing creative writing is important to me because it's a block I have; it's not something I ever felt comfortable with.

PASEO REFLECTIONS

Hunts Point
Greenpoint
Worlds apart
But are they really?

My point is that my point is Greenpoint.
But I have come to love Hunts Point.

Do I really know the point
About the Point which is Hunts Point?
Maybe not.

White boy from Greenpoint, Brooklyn,
Polaco Italiano
Skin mas oscuro en el verano
Hablando español que
A veces sueno a un boricua.

But my point is that the
Point from which I come
Is not the Point
Which is Hunts Point in the Bronx,
A barrio much maligned
In the time of my youth.

Much fear bred in white boys
From Brooklyn.
The point was not to
Point myself in any way
Towards any point in the South Bronx.

But the Point which is Hunts Point
Now welcomes me,
Makes me feel at home,
Makes my students get the point.

Greenpoint or Hunts Point?
The point is not to miss the point.
White boy can get along with
Black or Brown boy if he
Really tries to extend himself,
Learn the history,
Learn the language,
Learn the culture,
Love the people.
Get the point.

I was giving the address of the Community Center in Hunts Point to a student who was writing a thank you letter, and it clicked in my head. I grew up in Greenpoint, a neighborhood in New York City that was very different from Hunts Point, and probably still is, in perception and reality. Greenpoint was very much a white community, a European ethnic neighborhood: Polish, Italian, some German and Irish. Anyone not identified as white would not feel welcomed there. It was a strong part of the culture of the neighborhood to fear and loathe Puerto Ricans, whom we usually referred to as "Spanish" out of our own ignorance, or sometimes a harsher term beginning with "sp—." That was the main prejudice when I was a kid. Puerto Ricans lived on the fringes of our neighborhood in Williamsburg, one of the first big Puerto Rican communities in New York City.

*John has some mannerisms, a style of speaking, and even aspects of his appearance that seem more stereotypical of Latino or Black young men than most white men. We ask him about this.*

It's a fair question, and I'm a little self-conscious about it. My skin seems to be getting darker, especially if I've been out in the sun. I don't know if it's because of aging or some kind of internal chemicals or whatever poisons I put into my system, but some of the youth I work with think that I'm some sort of Latino. I try to quickly correct them, just because I don't want anyone to think that I'm fronting, that I'm something I'm not.

Unconsciously to semiconsciously, I fall into mannerisms if I'm around a certain group for a while. On one of my first visits back home after I had left Brooklyn to go to college, my mother almost cried because she felt that I was losing my Brooklyn accent. Now, mind you, my mother was just a few years short of completing a ph.d. and had been an English teacher at one of the academically elite public high schools in New York City and prided herself in knowing and using so-called proper English grammar and diction. And to a certain extent, I was trying to lose my Brooklyn accent because I wasn't proud of where I was from. Nobody else I was with at Georgetown reflected my working-class, Polish and Italian American neighborhood in Brooklyn. Initially, some people made fun of my accent. I didn't stand up for myself.

Working with youth of color here in Boston—mostly Latino and African American, some raised here, some recent immigrants—I do find myself picking up some of their mannerisms. I have to be careful about this because I think it may not be appropriate. When I think about my first few years of teaching in this program, if I had a tape of it, I'd be embarrassed. I wasn't trying to, but I was speaking exactly like they do. There's nothing wrong with the way they speak, but it's not my way of speaking. They didn't mind. But after teaching a few years, feeling more comfortable about myself as a teacher and as a person, I feel like I'm between different worlds. That is definitely awkward for me some times.

Part of my comfort level of being an Anglo and working with Latino students is the feedback I get from the students and other adults I work with. That feedback indicates that what I'm doing is respectful and that I should keep doing it. Now, I could run into places in this world where people would tell me, "F— you, you shouldn't be doing this." If somebody else came along who was from my students' ethnic background and could do this anywhere near as well as I think I do this, they should do it. I'm in the fortunate position that I was there when the job was there, and I got it. But I'm willing to say, "Hey, screw my privilege; somebody else should be doing this. You should have somebody who's a role model from your own background. You don't need some white boy coming in and teaching you about your own culture."

Teaching can be an extremely revolutionary act. I have a friend—a political *compañero*—who likes to joke that teachers are the class enemy. Sometimes they just prop up a system that keeps working-class people down and divided. I see it as my job to encourage youth to really express themselves about the world, giving them an opportunity that they generally don't get in school to say, "This is how it really is. This is how I see the world. It ain't like something that's in this textbook or some standardized test. This is the way my little piece of the world works." And then I help direct them to alternative perspectives in terms of analyzing past, present, and future societies. That's revolutionary to me.

Young people in adolescence have a fair amount of world knowledge, some literacy skills, but a lot of critical thinking capacity. And they typically have little or no illusions about democracy in reality versus democracy in books, and rights in reality versus rights in the Constitution. So I help them cultivate that latent critical thinking capacity and direct them to the resources to fill in the blanks in their knowledge. I encourage them to take it where they need to take it and not believe what I say just because I say it.

I'm helping them develop skills to challenge capitalism. They are so overwhelmed, as are people in general in this country, by the ideological apparatus—the media and the public and private education system—that they can't see the possibility of building a society that is for human needs. So they try to get the most they can for themselves. I cannot possibly convince them, on my own, that that's wrong. And it's not my job or role, and it would be irresponsible of me to try to do that as a teacher in a public school. But what I can do is to put them on the spot when they repeat tried and truisms, whether it's about the economic system or about race.

For example, in the newspaper today, on May 30, 2001, the only image you're going to see of an Arab or Muslim man is of a so-called terrorist. What's that all mean? What is terrorism? What is socialism? What is communism? What are rights? What are privileges? What's freedom? What's race? What's white? I try to get into the deeper meanings of all these terms that are thrown about loosely in the media and education system and encourage them and cajole them to think twice about things and provide them with alternatives to the crap that is spoon-fed in most textbooks. My students love the title of the book *Lies My Teacher Told Me*.

I also think it's important that my students not fall into simple tried and truisms that all white people are bad. It's not about saying, "Don't struggle against racism" or "Trust white people." No. I say very honestly, "You have every right to have doubts about me and a lot of other white folks because we, as a people in general, have done you and your people wrong." I don't spend a lot of time on this, but I do want them to know that there are white folks who have made ultimate sacrifices in the struggle to support freedom and equality. They didn't lead the movements, they didn't make the movements against slavery or for any type of empowerment, but there have been important allies. Schools don't teach about John Brown to white kids or kids of color.

As a teacher, there are a few things I always try to come back to. Students will often ask me, "Are you white?" I don't give them a simple answer to that question. I make sure that they understand the historic origin of the term as something that, in this country, was first developed by the British aristocracy to divide poor and working-class European immigrants from Native Americans and African Americans and to destroy potential alliances between them. I tell students that I try to reject the label "white" but that's what society identifies me as. Growing up, I was considered a white kid by most definitions of the society. That's who I am—a white man—no matter how long I'm out in the sun or how well I can speak Spanish with a Puerto Rican or Dominican accent. I'm a white man.

I tell my students that I grew up in a racist society and that I've changed because of my experiences living and working with people from different communities. When I was their age, I was a scared, confused young white boy who would never want to hang out with any of them. Ultimately, that's what I am. I've been given race and class privileges in this world that I can still resort to. The guys I work with don't have those, and I have no illusions about that. I own those privileges with them, straight up.

It is a conscious decision on my part to live in the city in a multinational neighborhood. I think it's important for public school teachers, to all reasonable extents—because I can't judge everybody's individual case—to make an effort to live in a community where our students live, or at least in a community that is similar to where they teach. It's important for them to see me shop at some of the same places they do and walk around the same places. Not to say that I am like them or whatever, but their teacher doesn't have to be someone coming in on a spaceship from somewhere thirty miles away, some gated community. The students can relate better to people they see outside of school.

I try to set certain rules for myself and others, but I break those rules sometimes. It's a complicated process. I have to constantly check myself: did I go a little too far? I know I do sometimes. I am inspired by the Spanish language and many Latin American and other cultures not my own. I am inspired by hip-hop culture. So when I write, like poetry or something, there is no John Allocca culture per se. I am a series of different cultures that I'm trying to put together to make some sense out of the world.

# Bill Johnston

*Bill spent thirty-one years in the Boston Police Department in the Tactical Control Force (the "riot squad") and the Community Disorders Unit. Now sixty and retired from the Department, he works with Facing History and Ourselves, an educational program about bias and oppression. "From a white Irish cop, the words coming out of my mouth have a big impact. Racism is our problem."*

*Bill has received many awards, including the Courage of Conscience Award, Friends of the Gay and Lesbian Community, and an award from the ADL. The last is particularly important for Bill; when he wasn't getting much support in the Police Department, his strongest ally was the ADL He had great admiration for the now deceased executive director of the ADL, Lenny Zakim. Bill says, "Through Lenny, I learned that it wasn't about the 'Jews'; it was about me and you and everybody else. When other groups, like the Cape Verdeans, were having problems, the ADL would call them and ask them how they were doing. I realized that even though there are cultural differences, if we can't get together on an issue, the bigots win."*

. . .

I hear excuses for hate crime. "It's only an isolated incident. It's only a childish prank. It's only vandalism." Those swastikas painted on the temple? That's not vandalism. That's a message of hate. Vandalism is when you're trying to destroy property. The swastikas are trying to destroy people.

When you're dealing with haters out there, very few specialize. There's no hater who goes, "I only beat up Cambodians. I don't beat up Vietnamese or Chinese. I don't beat Blacks or gays." It's whoever is different. It's whoever doesn't have power. It's whoever is the most vulnerable.

That young hater, that young coward—that's how I define him. You gotta put those words together: a hater is a coward. When they make you different, they make you less than them. To prove it, look at the haters. Hiding under the sheets of the KKK, under the cover of darkness, in a large group.

Then there's the community response. Look at Laramie, Wyoming, and Jasper, Texas. "Oh, my God, it's terrible." But wait a second. Who's responsible for that? What were the parameters of behavior expected within those communities? Did those kids in Laramie say, "Hey, listen, I'm going to crucify a gay guy, and I'm going to get away with it?" Or did they say, "I'm going to crucify a gay guy and go to jail?" Somewhere along the line, they said, "We can get away with this."

It starts when we say, "They're only words. They're only jokes." As a young police officer, I learned very early that weapons kill. It wasn't until I was a member of the Hate Crimes Unit that I realized that words kill. Please don't tell me that sticks and stones will break my bones but names will never hurt me. Tell that to a six-year-old Black kid who's just been called a "nigger." Tell that to a Jew who's just been called a "kike." I'm telling you, I've seen the physical scars heal. People carry the emotional scars for the rest of their lives.

Which one of us hasn't been there when someone used one of those words or told one of those jokes? And we cringed but kept our mouths shut, rather than saying, "Don't you ever use another word like that in front of me." You say that it's only a joke? Well, if it's only a joke, then how come when you started telling the joke, you looked around to make sure that no Italians, no Blacks were there? Nobody speaks up, nothing happens. It escalates up to the point where somebody dies. And then we, the community, point and say, "He killed him." In fact, we killed him. The blood is on the hands of people in Laramie and Jasper. Somewhere along the line, no one said, "In the confines of this culture, this behavior is not acceptable." We can really make a dent in this if we as a community have the moral courage.

I think that white America is petrified. We're really scared. You look out the window; it's not Mrs. O'Reilly from County Cork; it's Mrs. Tran from Vietnam. I believe that some demagogue could grab on to that and play to their fear. You watch *Eyes on the Prize* and you realize, "For the white guy, this is all about power." It would be idiotic just to give it up. I keep on hearing that over and over again: "This is all about power."

And I keep hearing white people talk about Affirmative Action. It's a drumbeat every single day. "All the Blacks are taking our jobs." I look at the Police Academy and say, "Where are all these Blacks who are taking our jobs? What are you, nuts?" It just isn't happening. I'm a veteran, so I get two points on the civil service exam. The son of a police officer killed in the line of duty automatically gets points. If I score ninety, I get ninety-two. Two points is a monster. I became a sergeant because of those two points I got as a veteran. But they don't see that as Affirmative Action.

We've done a great job of spreading this disease called racism. If white America doesn't understand this, they don't understand American history.

We've done such a good job that young Black males have caught the disease. Young Black males are killing other Black males. Why are they doing that? Well, they certainly aren't doing it because of the color of their skin. They're all the same. But they've got to find a difference. They've got to make them less than human. So they don't kill each other over the color of their skin; they kill each other over the color of their jacket.

The police are taking credit for the drop in crime. The nerve of us. I honestly believe that if we had said three years ago, "Every police officer in the Boston Police Department and cities throughout the country is going to eat Cheerios and by eating Cheerios, crime will go down." And crime would have gone down. How about giving some credit to the people within that community? Even young kids have turned around and said, "So if I live this life, I die? I don't want to live that way."

In the 1960s, when those white officers turned their German shepherds on citizens trying to exercise their rights under the Constitution, were they doing community policing? Yeah, folks, they were. They were doing exactly what the white community wanted them to do.

. . .

As I look back on my life and career, [I see] I was the victim, I was the bystander, and I was the perpetrator. I grew up in Roxbury, one of twelve children. The Catholic Church was all-important. We were extremely poor. The derogatory terms used to describe Blacks, to describe Italians, to describe Jews—I heard them every day. My world was relatively small—maybe six blocks. My ambitions, I guess, were that of everybody else: you go in the service, you get out of the service, you get married, you get the second floor of a three-decker and a secure job. That's all I wanted. That's all I knew. I wish I could say that I came to policing as a vocation, but it was just a secure job. I thought I could become a priest, a prisoner at Walpole, or a police officer. I became a police officer.

I came to the department in 1966, when the training wasn't quite as much like the military as it is now. I think the reasons it became more military was because of the riots, because of the SWAT teams. I remember being at the Police Academy, and an instructor got up and said, "This is going to be one of the last all-white classes. The Blacks are coming." I went through the training; we marched together, ran together, did everything together, as if that's the way we did our job. And policing had nothing to do with that. You're out there by yourself.

The elite in the Boston Police Department were the officers in the Tactical Control Force. They were interviewed and handpicked. And I got picked.

I think they were looking for someone over six feet tall, young, aggressive. To belong to the Tactical Control Force, to be embraced by that club was all-important to me. I went in there and looked around and asked myself, "What does it take to be a good cop?" It was us against them. And them—people of color—had no power.

As a member of the Tactical Control Force, I was in the riots in the neighborhood where I grew up. During the riots, we pulled out of sections of Roxbury. Think about that. Would we have pulled out of sections of Beacon Hill? Never. And I remember being scared, really scared. All that training they gave us fell apart.

I remember the language they used to talk about the Blacks. I realized that the department—and I—could make them less than me, less than human. And basically, we could do almost anything we wanted to. There were times when my stomach told me, "Something's really wrong here. I mean really, really wrong." But I didn't have the courage to stand up to my brother officers when they were using that language. In fact, I didn't have the courage for *me* to not use that language. If you want to be part of the club, you use that language.

My department kept on telling me what a great cop I was. They gave me the awards; they wrote me commendations; they gave me the William Taylor Award for police excellence. I was the cop of the year. So I thought maybe there was something wrong with me.

A couple of seeds were planted when I was a member of the Tactical Control Force. They started a decoy unit within the Tactical Control Force. That's an officer going out and doing whatever it takes to look vulnerable so the bad guy will come along and rob him. Two things happened to me as a decoy. For the first time in my life I realized what it meant to be a victim of a crime. I had not experienced that.

The other thing I realized was that if people even perceive you to be different—you do not have to be different—you're treated differently. As a decoy, when I was coming out of a straight bar, I was robbed. Roughed up a little to get the money, but once they had the money, it was, "See ya later." But when I was coming out of gay bars, the whole dynamic changed. It was always the words, "Kill the fag." All the injuries I received as a decoy happened when I was decoying at gay bars. Why? They perceived me to be gay; therefore I was different; therefore I was less than human, less than them; they could do anything they wanted.

As bad as the injuries were, that was not the worst thing that happened in those decoy operations. A worse thing was what the perpetrator said to the cops. The perpetrator was oftentimes a white male between the ages of sixteen and twenty-four. When the backup police had arrested him, he'd actually ask why he was being arrested. They'd tell him, "You just robbed that guy over there." And he'd say, "Yeah, but he's a fag," as if the police officers at that moment were going to say, "Geez, I didn't know that." This hater honestly believed that the cops agreed with him. In his mind, there was no sin, no crime. There was absolutely no shame.

. . .

So I make the Tactical Control Force, then sergeant. Then I go to a unit called the Community Disorders Unit. It was formed in 1978 to deal with bias. But it was basically racial bias, and in Boston, that meant Black people and white people. It wasn't formed because the commissioner or the mayor woke up one morning and said, "My God, what's happening? Our city is horrendous." Remember people were dying over this issue. The Community Disorders Unit was formed because we got sued, and part of the remedy was to create the unit. It was supposed to be a public relations gimmick in the minority community. Originally only two officers were assigned, and they were going to be bean counters. They were going to count how many Blacks were attacked, how many whites were attacked. Period.

When I go into this unit, they tell me, "You really don't have to do anything" as far as police work. It is nonarrest oriented. And I remember thinking, "What the hell does 'nonarrest oriented' mean?" Basically they're saying, "We don't know how to handle this issue, so we'll just do a song and dance. If the rabbi has a problem, we'll go down and dance with the rabbi. If a minority family has a problem, we'll go down and hold their hands." Afterward I learned if you do that, you might as well be the perpetrator. You're just continuing the problem. You're just traumatizing that family or that victim again by not responding properly as a police officer and not treating this incident as what it truly is: one of the worst crimes that can be committed.

In the early months in the unit, I do my bit. I'm doing enough. You have to understand what civil rights meant to me then. Civil rights was a weapon used against police officers. So I want to make sure that I don't get hurt. Believe it or not, I'm doing the right thing for the wrong reasons. If I get sufficient facts to support a complaint, I'm going to go forward. I'm not playing with this. That way no one's going to come down on me.

Am I a bad guy? No, I'm doing what the community wants, although I admit it's the community in power. I'm also doing what my department wants. You have to realize we haven't even admitted we have a race problem. The court had told us we had to have this unit because of the suit.

I guess dealing with the families is what changed it for me. I remember one time going to see a family after an incident—it's one of those rotten February nights—and the father is crying while he's telling me what happened. He has two children; one was taking a bath, and the other was watching TV; his wife was cleaning up after dinner when all of a sudden eighteen windows were taken out. He says to me, "The windows are breaking; the kids are screaming for me; my wife is screaming for me. And I stood here paralyzed, not knowing which way to go. My wife told me she wanted me to do something. She said, 'Do something.' Please, officer, explain to her that if I had gone out that door, I would have killed somebody."

As corny as it sounds, I think that at that very moment, when I really looked in that guy's eyes and saw his fear and desperation, I understood. I had been making the mistake a whole lot of people make when you deal with the issue of crime. You steal $100,000; it's a major crime. You steal ten bucks, who gives a damn? What was stolen from that family was their dignity. When you talk about these kinds of crimes, that's what's stolen here. The police department still classifies incidents like this as "shattered windows." They're looking at the wrong thing. It's not shattered windows. It's shattered families.

While this is going on, my childhood sweetheart, who I married and had five children with, gets a terrible disease called cancer. I had believed that nothing would ever happen to her. Every morning I'm waking up and realizing that I'm looking at the same fear and desperation in my eyes that I saw in that father's eyes. There was nothing I could do to protect my wife. And there was nothing he could do to protect his family. My family had a disease that was going to take them. His family was carrying the reason for their victimization around with them all the time: the color of their skin.

My wife dies. I remember talking to gay friends at the time. For me, it was like this person inside me coming out of the closet. I realize that no one can ever hurt me again. So I decide to stand up.

. . .

In 1986, I remember going to court and having a clerk say, "Show me in the Constitution where fags have civil rights." I said, "One person cannot violate the constitutional rights of another person. Prove to me that gays aren't people." And we fought and we won that. That was long before there was a law about gay civil rights.

Through that and listening to gay men, I'm thinking, "God, what must happen to women every day?" I go up and grab some domestic violence cases, and I read them. And something jumps out at me. If I take gender out of this, some of these cases scream to me, "Civil rights violations." If women have to leave their homes for their own safety and then can't afford housing, that's a fair housing issue. If they're so badly beaten that they can't go to church or temple and they lose the support of family and friends—that's Article Two of our Constitution that guarantees right of association. I thought I was onto something.

Why do we allow these crimes to be called "domestic violence"? I have no idea what that term means, but it's got to be thrown out. Women die as a result of a domestic dispute. Geez, folks, ain't that murder? If these perpetrators don't fall into the category "haters and cowards," there is no such thing. When you're dealing with the issue of civil rights, words are so important. Words either define or they dismiss the problem. And I think the words "domestic violence" dismiss the problem. Under domestic violence law, if you slap her, it's a misdemeanor. You get two and one-half years. But if I can make it a civil rights violation, it goes from a two-and-one-half-year misdemeanor to a ten-year felony.

So I figure I'm onto something, and I present it. Then I run into barriers that I never thought I'd run into. Males, they're looking at me like I've got eight heads. "Billy, you can put all the poor Blacks, poor whites, poor Asians, poor Hispanics in there. We don't care. But don't cross this line." And I run into female lawyers who are saying, "Well, she's got to be doing something wrong." I ask myself, "What the hell? Why are you saying that?" And then I realize the reason they're saying that is that if she isn't doing something wrong, they could be victims tomorrow.

It took five years to get the first case. I had to show multiple relationships —a guy who had attacked and raped and beaten women. They wouldn't give me the guy who beat and raped the same woman three times in a row.

Why did it become so important for me to identify that as a hate crime? Where are my young haters coming from? They're coming from homes where they're watching their father beat up their mother. And they're watching a law enforcement system that doesn't do a hell of a lot to protect her. In fact, that injunction against him, that piece of paper we give to women to protect them, we're oftentimes wrapping that around her when we're burying her. I don't think it's a gigantic step for the same kid to hit the street and start assaulting people by the dozens.

• • •

Boston Area Gay and Lesbian Youth were marching in the Gay Pride March and invited me to march with them. "We'd like you to march with us, you've been supportive of us, but of course we know you won't." I said, "I'll march.

Who's going to see me?" I arrive there, and there's a big banner with my name on it. I marched with them not as a police officer but just supporting.

In front of me in the march was a very good friend of mine, Rob, who I had brought into the unit. He was gay. He was marching in uniform. As we're going down the street, the officers on duty are turning their backs as we approach. So I go up to Rob and say, "Rob come with me. Everyone who turns their back, we're going to walk over to them; we're going to turn them around and shake their hands." In the department, I became gay. "The only reason he's involved is because he's gay." They couldn't understand that I'd be willing to do that.

The question I always got was, "Why are you so embroiled in this? What are you, nuts, Billy? You don't have enough problems already? You're making an appointment with the commissioner to bring up this stuff? Why, Billy?"

I think 80 percent of the department—it may be higher—at one time had the moral courage to raise their head. And they got slammed. It's almost like that carnival game. "I'm not going to put my head up there; there's a guy with a hammer." I was always stupid enough to believe, "Well, maybe this time it's going to be different." And there were times I got slammed over the head.

And I saw officers give up their identity. People in the community used to think it was going to be great when Blacks and gays and women are in the force. And I used to run into them two years after they'd been on the job, and they're all cops. Teaching that institutional loyalty over personal integrity. If people show moral courage, we don't give them awards. We just give them names. We call them "rats" and "snitches."

At times I would get tired and not want to fight anymore. Why should I say anything? I pretty much had it made. But I'm thinking, "Wait a second. I'm not going to let this slide." So you get up every morning and say, "Hey, listen, I'm going to fight. I'm not going to allow this to happen." Because it's so easy to think, "I'll pretend I didn't hear that. I didn't see that. I don't think he really meant that. Let me just get on with my life." And no one will think less of me. No one would know. But I would.

When I was retiring, at the ceremony there were all these messages from people around the country who said what a wonderful guy Billy Johnston was. My son got up and said, "I can hardly wait to meet this guy." Now the reason he said it—and I know why he said it—I wasn't there many times for my own family. That's a regret. That's a price I paid. I always say to people out there, "If you're going to have moral courage, understand that there's a price to be paid, and you're going to pay it." Even doing the right thing can have negative consequences for you or someone you really care for. You have to survive. But you can't be silent.

I remember when women first came on the force. I was a young officer then. The men wouldn't even stand next to the women during roll call. No other group paid the price that women paid. Women paid a horrendous price. I didn't speak out at that time. I thought, "If I don't curse them or use derogatory words around them, then I'm okay." By my silence I condoned it.

In the privacy of command staff meetings, I should have been more vocal; I should have stood up; I should have done more. I didn't. That's my shame in my gut. And I beat the living daylights out of myself. I would absolutely crucify myself. I would work it until my stomach's in knots and I'm almost physically ill. Why didn't you say something? Why didn't you do something?

I have a vision that when we arrive at the Pearly Gates, we're going to find out that God is everything that we're not. If God made us all, then he is all of us. At my moment of death, the God who comes to judge me will be young, gay, Jewish, African American. And she is going to say, "How the hell did you treat me?" Ultimately, I think that's the only sin that will keep you out of heaven. I really mean it, and I believe in God. How you treat others is what really matters. If you think, "I was really good to Blacks and Jews, but I had a tough time with those gays," that ain't gonna work.

# A. T. Miller

*A. T. is currently the coordinator of Multicultural Teaching and Learning for all nineteen schools and colleges at the University of Michigan. Before that, he was the director of Africana Studies for eight years at Union College in Schenectady, New York, where he also served on the Schenectady Human Rights Commission. At the age of twenty-two, immediately after college, A. T. went to East Africa to teach in an African Quaker secondary school being established in a small community. (There are over one-half million Quakers, more than one thousand Quaker primary schools, and over four hundred Quaker high schools in East Africa.) He also worked with the Kenya National Music Festivals for ten years. He is forty-three.*

*His PH.D. dissertation was on African family patterns in the diaspora: the parallels between the patterns of family organization in Africa and decisions made by African Americans and other African-heritage populations about their families. The research turned the prevailing view of the pathology of Black families on its head. Instead of defining Black families as "disorganized" because children were sometimes living with relatives other than their biological parents, A. T. came to the conclusion that Black families were, in general, well functioning when seen through an African model of putting children's needs first. For example, African American parents might place their children in informal foster care situations with relatives or friends so that the children can go to a better school or spend time away from an urban environment for an extended period of time. And he came to believe that what white American families and generally American cultural values do to children is often horrible: the privatization of children, thinking that children are the parents' property, putting material needs first.*

*Ironically, the interview took place on Fathers' Day at a small coffee shop near the University of Michigan campus in Ann Arbor. We walked in and saw a man standing near the counter who, we realized later, had a resemblance to popular European and white American portraits of Jesus Christ. He has long blond hair and a dark beard and was wearing an African shirt. A. T. told us later that when people first meet him, they often say that they have met him before. He suspects that it's because of their familiarity with the pictures of Christ.*

• • •

I joke with friends that my classes always come down to love and faith and hope. Teaching Africana studies, I get students asking, "How did people live through this? How can people keep going?" Well, you get that bottom line: it's built on love, faith, and hope for each other. Love is a big part of teaching for me. It isn't the kind of love you have for intimates or family, but I really do love my students, and I came to grips with that about ten years ago. That's what it is for me—it's not some analysis of oppression, although I'm well schooled in that and teach that to my students.

I also experienced a strong sense of faith when I was in the Jesse Jackson for president campaign. It had this astounding flavor to it, even though the result wasn't the greatest. There was this sense of having faith in each other and that this campaign made sense.

I don't talk about love, faith, and hope up front. It's a personal thing; it's not necessarily what I espouse in official occasions or in my classrooms. I must confess I do try to communicate it, but it's mixed into a much more complex message. It comes out after some deep wrestling with the complications and complexities of history and bizarre notions of race and gender and inequality and all of that kind of thing. I don't think that this is anything you can fake or strategically plan.

In my first year of teaching, a white male student said something that was very naive about race and a little off-topic and semi-offensive. I can't even remember what he said. And I slightly turned it into a joke; I didn't make it a big ha-ha joke, but it was dismissive. He was an athlete, sitting in the back of the room, and I felt free to do that to him. That kid was so hurt by that and sent me a note about it at the end of the class. When I made the comment, I had seen the look on his face, and I really regretted what I said. But then I thought, "White guys can take it" and justified it to myself. And, of course, most white men don't know how to deal with it. I see white male athletes as people who constantly get disrespected academically. It's hard for me to take care of the privileged, but it's a responsibility in the classroom.

I try to teach classes in an African or African American way so that students grasp that it isn't just the history of Africa; it's African history told in an African way. All of my classes are structured circularly rather than in progression. I start with some kind of historical dilemma or something and look at it from all different angles during the course of the semester and come back to where we started. And I include spiritual expressions in the classroom. I incorporate poetry that I've written or sometimes things that I select, and I sing fairly often and make the whole class sing and even dance.

I tell students up front when I'm teaching African history, as well as African American history, "We're not just going to learn the content; we're going to learn the method. So I'll tell you a story." Often I'll first tell them a story and then say, "And that story is really about this historical incident. And that's an example of traditional historical practice in this community." Or I'll sing a song and then tell them where that song comes from and what it means and that these are key ways that history was preserved among people where there weren't the formal, archive types of records. I want them to experience the meaning of music, which is fundamental both in African and in African American culture. I want them to understand that this isn't just good rhythm or fun but that music is profound in these cultures. For Black students, knowing that heritage is very meaningful. Sometimes they know the songs but don't know the historical context, and vice versa.

I usually just start off with singing and make everyone sing because I think it's helpful for everyone to be embarrassed in front of each other. It means that we'll get used to being vulnerable in class, and they bond because they think I'm the weirdo. They get to exchange glances with each and think, "What is this?" It's a way to drop guard at the beginning of class, and there's a bonding feeling when they all sing together. Singing is a communal process. I always tell the students, "We're going to keep singing until everybody's singing," and so we'll do it twelve times if we have to. These are university students, so you've usually got a lot of reluctant people on the first verse. There are a few classes—like when we get to freedom songs—when, for a whole day, we'll listen to recordings and sing. Often students react with, "Now I understand why those songs were so important." They talk about how they felt, that singing those songs was so cool.

When I was director of Africana Studies at Union, I took it as my responsibility to teach and lead in an African-centered style. I really like the founding intentions of the field of Africana Studies: there is no ebony tower; this will always be community linked, always accessible; knowledge and research will always be shared. There are many departments that operate that way, but it isn't universal. Some have become very professionalized in the institution of higher education, and I wanted to be sure that didn't happen. So at Union, I tried to make sure that we never had a faculty meeting that didn't include the students. I expected every declared major to be at every department meeting. Every student majoring and minoring in Africana Studies had to be active in some way on campus and in some way off campus. That meant, of course, that I had to have all kinds of connections in the community and on campus because you don't just send students out to tromp on toes. It's very important that there's open communication, so that people can say, "I can't have this kid at my agency."

And our semesters abroad were very different from the programs typically offered at universities, the "drinking in England" semester. Even lots of universities that do things in Africa simply send students to an African university. I wanted to be sure that we did nothing of the sort. For example, in our program in Kenya, we were six weeks in Nairobi and six weeks on the road. The students had three different home stays: ten days living with a rural family in a village; ten days living with a middle-class family in the city; four days in Kampala, Uganda, with families.

Then the students all did internships in their area of interest. We had students do all kinds of amazing things, from linkages to World Health Organization AIDS projects to being an actress with a drama troupe in Nairobi. That meant that the students were very connected to communities. It also meant that they were all spread out and not hanging out with each other. We did similar things with programs in Brazil and Barbados.

We made sure that everything we did was contracted locally, so that students would get the wisdom of the people in the country. It was also to make sure that the money the program spent stayed in the country and built up African businesses and institutions. The people who did the transport, the places we stayed—we didn't use American tour companies or American student-run operations or British-run programs. I was able to do that in East Africa because I had lived there eight years, so I knew local people and had lots of local connections.

. . .

When I moved to Ann Arbor and was looking for a place to live, there were all kinds of places I ruled out. Not that anybody there was some horrifying Klan member or something, but I just thought, "If this neighborhood is all white, especially since we're close to Detroit, then it's not a place I want to be. I want to live in a place where my friends can come over, my cousins can come to town and stay over, and no one is raising an eyebrow or doing their double take or anything like that. I know that I can get away with living in a white suburb, but I want to feel comfortable with my friends." So I live in an apartment complex toward Ypsilanti that's very mixed.

I travel in very mixed company, and I've had the experience of accidentally bringing people to some place that I thought was nice, and then I realize, "Oh, no." We've been treated horribly—people won't serve you, being followed around—all the standard stuff. That's part of it: realizing that I can't come to this place anymore. And sometimes that isn't it. When I'm in Maine, for example, I know that it's unlikely to be a mixed environment wherever I go. But I always notice. And when it's a few people of color, I know how many. I don't do a lot of actual counting, but I take it in quickly.

So I'm very uncomfortable in an all-white environment. Very. And I notice it if I go to a concert and the audience is all white, I notice it. It's not like I want to leave; I just notice it. It makes me wonder if this is a hostile environment. Why would this be all white? It makes it a suspect environment for me. I think things like, "I'll hear stuff I don't want to hear; it's not a place I'd want to bring friends."

People joke that every administrators' meeting I go to at the University of Michigan, I point out that the men and women are sitting separately. And it's true that at almost every meeting I go to, they are. I point it out because I find it uncomfortable. It's uncomfortable for me because now that I've noticed, I have to make a choice. Who will I sit with? I don't want to make the women uncomfortable by plopping down in the middle of them, but I also don't want to be like, "I'm going to go sit with all of the boys." My way of getting around it is to joke about it, to come in the door and say, "I'm glad the boys and girls are sitting together today!" And people are chagrined.

Sometimes my white male friends make insensitive comments. When I've tried to call them on it, I've had them throw it back at me or say things like, "Lighten up" or "I was just joking." I am guarded in those kinds of friendships because of those moments of disappointment. I'm slow to become friends. There is a little reserve that it takes me a long time to let go of, so that if something happens, it doesn't hurt as much. I have so many Black friends who wait for the other shoe to drop with white friends. And I think I do the same.

I feel sad about the impact of racism on white people, about what the society has done in making them white. And I feel disappointment about my loss of trust: "Okay, you really don't believe that all people are people." I don't say that out loud, but realizing that hurts. I guess the only way to deal with it is sadness. And I've certainly disappointed African American and African friends in profound ways. I've been told where I dropped the ball. It's painful for me when I do that.

There's this concept about "having someone's back." It's great when it happens. But as I've understood it more and more, I think it's really too far of an expectation. As director of Africana Studies at Union, I was the target of all kinds of complaints and stuff. There were times when I thought, "Where is she? Why didn't somebody say something? Why did I have to be the one to take the fall?"

Well, the Black faculty are all kinds of other targets. While one part of me says, "Why aren't they standing up for me? I need some defense here!," I try to let that go. You can't expect that. It does happen, but it's stretching the demands within our context, expectations that are beyond general social accommodation. So when Black colleagues don't stand up for me, that to me is not a disappointment. Now I think, "I can take this fall. That's my job," especially in an important position like mine. I'm the one who's supposed to be fried, not the assistant professor who is just working to make it through the system to get tenure.

The same is true with my students. I was the faculty sponsor for the African and Latino Alliance of Students at Union. The students chose me to be their sponsor, and I refused for four years. I didn't think it was appropriate. And at a certain point, they were like, "Well, who's going to do it?" When they were raising issues and the administration was starting to come down on them, I really saw that part of the job was, "I'll take the flack. What is this institution doing attacking some junior who's here to get an education?"

. . .

I knew as a little kid that I was gay and pretty much accepted it by high school. I even had a boyfriend in high school. We were horny little adolescents, so every once in a while we'd be making out somewhere, and some friend of mine would see us. Because I was an athlete and didn't fit their stereotype of who would be gay, especially then, they would say, "You're not gay. You're just messing around." And I would tell them, "No, I'm gay." It wouldn't register on them.

Here at the university, I'm very out, but it's hard to say how related that is to my understanding of African and African American culture because it's so different. My being gay is not something that anybody automatically sees. I never made the link until people started asking me about it, although I guess I wondered about it.

I think there is a certain level of empathy and understanding that I have about some things. But I do think that it's problematic to make certain kinds of links unless you're talking about gay and lesbian people of color. That's the link. There are people who are the link. It's like the link of racism and sexism: "Well, women of color. How's that?" There are people who simply are the link.

My research and passion is mainly around race issues, although all my Africana courses include issues of sexual orientation and gender. It's not a unit that's separate; it's mixed in. I help students think through the combinations and the interactions. But if I'm talking about issues of race for a gay, lesbian, bisexual, and transgendered (GLBT) audience, I don't think I make gay and lesbian analogies. I don't think it's productive because it is different. Analogies may be a way in, but many GLBT people think, "I can't be racist. I'm one of the oppressed people." I think that that is a problem we have to deal with, and making analogies plays into the problem. So people have to understand, "This is a different oppression, and you can do it."

People of color led the gay and lesbian liberation movement. Stonewall was all people of color, and some of the earliest out people were the lesbian and bisexual blues women who later became part of the Harlem Renaissance.[1] In fact, that was entirely a gay movement. Later, it was James Baldwin who published a milestone in gay male literature, *Giovanni's Room*. That book meant a lot to me. Those are important parts of African American history but also important parts of GLBT history. Women like Barbara Smith and Audre Lorde taught us all to think more clearly about the intersections of gender, race, and sexuality.[2] They really developed intellectually the concept of multiple simultaneous identity. I think there's a complete legitimacy to focusing in on a particular group's history, but you can't do any one group without everything else. You can't do Black history without women and gay people. You can't do gay history without both sexes and people of color. People often miss those connections, and I try to remind them of that. My job is to coordinate multiculturalism, so it's making sure that all of those links are there.

• • •

*We ask A. T. how he came to embrace and embody an*
*African-centered worldview.*

There's an old saying: you can think your way to a new way of acting, and you can act your way to a new way of thinking. It's really both for me. Very young, I had crossracial friendships that my parents very much encouraged. In fourth and fifth grades, I stayed overnight in homes of Black kids. It seemed normal to me. My father's mother's family is racially mixed, so I have Black cousins. In high school, I became very fascinated with Africa and African American history and culture. Some things came to me through poetry and reading.

Then I lived in Africa for a long time. I remember the first meal I had in the village. People said to me, "It's going to be African food. We hope you can eat it." The meal is fried chicken, greens, ugali—which is made from cornmeal—so I thought, "Okay. Who was cooking in North Carolina?" It revealed a lot to me about African roots in the U.S.

When I was there, I was very clear. "I'm an American. I'm not trying to pretend to be African." But I was very much treated, especially in the village, as an insider and was made an elder. It was strange: the more I made clear that distinction, that I'm American, the more it made me an insider. I really can't explain how or why that happened. I think that if I had been trying to play at being an African, then the line would have come down: "This is offensive and don't pretend." People knew that I had sincerely learned the local language, and I loved the local music, so when I started singing and dancing along, it wasn't a show. I was doing it with my friends. I first started singing with the local church choir that I was simply a member of. I wasn't conducting it, I wasn't recording it, I wasn't researching it.

I miss being in East Africa. I go there once or twice a year. I miss it a lot. Some of my dearest friends are there. My kids are there. They're not my biological children; these are students who lost their parents and I became their guardian, and they're grown now and have their own kids. I'm very close to them.

There are also people and places that I love very much here in the U.S. In the overall scheme of culture and politics—when you're talking macro— yeah, it's horrifying to be in this violent empire. I dislike that. But when you're talking personal, I love being near my family, and I'm very close to my siblings. They're just two completely different levels, and it's not as if the politics of Kenya are wonderful.

One fascinating thing for me was living in the village and loving people who were so wise. They could really give you good advice about life and psychology, if that's what you want to call it. And then I would step back and realize that this person has never been to Nairobi and will live their whole life in this rural African place as a wonderful person with none of that American "Will I be famous? Will I accomplish this? Will people remember me this way or that way?" That person will be remembered by their relatives in their village. The whole point is, "You only exist in the eyes of others." So what matters is everything you do in relation to others.

I had to come to grips with the fact that I know these wonderful people, and they're never going to be out in the big world in that U.S. sense. Those kinds of values really affected me profoundly. Going through the U.S. college system and being pushed toward all this ambition. And the ironic thing is that now I have this big job at the University of Michigan. Yes, I'm climbing the higher education ladder!

. . .

I got a very nice compliment two or three months after I was here. There was something I was planning I and asked some pretty high-up people in the administration if I needed to run it by them. They said, "No, we trust you." That took me aback. I thought, "Uh oh. You don't know what you just said because I'm somebody who will keep going until someone tells me 'no.'" I told them at the beginning, "Look, I'm going to push." One of the first things I did was to review the salary structure in our office and uncovered questionable stuff. The women of color seemed to be the lowest paid in every job category. I believe in going straight to the heart of stuff and not being slow or pretending you don't know or you're too new or something like that. To me, the things I say and do are common sense in my sensibility.

My being in this position reaches white people who think, for example, that they could never attend the King celebration or go to a Nina Simone concert. Segregation has played so much in their minds that they think they can't participate in it. King's birthday is a national holiday. A Nina Simone concert is a public event. People want you there. It's not like you're crashing the Black caucus. It's a community event.

I guess part of the disjunction of being a white man and what I do is that I can't possibly kick back in my job. People can get in a pattern of thinking, "Well, here's how I do my job, and I'll just do it this way for the next ten years." I just can't do that. I like that my job keeps me on my toes. I like that every seminar has to have the right hook in the first ten minutes or there's going to be some people who go out the door. I think it's good for me, and it makes me good for what's being done.

I often bring up my race and gender at the beginning of class. I make clear to my students that it's an issue and that I think it's appropriately an issue. I'm willing to be challenged and questioned about it, and I often say to students, "You should be just as skeptical of your economics professors. What qualifies them to teach what they're teaching?" I don't say that to be arrogant about it, but I often think, "Who am I to be doing this?" And I share that question with my students. One always has to be respectful, so I don't claim my position as African Studies teacher as a right. As I tell students in classes, I think it's healthy to constantly be checking back with yourself and in the community within which you're working and asking, "How am I doing?"

I know that I've been a model for a number of white men. I take that role seriously and try to be a model in such a way that it's respectful. And as I think about this interview appearing in your book, I'm not completely comfortable being in the spotlight or thinking that what I've done is extraordinary. But it's worth it. White men need this.

# Ken Kimerling

*When we first contacted Ken, he said, "I do what I do," downplaying the significance of his work and implying that it wouldn't be worth our time to interview him. But when we called him back to schedule an interview, he agreed to talk with us.*

*Ken's an attorney who represents exploited Asian workers: garment workers in sweatshops, restaurant workers in Chinese restaurants, and Pakistani, Bangladeshi, and Indian cab drivers. He also does things that are closer to traditional civil rights work, like representing Chinese workers who are trying to get language assistance to access the unemployment insurance system.*

*In 1971, as a young attorney, he commuted daily to Attica after the rebellion there. He spent time with prisoner leaders and did litigation around conditions at the prison. But by 1972, prison officials had shipped the leaders of the rebellion out to other prisons. He got hired at the newly formed Puerto Rican Legal Defense and Education Fund and worked there for twenty-five years, until 1997. He now works at the Asian American Legal Defense and Education Fund. Because he is well known in civil rights work in New York City, he frequently gets called up and pulled into different projects, like fighting the mayor on his efforts to sell off the public hospital system. He's fifty-six.*

*We met in his office in Lower Manhattan. Based on a brief phone conversation before the interview, we were aware of making four assumptions about Ken: (1) he came from an activist Jewish family; (2) he made a decision a long time ago to go into this kind of work; (3) he's quite humble and humility is an important value for him; and (4) he sees himself playing a supportive role in the context of a larger struggle rather than being a leader. We asked him about this.*

．  ．  ．

You're right on some. I'm Jewish, but my parents were not activists. My father worked hard in the garment industry. He sold cloth. My grandfather was a presser. The garment industry has been an entry point for lots of immigrant groups. So working here is sort of like coming home.

In terms of the timing of my career decisions, it's hard to know. It wasn't like it was a cathartic event in my life that made me do what I do. I found myself where I was. I've been involved in discrimination issues since about 1966. Humble? Yeah, I don't think I have enough ego sometimes to do what I need to do. And I do see myself as supportive; I'm more involved in supporting things that are happening than leading them. I've just sort of figured out what I can do and do well, and I'm not interested in leading something. I know what my strengths are, and that's not necessarily one of them. I feel I'm a better team player than the captain of the team. So you're pretty right—you got about a seventy-five.

I think I work well and get along with most people. I think I have some kind of humor and perspective that some people at the front end don't share. And I like what I do. I'm not the brightest person out there, but I can think. I'm not the person who can create the paradigm, but I can understand it. I've been in lots of settings where there are people who have great insights into every situation we're in and can describe it; I'm not that, but I can understand what they're saying.

There are lots of people who are real "A" types; they can't pull back; they can't rest; they can't not do something all the time. I'm not the kind of person who has to constantly be doing either this or something else. I don't think that's a good quality necessarily, but that's who I am.

I don't take work home at night, in part because I don't have that many hours that I'm awake. I eat and fall asleep like most people do, even if they take their briefcase home and then carry it back to work the next day without having opened it up. I don't even pretend that I'm going to do much when I go home. I have a wife; I have a daughter—she's fifteen and a half. That keeps me occupied. And I have a carpentry shop in my basement; I ride my bicycle; I read fiction. I cook, clean, run chores, change the kitty litter.

I certainly live my job. Most of my waking hours, like everyone else's, are spent working. But this work is not something that I woke up one day and said, "I've got to go out and change the conditions of garment workers in Chinatown." I spent a long time at the Puerto Rican Legal Defense and Education Fund, which is located in this building, and I knew the folks here at the Asian American Legal Defense and Education Fund and what they did to some extent, and I had the opportunity to come work here. I've grown to appreciate what I do. I like what I do. I think it's really important work. But I don't think I've ever felt that it was essential to my being.

. . .

When I was at the Puerto Rican Legal Defense and Education Fund, I was essentially the only white guy there. There would always be one or two others at points in time, but I was the only guy that stuck it out and stayed there, so I became the white guy. Not that I was ever identified that way or ever felt that way, but it's clearly what I was. Given the fact that I was there for twenty-five years, I became identified with the organization. A lot of people who knew the organization knew me. People would call me because they wanted the fund to do something.

I never felt any sense of being separate from anybody there because I wasn't Puerto Rican. It was clear who I was—I wasn't Puerto Rican—and it never became apparent to me that somebody treated me differently because I wasn't Puerto Rican. So it was never an issue. I made it an issue in part when I first got there, and there were some other white lawyers. We had a legal director who was white. At the point in time when it became apparent that I would take that job or would be in that position because more senior people had left, I said, "I don't want to be the legal director" because it had always been this white person in a Latino workplace. I didn't want that. I said, "I'm happy to do what a legal director does, but I don't want that title or that position." Because I refused the job, the organization didn't have a legal director until I left. Nobody really talked about it; nobody said, "Yeah, that's a good thing he's doing." But I think people understood what was happening.

I don't think I ever pretended to be Puerto Rican. I didn't even try to become bicultural. It seems to me that I could have spent time in Puerto Rico, read a lot of Puerto Rican history, and become fully, culturally Puerto Rican. But I didn't want to. I realized it was false. It's not like I have my own identity that I can clearly define, but I am who I am. I'm clearly white and middle class.

Part of the joy of what I do is learning about the culture of the people I work with. I have friends who are Puerto Rican, and I enjoy lots of the cultural stuff—the music and food—and there is a kind of ease and softness in the Latino community that is wonderful. I'm reluctant to stereotype, and I'm not sure how to describe it, but there seems to be among the Puerto Ricans I know a quick acceptance, a "bringing in" of someone like myself who is not Puerto Rican.

I wouldn't say that my very best friends are Puerto Rican or Asian, but I have good strong feelings, and love, for people I've worked with. When we see each other, we hug; we party together. In some ways, I want to have as many multicultural relationships as possible. I've just grown and learned so much from them. We have the strongest tendencies to hang with the people with whom we share a sense of humor, a background, common touchstones. My closest friends are people like me: people who are involved in civil rights, white lawyer types. I think the reason that white people get into the fight against racism is that they recognize the importance of race and the way that it affects people's lives and how much we're all missing by not having integrated lives. New York is a wonderful city in many ways just because everyone is forced to live and grow together. If you just listen to the language, you realize that cultures come in and affect the lives of other people. If we could somehow break down some of the enclaves, it would be great.

• • •

There's a tension in the legal community between lawyers who are lawyers and lawyers who are organizers. There are lots of lawyers who see themselves primarily as organizers. To me, it's okay. It's maybe who they really are at heart: they're really organizers, and they have this legal skill. And then there are lawyers who just say, "I'm the lawyer." And then there are lawyers who say, "I don't want anyone interfering with my clients; I don't want any organizers." In a lot of lawyer groups, there are one or two people who say, "I work in the community. I'm going to all these meetings at night. I'm doing this, I'm doing that." I say, "I'm a lawyer, so I go to court."

It's not quite as stark as I make it out. But there is this way in which some lawyers find it easier to be organizers or political people and not use their legal skills. I think that there are people who should be organizers and political. But if they're lawyers, they should use their legal skills. It can't be a lawyer who uses their skills in the "I know what's right, and I'm going to take over and use you and the law to move this agenda forward" kind of lawyering; it has to be in the context of other political and social considerations and other organizing that's going on. Lawyers should use their legal skills to support organizers, but they shouldn't necessarily be organizers themselves.

There are tensions I experience between what I think is good for the case and what they see as good for organizing. You have to be able to live with that tension and work through it and have some kind of trust relationship with the organizers so that you can talk to them and challenge them and let them respond and try to find how it works together.

Sometimes I'm judged by organizer lawyers as not being political enough and not involved enough in the community. And an element of this is that I'm white. There are some lawyers who think that lawyers who aren't organizers aren't moving the struggle forward, and I'm saying that that gets complicated by the fact that you're not part of the community either.

There's no way that most lawyers give up control completely, even though they say that the client makes the calls. Whatever the context is— whether you represent IBM or Grandma Moses—the lawyers make decisions about what's going to happen in their cases. If you talk to most lawyers, the bottom line is that because they control a lot of information and are involved in a process that's alien to most people, they can make decisions by the way that they structure the discussion. But it was never thrown up at me that we were doing something that was against the interests of the community.

*Given the money you could make as an attorney, why do you continue to stay in this work?*

Well, it's a decision a lot of lawyers would like to make if you talk to them. I like my work. I like what I do. And I get paid. Even if I'm at the low end of the lawyer's scale, I'm still not a poor person in any sense. I think I'm making $55,000 this year. I made more when I was at the Puerto Rican Legal Defense and Education Fund. You know, it's not an insignificant amount of money. I'm comfortable with it.

The thing you have to know about New York is that the most important thing is to have an apartment that you can afford. I've been very lucky in finding places to live. I used to have a rent-controlled apartment, and then in the early '70s, my wife and I borrowed some money from her parents and bought what was raw space in a building that was a warehouse converted into co-op lofts. We got in before everything went crazy. What I pay for maintenance is less than what people pay for a studio. I'm just lucky. It makes me able to do this. I don't have a car—I don't want a car; my daughter goes to public school. I don't have a second home. But I have a comfortable life. I have enough money. I can go out to eat on the weekends; I can go to the theater and the movies without really thinking about it.

It means that I can do work that I want to do, that many lawyers would like to do in terms of satisfaction. I don't charge my clients, which is an incredible luxury. I can say, "I want to represent you, and you don't have to pay me." I have the luxury of taking on cases that I think are important. It's really an ideal situation if you're not interested in making lots of money but you're interested in doing good work.

And I get the satisfaction of sometimes winning cases. One I worked on at the Puerto Rican Legal Defense and Education Fund involved 4,500 apartments in a housing co-op on the Lower East Side of Manhattan. These buildings were built with money from the International Ladies' Garment Workers' Union and populated initially by the Jewish community, some of them who were in the union and some who weren't. The buildings became the center of the Jewish community on the Lower East Side. The neighborhood in the vicinity of the co-op was at least 50 percent minority, while the co-op was 97 percent white and predominantly Jewish.

This community had completely shut itself off from its neighbors. They had an agenda of maintaining the Jewish community. When Blacks and Latinos who lived in the neighborhood applied to buy one of the units, they were told that there's a twenty-year waiting list. But if you knew people there or if you had grown up there, you could get in within months or within a year of your application. So the young Jewish family or the yeshiva student could get in, but the Puerto Ricans who lived across the street in public housing or a tenement couldn't get in, even though they could afford it and wanted to stay in the neighborhood. I worked with groups on the Lower East Side who had done the organizing and filed a lawsuit. We got a settlement that opened up those buildings, at least for a short window of time. We were able to increase the percentage of Latino and Black residents from about 3 or 4 percent to close to 15–20 percent.

I also worked on six or seven cases involving civil service jobs while I was at the Puerto Rican Legal Defense and Education Fund. Civil service jobs have always been the entry point for groups, often immigrants, who are moving up economically. It's a way to get into the middle class. Blacks and Latinos were being kept out of these jobs because of discriminatory civil service exams that really didn't measure who would be a good police officer or firefighter. The history of those kinds of written tests is that Blacks and Latinos don't do well on them even though they have the skills to do the jobs. Over time, we brought a number of cases to court. We were able to increase the numbers of Blacks and Latinos in the police department. Unfortunately, we were only able to get a few more Latinos and Blacks into the fire department, which is very racially divided in New York. Still, it felt great to accomplish what we did. And it really served both the people who got those jobs and the city as well.

. . .

In the current work I'm doing, although some of it involves issues of race and discrimination, a large share of it has to do with people who are just being exploited, albeit by their own. It happens here in the Chinese community in a dramatic way. The garment factory owners are Chinese. The domestic workers are often brought in by others from their own country. So it doesn't have the same racial overtones that most of what we know about labor and exploitation often does. But what's damning about sweatshops is in part the fact that the workers don't make much money. The Department of Labor did a survey of garment factories. Abysmal results nationally: only about 35 percent of them are in full compliance with minimum-wage regulations; in Chinatown, only about 10 percent are in full compliance. Now, these are primarily unionized shops. And then there's a large cash economy on top of this: "I'll pay you cash, but if you complain, this is all going to collapse around us."

Almost as important, if not more important, is the fact that the workers spend their lives there in the factories. You're working six and seven days a week, ten and twelve hours a day—you don't have a life. Your life is being taken over by your economic need, which is not really being fulfilled by these low-wage jobs. It's terrible.

So when workers stand up to protest conditions in these sweatshops, they're not only threatened by the boss, but they're also threatened by other workers, who say, "If you complain, this factory's going to close, and if we complain enough, this garment work is going to disappear and either go overseas or to another part of the city or underground. So don't complain. It may not be ideal, but it's okay, and it's the way it works here." And so you have very few people who will complain. It gets played out in the Chinese newspapers—the papers are more aligned with the managers because they get their advertising money from them. So the papers will play up the workers as bad guys for fighting for minimum wage, that they're liars and crooks, and really attack them. When we do press conferences, nobody will let their picture be taken so that they don't get blackballed in another job.

Language is so important for economics. How many jobs can you get if you can't speak English? What I find most difficult in what we do is that Chinese is the most alien of languages for the large majority of people in this country, as opposed to Romance languages or East European languages that at least share an alphabet with us. There are very few people who can employ somebody who speaks a language that is completely different. So the Chinese workers come to the U.S. and are exploited by their own, who speak more English, and it makes it impossible for them to complain because it's a closed community. You can't find work outside the Chinese community if you only speak Chinese. So you're either going to work in the garment factories or you're going to work in the restaurant industries, but that's it. There's not a lot left. If you become a troublemaker, you're dead.

It's unlike Spanish, where the language shares the alphabet and sound system. Many New Yorkers who aren't Latinos can speak some Spanish. Not that you're not as exploited, but your mobility is much greater. If you screw up with one guy, there's another guy three blocks away who doesn't know that guy because it's not a closed community the way it is in Chinatown. So it's really an almost insurmountable task that we face in trying to break up that system.

I represent workers where we go in and win a lawsuit and we get some money. Two years later, they're doing exactly what they did two years before. The situation may even be worse. There's no option. People come and complain sometimes because that factory is closed; sometimes they're working without pay on the basis that the manager has told them, "The manufacturer has stiffed me; I can't pay you right now; I'll pay you later." The workers don't want to leave because if they do, they'll never get that money. And then the factory closes, and then they come forward. Even though they've learned about what their rights are theoretically, if they can get a job, they'll take that job, and that's it.

Recently, we were brought in to assist some workers in factories run by a Chinese woman in Lower Manhattan. During the years that she had run the factories, the workers had worked seven days a week and incredible hours: 8 A.M. to 8 P.M., sometimes through the night. She didn't pay them overtime, and when things were slow, they didn't get paid minimum wage. These were people who were strong enough individually to come forward and strong as a group because they'd been organized by the Chinese Staff and Workers' Association, a group I work with in Chinatown.

In that case, we were able to go to federal court, force her to sell some machines, and give that money to the workers in back pay. And then we sued one of the manufacturers who we believe had given money to this woman to set up and run the factories. We collected $400,000 in damages, about $20,000–30,000 for most of the workers. It was great to celebrate their victory.

Sometimes we try to negotiate a settlement, and I find negotiation in the Chinese community to be a very difficult process. The styles of negotiating are different from what I'm used to. There's often a hard positioning, and you're not sure whether it's negotiating posturing or a real position. It seems difficult to get someone to even indicate that there's room for movement. People position themselves as if there's no room. It's as if they're saying, "This is it. We can't give you more." Needless to say, things get resolved, but it's a posturing that I'm not used to or familiar with enough to fully understand all the signals. The signals that I should be able to hear are not coming through to me. I have to rely on my clients to tell me the signals and cut through the posturing.

To some extent, the fact that I'm doing it in the context of a law suit in which the lawyers are generally not Asian makes it easier because lawyers, even when you're representing clients, have a lot of similarities about how they approach things. And so you can sometimes get stuff done that wouldn't get done if the two parties were meeting head to head because the parties would never compromise.

I work with this organizing group that tries to work with different groups so that they can strengthen each other and picket with each other and go out and attack these other industries. But organizing them is so slow. It's hard to compete with the economics of exploitation because there's always other workers to take your place. If this guy wants to make minimum wage, you can find someone else willing to work for less than minimum wage. Right now in Chinatown there's great numbers of Fukinese workers from Fujian Province in China. They speak a different dialect and are sometimes looked down upon by the existing Chinese community, where Cantonese is spoken. Almost all of the Fukinese workers are smuggled in; they owe $30,000 or $40,000, and they'll take whatever they can get.

*Does it feel hopeless?*

I don't feel that way, just because I'm lucky enough to work with some strong organizers who have been at it and will continue to do it. I get energized by their positiveness. But it's real hard. It's like the debate about racism: is it hopeless or not? No one can be optimistic about it changing dramatically, but you've got to fight. It doesn't go away. What's the alternative?

# Monte Piliawsky

*Monte is a teacher and a political scientist. He grew up in New Orleans in the 1940s, taught at two historically Black colleges and three historically white colleges, and now teaches at Wayne State University in Detroit. Many of his students are teachers working on their master's degree; about half of his students are white and half are African American. Monte is fifty-seven. In addition to identifying himself as having been raised working class and Jewish, he considers himself a feminist. "Almost all of the women I've known in my life have really suffered, even though they may have achieved a great deal. Men have not taken women's minds seriously."*

*While teaching at the University of Southern Mississippi (USM) from 1970 to 1972, he wrote* Exit 13: Oppression and Racism in Academia. *In the introduction, he writes, "The University was blatantly racist, an ideology symbolically exhibited in the school's mascot, Confederate General Nathan Bedford Forrest, the founder and first Grand Wizard of the original Ku Klux Klan. Sexism pervaded the college community of USM. For example, a married professor of music was fired for having a baby, even though she did not miss a single day of work because of the pregnancy."*

*Almost all of his writing is on race and has been published in Black journals. And almost all of the organizations at which he's given speeches have been African American. In fact, he's soon going to be the first white president of one, the Southern Conference on African American Studies.*

*In preparation for the interview, Monte had pulled a couple of dozen books about the Civil Rights Movement from his shelves and laid them out on his kitchen table. He began the interview by talking about one of his favorite subjects: why some white men in the twentieth century have challenged racism and joined the Civil Rights Movement. As he talked about some of the white men he's studied, he pulled out one book or another and read passages about their lives.*

· · ·

There are at least three paths that I've identified that white men have taken on the transformative journey to becoming committed to racial justice. The first path involves coming to view racial justice as a moral imperative and supporting African Americans because it is right and just to do so. Like the abolitionist movement, the inspiration for this commitment is located either in the egalitarian idealism of the church or in secular humanism, sometimes linked with socialism or communism.

One of the leading white southern male activists in the generation before the Civil Rights Movement of the 1950s and 1960s was James Dombrowski. In 1932, he cofounded the Highlander Folk School. Later, he became the executive director of the Southern Conference Education Fund, the South's primary biracial civil rights organization. Dombrowski came to his racial views out of a religious concern for social justice. At one point in the late 1970s, he described himself as a Christian socialist and a radical.

A second path in the transformative journey is a single event akin to a religious conversion experience—one very specific, often profoundly painful event. Henry Leland Mitchell, son of a Tennessee farmer, was born in 1906 in a two-room shack. Raised in abject poverty, he went from high school almost directly into a lifetime of organizing tenant farmers. In the 1930s, he helped create the Southern Tenant Farmers' Union, a model of interracial cooperation. At the age of eleven, he traveled with his family to Dyersburg. Tennessee, to witness a lynching of an African American youth accused of making sexually suggestive remarks to a white woman. John Egerton, in his book, *Speak Now against the Day: The Generation before the Civil Rights Movement in the South,* described the impact on Mitchell this way: "He saw the flames, caught the nauseating odor of burning flesh, heard the victim's screams of suffering and the cheers of the morbidly excited throng. Sickened and terrified, he bolted out of their midst and fled. The atrocity was branded in his memory for life" (p. 155).

Will Campbell was born in a rural, poverty-stricken county in southern Mississippi, became an ordained Baptist minister, and eventually an advocate of racial equality. In his autobiography, *Brother to a Dragonfly,* Campbell describes the impact on him of a book called *Freedom Road,* by Howard Fast, which he read in 1944 while stationed in the South Pacific. The book is a historical novel about an illiterate former slave who allied poor whites and African Americans in opposition to the plantation class until the Ku Klux Klan slaughtered all of the families involved. In his autobiography, Campbell says, "I knew that my life would never be the same. I knew that the tragedy of the South would occupy the remainder of my days. It was a conversion experience comparable to none I had ever had, and I knew it would have to find expression" (p. 98).

A third path is a series of interactions with African Americans that leads white men to dedicate their lives to racial justice. For example, Moon Landrieu, the progressive mayor of New Orleans in the 1970s and then secretary of HUD in the Carter administration, recalls growing up in a racially mixed, working-class New Orleans neighborhood where his mother ran a corner grocery out of the family's house. He remembers his mother kissing and hugging the Black children. But it wasn't until he attended meetings with African American students in college, when he was having contact on an equal level, that he realized—and got angry—that they couldn't eat together because of Jim Crow. Later, in the summer of 1960, at the age of twenty-nine, Landrieu was one of only two members of the Louisiana State Legislature to vote to keep the New Orleans public schools open. All the other legislators wanted to close down the schools because of federal desegregation orders.

Finally, there was John Howard Griffin, the author of *Black like Me*. He was born in Dallas, Texas, in 1920. In 1939, as a medical student, he helped rescue Jews in occupied France. However, by his own admission, he didn't see any connection between anti-Semitism in Europe and racism in the United States. It wasn't until 1959, when Griffin darkened his skin and passed for a time as a Black man in the deep South, that he converted to becoming a champion for racial justice.

I have asked almost every white person I've met in my life who also fights racism, "How did you develop your commitment?" The most frequent single answer is that they read *Black like Me*. So I believe that individual books and certain epiphanylike experiences can have some impact. But I think it's hard for those single experiences to be life sustaining, especially as you get into your thirties and forties and all the mundane things about living start to happen.

In my mind, the single most important factor in sustaining political activism is developing an ideology. You have to see the connection between discrimination against Blacks and discrimination against working-class whites. The goal of racism, basically, is to maintain capitalist oppression. More than anything else, racism is there because people in power realize it's useful to keep working-class whites and Blacks apart. Well, many people who see racist actions are not going to see the connections between these things. Once you get caught up in the rest of your life—like making a living and having a family—it's hard to sustain your antiracist actions unless it becomes crystallized in a core philosophy.

You obviously don't have to have a left wing ideology to commit yourself to fighting racism. But I think it helps. I think it's hard to have the kind of lifetime commitment unless you see your work as part of an overall effort that has continuity among the generations and relates to changing history in a positive way.

. . .

My own development into a white man challenging racism happened gradually and in stages and was kind of subconscious. I didn't actually realize it was happening. Eventually, however, I did develop a left wing ideology.

I was born in 1944. I grew up in a white, working-class neighborhood in New Orleans. My immediate blocks were all white, but two blocks away was an all-Black neighborhood. The person who ironed for my family was Genevieve Rochelle, who was also my babysitter. Her husband, Anthony Rochelle, cut our grass. They were Creoles, light-skinned African Americans, who lived two blocks away. So I had contact and affection for people who were African American. But there were barriers. I never went to their place; they always came to my place. We called them by their first names, but they called my mom "Miss Sadye" and my dad "Mister Nat."

My father had a couple of businesses on the major Black street in New Orleans. The first was a shoe repair shop, and then later he converted it into what he called a fix-it shop. All of his customers and his employees were African American. From the time I was born, I would go down from my house in a white neighborhood to his business to see the Zulu Parade on Mardi Gras day, which none of my peers ever saw.[1] My father's Black employees were at my bar mitzvah. At the time, I didn't know what all that meant. And I didn't understand the significance of the superior-subordinate relationship that I had with African Americans. But at least it was better than not having contact.

The first key event in my life in terms of understanding racism was when the New Orleans public schools desegregated. I was a senior in high school. In the summer of 1960, the state legislature voted to close down all the public schools in New Orleans rather than allow desegregation. I wasn't going to be able to finish high school, so my parents enrolled me in a military academy, which fortunately I did not actually attend.

I remember the day of the desegregation. Four African American kids went to two white, working-class public schools. Race riots ensued in the city. It's so interesting that those white, working-class neighborhoods were picked. Wealthy white kids went to private schools, middle-class Blacks mainly went to private schools in New Orleans, and about 40 percent of the white kids went to parochial schools because they were Catholic. So who was losing out on education? Working-class whites. And which neighborhoods did they target? Working-class white. And who were the rioters?

Working-class whites. It was the first time I had some understanding of how race was used to divide whites and Blacks. I began to understand a little bit about the intersection between class and race. I didn't intellectualize it yet, but I began to gain some understanding of it.

I went to college and then on to graduate school in the 1960s. At that time, the Vietnam War was the dominant event. Through my studies, I began to see the connections between race and class in terms of who were the soldiers actually fighting the war. I understood what Dr. King said about the giant triplets of militarism, racism, and materialism.

In 1968, at the age of twenty-four, I got my first teaching job at Xavier University, a Black school in New Orleans. Then I began to see how class gets convoluted within race. The Black community in New Orleans was as stratified as the white community—along color lines. Dark-skinned Blacks were often at odds with light-skinned Creole people economically, religiously, and politically. Almost every major Black political leader was a Creole, Catholic with French names, and their kids learned French as almost a native language.

Then I went to teach at the University of Southern Mississippi in 1970. I was twenty-six when I got to the school and twenty-eight when I left. That was the radicalizing experience of my life because of what I saw and learned there. That's where I saw the barbarism of racism.

While I was there, I researched and started writing *Exit 13*. It's the story of the killing of Clyde Kennard, the first African American student who tried to get into the University of Southern Mississippi at about the same time James Meredith was trying to get into the University of Mississippi. He was framed by a conspiracy involving the governor of Mississippi, the president of the University of Southern Mississippi, and the local police, who put bootleg liquor in his car when he came to the campus to try to enroll in the school. When the police "discovered" the liquor, he was fined and released. They thought that would discourage him from trying to enroll, but it did not. So then they arranged to sell him $25 worth of stolen chicken feed. He was arrested and sentenced to seven years of hard labor at Parchment Prison for being in possession of $25 of stolen chicken feed. While in prison, he developed cancer, and they refused to treat him. He died on July 4, 1963.

When I began to write *Exit 13*, I was a little scared. I don't want to be grandiose about it, but I was slightly concerned that they would plant something in my house when I was writing this book. I was white and this was the early 1970s, so it was different than Kennard. But I was concerned. I never felt a threat on academic freedom grounds to my political ideas. I only felt the threat of what I was doing if I were challenging people in the administration, hurting their careers. They didn't really care about my left wing ideas because they had right wingers on the faculty who could counter me and other leftists.

I came back to New Orleans, and from 1974 to 1987, I taught at Dillard University, a historically Black institution. I didn't pick the school because it was Black. It was a job. Fortunately, being at that school for thirteen years allowed me to learn a lot about race and class. As one of the comparatively few white professors and the only white administrator at Dillard, I had a rare opportunity to become immersed in the African American experience.

In 1981, I was the only white of a group of twelve educators who spent six weeks in West Africa—Sierra Leone, Mali, and Senegal—developing an educational curriculum. While at Goree Island, the last holding place for millions of West African slaves transported to America, I experienced another transformative moment. I recognized that class, even more than race, divides people. I was the only white in our group. However, I was treated well not because I was the only white, but because I was part of a group who were viewed as rich Americans.

Finally, I adopted an African American daughter, Rachel, in 1989, when she was six weeks old. That meant that I continued my immersion in the African American community. It was as if I had been reinforcing, over many years, the cognitive and emotional experiences that I had begun as a youngster visiting my dad's business in the New Orleans Black community.

I guess the point is this. We often talk in this country about treating people as equals. I don't think that's the goal. I have an African American daughter. I raise her differently than if she were white. I'm more concerned about her self-esteem. The key to my becoming antiracist was understanding that the white power structure and the capitalist power structure treat Blacks and whites differently. Blacks were slaves and whites were not. As a young person, I didn't know Blacks as my social equals. There was a tremendous social distance. Contact was one thing, but it was a very awkward situation. It was a superior-subordinate relationship. That has to be understood. It's easy to treat people nice when it's half condescending and half patronizing.

I can never truly empathize with a Black person. We have to start there. We can't say we understand. It's not so. I intellectually know the racial history. I emotionally have feelings. But we have to act with the understanding that we have had different histories and divergent experiences.

• • •

The only thing I know how to do well is to teach. And the most exciting thing as a teacher is to see when a light bulb goes off in someone's head and you've made a connection; you've reached someone. The "ism" I know best is racism. Other people know other "isms" better than me, but I think I understand racism better than most white men. When I explain racism to a class and they begin to see for the first time that they have been victimized and how race is used to divide whites and Blacks for the benefit of capitalism and for their disadvantage, I feel alive. I feel that my life has had meaning. It's as simple as that. It's the one thing that I can do that no one else seems to want to do or know how to do or be willing to take the risk to do.

When I have Blacks and whites together in a class, as I have now, I have them talk with each other about meaningful things. They shed their inhibitions, and Blacks will talk about why they don't like whites, or whites will talk about why they're racist. They'll try to demystify all of these stereotypes they have about each other. And sometimes it will get heated. I encourage them.

My whole teaching approach is to try and be confrontational and sometimes even somewhat outrageous, but about something I believe. For example, I'll say to Blacks in class, "You're really making a mistake when you give your kid one of these made-up names. Shaquille O'Neal, if he didn't weigh 350 pounds, would have been beaten up with that name. White employers are the gatekeepers to your future, and so everything else being equal, they're going to hire John rather than Latonya." When I say things like that, the Black students in class say, "This guy's got courage. He's willing to take us on. And maybe he's got a point."

*Do you ever get scared that the African Americans in your classes are going to think you're a racist?*

Yeah. Yeah. All the time. I take that risk. On the first day of class, I walk in and tell them, "You're my pulpit. These are my convictions. I'm going to try and convert you. You're going to be afraid that if you don't share my left wing views, you're going to get a poor grade. Well, it isn't so. I've had right wingers in my class, and they get some of the best grades because I'm afraid that I'll give liberals the better grades. So I'll bend over backward not to grade you down if you have reactionary positions." I say all of that, and I believe it.

I think what students respect is my honesty and my convictions. They come in thinking that we're going to deal with facts. The first thing I tell them is, "There is no such thing as objectivity. It's a social construction of reality. What passes for knowledge often represents the biases of the dominant, white, European American culture. Everyone has a bias. These are my biases. You should know your own and others' biases." I tell them what

Howard Zinn says about history: that it's a selection from an infinite number of facts, reflecting the interests and values of the privileged—in other words, the victors of the wars.

In the course of a year, I now work with about one hundred teachers. Think about that as a platform for change. Each teacher in a lifetime teaches thousands of students. If I can change the values of one hundred teachers each year, that is a much greater impact than I ever would have imagined in my life. My writing is only going to be read by the people who already agree with me. It's like preaching to the converted. A pastor only has the same parishioners. The idea that I'm teaching teachers is exciting.

To some extent, I know I'm not really changing their values. On the other hand, you never know. It happens. And people come back and tell me that I made a difference in their life.

*Who is your audience? Black folks or white folks?*

That's a very good question. I've thought about that and finally dismissed it in my mind because I've never really figured it out. Most of the time I think that I have nothing to offer Blacks because they understand race a lot better than I do. And so it would be better to have an all-white audience.

It's such a complicated thing. I taught for three and a half years at Trinity College in Hartford, Connecticut. Almost all of my students were white. They were very wealthy; they had gone to the finest boarding schools in New England. They were ultraconservative. I had a class with 180 students— more than 10 percent of the college enrollment. I was very popular. They loved my passion and convictions, even though they didn't agree with me. I had no impact there at all. At least I don't think I had any impact. These students were young. Very few of them would ever talk in class. All they cared about was their image, and they didn't want to say anything that would embarrass them.

I guess I'm pretty angry at elite whites. It's my prejudice, and too much so. If I have a part of my background which is marred with an undeserved prejudice, it's about class. As a kid growing up, I felt that I was made fun of by the wealthier Jews. My father was a compulsive gambler. We weren't exactly the crème de la crème of bourgeois society. I was pretty poor. I never had the fashionable clothes that some other Jewish kids had. My parents made things for me. I wasn't let in to the fraternities. In a sense, I didn't want to be, but I wanted to be asked, and then I could have turned them down. And so I suppose I did have some resentment about that.

Today, yeah, I think that very rich people, almost by definition, are bad folks. I believe in a confiscatory tax. I think that no one has a right to inherit great wealth and certainly no more than, say, $500,000. Most people who are wealthy didn't earn it; they inherited it. That's unfair. I not only dislike the rich for being wealthy, but now I also resent them for propagating the myth that the tax changes they propose will help working-class people.

When I first got to Trinity College, I felt like an imposter. This was the second school founded in Connecticut after Yale and the eighth school in the country with a Phi Beta Kappa chapter. To be honest, I internalized their standards, and I felt inferior. It's a cruel joke. I didn't want to show my ignorance and my lack of social poise.

I developed a strategy with the faculty there. At meetings, we would sit around, and they would talk about all of this erudite stuff that they knew but which I didn't. I didn't like being there and felt uncomfortable, but it was part of my job. I would wait for my moment, for the one thing that I know something about that they didn't know. I would wait for the one thing that would be provocative and win me a lot of points. I would get it in early, make my spiel, and then say very little for the next hour. I would get my best shot in and manage to be respectable.

I also like to think that whites want to be challenged. Deep down, many of us don't think we're very good people. But we want to be better. We want some redemption. So we like someone to confront us, and maybe in this way we will find a way to work through our insecurities.

· · ·

Teaching and writing are what I have to contribute to the Movement. As a dear friend of mine says, "We all contribute a little bit to the Movement in whatever way we can." Some people are union organizers; some people are lawyers who defend people who otherwise couldn't do civil disobedience without risk. Teaching and writing are the only things I can do to contribute.

Marion Wright Edelman says, "Service is the rent we pay for living, the very meaning of life."[2] So how can I serve? It's an interesting issue. The concept of service has a noblesse oblige quality to it and sounds like a superior-subordinate relationship. I oftentimes can't quite find the right balance between serving in an intellectually superior way and serving on an equal playing field. And sometimes I serve from a subordinate position because I'm ignorant and begging for understanding from those I'm supposedly serving.

I'm Jewish, and that definitely impacts how I think about my contribution to the Movement. There are three basic factors about being Jewish in a secular sense. One is charity or tzedakah. It's a critical thing. Jews believe in serving others. The second factor is education. The Torah teaches us that we should pursue truth. We don't live very long, and our ideas will persevere after us and hopefully have an influence and improve people's lives. The only thing we have to offer is the relentless pursuit of the truth, understanding things, and writing that down as we know it.

Once you start pursuing truth, you get the third factor: you see the world as a place where there is injustice. That's true for anyone, but if you're Jewish, you're likely to come to that realization sooner, partly because Jews have been discriminated against, but also because if you look at the history of the world from a Jewish lens, you're going to see injustice. So it's a small step from that to "part of my mission in life is to combat injustice." Jews believe that they are God's "chosen people," selected not to receive but to heal the world.

There's a line in the movie *Norma Rae* where she asks a union organizer, "What does it mean to be Jewish?" And he looks at her and says, "History and tradition." That's the point. There's a sense of the continuity of generations and the meaning of injustice and suffering and therefore combating injustice. So what Judaism gives to Jews is an understanding of that. And that becomes a factor in the relationship between Blacks and Jews because Jews are going to see a similarity of their experiences. Jews develop, almost by definition, an oppositional identity, a sense of being different and being discriminated against. Almost no other white group is going to get that same sense as readily.

Being Jewish and knowing that the purpose of life is to try and help, having the knowledge I do and the forum I have of teaching and writing, what else can I do? If I did anything else but try and help people understand and then act in a more humanistic way, I'd feel guilty. In my subconscious, I think I do have some guilt for having survived the Holocaust. I've been spared. I'm alive. I didn't deserve that. And so what I do is the little bit that I can do to pay back.

# Lonnie Lusardo

*Lonnie is a management consultant and community organizer in Seattle, Washington. As a consultant in Strategic Diversity Management, he also conducts training programs on diversity. As a community organizer, he has been the president of a local gay and lesbian business organization, a cofounder of an alliance of West Coast gay and lesbian business organizations, and one of the early organizers of Hands Off Washington, a statewide coalition developed in response to an antigay political campaign. Hands Off Washington was formed in the early 1990s in anticipation of an initiative campaign organized primarily out of Oregon to repeal all gay rights laws and bar future laws. Hands Off Washington was successful at preventing the campaign from taking hold in Washington. But in its attempt to later enact a statewide gay rights law by initiative, Hands Off Washington was unsuccessful. Hands Off Washington then became inactive. It later became the Fairness Lobby, a political action committee.*

*Although much of the work he does is in the gay and lesbian community, Lonnie believes that it's very important for out gay people to work in the mainstream rather than always within the context of their own organizations. At one point, he was appointed by the mayor of Seattle to the Police Community Relations Task Force; his peers elected him chair. He grew up and spent the first thirty years of his life in Norwalk, Connecticut, and moved to Seattle in 1979. Lonnie is fifty-six.*

• • •

Seventeen or eighteen years ago, I was up for a promotion at a secretarial job I had in a government organization. The promotion would have been to a training coordinator position, and I knew I was capable and competent. I was teaching in several colleges and a university at the time, so I had the skills, experience, and lots of awareness. I knew I could do the job, and foolishly, I thought the job was mine. The job was publicly advertised—anyone could apply—and I wasn't even interviewed for the job. An African American woman got the job, and I resented that. I didn't say anything about it, but I resented it. I believed that this woman was selected because she's African American, not because of her qualifications.

I remember talking to friends about my feelings, telling them how challenged I was by this, and saying to myself, "I'm a supporter of Affirmative Action, and I'm challenged by this?" Then something really odd happened. I ended up loving her and really, really enjoying her contributions to our team. I stayed on the team as the secretary, and after about a year, I came to realize that she really was the right person for the job. That was a lot of learning for me, a lot of self-discovery. To this day, we are close friends, although I've never discussed my initial resentments with her. I probably will at some point. I haven't reached the comfort level to discuss that with her.

I have this very, very vivid image of racism when I was a young child. I don't think I could have been more than six or seven years old. I remember asking my older brother, "What does 'nigger' mean?" All I remember him saying to me was, "Don't say it around Black people." So, defiant little brat that I could be, I remember planting myself out on the sidewalk near the street, watching the cars go by. A car went by with our Black neighbors inside it, and as the car passed me, I said "nigger" as loud as I could. I did it just to find out what the word meant—I really didn't know. So the car stopped and I was in shock, but I was also defiant and I didn't want to leave. The car stayed there for what seemed like an eternity—it was probably only a couple of minutes—and then it drove off. As soon as the car got out of sight, I went running in the house and realized at that point that the word was a really bad word and probably meant something bad about Black people.

Although I was told not to use that word in public, it was used freely in the house. I didn't understand. It was very disconcerting to me. My mother was a very loving person, and I just couldn't understand how she could use that word. It just didn't add up. When I got to high school, I began to understand. Everything changed to make me see racism. What happened was this: I had a very strong attraction to one of my closest male friends, but I could never think of myself as being gay. I saw myself as somebody who would be the "nigger" in the family if they ever found out about this.

That was the bridge for me between racism and homophobia. From that, I was able to see how people in my family and in my sphere of influence treated women. The realization that it's not their fault for being prejudiced— that took me a very long time to get. I can't blame my father for being a racist. I hated him long enough to know that he was a racist, but the reality is he had no choice. Through that understanding, I was able to forgive my father.

Eventually, I came to the conclusion that it's our institutions that make us racist. If you grow up in an environment where women are treated like second-class citizens, where people of color are treated like they're less than white people, then of course you will maintain that behavior as an adult. So we don't embrace gender, sexuality, or race very lovingly or openly in a way that teaches us to value everybody evenly. We are actually acculturated to not treat everybody evenly.

An opportunity I had to understand this dynamic about racism was when the previous mayor of Seattle, Norm Rice, appointed me to what was then called the "Police Community Relations Task Force." The purpose of the task force was to assess and try to improve relations between the police department and four specific communities in Seattle: the African American community, the Asian American community, the Latino community, and the gay and lesbian community. There were fourteen of us on the task force. It was the most challenging organization I've ever been a part of, and my peers elected me chair. I think that may have had something to do with the way I can connect issues together and try to be objective and fair.

We conducted public hearings and focus groups in these four communities. We asked them, "How do you think you're treated by the Seattle Police Department?" We'd hear the same things over and over again, and people were learning from each other in the process. For example, a white man told this story about how he was jogging with a Black male friend of his when they noticed that a cop car was following them. The Black guy stops running, but the white guy keeps going. He returns and says, "What's up?" And the Black guy says, "There's a cop car over there." So the white guy says, "We're not doing anything wrong." And his friend responds, "You're not doing anything wrong, but I'm Black; you have to understand that I'll get stopped." It was a whole new level of understanding for the white guy.

In the Asian community there were stories about cops not understanding cultural dynamics. A male would almost always respond to challenges, but Asian women would feel threatened just by the presence of a cop and didn't know what to say. Latinas had stories about cops who would talk to them as if they lacked intelligence. Hearing all these stories over and over again gave me a clear sense about the presence of racism.

Is it a cop's fault if he or she is racist? Or are they a product of their environment? Consider the environment of a police department. I'm saying nothing against the police or individual police officers, but the environment they operate in, where white men are the majority, promotes a feeling of racism and sexism and homophobia.

I've tried to get other white gay people to understand this. For example,

when we started Hands Off Washington, I was adamant that the organization should support gay rights but be inclusive of other oppressed groups. I
believed at the time, and said so very strongly, that the organization would
fail without the support of communities of color. We needed their support,
and the only way we could get it would be by giving them our support. We
had not done that very well in the past. So we had to reinvent the way we
interacted with community and religious groups if we truly wanted their
support. Many of them had supported us in the past, so I said, "Let's in this
campaign create a process that is very user-friendly to people of color and
attracts them to our organization." So, for example, I pushed to make sure
that on our board we had a wide representation of women and men of color
and people from different community groups.

We started forming coalitions around the state. I remember a meeting
east of the Cascades that changed my life. There were about two hundred
people there, and we were talking about the need to get people of color
involved, and this one Black woman stood up. She said, "If you want support
from the Black community, you need to go to the places where Black people
hang out and show that you really care. One of the places you may think
about going is to a Black church. How many people in this room have ever
been to a Black church?" Not a single hand went up.

Within weeks I went to a Black church and have gone back there at least
once a year. What I discovered is that it's filled with people I know and
people I've known for a long time and truly admire. When I go there, I'm
treated like royalty. I am so loved by people who recognize this white guy is
now walking the walk. I know I can call the people from that church if I need
support.

• • •

One of the things I do when I'm leading diversity awareness training is to try
to get people to examine their own cultural identity. In a racially mixed
group of people, the ones who are most likely to not understand the question will be white people. They ask, "What do you mean by cultural identity?" Well, from my experience, a person of color will grasp it right away;
they know that their cultural identity is different than the mainstream. They
have had to adapt to the dominate U.S. culture. For those white people in the
group, we don't have to adapt; the culture is us. For those reasons, many
white people will say, "I don't have a cultural identity; I'm just white." Well
that's your cultural identity. How white are you?

I never asked to be white. My choices are to be white and act white or to
be white and not act white. Acting white is a very strange thing in dominant

U.S. culture. What is acting white? What is acting Black? What is acting Asian? Many white people fall into the trap of not consciously thinking about themselves as being white. You're in the dominant culture, and you don't even realize it. You're trapped into seeing everything through the white prism.

It's very hard sometimes for white people to conceptualize this. A person in a minority group or an oppressed group—a woman or a person who speaks English as a second language, somebody who's disabled or a sexual minority, somebody who's experienced the challenges of their minority status—will understand cultural identity. For white folks it's not a big deal; it's just like, "I do what everybody does because I am in my culture." We are so accustomed as white people to thinking what white people do is the right thing to do. We just don't question it anymore.

It happens to me, too; sometimes I don't see my cultural identity. But what I'm trying to do is be more aware of my identity. So rather than going to a church that's going to be all white people, I will go to a church that I know is going to be some other group of people. Rather than going to some function that I know is going to be attended by white people, I can go to something that is far more likely to have a wider representation of people. It's not easy, and I wouldn't call it a natural thing to do. With time, however, it becomes natural.

If you were to ask most white people to identify the cultural identity of all the people they go to for services—their doctor, dentist, veterinarian, hair dresser, dry cleaner, grocer—[it would become clear that] the vast majority of them gravitate toward providers who look and act like them. You want a good doctor? You go to one who's white and male. I don't think that way anymore. And I want to break those myths because I think they are only myths and because they're damaging to people. Sometimes I believe that I can get better service from an African American doctor. I think I can learn more. I learn to be more trusting.

I've also found myself patronizing or condescending toward people of color I'm going to for services, thinking, "I feel sorry for them because they don't get as much business as a white person would." Is it right to think that? No. Do I do it? Yeah. We're all creatures of habit. Yeah. I do that. I've also made a lot of mistakes, and I've gone to people who are really lousy providers. Are they lousy providers because of their race or gender, or is it because they're just lousy providers?

When I first moved into this house, I wanted to have a sprinkler system put in the courtyard in front of the house. I had recently met a member of the gay business association, a woman plumber, and I thought wow, that's cool, I would like to have her do this project. And I was very dissatisfied with the project. I remember thinking about this afterward: Are you dissatisfied because she did a bad job? Are you dissatisfied because you didn't give her good instructions? Are you dissatisfied because you're accustomed to men doing this kind of work? That was a hard one for me. It was a real test. I don't have the answers for it. All I know is I was dissatisfied with what she did. It takes a lot of soul searching to really figure out if it was because she's a woman or because of some other factors. To what extent was I responsible for her failure?

. . .

As a consultant, I've seen countless situations where somebody doesn't feel whole, and their effectiveness and productivity and profit at an organization are diminished as a result of this. To create the conditions where everybody feels whole represents an extraordinary shift in thinking. Many organizations have tried it, and about every one of them has failed. What gets in the way is this shit that we carry from day one in our lives that tells us we can't treat everybody evenly because there are the haves and the have-nots.

If we violate someone's sensibilities, how can we make that person whole again? How can we regain some stability in a work relationship or a personal relationship? When I apply this to organizations I work with, I ask them about the processes they have in place to address stereotypes. So, for example, if an organization truly values differences and they have a mission statement that includes how important people are and how important diversity is, then what processes are in place to do performance appraisal that rewards the managers who truly recognize and value everyone on their staff? Does everybody get a shot at being mentored by somebody they see as a hero or a heroine within the company? What are they doing to accommodate the needs of single mothers? What are they doing to accommodate the needs of someone who speaks English as a second language? What are they doing to make the work environment easier and more comfortable for a person with visible disabilities or invisible disabilities?

How do we create an environment with a sense of wholeness, where everybody feels they can be everything they want to be? If I go to work feeling great, the people around me are likely to feel at least good. I don't go around singing "We are the world"; I get pissed off at people; I'm human. But I often think, "Wouldn't it be great if everybody at an organization felt as though they owned the company, truly owned the company, and enjoyed it?" If everybody who worked at an organization truly loved their job, what would the productivity be like? What would the profit be like?

# Lee Formwalt

In 1984, while on the faculty of Albany State College (ASC), a historically black institution in Albany, Georgia, Lee got a National Endowment for the Humanities grant to write a history of the nineteenth-century African American experience in Dougherty County, Georgia. Beginning with the 1840 census, the county became majority Black, and yet the published history of the county was almost exclusively about white people. Lee set out to rewrite that history. He was motivated because of what he was learning from his African American students at ASC. In his historical methods course, he was assigning students to do original research using courthouse records, and he was finding that the stories emerging from those original sources were quite different from the published history. Lee's research on southwest Georgia resulted in articles published in scholarly journals and an essay in the New Georgia Guide, published in preparation for the 1996 Olympics in Atlanta. He continues to work on a book-length study of the history of Dougherty County. He's fifty-one.

Lee taught at ASC, now Albany State University (ASU) from 1977 to 1999 and was dean of the graduate school for his last two years there. In the 1990s, he was instrumental in the establishment of the Albany Civil Rights Museum at Old Mount Zion Church. In 1999, he moved to Bloomington, Indiana, to become the executive director of the Organization of American Historians (OAH). Three months after his arrival, he found himself embroiled in a civil rights controversy. OAH was scheduled to have its 2000 annual meeting at the Adam's Mark Hotel in St. Louis, Missouri, but the U.S. Justice Department had just sued the hotel chain for racial discrimination. Lee led the organization in its decision to move the meeting to another site.

The interview took place during the Prison and Jail Project's annual Freedom-walk, a week-long "journey for justice" where a small group of activists walk about one hundred miles through several southwest Georgia counties. On this particular day, we were in "bad" Baker County, walking through Newton, Georgia, and visiting the old Baker County jail. The jail was in use until 1994 but could have been built in the Middle Ages; it looked like a medieval torture chamber. The old jail was the backdrop for the interview.

. . .

I was born and raised in Springfield, Massachusetts, and ended up in southwest Georgia in 1977, when I was offered a temporary job at Albany State College. At first, I didn't know it was a historically Black college. I had applied to over two hundred institutions. I found that out when one of my references was asked if he thought I'd have any difficulty working with Black students. He assured them I wouldn't because I'd been at Catholic University in Washington, D.C., where there were African and African American students.

Prior to coming to Albany, I wasn't very interested in or concerned about race. I was aware that racism existed, but I didn't think it connected with me at all. I grew up in a household where there were some basic racist assumptions. Things like, "Blacks are lazy, shiftless. You certainly wouldn't want to live with them. You wouldn't want to work with them or become intimate with them. You should tolerate them; you shouldn't harm or hurt them."

I came down here not with any intent to deal with the issue of race. I just wanted to be a teacher. But after I was here for a while, I became aware of the significance of race in this community. Early on, while I was investigating the area's local history, I found out that there was no published local Black history, and yet, for most of its existence, this community was predominantly Black. The published history was a white history, done in 1924 by the local chapter of the Daughters of the American Revolution. It was four hundred pages long, with a three-page chapter at the end on "The Negro in Albany." I was trying to get material for my students to teach them how to do historical research. The idea was to give them a historical problem and send them to the courthouse, where they would use deeds and probate records, and to the library to use newspapers and U.S. census records on microfilm.

One of the things that came out very clearly in the preliminary investigation of these records was just how significant the Black population was in the history of this community. As I started digging, some white people wondered, "Why are you digging into this? Why do you want to know this stuff?" This reaction was more covert than overt, but there have been some cases where I received information from certain individuals who said that if asked, they would deny they were the source of that information.

For example, I had heard that when Martin Luther King was in jail in Albany in the 1960s, his point was to stay in jail as a statement about an oppressive system that would put someone in jail simply for protesting injustice. He was given the option of paying a fine or staying in jail. He chose the latter. Shortly thereafter, the word went out that a well-dressed Black man had come and paid his fine, and Dr. King was tossed out of jail.

One day I had the opportunity to meet and talk with B. C. Gardner, a white attorney in Albany, who told me of his role in the release of Dr. King. Gardner wanted King out of Albany because if he stayed in Albany, there was significant potential for violence. So he—not a well-dressed Black man—paid the fine. But he went on to say that if I told this to anyone, he would deny it. This was one of white Albany's secrets, and he didn't want to be known for revealing something that was supposed to be left hidden.

. . .

Moving into this community and getting settled in, my wife and I had to make certain arrangements, like getting credit at several stores and finding a doctor. People would ask us where I was employed. When my wife or I would say "Albany State," they would say, "You mean the junior college," referring to the two-year, predominantly white institution on the other side of town. They couldn't believe that a white man would be working at the Black college. So right from the time we moved here, we had a heightened sense of race in our lives because I was working at this predominantly Black institution and because, in a sense, we were "the other."

For a while, there were two kinds of developments going on inside of me. One had to do with how I thought I, as a white person, was being treated at the college. I'd started at a very low salary, and there were other whites at the institution who were unhappy with their salaries. From our perspective, there seemed to be a pattern of Black discrimination against white employees. So there was a sense of relatedness among the non-Blacks at the institution, an "us versus them" type of thing. It's the kind of thing I look back on now with some embarrassment. Basically, for us whites, there was no difference: Blacks were being discriminated against out there, and we were being discriminated against in here. I saw these two things as equal and believed that neither one was right. In fact, several white professors filed lawsuits against the college and won in federal court. And, sad to say, I think there really was some discrimination. We heard comments by administrators saying, "This is what they do to us out there, so I'm going to make sure that I hire Blacks in here."

The second development for me was a growing awareness of just how pervasive discrimination was against Blacks in the larger society. I began to better understand this when white acquaintances in Albany asked me about working on the Black college campus: "Aren't you scared? Isn't it dangerous over there in the parking lot at night?" It was weird because I recognized that I might have said the same thing a few years earlier. But I was in there, and I knew very well that it was a safe environment. It's probably one of the safest places in town. It's a college campus, for heaven's sake! But because white people have the concept of Blacks as "the other," dangerous ones who can't be trusted, they can't imagine a Black college campus being safe.

As I heard more and more of that kind of stuff, I began to have a greater sense of what African Americans experience in the larger society on a personal level. It's hard to say when the turning point came, when I really rejected any sense of being a victim myself and began to see very clearly that the real problem was the racism in the larger society. Whatever was perceived as racial discrimination against whites was nothing compared to what African Americans endured on a daily basis. I guess it was when I finally recognized that I have a choice: I can leave this campus, and whenever I do leave this campus and walk into my white society, I'm treated just fine, thank you. My African American colleagues, however, would feel fine on the campus, and whenever they left, they were going into hostile territory.

A big step for me in raising my consciousness about race was getting involved in the development of the Albany Civil Rights Museum in 1993. Working with local African Americans was difficult for me at times. Here I am, I thought, a local historian, an expert on African American history in Georgia. I'm going to help bring this museum to fruition; I'm going to help people get to know their African American history. But on several occasions, I have been challenged for my work.

For example, in 1993 I put together a program for the following February where we planned to have four major speakers from around the country come to Albany to talk about the Civil Rights Movement in south Georgia. I had put a lot of work into the planning for this. I was proud of it. Then I heard rumblings in the Black community that some folks weren't happy. "Who was this white boy doing our history? And why is he inviting people from outside to talk about the Civil Rights Movement in south Georgia? What about our people right here?" The more I thought about it, the more I came to see that they were right. I can't help being white, and I couldn't change the fact that I was excited about this history, but they were absolutely right about me ignoring the important role local sources could play in telling the story.

It was humbling for me. I was forced to admit, "I wasn't right." I was able to overcome my professional and personal pride and say, "They're right. Now what do we do about it?" That's when I got together with African Americans in the community and said we need to do some kind of follow-up series in March, April, and May where we bring local people to this forum and have them talk about their experiences. We'll video tape those, just like we videotaped the four major speakers who were coming in February. The mind-blowing thing for me was that those three sessions with the local people were much more powerful than the February talks. The major speakers, as good as they were, paled against the tales told by the local folks. There was a woman who talked about her experience as a high school student being put in a jail cell with a German shepherd. The horrible accommodations in jail, the beatings they had to endure—they were incredibly emotional tales. Their stories made the Movement come alive. February was good, but these were better.

During that February series, another important thing happened to me. One of the four major speakers from the outside was Michael Chalfen, a student from England who had written his senior thesis on the Albany Movement. He had argued that the Albany Movement had been a success. Now I had taken the position as a professional historian—along with other professional historians—that the Albany Movement had been a failure. I was doing it from the perspective that things were so bad here that even Martin Luther King comes here and he can't make a difference. He admitted failure. And so I described the movement as a failure. In saying that, I was hoping to demonstrate how oppressive racism was. But what I was doing instead was insulting local Black people. In effect, I was saying to them, "Look, you feel badly that it was a failure, but own up to it. It was a failure. It didn't achieve what it was supposed to." That was my attitude.

I had read Michael's work, and it changed my position. This white, twenty-three-year-old Englishman put the argument in a way that was convincing to me that it would be erroneous to call the movement a failure. So when I introduced him as a speaker in this series, I stated that I had been wrong in my position about the movement and that I had him to thank for my change of attitude. At that time, I wasn't yet aware of my own racism and missed the obvious irony of changing my position because of what a young white Englishman said when I had been discounting the same thing when local Black people had been telling it to me.

I had asked McCree Harris, an older Black woman, to be one of the commentators at Michael's talk. She was so happy to hear my change of opinion. After that, there was a strong bond between us. She trusted me very deeply, and I trusted her very deeply. But that trust didn't exist before that night. And, unfortunately, McCree died in July 2000.

If a person of color were to say to me now, "Lee, your behavior is racist," it wouldn't be easy for me to hear. I do think that I'm more ready to deal with that than I used to be. I think of myself as a recovering racist. When you begin to understand your own racism, then part of that understanding is realizing that you can slip back. I try to catch it as much as I can, but there will be moments when it hits you, and you say to yourself, "I can't believe I did that." I see some Black guy pull out in front of my car . . . wait a minute, I can't believe I just thought that thought. I think the person who identifies his prejudice has come much farther than the person who thinks he's cured. And so if someone called me a racist, I would hope that I would be able to reflect on that without being defensive and hostile.

. . .

When our oldest daughter was ready to go to high school, we had some decisions to make. The public high school for our district was Monroe, the city's Black high school before desegregation. Although it was racially integrated, as were the other three high schools in the area, 85–90 percent of the students at Monroe were Black. We were hearing tales from people about how terrible this would be to send our daughter to this school. We even had a white lawyer in our church offer to adopt our children so that they could go to a predominantly white school in another district.

We thought this should not be just our decision, but that our child should have a say in it too. So the oldest and youngest, both girls, went through the process of looking at one of the private schools in town. We said that the only way you can go to the private school is if you win a scholarship because we can't afford to pay the tuition. In both cases, they didn't win the scholarship, and I'm glad they didn't. I felt we had to offer that option to them, so they wouldn't resent us for making them go to a school that they were not that sure about.

At about this same time, my understanding of the extent of racism in this community was developing, and I thought it was important not to make decisions based on fear. Since Monroe is a public school, I believed that parents should have the right to participate in activities. My wife and I have always thought that parents who play an active role in school usually feel better about those schools than other parents do.

Unfortunately, our oldest daughter Jennifer's first year at Monroe was a disaster. But, ironically, it was a disaster because of the white kids she was hanging around with. In Albany, if you're white and middle class and you're zoned for Monroe, you sell your house and move or you send your children to private school. So most of the white kids who go to Monroe are those whose parents are too poor to either move or send them to private school. Jennifer started hanging with some of these kids from a different socioeconomic background with different academic goals, and she was easily swayed. We found out one day that she skipped school. Her grade average dropped that year—this was a student who had done extremely well before high school.

The next year, our son Zachary started at Monroe. Now we had to deal with our children coming home and telling us about the things that Black kids were doing to them. We had to sift through what they told us to find out what was perception and what was reality. I tended to be more skeptical and my wife tended to be more sensitive to their concerns. There was nothing really seriously bad that ever happened. We were very involved in the Parent-Teacher Association; if we had difficulty with a teacher, we talked to the teacher or the principal, and things got changed right away. We were pretty satisfied with the school.

Afterward, as the kids got older and graduated, I began to hear more about the fact that they were unhappy with my lack of sensitivity to their needs. They thought that I was more concerned with racial sensitivity than their particular concerns. That was a tough issue for me to deal with and still is today; our youngest daughter Meghan is a senior there now. When our son and other daughter are home and Meghan starts talking about these issues, they say, "Yeah, Dad, you never listened to us."

. . .

There are moments when white people I'm with who don't really know me suddenly realize that I'm the only white administrator at a historically Black college, and they ask me, "Aren't you uncomfortable?" I tell them, "No. I've been working in this African American environment for twenty-one years now, and I feel very comfortable." There has always been Black leadership at the college; I've never worked under white leadership. My immediate supervisors have always been Black women and men. This was my first job—and doesn't what you do first become the norm by which you judge everything? I'm 48, and as a professor and administrator, I've never worked for a white person.

Sometimes, my current Black boss has to remind me that I'm white. We were talking about another dean with whom I was having a real problem. He says to me, rubbing his hand on his skin, "Don't forget that this is very important," implying that it was my colleague's attitude about my white skin that was the problem. It's been a wonderful experience, and I wouldn't change it for the world, but if I had been offered another position in the first five years I was here, I would have been out of here in a second.

There are white men who are supportive of what I do, but most of them live outside this area. The group of people with whom I'm most comfortable are the historians I met last summer at the Du Bois Institute at Harvard University. We were together for five weeks, talking about the southern Civil Rights Movement. Sometimes I'm in daily communication with them.

There are also some white people in Albany who honestly value what I do when it comes to race. There are enough people so that we can make a difference. But we don't always agree on strategy. For example, there's a white male professor at Albany State who has actively promoted diversity. We've worked together on several projects. I talked to him about a white male banker in Albany who despises what I've written about racism in this region and as a result has told people not to support the Civil Rights Museum because I'm one of the key people associated with it. My colleague was willing to get the word out about what this guy is doing. He got back to me the next day, telling me that another white man—a prominent business leader—had warned him not to get the word out about this banker, strongly suggesting that he reconsider his decision. And so my colleague told me that he wouldn't say anything about the banker.

I don't know whether he was right or wrong in his decision to stay quiet. He was more cautious than I would have been. I've gotten to the point now where I don't really care what people like the banker and the business leader think about me. They already think I'm a lunatic because of my views. Why should I be sensitive about what I say in front of these conservative white individuals?

I have found, however, that having a leadership position at the museum makes me more cautious about things than I might have been otherwise because I have this responsibility now for making sure that the museum succeeds. One of the things that has been a hallmark of the museum so far has been the racial integration of the leadership, so the last thing we want to do is alienate either Black or white people by saying things that might upset them. When we're asking white people for money, I'm not sure that it's a good idea to rub racism in their faces. So as I think this through, maybe I react differently depending on the situation. Sometimes I don't care what people think, and other times I'm quite cautious.

So when it comes to being around other white people in Albany, there are some I challenge and others I avoid rather than dealing with their racism. I've been accused of being antiwhite, although I don't think I am. I don't feel like I ever went through a stage of hating my whiteness or hating white people. But I do find myself sometimes feeling very awkward and being very quiet around white people who I know don't have the same feelings I have about the issue of race. I just went out to lunch with three white men where this happened. They were talking about a situation where they might sue ASU for discrimination. I felt uncomfortable because they were unaware of their own racism.

There are some people you simply can't have a conversation with about race. They just aren't going to listen to you. There are people who are so flagrantly racist that what's the point of talking to them? I wish that wasn't the case. There may have been a stage in my liberalism when I felt that everyone could be convinced of a just cause, but I don't think that any more. As I get older and see older people in their sixties and seventies, I wonder, is it worth the energy to try and change their minds? I only have a limited amount of energy, and so is it worth the energy to try to change someone like that? Do you just cross them off the list? That's hard to do, too.

Like with my own parents. They say that they're very proud of me. And I do think they are, much more so today than even five or ten years ago. My father wasn't sure what I was going to do with a Ph.D. in history. As I moved through the ranks, publishing, and now getting to be dean—they were just so proud! It's a Black school, so not as prestigious in their minds, but still I'm a dean! And I have been open with them about racial problems that I have faced at the school. I've talked to them matter-of-factly about racism, as if they believe the way I do, knowing full well that they don't. They weren't about to challenge me or even agree, but they did listen. They've seen me changing. Every column I write in the *Albany Herald,* even the one about whiteness, I've sent to them. What they've told me is that they think the columns are great.

# Nibs Stroupe

*Nibs was born in Memphis, Tennessee, in 1946 and grew up in Helena, Arkansas, in the Mississippi River Delta. In 1974, he married the Reverend Caroline Leach. They have two children: David, a senior in high school, and Susan, a first-year student in college.*
*Nibs has been an activist for homeless people and prison reform. In the early 1970s, he helped found Opportunity House, a halfway house for men getting out of prison in Nashville, and served as its first director. In the late 1970s, he and his wife served as the first wife-husband team at St. Columbia Presbyterian Church, a small church in a housing project. After working with prisoners on death row and for prison reform as a staff member of the Southern Prison Ministry, in 1983 Nibs became co-pastor, with his wife, of Oakhurst Presbyterian Church, a multiracial church in Decatur, Georgia. With his friend and colleague, Inęz Fleming, he wrote* While We Run This Race: Confronting the Power of Racism in a Southern Church, *a chronicle of his experiences at Oakhurst. In addition to speaking out about racism from the pulpit and at church functions, Nibs has led many workshops and seminars on racism around the United States, especially in the South. He's fifty-five.*

• • •

Race has always been, and always will be, the center of my life. I won't get rid of whiteness. I will have race in my marrow until I die. It is a given. I can't envision ever getting past that.

I grew up in the white South, on the Mississippi River. I don't remember when I first thought about race, but I do remember that race was always this kind of presence. It was part of me, part of my blood. As a child, I noticed that there were dark people. I wasn't quite sure what they were. The "code" said that they were not the same species as me—that they were sort of like cats or dogs, something like that. But I wondered—they acted and looked like me. Of course they had a different colored skin, but they seemed like human beings to me.

So there was always this sense that never came to consciousness. What's going on? What's inside them? Are they like us? I believe that my mother was the first person in my life to challenge the codes. Although her folk were from Mississippi and she grew up under Jim Crow, she would never let me call Black adults by their first name or even using "uncle." I had to call them "Mr." or "Miss" or "Mrs."

The first time I remember really wondering about all of this was in 1962, when James Meredith wanted to go to the University of Mississippi in Oxford. I was a sophomore in high school. A group of us decided to go to Oxford—about sixty miles away—to defend southern white manhood against this guy who was trying to get into a white school. Fortunately, we didn't go, but that kind of fevered talk about the "niggers" really made me start to think about race. I didn't like how I got caught up in it.

The next thing that changed my consciousness was watching Dr. Martin Luther King's speech in Washington in 1963 on television. I had heard that King was a communist. I believed what the codes said—that there were these communists and northerners out there, these monsters, who were trying to destroy the South. But when I saw the sea of people on the mall—and that there were white people and Black people and all kinds of different people—I began to wonder what was going on. I wasn't ready to sign up, but I thought maybe there was a little more to the story.

And then Kennedy was assassinated. That sort of broke things open. I knew then that the world isn't this nice little place. In fact, we dedicated our high school annual to Kennedy, a president who was invading the South and was making us integrate. It really had a formative effect on me and began to break things open.

One of our teachers in high school was a Jewish woman named Vera Miller. She helped me see things differently. She had us reading [Alan Paton's] *Cry the Beloved Country.* It really shocked me. Here was a Black minister who was portrayed as a human being; that was a stunning thing for me to think about. She was the person who helped me see that there was more to life than what I had seen in a small southern town.

At the end of my sophomore year at college, I got a job up north. My friend David Billings and I had heard about a church in Brooklyn—Lafayette Avenue Presbyterian—that hired southern white guys to work in a summer program where we would be working with Black people. I contacted them, and they said we could come. I don't know if either one of us would have gone by ourselves. I mean, Helena to Brooklyn is quite a jump! It was scary and exciting to be working with Black people on a peer level. In fact, our supervisors were Black. It was that summer that really changed me.

. . .

In 1983, I was called to be the pastor at Oakhurst Presbyterian in Decatur, Georgia. About a year after that, my wife Caroline was called as the associate pastor. What intrigued me about the church was that it was already integrated. It's been my experience that one of the hardest things to do is to get white and Black folks together on some sort of consistent basis. When I became pastor here, I recognized that I had only dipped into the surface of racism. I thought I knew a lot, but I really did not.

I've been here at Oakhurst for thirteen years now. What's been a revelation to me is the way that we have encountered each other on a human level: how Black people have opened up to me and how I have opened up to them. That's been a long but hard and good journey. And it continues. I've learned the most about racism since I've been here: how racism affects me and other white folks. I had just assumed that everybody responded the same to racism, but they don't; Black people have different responses to racism. That was strong learning for me.

It's difficult at first when I get challenged for doing something racist. Inez Fleming, a member of the church and training colleague, was the first one to really call me on something. I remember a phone call; I don't remember what the issue was, but she had taken issue with something I'd done. I said, "Why are you mad about this?" And she said, "I'm not mad about this. Why do you think I'm mad?" I said, "Well, you sound angry." "No, I don't sound angry," she said, "but if you want me to sound angry, I will. I think the problem is you're not used to getting this from a Black person."

Of course, I was defensive, but I began to percolate that around and discovered that it was true. I was not used to getting that from a Black person. In these kinds of situations, I think that you ask yourself, "Is this racism? Is this white man stuff?" I think you have to keep sifting through that. A lot of white people don't ask these questions because most of us don't operate this way with Black people.

Inez has been a friend to me. She has really opened my eyes to how much race has played, and continues to play, a part in my life. I have really appreciated that. She didn't have to open up and make herself vulnerable to me, but she did. She is always pushing me and asking, "What are you really thinking? I don't want this 'preacher stuff.' "

The gift I have given Inez has been to encourage her to be honest with white people and not let us off the hook. When I've pushed her to do this, she has pushed me, saying, "That's easy for you to say. I get crap for being honest with white people and you don't." I have been at workshops where she takes no prisoners, and even though it may not be helpful at times, I think it has been good for her to be so outspoken. I think that is the gift that I gave her. If you ask her, I think she would say she was astonished that she got that from a white man.

I think that for the Black people that come to this church, what I offer them, and the other white people who engage with them, is a possibility of being ordinary human beings. That there may be a time and a space to just exhale, to just be a person and not worry about all this mess. I think that is part of what Inez gets from me—that she can put some bridges over the wide chasms. She might have to tiptoe precariously, but she can get to the other side.

One of the dangers here at Oakhurst is that since I am a white person trying to deal with racism, I'm given more credit by Black people than I probably ought to have. I think it comes out of their longing to be seen as human beings. So when somebody makes a few steps toward them, they are very open to it. I'm often told by the Black members of the church that they've learned more about their history from me than from Black folks. I have a background in history, and so, for example, I've been talking at church this week about today being the one hundredth anniversary of *Plessy vs. Ferguson*. Maybe it's true on some level that I have taught them more about their history, but for me, that's scary and dangerous. I'm very careful to let them know that it's a problem that they're learning this stuff from a white guy, that they need to go back and see how white folks have kept them from knowing this history.

White members of the church have had different reactions to what we've done here. When my wife and I arrived, it was an old church in terms of the age of its members. Most of the white people who were here when we arrived have either died or left in disgust. I think the white people who have stayed have done so because they see that the church is reviving. They like that. Most of them don't agree with my preaching about social justice. I think they would say I'm a good pastor, but in terms of how they believe the gospel is proclaimed to the world, most of them are not comfortable with my focusing on issues of social justice. They stay because their roots are in this church. I'm just too much of an activist for many of them.

I am fairly relentless on white people. Sooner or later they get upset with me on my approach to racial issues because they want Oakhurst to be a place where everything is solved, whereas I see us being on a journey toward racial justice. They wonder why I'm so hard on white people.

I believe that race is central in this country, and yet I try to get all of us here at Oakhurst to see that there is oppression in our lives and we participate in it. So in addition to racism, we emphasize women's rights here; we have a strong stance on gay and lesbian folk here. I think we were the only church that joined with the ACLU when they sued the state of Georgia to overturn the sodomy law that was being used against gay people. We've also tried to do that sort of thing on abortion rights. There have not been many churches in Georgia that would routinely join legal briefs in support of abortion.

I think our central proclamation is that we are defined by God. We've been given life and identity by God, and that includes our sexual orientation. We need to keep that in mind and not let the categories of the world tell us or dictate to us as individuals or collectively who we're going to be and what we're going to be.

We emphasize race here because of who we are and who we've been, but we also emphasize class, gender, and sexual orientation as much as we can. Usually, at some point in a sermon or during worship, we will talk about the categories of the world. We usually list those four. We try to put them together. We try not to say that race is more important than gender or sexual orientation, but historically, and in this particular community and in this country, it's central. Some of the members haven't wanted to make lesbian and gay issues or women's issues central to our mission. I don't believe that it's so much being antigay as it is our desire to stick with race.

We try to weave the various oppressions together. That doesn't mean it's always a nice weaving. We've had clashes and continue to have clashes. Some of our Black women think that the white feminist issue is a place where privileged people are dabbling their toes in oppression. We've tried to get deeper than that, but it's hard because the white women don't want to yield and the Black women don't want to yield, and here I'm a white man trying to help mediate that.

It seems to me that the major conflicts that float around here are between the white women and Black women. The Black men and the white men are not nearly in conflict as much because we are so distant from each other. White guys are not supposed to show anything anyway. As a result, we don't engage with each other, nor are we even willing to engage. I believe that the Black and white men actually have more struggles, although they're not open struggles. That's where the struggles ought to be because that's the dynamic of racism.

The most open clash we have here is between the gay white men and some of the Black folk. About a year and a half ago, we had a forum on race and gender and sexual orientation and how they intersect. We had a fiery discussion, and it really came down to white gay men feeling that their oppression as gay men was the same as Black folk. I don't know whether that's true or not, but the thing that interested me was that it really opened up a fierce and good discussion about oppression. We talked about stereotypes and the issue of choice when it comes to being gay or Black. The continuing question is who is going to feel welcome here?

When I'm in these kinds of discussions, I try to remind myself that these are real people who are hurting and want to find some liberation. Now, that's easy here because I've seen folks give time and energy to all kinds of causes. Sometimes I slip into judging other people as being wrong, but I try to catch myself. I don't want to be in the situation where people always feel like, "Here comes Nibs; we're going to hear about race." Instead, I try to remind myself that people may be misguided but are trying to understand. The scary part of this for me is that I have become responsible for other people and what they have become, and that I think, and they think, that I have some answers.

. . .

Most of my life I've felt like I'm on the fringe. Because of my father's abandonment. I have felt that I was always the worst kid on the block, and it made it easy to leave the little southern community where I grew up. My friend Ed Loring has pushed me a lot and said that my absent father has really given me a great gift in that I don't have all the trappings of a white man. I was taught how to be a man by white women, which is real different than being taught by white men.

I also learned that the way you survive is to keep on the fringes. And now I find myself in the center of things, a leader with responsibility. I am going to have to have answers; I am going to have to take responsibility for mistakes. When members of the church have come to me and wanted spiritual guidance, I've often wondered, "Why are they picking on me? They don't know what they're getting into. I don't know anything!" But of course I do know stuff. And so over the last couple of years, I have been trying to shift on that.

My relationships with white men are a way for me to try to verify who I am as a white man. I have a couple of friends like that—Ed Loring and David Billings, for example. Ed has been the one with whom I have shared the most about my journey as a man. He has been a good friend for several decades. One of my dynamics is that I don't think I am worth much. Over the years he has helped me to see that I am worth something in the categories where I want to be worth something. That's been very important to me because I tend to think that I am not worth much. Other than Ed and David and Inez Fleming, I don't have many peers that I really trust. There is a loneliness I feel, though my friendship with my wife is powerful.

One of the things I wrestle with is that I am not very good with my hands. I remember reading one of Scott Peck's books, and I remember he talked about not being able to repair something in his car. That brought up his anxieties that he wasn't a man. I understood that. It's one of the issues I have. There's a voice in myself that says, "See, you are not really very strong. You can't handle this." And so I think I will be judged by other men as less of a man.

I would like to work more with white men, but it scares the crap out of me. When I talk with or about Black people or women or gays and lesbians, I am not one of them. There's an intellectual distance that I can keep. But when I am talking about white men, I am one.

When I first began doing racism workshops, we would usually get the most resistance from the white men. I would try to go lick for lick with them, showing them how much I know and how little they know, and try to crush them. I have shifted over the last year or so, trying not to be so judgmental of the white men that we work with and trying to give them more space to deal with racism. It is hard work to do that.

• • •

My kids get uncomfortable with my work sometimes. I think their view of me is that I am really strange on the race stuff. My son attends Decatur High School and is in all of the advanced courses and doing well. In my view, he attends a private white school in the midst of an integrated public school because of the tracking system. When I call it a "private white school," he says, "Dad, don't say that." My son is in a history class where they are talking about Plessy vs. Ferguson and Brown vs. the Board of Education. Last week, the teacher quoted something from Vincent Harding, and my son mentioned in class that Vincent wrote the foreword in my book. The teacher was excited and asked David to bring her the book. When David came home that day, I'm not sure he had a sense of pride about me, but he seemed to feel like, "Oh well, maybe my father isn't so bad after all."

They get mad at me because I will acknowledge people when we pass on the sidewalk, and they ask me, "Did you know that person?" I say, "No." And they say, "Well, why did you say hi to them?" I answer, "Well, just to say that they are a human being and I am a human being." I think that is embarrassing to them because they are teenagers. But I hope I have given them a sense that this is how life really is—not what we have developed in this culture, where we are afraid of everybody.

They don't want me to get arrested. It is interesting how afraid they are of that. I've often wondered if they would be embarrassed if that happened. If they had just started that as teenagers, I would have just thought it was about their being teenagers and their father's behavior, but their fear started a long time ago. So I think it is just fear of jail and prison, and they don't want that to happen to me. So I have refused to get arrested, even though I have had many opportunities.

I believe that my children gained a lot from being in a church like this. I don't know if they associate that with me, but they are much more comfortable with Black folk than any of their friends. So I think that is a gift I have given them. I have been very involved in their lives.

At this point in his life, David wants to be a pediatrician. Susan really likes money and is an artist. Those two don't go together—being an artist and loving money—so she will have to come to some kind of decision. I don't have a need for my children to do the work that I do in life. But I do want them to see people as human beings. If they have that grounding, then whatever they do, their care for other people will well up.

. . .

We are in a culture that is very dangerous. To be a white man is to be driven by the sense that you have to earn things in order to be somebody. I think that is one of the reasons white men are so hostile now: we feel like the ground on which we earn our livelihood is being pulled out from underneath us. Although that is not true, we feel like it is. Newt Gingrich can easily exploit that because we are so insecure.[1]

I think for white people one of the main curses of being white is that we have divorced ourselves from being human. We've obviously crushed Black people, but we don't recognize how much damage we have done to ourselves. We really don't think we are a part of humanity. That is a major curse for us. We've developed a culture where we are lonely and hostile and can't be a part of community. All of our technology is driven by empowering the individual and divorcing ourselves from the rest of humanity. Our goal in life is to encapsulate ourselves and not need anybody. That is part of the legacy of being white. I want to help myself and others to see that not only is it necessary that we be dependent on one another, but that being dependent is part of our calling as human beings.

I believe that I have been called as a white person to go into my community and deal with the racial craziness there. The hardest part for me is to get over trying to beat up everybody. I think I have begun to find some creative ways to make change. Above all, I try to be a witness against racism. I'm relentless on that. I try to put it in terms of our sake, our children's sake, or grandchildren's sake—and that the racism is linked with loss in our culture. That is central for us. If we don't help people understand that, we've got some terrible times ahead. Not just in terms of what will happen to Black people and other people of color, but for ourselves as white people.

There is a line where you lose the ability to have strategy that will be effective because you are only witnessing. You go out and do political actions so that you can be a witness, but you might do a political action a different way if you thought you were going to transform or make a big difference. That is hard to know. I am at the point now where I am not sure what will make a difference. And that is dangerous because there are some strategies that might make a difference, so we need folks that are looking at those and thinking about those and developing those. They will be the central movement for change. I don't know what those are at this point.

I have had to temper the sense of what I hope, and I don't have much hope for this culture. I think we are going to collapse. What that is going to look like I don't know. I think we are going to have to go through a really rough time. I grew up in the '60s when you felt like if you marched around a few buildings, you felt like the whole society would change, which is hopelessly romantic.

I read a chilling novel, *The Parable of the Sower*, by a Black woman named Octavia Butler. It scared the crap out of me. The story is set in a time maybe 20–25 years from now. There is still a veneer of culture, but there are little fortresses around the United States where people with money—or who are servants—are living together and are armed against marauding desperadoes, some of whom are real criminals and some of whom are revolutionaries. But the clear understanding of the book is that people don't belong to one another. You only have camaraderie because you are surviving. I believe that could happen in this culture. In some communities north of Atlanta, like Lenox, you already have things that look like castles with moats. I believe that the people living there are really scared. And there is evil in the jails in places like south Georgia, where every day people die and lives are crushed, and it is considered normal. That is terrible evil.

So on that level, I don't have much hope that things will improve in our society. But my Christian faith encourages me to know that life belongs to God, that we belong to God, and that we belong to one another. As a result, I have hope in the grace and power of that. Grace and power may not transform this culture, but it will call forth some communities of faith.

I would wish for us white men to be able to hear about grace more. I think that is what keeps me going—the sense that there is a love and a power that wants us to be a human being. I feel that most of the time.

On one level, I long for a life where I don't have to deal with racism. Carol

Etzler, one of the first open lesbians I ever knew, wrote a song with the line, "Sometimes I wish my eyes had never been opened." Once I crossed that line, for me, it was not a possibility of going back. There is no possibility of ignorance. It is like saying, "I wish I was on Mars." It's nice to fantasize, but you can't do it. I think the real issue is energy: how much do I want to take on? We get a fair amount of requests to do workshops in other parts of the country. Well, I don't have a whole lot of energy for that, and there are a lot of people doing it. So we do a few but not a whole lot.

This work is a calling for me on a theological level. It is also a psychological part of who I am. The people who taught me about God were strong, racist people. But they also taught me that God is the power of love. They gave me a sense of a God who loved me and cared about me, no matter what I had done or what I would do. That keeps me going in this work now. My calling is to share that kind of love.

I was thinking the other day that I would like to do a book on individualism and the culture, and that would be sort of breaking away from antiracist work, breaking out of being a "race man" of sorts. But I'm comfortable with being a race man because white people are in so much denial about race that there is plenty of work to do all over the place. I don't find myself longing to get out of antiracist work. It is in me now. It is going to be there.

Challenging the System from the Margins

# John Cole Vodicka

*When John introduces himself to community groups in southwest Georgia, he says, "I'm with the Prison and Jail Project (PJP) in Americus." In truth, John founded the PJP, and from the perspective of many grateful citizens, he is the PJP. John has received "three or four" awards from southwest Georgia civil rights organizations, including county NAACP chapters; in 1999, he received the Georgia ACLU Bill of Rights Award. When asked about the awards, John characteristically said, "We were awarded these." At the ceremony for the ACLU award, John asked local African American women to accept the award with him.*

*In the mid 1970s, while working at a New Orleans halfway house and making visits to Angola State Prison, John founded and directed the Louisiana Coalition on Jails and Prisons, advocating for prisoners, challenging inhumane living conditions, and opposing the death penalty. In the 1980s, he was a lay chaplain at Alameda County Jail in Oakland, California, and then lived at the Catholic Worker House in West Virginia, providing hospitality to families of prisoners. With his wife Dee and three sons (Gabe, Luke, and Sam), he moved to Americus in 1993 and with his wife founded the PJP. John is fifty-three.*

*In 1996, John and members of the PJP organized the first Freedomwalk, a one-hundred-mile "journey for justice" through several southwest Georgia counties where the PJP works. Since then, the walk has become an annual event, drawing up to two hundred participants from local communities and across the United States. The goals are to call attention to the injustices in the criminal control system, the jails, and the courts, and to be in solidarity with those caught up in the system: those in jail and the families, friends, and loved ones of those in jail. It was during various Freedomwalks that we met other white men we interviewed for this book, like Lee Formwalt and Si Kahn.*

• • •

My personal experience of being in prison for a year during the Vietnam War fuels the rage I feel. That was almost thirty years ago. I don't have a vivid memory of my day-to-day experience in this little military prison, but that time keeps me going because I remember what it was like to not be free and to be abused psychologically. I think I would be even more angry or more explosive if I were not challenging racism in the so-called justice system. Frustrated, I guess, without a purpose.

In 1970, I dropped out of college and went into the navy for fear of the draft. In the navy, I was in a living situation with African Americans: we had to eat together, go to classes together, do push-ups together. I had to notice their humanness and that there isn't too much difference between us. I'd never before experienced that closeness, having grown up in Louisiana.

Through a series of events, I went AWOL for eight months and then got caught in Baton Rouge. They shipped me down to New Orleans, where I was put into the parish jail. For two weeks I slept in a dormitory built to hold twenty that had sixty people in it—almost all African American. Toward the end of those two weeks, I had made a couple of relationships with fellow prisoners.

The whole time I was there, I watched how the guards were treating these guys, how the chaplain treated me versus them. I talked to some of the guys about what they were in for. I said to myself, "I know New Orleans has white people. Why is this jail full of Black people? What is this?"

When I got sent to the navy brig, I saw the same sort of dynamic. A few more white people were included, but it was pretty much poor whites and African Americans. The African Americans were mistreated, set up by the guards, got the longer sentences, the worst discharges. We had a young Black kid commit suicide the second or third night I was there. He had been AWOL for seven days, and they locked him up. He tried to cut his wrists the first night he was there, and they caught him before he could do any damage. The guards' response was to put him in solitary confinement, where he hung himself. A couple of us wrote a bunch of letters to congresspeople and said this shouldn't have happened; no way this suicide should have happened. No way they should have put him in solitary confinement. Nobody ever wrote back. So I said to myself then that somebody has to be out there at least paying some attention to what is going on in these places.

. . .

I try to visit twenty-four jails in this part of Georgia, off and on, some only once or twice a year. When I first started going to the jails three years ago, I would be the only white person there. You visit at most of these jails through a chain-link fence. You come up from the street or the sidewalk to your side of the fence, and there is a space about ten feet wide that you holler through to the prisoners standing at another fenced boundary. On a Sunday or on a busy visiting day, there is a lot of hollering going back and forth. No privacy, no being out of the elements. If it rains, they miss their visiting, but if it is cold or hot, then you are stuck out there trying to relate to that person in the jail.

Sometimes you just see people wondering, "What is this white man doing at the fence? If he is not an attorney, he might be a minister; he might be a cop; he might be an undercover cop; he might be a private investigator. Who is this guy?" At times, everybody has just moved away from where I was standing.

All the time, we see fifteen-, sixteen-, seventeen-, eighteen-year-old African American kids, if not going to prison, then on probation for the rest of their lives almost, or certainly the rest of their most productive lives, getting fifteen, twenty, thirty years of probation. White probation officers can call them at any time and put them back in prison. If they don't report, if they don't pay their fine, if they don't have a job, if they are not where they are supposed to be, if they get picked up for something else, they go right back to prison. A Black woman told me, "It is just another form of slavery. It is just a sophisticated way of keeping us enslaved." I agree with that.

The system uses the sheriff and his employees to maintain control. There is a lot of fear connected to that title, that office in south Georgia. I think that somebody, some entity, is saying, "Well, we have to let them drink out of the same water fountain, we got to let them come to school with us, we got to let them work alongside us, we may even have to pay them a decent wage, but we can keep most of these Black men out of the job force; we can keep most of these Black men from ever threatening our jobs, or our families, or whatever we want to protect."

I don't know that any one person is responsible or that any one group of folks is responsible. I usually lay blame on the courthouse, which is symbolically a good place to point the finger. These courthouses are mostly white, and they don't even hire African Americans as assistants. You point to the courthouse and say, "This is where there is a conspiracy to keep Black folk, particularly Black men, on the plantation. This is how they do it in 1996."

• • •

Victories are few and far between, but sometimes we have a victory in the sense that something changes. A sheriff is run out of office, and for an instant, something is better for those who are in that jailhouse. Or we get a federal judge to order some improvements. We got the Justice Department down here last year, and they investigated ten jails and have ordered dramatic changes in all of them. Now we struggle to get the sheriffs to follow the Justice Department order. But those things are gratifying.

Even if those folks aren't run out of town or office, we *can* shake things up and get people asking questions. Folks *will* come to meetings and speak their minds about what has been bothering them for ten or fifteen years. That is really gratifying. It feels like we had a part in that, whether it was direct or indirect. That is a big part of what keeps me going.

When we got rid of a magistrate judge, I did a dance in my office. Here is a judge who had been there for thirty-two years. Before that he was a state trooper; before that he was a Georgia Bureau of Investigation agent. He'd physically slap little African American kids when he was a state trooper because they were on the sidewalk and wouldn't move off when he passed by. Then he became a magistrate judge for thirty-two years. We got rid of that sucker!

The heroes were not me or the others who documented his behavior. The heroes were the five or six African Americans who actually said, "Yeah, I'll sign an affidavit as to what happened to me when I went into his courtroom." Some of them, two years later, are still being harassed because they stood up to the racist judge and put their name on the affidavit saying he needed to go that we sent to the Georgia Supreme Court.

So when I see a white county judge turn his eyes down to the pavement when I walk past him, I say good. It is good for him to feel some sadness and discomfort that he and I can't relate in any way. There is also this feeling that he has got his eyes to the pavement because for too long Black people have walked past him with their eyes to the pavement. Now, he has to put his eyes to the pavement because he is ashamed, maybe of something he is doing in the courthouse. Let him pretend that it is anger toward me or that he hates my guts. But maybe we are forcing him to come to grips with a little bit of his behavior in that courthouse that he has never had to deal with before. Every time there is a court date in Sumter County, somebody from the Prison and Jail Project is sitting in that room watching. We might not be sitting with the defendant's family member, but we are sitting there and watching.

A friend of mine who used to work in Florida, Scharlotte Holdman, was once asked why she decided to spend her life fighting racism. The interviewer was looking for the Christian "This is what I am supposed to be doing" response. She said all of that, and then she said, "Ya know, sometimes it is just really, really gratifying to pop the motherfuckers." When I've been asked the same question, I've always used her answer. Part of what makes me feel good is popping those motherfuckers who are hurting people, who have had no sense of what it is like to be down to the bottom, who have always had the ability to control and manipulate and oppress.

The other thing that keeps me going is ego-related. There is sometimes press coverage that is flattering. An award came to me from the NAACP as Humanitarian of the Year. I don't go into this work expecting that to happen, but when it does, it certainly gives you a little boost. It tells you that even if people aren't coming up to you and saying thanks a lot for all that you are doing, at least there is recognition. If my work was totally unrecognized, I don't know if I could continue over the long haul.

. . .

There have been several times when I've been able to be in dialogue with other white men who disagree with what I'm doing. These conversations aren't finished, and I don't know if they will continue. A couple of white male ministers who are not on the far right of the spectrum in terms of race relationships or politics but are simply part of the status quo have simply accepted what happens to the Black community. For example, they've been to public events with the county judge as if they supported what he was doing. Partly out of my confronting them on this, the dialogue has begun. They have written back or called back and said, "Well, I am sorry that that offended you or didn't seem right. Here is why I did it, or here is what I was thinking." We discussed a little bit why I felt the way I did about somebody appearing on the same platform with this judge. I felt like they should have been out there holding a sign or something.

Those kind of things start the conversation. Sometimes I don't have the time or see it as a priority to continue the conversation. If I see them again and it seems right, the conversation may continue, or I may initiate it. An incident might occur where I feel compelled to call up so-and-so or write so-and-so a letter, or I bump into them in the grocery store and say, "Hey what did you mean about what you said or what you did?"

Occasionally, some white man will come to me and say, "What are you really all about? What are you trying to do? I agree, yeah, we are probably locking up too many people, but Black people commit all the crime in this country." That starts the dialogue. Hopefully their eyes open, and I see why they feel the way they do.

When I go to the jails and see the white jailers, I always try now to recognize their humanity. I didn't used to be able to do that at all. I worked for almost two years in Oakland, California, as a lay chaplain in the largest county jail in northern California. I was employed by a consortium of churches, not on the sheriff's payroll. I was in the jail four days a week, going from cell block to cell block.

I got to see how the keepers are dehumanized—certainly not as much as those who are the caged or the kept, but it is a totally dehumanizing existence and experience for everyone. It is an awful place to be locked up in or work at. I had guards come to me in tears and say, "Chaplain, I can't deal with this anymore. I go home and I drink and I beat my wife." Of course, some guards really seemed to relish their keys and their clubs and the pepper gas. I could see that they have chosen to be the jailer. In most county jails, the jailers are the sheriff's cronies or people who can't be employed anywhere else. They put a few signs in their yard to elect the sheriff, and then the sheriff makes them the jailer. There is a very fine line between the ones in the cage and the ones on the outside of the cage. It's who is wearing *which* uniform.

The sheriff here, Randy Howard, and I have gone head-to-head for about five years. Before the Prison and Jail Project was even an idea, I would go with some volunteers into his jail and start complaining about what we were seeing. We have sued him a couple of times and have gotten him under a federal court order. We have done everything to change his ways. He trained under Fred Chappel, a sheriff back in the '60s whom Martin Luther King called the "meanest man who ever lived." Randy Howard was his protégé and has been the sheriff for twenty years in this town. I and others have challenged him every chance we get, not just on jail issues, but on his arresting people without any search warrant and making sweeps in the housing projects. I have written editorials and been quoted in the paper about how he just doesn't understand the Constitution of the United States.

His son Randy Jr. is a deputy now. Four times a month we set up a table behind the jail where we provide refreshments to visitors. One day, I was out there, and little Randy Howard comes out with three other deputies. Now, I had never met him, but I thought I knew who he was. He comes right up into my face, and he says "I am Randy Howard Jr., and Randy Howard Sr. is my daddy."

I said, "Well, it's good to meet you." I reached out my hand, and he reluctantly shook it.

He said, "I want to know why you say so many bad things about my daddy."

I said, "Well, give me an example."

He said, "You just said something in the paper about my daddy having too much power in this county."

And I said, "Well, I said that the sheriff has too much power in this county, and your daddy happens to be the sheriff right now. We need to take some responsibility so that y'all don't have to go into our neighborhoods, busting people left and right. I need to be going to my neighbors and walking with them rather than waiting until the sheriff comes out to harass or arrest them." I wanted to be philosophical with him.

So he says, "Well, I love my daddy. My daddy used to throw the football with me when I was a little kid."

I just said, "That's wonderful. I've got an eleven-year-old kid and a seven-year-old kid and a five-year-old kid. I hope they can say the same about their father."

He turned and walked away. Those are the kinds of interactions that need to happen.

. . .

In southwest Georgia there is still very much a dividing line between African American and white, although some white people say that we all get along with one another. They "get along with one another" as long as the African Americans "know their place." There are still communities in southwest Georgia where African Americans step off the sidewalk when a white person is walking toward them. When that happens, I generally try to greet the person, acknowledge their presence. I've never said, "You don't need to step off the sidewalk." I don't know that I would because I don't know what good it would do in terms of getting to meet that individual. But at least I let them know that I acknowledge their presence.

Learning that Black people's trust of me will always be something short of 100 percent has been a long process for me. In 1975, when I was twenty-something, I started a project at Angola Prison in Louisiana. The prison held about four thousand mostly Black men. I felt like I was the "great white hope." I was the savior. The feedback that I was getting from the inside was, "We finally got someone on the outside who is going to speak for us." I look back now and say, "What an asshole I was."

In 1978, an ex-convict showed me a letter from a lawyer that basically suggested that if he gave the lawyer $10,000, he'd get a pardon. With this ex-convict's consent, I took this letter to the bar association. I said, "This is unethical, probably illegal." I pointed to another firm that we had heard was taking $10,000 from convicts' families, and the head of that law firm was on the governor's Executive Council. We got lots of publicity.

The editor of the prison news magazine—a nationally acclaimed publication that won the John F. Kennedy Award for journalism—wrote an editorial called "Vodicka: Friend or Foe?" They just raked me across the coals, saying that I had closed an avenue that some folks had for getting out. Even though it was unethical and illegal to sell and buy pardons and even if it cost $10,000, prisoners were willing to risk it. Apparently some were successful in getting the governor's signature on their pardon. That was probably the closest I've come to saying, "I can't deal with this if these folks that I'm 'saving' and walking with and working for are going to put up with this illegal stuff." I was going to take an indefinite sabbatical, but it turned out to be just six months.

I learned from this experience. In hindsight, I probably should have consulted a whole lot more folks before I went to the bar association and exposed the lawyers. All I had was this one ex-convict who had nothing to lose. I feel that that experience, among many others, told me that I can't always be trusted!

• • •

One of the most painful events in my entire life occurred at the Highlander Center in Tennessee at a Southern Coalition staff meeting back in 1980. It was a wonderful learning experience, but it was just awful.

The Southern Coalition decided in the late '70s that we needed to hire some lawyers to help death row prisoners who were going to be executed. So we set up a law project and hired a white male lawyer to direct it, a white male lawyer to be associate director, and an African American female fresh out of law school to be their assistant attorney. The associate director did not like her, and they had one conflict after another.

Before we got to Highlander for the meeting, I was asked by the director of the Southern Coalition to be on a three-person committee with another white man and a Black woman from the Southern Coalition staff to make a recommendation about what to do. The associate director of the law project had recommended that the Black woman be terminated. Well, the other white guy and I outvoted the African American woman on our committee to uphold the white associate director and fire the African American lawyer on the grounds of incompetence, inexperience, and belligerence.

As the committee spokesperson, I announced at the meeting to the forty African American and white volunteers and staff that we recommended termination. Two of my closest, closest friends on the Southern Coalition staff, Scharlotte and L.C.—one white, one African American woman— immediately exploded at me. They said, "John, how could you do this? I can't believe you are doing this! Can't you see what you are doing?" It was devastating. I was hysterical, sobbing tears, as they were berating me. They were probably trying to teach me as well, but I couldn't hear that because I was sobbing, just sobbing. Our committee's decision was rescinded by the whole staff after some very painful discussion.

This was an example of how I expected people to trust me without realizing that I could let them down or betray their trust. In this work, there are so many pits to fall into. I was learning this twenty years ago, and I am still learning this. There is something about being white, being male, and walking with African Americans while trying to gain trust, or build on it, that is full of land mines. And sometimes I don't even know that I've triggered one.

Like it or not, I am a part of the dominant power structure in this country, in this state, in this part of the state. As much as I resist that, as much as I try to challenge that, confront it, walk away from it, I am still a part of it.

. . .

I'm not feeling tired. There are times when I feel overwhelmed and times when I feel frustrated to a point where it almost immobilizes me. I don't know what the next step should be or could be, or if there should be a next step. But I don't feel tired. Very seldom have I gotten out of bed or come home at night saying, "Man, I just don't feel like I want to go back to work tomorrow." Every day there are new connections being made, relationships getting closer and stronger.

It took me until my mid-twenties to experience what my three kids have seen and heard and learned. They have made friendships with African Americans that I never had to at their ages. So my hopes and dreams are that some of the barriers that I have had to struggle with and overcome will not be quite as prevalent for them, that they will have some awareness of these issues as a result of what my wife Dee and I have been doing. Dee and I are parenting a whole lot differently than my parents were able to or wanted to or knew how to do. I hope that there is a place for my sons as white men that will make it easier for them to have friendships and relationships with people who are a different color.

# Richard Lapchick

*Richard has been called "the racial conscience of sport." For over twenty years, he was the U.S. leader of the international campaign to boycott South Africa in sport because of apartheid. He was among the two hundred guests specially invited by Nelson Mandela to his inauguration.*

*Richard is a prolific writer. His tenth book came out in September 2001 with a foreword by Muhammad Ali. Richard is also a regular columnist for* The Sports Business Journal *and* The Sporting News. *He has written more than 450 articles and given over 2,600 public speeches.*

*He brought his commitment to equality and his belief that sport can be an effective instrument of positive social change to Northeastern University in Boston, Massachusetts, where he was founder and is now Director Emeritus of the Center for the Study of Sports in Society. In August 2001, he accepted a new role at the University of Central Florida as the DeVos Eminent Scholar and Sport Business Management Program Director. In the tradition of his human rights activism, he is making sure that the curriculum will include courses with an emphasis on diversity, community service and philanthropy, social issues, and ethics. Richard is fifty-six.*

. . .

I was absolutely convinced at the age of fourteen that I would play in the National Basketball Association. There wasn't any doubt in my mind. Not because I'd shown any talent—I was tall at that point—but because I was the son of Joe Lapchick. He was the first great big man in the game, and everybody figured I was going to be 6′7″ to 6′10″. Clearly, something went awry! I wanted to stay home for the summer to work on my game, and my father wanted me to go to Germany to visit my sister. My father prevailed on me to go because of the Olympics in Rome.

After visiting my sister, we stopped in Dachau. I was never the same person after I saw what people were capable of doing to other people. And then we did go to Rome, and I saw what could happen on a sports field. The athletes in the Olympics ignored religion, race, gender, and ideology. They transcended all those things that divide people. They were just athletes. I didn't think much about that at the time, but I now think that those were moments of planting seeds that would later grow to become significant in my life. It also helped me understand some of the things that my father had done. We had talked about race at home but had never talked about race in sports at that point in my life.

My earliest memory is when I was five years old, looking outside my bedroom window in Yonkers, New York. I saw my father's image hanging from a tree, and people picketing under the tree. I also remember answering his telephone in the house for a number of years, hearing people say "nigger lover," and being real confused about why so many people didn't like him. He had brought Nat "Sweetwater" Clifton onto the New York Knicks basketball team—that's what the hanging and picketing and calls were all about.

Twenty-eight years later, in 1978, my own son, who was five years old and named after my dad, came to me one day. He asked me, "Daddy, are you a nigger lover?" I stepped back, paused for a few seconds, and asked him, "Joey, what do you think that is?" "I don't know, but some mean man just called me on the phone and told me you were one." It was as if the three generations of Lapchick boys and men had a circle drawn around them.

I was getting those phone calls because I was the national chair of the coalition that had come together to boycott South African sport. The first South African team was coming to play in the United States. The anti-apartheid movement was very small at that point and not popular at all. We had had our first demonstration the year before, protesting some South African individuals playing in the U.S. Open. Seventy-five people were there, and we thought it was a big success. But by 1978, Steve Biko had been killed, the Soweto uprising had taken place, and Americans were starting to learn more about apartheid. So it became critical for the South Africans to have a successful Davis Cup.

I went down to Nashville, Tennessee, where the Davis Cup matches were going to take place, to organize the protest, do some speaking and news conferences, and try to build up interest in it. I had also been asked by the African governments to announce that they would boycott the 1984 Los Angeles Olympics if the South African team was allowed to come. When we were announcing that boycott on Monday afternoon, all three major television networks were there. A reporter came up to me after the press conference and told me that the NLT corporation, the financial backer of the Davis Cup, had pulled out. I announced that, and everyone went crazy. I went home that night feeling that maybe for the first time in my life I had done something worthwhile.

The next day, I was back in Virginia, working late in my office at Virginia Wesleyan. I was trying to prepare an exam I was going to give to my urban politics class the next day. My office was in the school's library, which closed at 10:30 P.M. I had told the librarians as they were leaving that I was going to stay late. There was a knock on the door, and I assumed it was the campus security police, who routinely checked if they saw a light on. Instead, it was two men wearing stocking masks. They attacked me and caused liver damage, kidney damage, a hernia, and concussion. And they carved the word "nigger" on my stomach with a pair of office scissors.

Being involved in civil rights, I knew that some form of violence was a possibility. I didn't think it was likely, but I assumed it was possible. I didn't expect what followed after the attack, even though it was part of the fabric of other civil rights stories. The police leaked to the press that they thought I had self-inflicted my wounds and asked me to take a lie detector test. After consulting with major civil rights leaders, I said I wouldn't do it.

In announcing the decision not to take the lie detector test, I said that I thought I now had some understanding of what it must be like for a woman who has been raped to prove that she has been raped. I was flooded with letters and phone calls from women who had been raped, thanking me as a man for saying that. I'm sure that that planted more seeds for what eventually became the Mentors in Violence Prevention, a program working on men's violence against women at the Center for the Study of Sports in Society. When Jackson Katz, a Boston activist, came to us at the center with the idea for that project, we were definitely ready to do it.

I went back to Nashville a couple of days later and realized that nobody cared anymore whether the South African team was coming. It was, "Did Lapchick self-inflict the wounds or not?" So I flew to Washington, D.C., took a polygraph, and flew to New York City to have the New York medical examiner examine me. Before we had a chance to release the results of that, Connie Mulder, the South African minister of information, came through New York City. He held a press conference and talked about their successes, including the fact that the South African tennis team would be playing in the Davis Cup—it appeared that they would—and that Richard Lapchick's credibility had been destroyed and that that was a victory for the South African government.

That brought the U.S. Justice Department into this, to look into what was going on in the investigation of the attack on me. I found out months later that the Grand Wizard of the Virginia Klan was welcomed as a guest of state in Pretoria five weeks after the attack. Soon after Mulder's press conference, we held our own press conference at the United Nations, announcing the results of the lie detector test and the medical exam, affirming that the attack had taken place as I said it had.

On a Sunday, I went back to Virginia. Right after the attack had taken place, we had sent my son and daughter—he was five and she was three—to my wife's grandparents' house in Ft. Myers, Florida. They were now back in Virginia. We thought things were going to calm down. Later that week, on Friday, I got a kidnap threat on Joey at my office at Virginia Wesleyan. I called my wife, she couldn't find him, and I drove home. I walked through the neighborhood looking for him. This was a kid who hadn't wandered away before. So then I called the police to report that he was missing and that I had received a kidnap threat. He wasn't kidnapped, but he was missing for the worst two and a half hours of my life, before or since. We decided that night to leave Virginia. Up to that point, we were going to stay, but there was just too much risk involved. It seemed like the whole world was collapsing around us. The police didn't return my phone call to report the kidnap threat until two weeks later.

On Monday morning, the United Nations called. They knew what was going on and literally tried to rescue me out of there by offering me a position with the Special Committee against Apartheid. Of course, I took it, and we moved north. A lot of people thought that the attack and kidnap threat were a "southern thing."

When we were living in New York City, the second South African team—a rugby team—was coming to the U.S. We built a large coalition of groups that met every Thursday night at the Church Center for the United Nations across the street from the U.N. I was the chair of the group, so anyone who wanted to know where I was on Thursday nights could easily find out.

My family was away for the summer in upstate New York. They decided that they were going to come back and surprise me on this one Thursday night. What they found when they came to the apartment was that it had been broken into and nothing had been touched except my things. The only thing that had been taken was a manuscript for the book *Five Minutes to Midnight*, which I was writing about what had happened. The police told my family that they should get out of town for their own safety. We immediately got bodyguards.

I had purchased a used car from a colleague at the U.N. and parked it on the Upper West Side that night. My wife was driving on the New York State Thruway the next day when the engine seized up because someone had tampered with it. Thank God they weren't hurt. Five days later, the New

York City police—who were acting much differently than the Virginia police—found two men under the hood of another car I had bought to replace the other one.

• • •

At the time of the attack, there was a tendency in the Black community not to have white people involved in the Civil Rights Movement. I was not thrilled to go along with that, but that's the way it was. One of the ironic positive impacts of the attack is that after the attack, the level of credibility that I had as a white person went up. It gave me an entrée in the Black community that was, I think, fairly unique in this country. I frequently found myself as the only white person speaking to an all-Black audience or just being in an all-Black group. I consider that one of the blessings of my life.

I was given a great lesson after the attack and particularly after the police accusations. A lot of white people who I thought were my friends were afraid of being associated with me and disappeared from the landscape. That was one of the more painful parts of that experience, of having to adopt as a self-defense mechanism, to some degree, a cynicism about people that I never had before. That was a hard lesson for a while.

I think I've tried to shed that since then. My philosophy of dealing with people is to let them prove that they're wrong and to assume that they're good. I think that's a lot healthier way for me to go about life. I don't think a lot of people have that philosophy. I think many people tend to be cynical to start with and then let people prove they're good, as opposed to the opposite.

There are many white men I consider good friends. But I assume that there are a lot of people who are unhappy about things that I do, even though I might not hear about it. I know there are people who believe, for example, that if you're a white male in our organizations, you're going to have less opportunity for promotion, salary increases, etc. I think that's crazy, but I know that there have been white men who have felt that way—that Black people in the organization will get second chances and they won't. I happen to be a horrible firer and give way too many chances for anybody, irrespective of color. But that's a feeling out there. You can go into any organization, and white men think that acting positively on issues of race or gender is going to impact them negatively.

I do try to use my role to give a voice to people of color in my own organization. The coo [Chief Operating Officer] at the Center for the Study of Sports in Boston is a Latino male; the coo at the National Consortium for Academics and Sports here in Florida is an African American male; the two associate directors of both the center and the consortium are African American females; and we make them very public people in terms of speaking to the media, going out on speaking engagements, doing a lot of the teamwork leadership training. So where I have direct control of it, that's pretty easy to do.

We have a major national conference that we stage here every year, and we will always make sure that Latino and African American athletes and lesbian and gay athletes have some voice there as speakers on the program. We have an awards program in Boston—it's a very high-profile event—and most of the award winners have been people of color or women. We've had three lesbian award winners in the last decade or so, and we're trying to make a statement with this. It's a very high-profile audience that attends. It includes media, people from the world of sports, and the corporate community.

I continue to do this work because I've seen enough examples of positive change, from little things to big things. When I was at Northeastern, I used to get a haircut at a barbershop across the street from campus. One day, in the middle of a haircut, the barber started a conversation with someone else. He made references to "niggers," and I just got up out of the chair and walked out. I was not very pleasing to look at!

Then my family moved to a different suburb of Boston. Soon after we moved, I went into the local barber shop. The owner was talking to a customer, and as a Black person was walking by, the customer asked the owner if Black people ever came in for a haircut. He answered, "I wouldn't know how to cut their hair, and I'm happy that they don't come in." I decided to handle it differently than I had the other time. I didn't say anything then, but I befriended the guy, just by coming back and having conversations about things like golf—he was a passionate golfer. Then I brought him a copy of *Five Minutes to Midnight*. At first, he thought it was about horse racing. And then he read it. It happened that one of our neighbors worked in the barber shop cutting hair on Saturdays. He told me, "Joe was really shocked by the book. He had no idea that you were involved in that."

When I came to the shop a couple of weeks later to get a haircut, a Black guy came in the store and asked the owner, "Can I use your bathroom?" You know, most store owners don't like anybody coming in and asking if they can use the bathroom. But Joe said, "Yes" and showed him where the bathroom was. He came out and then asked, "Do you have any towels I can use?" And Joe said, "Yes." I was waiting for him to lose his patience. And then the guy asked Joe, "Can you give me a quarter so that I can use your pay phone?" Joe gave him the quarter. He left, and Joe then said to me, "Before I met you, that would have never happened in my shop."

And then there are examples of big changes. I was on the steps of the

Union Building in Pretoria, South Africa, when Nelson Mandela was inaugurated. That showed me that anything is possible.

*Do you see yourself as a role model?*

I know a lot of people think I am.

*And you?*

That's funny. No one has ever asked me that question. And I talk about role models all the time. Yes, I think I am a role model.

For a long period of time, I stopped talking publicly about the attack and its aftermath in my personal life. Arthur Ashe and I did a lot of speaking dates together. In his last year alive, he told me, "You've really got to tell that story so people understand why you do the things you do, especially since the center is becoming very successful." I know that he was right. I could see the impact on the audience. They never thought that they could have a role in antiracist work but began to see that as a possibility.

I'll always remember one speech I gave in Tampa, Florida. There were about eight hundred people in the audience, a combination of college students and retired people. I was up on a raised podium, and sitting right in front of me in the audience were three young white men. While I was talking about the attack, I could see them writing something, but I couldn't make out what it was, and I wasn't really paying that much attention. Then the three of them simultaneously turned their notepads around, and they said, "KKK." I'm a pretty calm speaker, so I just kept on going.

After it was over—sometimes people will come up and say something—I saw this one older man hanging back. He was crying. After everyone else left, he approached me and told me, "I'm from a town in Pennsylvania. When I was growing up, if I had been around you, I would have been one of the people who would have attacked you. But I want you to know that after hearing you tonight, if I was around, I would have defended you." It is never too late for people to change.

# Chris Shuey

*Chris is an environmental health specialist on the staff of the Southwest Research and Information Center (SRIC), a not-for-profit public education center and public interest group. SRIC provides technical assistance, largely about natural resources and public health issues. It does policy research and analysis and targeted advocacy. Much of the work is at the request of Native people, especially the Navajo. SRIC has a policy that the staff and board of the organization should reflect the diversity of New Mexico and the Southwest, and they do.*

*When SRIC started in the 1970s, it was doing what is now called environmental justice work. The people that formed the organization were Naderesque folks from Washington, D.C., who believed that in a democracy, information is power. They had gotten some requests from Navajos living in the Four Corners region of the Navajo nation, near a coal-burning power plant, for information on what coal was doing to their health.*

*Chris is forty-six. He was born and raised in Ohio but has lived in Arizona and New Mexico for the last twenty-seven years. The interview took place at the SRIC offices in Albuquerque, New Mexico.*

. . .

When I was twenty years old, in 1975, I was working at the newspaper in Scottsdale, Arizona, and going to school at Arizona State. There was this thing called the Central Arizona Project, a series of big, concrete viaducts designed to move Colorado River water uphill across the Sonoran Desert and store it in a place called Orme Dam. The project was designed to provide both water and flood control for Phoenix. The proposed site for the Orme Dam was on Native land: part of the Salt River Pima-Maricopa and the Fort McDowell Yavapai-Apache reservations.

Anthropologists and tribal elders estimate that there were at one time millions of Apaches living in the Sonoran Desert. But they now number about 350 people on a reservation of just 25,000 acres at Fort McDowell. The Orme Dam would put 17,000 acres of the reservation under water most of the time, but when it was drained to provide water for Phoenix, the Fort McDowell people would be left with a mudflat. In the media, there was all this attention to the needs of the big, huge Phoenix metropolitan area of several million people. All you ever heard was, "We need downstream flood control." Of course, people wanted flood control because they had built homes and businesses in the flood plain.

When I began working on this story for the newspaper, it brought back memories of growing up in Ohio. My dad had a farm of about six hundred acres; there was a river called Buck Creek that formed the eastern boundary of our land. Buck Creek flooded every now and then. In the 1950s, it flooded out a portion of the downtown area that included a business employing a lot of people. Because of the impact on the town, the Army Corps of Engineers was brought in. They designed a flood control plan that included a dam.

They came out to the local farmers and said, "We need to take your land so we can build this dam." But for my dad and the other farmers, this was the best land they had; it was river bottom soil and consistently produced the highest yields. Even though this was a very conservative, Republican, Protestant work-ethic community, they were conservationists. They were land-based people, really connected to the land. They fought the Corps of Engineers plan and lost. The land was condemned, and the government gave them the agricultural value of the land. Although my dad wasn't the best of businessmen, that was really his undoing as a farmer.

I remember listening to a conversation my father had during this time with the congressman from that area, Clarence J. Brown Jr. He was trying to convince my father to take what the government was offering because it really was a good plan and was going to help everybody. Some of the people who worked with my dad had gone to Vietnam and come back maimed. I was just a young kid—I didn't really know what was going on—but I had this sense that there was something wrong with what the government was doing, with how it was interfering with my family.

And so a decade later as a young adult, I felt that it was important as a reporter to describe what these people at Fort McDowell were experiencing. Here again was government saying, "This is good for you." In the back of my mind, I was saying, "Well, it wasn't good for the white people back in Ohio, so how could it be good for the Indians out here in Arizona?"

There was a big internal tribal debate over this. I went up to the tribal headquarters and was met at the little dirt road going into the tribal office by a Bureau of Indian Affairs [BIA] police officer, himself an Indian. He said to me, "You can't come in." I responded, "What do you mean, I can't come in? I'm a reporter! I'm here to cover what the debate is all about." He told me again, "You cannot come in. You are an outsider. We don't observe what you think is legal. You're now on the reservation; you have to abide by our laws and our ways of doing things." I put up a fuss about this, and they brought out a couple of other BIA police officers and a tribal official. The official tried to patiently explain to me that there were things they had to decide without the outside world observing and that I didn't understand this.

I was pissed. But I had to write a story abut it, and so the next morning I came into the newspaper office and tried to explain what had happened to the managing editor. A few days later, I got a telephone call from the same tribal officer who had tried to explain the situation to me at the reservation. He identifies himself as Hiawatha Hood, and it turns out that he's the chairman of the tribe; he hadn't told me this when I was trying to push my way into the meeting. He tells me that he wants to explain to me what they're thinking about the proposed dam and would like me to come out to the reservation to talk.

I went out, and that led to a whole series of conversations I had with him. He explained to me that the debate they were having was about whether or not they were going to accept the government's offer of $75,000 per tribal member as compensation for the dam. They had to discuss many things about the land that would be flooded, including ceremonial issues involving herb gathering and burials—in other words, they had to debate the tradeoffs between money and their connection to the land.

This was the first time I had heard of the term "Mother Earth." I had heard of "Mother Nature" but never this notion that the people were a part of the earth, that they came from the earth and went back to the earth. It kind of made some sense, but I was also just trying to be a dutiful reporter. I believed that the major metropolitan newspapers were giving short shrift to the Indian side of the story. So it really wasn't politics that was initially driving the story for me; I just wanted to report the other side.

But that started an educational process for me and began to help me understand why there wasn't an automatic trust between Indian people and white people. Over and over again I have had to learn about this. It's taken me years and years of work, with all kinds of people of color and communities, for me to understand the distrust that people of color carry today, and will always carry, because of their dealings with the white dominant culture over the last five hundred years.

. . .

I joined SRIC in 1981. People at SRIC were doing research about the impact of mining and finding an epidemic of lung cancer among a group of Navajos.

Most people didn't know—and still don't know—about the history of Navajos who worked in underground mines digging uranium for use in weapons in the defense industry. Many Navajo people went to work in the uranium mines in the 1940s because they needed jobs and wanted to defend our country. They paid the price. By the 1950s and '60s, people were dying. We now know that the excess risk of lung cancer among the Navajos is 3–5 times higher than "normal," and most lung cancer among Navajos is attributable to uranium mining.

I made a lot of trips to the Four Corners area in the late 1970s and early 1980s. I stayed in people's hogans. The women who had lost their husbands to lung cancer were faced with tremendous obstacles. They often cared for large families of children and did all the work that was expected of women in a Native society. That level of work wasn't much different from what was expected of my mom in the farming culture where I grew up. But on top of that, the Native women had to do all the things the men did, like hauling water and chopping wood.

I couldn't understand this thing about hauling water. I thought, even if they aren't on the town's public water system, don't they have wells? In Ohio, where I grew up, you had a couple of wells on the family farm, and that supplied your water. In the Navajo Nation, there were community windmills where the people went to get water. The windmills were miles and miles away from where people lived. They used old oil barrels or lard buckets to haul their water. They didn't have running water in the homes; they had a bucket with a ladle.

At the time, I thought I had it rough. I wasn't making much money as a journalist; I had an old Volkswagen; I didn't have air conditioning in my house—in Phoenix, I thought that that was a real test of your endurance. But after spending time among the Navajo, I had the impression that I've got it made compared to some of the folks up there. When you overlay the impact of uranium mining on pretty abject poverty, it's devastating to people's health. I was blown away by all of the things that I live with and take for granted. It dawned on me that even in low- and moderate-income rural white communities, there is some level of privilege.

. . .

For so many white people, including myself, it was not difficult to pull up roots from where I was raised and move west. As a middle-aged guy looking back on my life, I often wonder if it was a good decision to leave Ohio as a young man. There were a lot of good reasons why I left, and I certainly have a much better relationship with my family since I moved here. Whether it was good or not, it's the choice I made and have lived with. But sometimes I feel like maybe there's part of my life that's now missing because I'm not connected to the land where I was raised.

Over and over again, in Native cultures, you hear, "We were born here, and we stay here; we're not like you white people. We're connected; our umbilical cords are buried here. We don't leave." This is a common theme in much of the opposition to a proposed uranium mine in Navajo country in northwestern New Mexico, an issue we're working on right now here at SRIC. The mining company injects chemicals into the ground to leach out the uranium. The uranium is indigenous to the rocks that are the only source of high-quality drinking water in the area. And so the Navajos say, "If you pollute our water, which is our life blood, the basis for our life, you essentially kill us—not necessarily in the ways you know, like cancer, but you kill us spiritually because we have nowhere else to go. If we have to go, then we leave behind our connection to the place we came from. You white people may find that comfortable, but we don't."

One of the frameworks we have as Europeans is a rigid system of laws. As a result, we white people couch things in legalistic and scientific terms. That's how we fight things like the proposed uranium mine, dealing with things like the scientific aspects of how groundwater flows and how the particles of uranium get from point A to point B. The Native people couch these things in spiritual terms. Unfortunately, we don't get to do battle on those grounds. We only have the opportunity to battle the uranium mine in the Western framework.

The Navajos who are opposed to the mining refer to their teachings as the principal basis of their opposition. For example, in their stories, there are references to substances that you leave in the earth. You don't let the air mix with these substances, and if you do, it will bring harm. The proof of what happens if you violate those teachings is manifest in the people who have died of cancer and respiratory disease. There are a substantial number of Navajo for whom uranium means death.

People in Native communities around the world—Navajos, Native people in Canada, aboriginal people in Australia and Namibia—are still locked in this horrible debate about what to do now about uranium mining. Wherever there's uranium where land-based indigenous people live, it seems to have brought out the worst of conflicts at the local level. Here in the Southwest, opposition to mining is a broad-based community effort. But, to promote the mining of uranium, the mining company has hired some local Navajos who are family members of the opposition leadership. And there is a group of Navajos who have leased their lands for uranium mining as a way to make money; it's one of the few options they have for making money. The impact, of course, has been a split in the Navajo community.

There are some things that you don't talk about in Navajo communities—it's bad medicine to do so. You don't talk about death. And you don't talk about how families are split. You don't talk about the hurt that goes on. And when you hear it—when they finally enunciate it—it's only because they trust the people around them, or they're so burdened by it emotionally that it starts to come out. It's tremendously debilitating to the folks out there. There are some who believe that their physical ailments are directly related to the disharmony that has beset them over this issue. There are people who have even withdrawn from dealing with the issue because of how they feel that their mental, physical, and spiritual balance has been disrupted.

There have been ceremonies designed to correct this imbalance. I've been asked to take part in some of these. That doesn't make me Indian. I treat it no differently than a close friend who is Jewish asking me to come to the temple with him and his family, or being invited to a different church. I do it because there is some sign of trust and respect that people are asking me to attend.

But in this case, it's even more important for me to attend. I believe that I'm being invited to participate because they are concerned for *my* health and well-being. They do not want the same bad medicine to befall those of us who are working with them. They feel that these ceremonies—the medicine they have to correct this disharmony—should also be directed to those who are close to them.

I am constantly reminded what a privilege it is to be trusted and respected enough so that I am asked to attend these ceremonies to protect me. There are some things about being white that bestow privilege on you in our society—that's absolutely clear to me. But so few white people are privileged to be taken in and trusted in this way. So it makes me feel good. I come out of those events feeling energized, feeling just good. I don't know how else to say it. Does that mean that I take up Navajo spirituality? No, it's not me. I have reacted negatively to white people who go around boasting about their Indian connections. I don't think that that's necessary. It seems self-serving.

Although I admire many things in Native culture—I've had the privilege to observe and even participate in traditional practices, and I have had much more exposure to their value system than the vast majority of white people—I'm not Indian. I'm of European descent. My mother's ancestors came from Ireland and England. My father's side of the family were persecuted French Huguenots from France; they didn't want to have their heads chopped off or become Roman Catholics, so they boarded ships and went to the New World. Some of them became missionaries and went to Africa. Some became Quakers; others became Methodists. That's my background.

I've never thought I needed to live in a tepee—that's a Plains Indian thing anyway; it's not Navajo. I don't want to have a hogan. I've read a lot of the oral histories that have been written down. I've learned some of the language. I try to understand what people say. But that's kind of academic, in order to be able to do the job I do a little better and understand a little more clearly what my role is.

When I'm meeting with people on the reservation, I'm mostly using English. They get a kick out of it when I introduce myself at meetings in Navajo. I botch up all sort of words, and I understand maybe 10 percent of what people say. It's a very difficult language to pick up. I get a little bit of respect for making the effort. That's not my motivation; my motivation is simply to be able to understand a little bit more.

. . .

Given different circumstances, I could have been a damn mining engineer who thinks that there's nothing wrong with taking uranium out of the ground for fuel to put in reactors to generate electricity. The guys who do this feel that they are tremendous contributors to society, even believing in some cases that they are doing God's work. My work with SRIC and all the contact with Native people have to some extent given me a different theoretical, conceptual, and philosophical basis for what I do.

It has also helped me appreciate the context in which I grew up. I developed a real negative attitude about that context because we worked so damn hard as kids. I was the oldest of five sons in the family. We were expected to work on the farm, and I was a big kid. We played all the sports and stuff, but we were expected to work. Now, my wife and I have these issues of what we do with our kids in the summertime, when there's no school. When you grew up on a farm in Ohio, your summer was planned. There was no question about what you were going to do. As a result of living here and being with the Navajo, I've been able to understand and appreciate what it means to be a land-based people.

# Terry Kupers

*Terry wears many hats. He is an activist, a psychiatrist, a writer, a husband, and a parent who has tried to raise politically conscious children. As an activist, he works with at least three California-based prison activist groups: Critical Resistance (CR), Stop Prisoner Rape, and California Prison Focus. Critical Resistance does political consciousness-raising and organizing on prison issues and aims to "get beyond the prison-industrial complex." Stop Prisoner Rape aims to do just that and to end the misogyny that prevails in men's and women's prisons. California Prison Focus struggles to uphold the human and constitutional rights of prisoners, especially prisoners housed in California's supermaximum control units, women prisoners, and prisoners suffering from HIV and hepatitis C. Since the criminal justice system discriminates against people of color at every turn, struggling to overcome racism is a central part of prison activism.*

*As a clinician, Terry struggles to make quality mental health treatment available to all, especially in low-income communities where shortfalls in public mental health budgets mean inadequate services. Two of his areas of expertise as a forensic psychiatrist are the psychosis-inducing effects of long-term solitary confinement in supermaximum security prisons and the dreadful consequences of rape and sexual harassment "inside." He serves as an expert witness and travels frequently around the United States to testify on behalf of prisoners. Terry has recently written* Prison Madness: The Mental Health Crisis behind Bars and What We Must Do about It *and has co-edited* Prison Masculinities *with Don Sabo and Willie London. He has also written books about public mental health, psychoanalytic psychotherapy, and men's issues.*

*Terry is fifty-eight and lives in Oakland, California. He is married to Arlene Shmaeff and has three grown sons. "Arlene and I grew up in pretty white environments. We made the decision to raise our kids in a multiracial environment. As a result, my sons now live in a very racially diverse world. Their friends come from all cultures. There is an ease and a comfort among them and their friends that was not true for me when I was their age, and even after years of struggle, and in spite of a lot of antiracist consciousness, I am not as comfortable as my sons are in diverse settings."*

• • •

Racism is the central issue in the prison movement today. After all, it's no longer acceptable, after the Civil Rights Movement, for whites to openly express racist sentiments. So who do they make poster boys for the "law and order" sensibility? Young Black males. They don't have to proclaim their bigotry; all they have to do is mention crime, and the public's fears are subliminally directed at young men of color. Then, in the criminal justice system—even in areas like drug crimes, where whites are equally represented among offenders—people of color are much more likely than whites to be arrested, to be prosecuted, to be convicted, and to be given a long sentence. And in prison, people of color are much more likely to be sent to punitive segregation and then to a supermax. You can't address what stinks in the criminal justice system without exposing the racism that pervades it.

I learned in the Civil Rights Movement to support leadership from people of color. Since the prisons are disproportionately filled with people of color, it certainly made sense to make ex-prisoners and people of color the major spokespeople for Critical Resistance. So when we were planning a major CR conference in Berkeley in 1998, of course that meant that I would not be a major spokesperson. I felt fine putting in long hours organizing the conference and leaving the major speaking gigs to others. I understood why it was important, politically to have Black and Latino and Native leadership. If you're white and really believe in developing a counterleadership, then you're going to find yourself in exactly the position I found myself. In such a context, I don't think it's time for a white man to tell everyone how to do it. And at other times I step forward and lead and get recognition.

Of course, I think secretly I'd like to be famous. I'd secretly like to be the one they call on to comment when major events occur—a pundit, so to speak. But as it's turned out, I'm not going to be the one they invite to share my views much of the time. I'm coming to terms with that as a loss, not because I don't want to be more prominent. I'm realizing that this is okay. I'm doing some good. The movement is growing. Personally, I've gotten many good things for my efforts. I'm getting respect and recognition. I've come to terms with it in the sense of letting go of it and mourning, not necessarily in terms of having achieved all I originally wanted to achieve. But sometimes I have to remind myself it's not about me.

I was just told that my current book about prison hasn't sold enough to justify paperback. Now all of my books have been very mediocre in terms of commercial success, and all of them have gotten the boobie prize: they've had "critical success." I get good reviews, the book has an impact—I get invited to talk about it—but the book isn't a blockbuster. In the past, it's been partly because I'm a little ambivalent about being "out there," and so I haven't gone to an agent, and I haven't gone to big publishers. So the book just sort of sits there. For this one I went all out. I said "Yes" to every radio show—I was on sixty or more shows—I traveled a bunch, and still it didn't sell a huge number of copies. The prison topic is just not a big seller.

I grew up in a family of six. My m.o. was to not take up more than one-sixth of the space, whatever it was—whether it was helpings of food at dinner or time in a conversation. I still use that formula. That creates an ambivalence about being out there. I both want to and won't let myself. I think that's why I miss some things. The timing's off or something, and I don't quite reach for the microphone. So when I became aware, on a political level, that there are times I just shouldn't be out in front, it all kind of came together.

There's a whole psychology here—and a politics. I'm sad that I've lived my life without putting myself out there as much as I might. My m.o. about taking no more than one-sixth of the space causes me to be slightly flat in various social situations. Of course, this dovetails nicely with my upbringing as a man—to not be too expressive, etc.—and all of this is sad for me. I've figured out the cause for that sadness by struggling with the women in my life. And the feminist struggle to make the personal political and vice versa has hugely increased my insight into all this.

Like many others of my generation, I learned about feminism at home. There were the large political issues—struggling for equal employment and an equal share of leadership for women, "take back the night," an end to domestic violence, etc. And then there were the multitude of tiny personal lessons men learn from women and eventually the ways we learn to be different without being oppressive. For example, my wife Arlene injects her emotions into her relationships. And therefore she sometimes has disputes with her friends. I also mix it up with her. I've learned how to do that. At first I thought hers was the politically correct way to be intimate, and I was doing things all wrong. But eventually I decided I don't want that kind of heat in my other relationships. I've observed her doing it with her friends, I get it, I admire her capacity to be so deeply intimate, but I don't think I want to spend the amount of emotional time she does. She spends an awful lot of time talking on the phone with friends. I don't. First of all, I hate talking on the phone, and second, I'm busy doing one thing or the other. I recognize that she just lives her life differently. So I learn from her, and I respect what she's doing, and then I've made some choices not to do it the way she does.

Because when I do that—for example, when I put out all that I'm feeling, especially negative feelings toward someone, before I understand the situation—I get into trouble. Now she knows how to get out of that trouble because she's been doing that all her life. But I don't know how to do that.

*Is your ambivalence about "being out there" also connected to being a Jew?*

I've not examined that very much. A friend accused me of being an assimilationist. It shocked me. An assimilationist? That's interesting. I don't even think about it enough to be an assimilationist. I'm definitely assimilated. I'm from the West Coast. You know, in my parents' generation (my father came to the U.S. from Russia when he was eight), the migration of Jews was to the West, where you'd be just like everybody else. I don't look particularly Jewish. I haven't struggled with the issue of being Jewish as much as I've struggled with the issues of race, class, and gender.

My friend Michael Lerner accuses me of having internalized anti-Semitism.[1] I think there's something there because I won't make Jewish statements. He will hear the anti-Semitism in any conversation and will point it out. He says I don't hear it and therefore won't make an issue of it. It's true. I'm not as aware of living in the world as a Jew, and my cultural background is pretty invisible to me. I'm working on that. Jewish Renewal—a movement within American Judaism that is politically progressive and spiritually innovative—offers me a chance to integrate religion and politics.

I've been struggling with a lot of Jewish people about this recently. I don't think being a Jew has been a major issue for me. Well, of course it has been on some level, but I don't focus on subtle anti-Semitism that's going on. In general, around Jewish issues here in the Bay Area, I'm not the first one to stand up and say, "I'm a Jew, and that's anti-Semitic." I don't see it as fast as others. Once I see it, I'll take a stand on it, but it's not where my head's at. I think that's my assimilation. So back to your question: I think, yes, I am ambivalent. I think it's a Jewish phenomenon.

. . .

I went to Stanford University as an undergrad, where I took literature courses from Robert McAffee Brown. He was my favorite professor and a mentor. He helped start the voter drives in the South. In his courses, he would have you read novels, and they'd be leftish novels. I didn't realize this until years later. Brown wasn't a communist; he was a theologian, an advocate of liberation theology. He really raised my social consciousness.

Then I went to medical school and put it on the back burner because I had to study. But I had a need to renew this interest that Brown had sparked, and so I got involved with the [United] Farm Workers, where I met a lot of radical activists. We were helping organize the union and taking part in demonstrations. I spent a summer tutoring migrant kids near Bakersfield, California, in the early 1960s. I was twenty or twenty-one, the same age as the other civil rights activists, but they were sophomores and juniors in college, and I was in the first year of medical school.

The next summer, I did civil rights work in the South. Black civil rights leaders were saying that whites were being paternalistic. I read about "the Moses Syndrome." I looked at that and realized that that was sort of how I felt. I was going to the South to lead Black people to freedom. There was this tremendous chauvinism. And so Black people were saying, "You know, we're not saying we don't want you. We're just saying that we want you to go organize white folks. We need you to do that, and you need to listen to us." I thought that was perfectly reasonable. They were also saying, "You don't get it because of your situation in society."

When I got back to Los Angeles, my radical friends took me aside and explained to me Marxism and the "National Question." They gave me the theoretical reasons why there needed to be Black leadership. They told me, "A lot of Jews are going to leave the Movement because Black leaders have taken a staunchly pro-Arafat position." I wasn't particularly anti-Arafat—I thought he was a fine revolutionary, even though I was Jewish. When Theodore Bikel left the Civil Rights Movement and took a lot of Jews with him, I thought, "Wait a minute. First of all, that's not even relevant, but second of all, it's just an excuse to leave."

When the bombing of Cambodia started in the early 1970s, things began to heat up in the United States. I was going to two meetings a night. I was in touch with really thoughtful Marxist organizers in Los Angeles. They were the heart of the Movement. They were the finest organizers around. One of them, a Black man named Franklin Alexander, started SNCC in L.A. and led the L.A. contingent to the South. He was a lifetime communist, from generations of Black communist leaders. There was also Dorothy Healey, a prominent communist leader. She understood what was happening at a very profound level and taught me a lot. I read Herbert Marcuse's *Reason and Revolution* and other books. I tried to figure out how to apply theory in day-to-day struggles. I wasn't alone. I met some wonderful people, many of whom are still my friends and still activists. We organized events, we demonstrated, and we studied theory.

All through this time I had good coaching. I knew that other activists knew more than me. I knew science and medicine. I didn't know politics. I was a novice. So I listened.

. . .

There are psychological as well as political roots to my choices as an activist. For example, my oldest brother—he's four years older; we were never very close, but I looked up to him. He was into hot rods, drinking in high school, and cutting classes. He was sort of a hood. And now I'm dealing with hoods—in prison. There's got to be some kind of a connection. These guys remind me of my brother, who is totally respectable today, by the way. And even though I'm pretty "straight" by their standards, I seem to be able to relate to prisoners pretty easily, even across class and racial lines.

*You're both a therapist and an activist. What's the importance of doing some personal-level work alongside doing activism?*

I've spent my whole life on that question. I've done a lot of work on Marx and Freud. They're both reflexive. They are the great postmodern theoreticians. And they both believe that appearance does not constitute reality, that what you see is not what's going on, that there's a systematic distortion going on in the way we see the world; and by studying the structure of the distortions, you discover the deeper reality. They both believe that practice is the only way to expand our knowledge and that practice has to be guided by theory, even as it becomes the empirical basis for an enlarged and improved theory. In a sense, though they focused on different objects of study, they're both saying the same thing.

When I was at my most radical and crazy moment—which is right when I was splitting up with my first wife—I went to see a prominent analyst in L.A. at a friend's urging. He talks to me awhile, and then he says, "Why do you have to go and be an outsider the way you are and not be part of the establishment? Instead of demonstrating about the prisons and being with the Panthers, you could be testifying in court, and your cases could go to the Supreme Court." I rejected his advice.

Well, in fact, now I am an expert witness, and some of the cases I'm involved in do go to the Supreme Court! But at the time, I was having trouble with the idea that if you're going to analyze the personal reasons why you're political, then you're going to end up not being political. Because what you're going to do is pathologize everything. Is your activism happening out of Oedipal rebellion or something like that?

What I now understand is that I *was* acting out my Oedipal rebellion. And so was everyone else. We were also doing something that was socially correct. So these two things happen to overlap, and there are actually theoretical reasons why they overlap, and I've written about that. But it's okay to do both. It's not either / or.

The other thing that catches up to me is that I'm getting older. Like the adults over thirty we debunked in the '60s, I have more at stake, more interest in the reigning order. Having kids is a big turning point here. I start having this modulated view of activism. I feel that I've settled down and I am more centered, and that's because of life experience, especially struggling with my wife and women friends about gender equality and raising children and therapy. As a youngster, I acted out to some extent. It's a puzzle. Do I just have a more sophisticated worldview? I definitely was wilder when I was young. And I was ambivalent about my success. Here I was a doctor, and I was willing to throw it all away, risking arrest or worse. My whole generation was.

When I was first doing radical activism—this is why revolutions are made by young people—it was extreme. It was all or nothing. The only meaning to life was changing the ruling order. There's something extreme and frantic about it. I lived a life for "The Cause" because at that time, I didn't know what life was about. So even though our Marxist analysis seemed to explain everything, on another level I didn't really understand what was going on.

Luckily, my early understanding came from Marxism and social struggle, and eventually I was going to integrate these with a personal and psychoanalytic view. But by learning the social view first and getting hooked on social struggle, I feel that since then I've been able to go back and forth between the two. Whereas if it had gone the other way around, if I'd gotten psychoanalytically informed first, I would have said, "Why do we have to make such a commotion out there in the streets?" I would have looked at my behavior critically instead of doing it wildly. Then I wouldn't have had such wonderful radical experiences, and I wouldn't have learned always to look for the radical analysis beneath the appearances. I believe if that had happened, I'd be a much different person.

I used to work with the Black Panthers. I hadn't really valued living yet, so I was willing to die, but I wasn't really conscious of that. I was willing to throw it all away for some heroic, romantic notion. I knew that there was a chance I could get killed, and I believed that it was a risk you had to take. Everybody thought that. I mean, we had guns.

The Panthers asked me to set up and work at their medical clinic, the Bunchy Carter Clinic in South Central L.A. I went to some Black comrades and asked them what I should do because it would require a tremendous outpouring of energy, and then I wouldn't be able to do other political stuff. They told me, "Do it—it's really important to keep the Panthers afloat right now."

At the clinic, I treated mostly infections, but I did sutures and referred people if they needed something more. I hadn't learned yet in medical school how to treat bullet wounds, so what I did was go to a surgery professor and ask, "What if someone got shot through the arm? What would you do? And what if they got shot here, or what if they got shot there?" And he would tell me, I would write it all down, and eventually it got published in some how-to book about revolutionary medicine. And I taught a class to Movement activists on health and how to handle any emergency.

What happened, usually, was that I'd just do triage. I'd patch someone up if they had a minor wound, but what I was there to do was to tell them when it wasn't minor. I remember one kid who got shot—he was a Panther. He had blood in his urine. I told him, "You have to go to the hospital. You've been shot in the kidney or bladder, but whatever it is, you might get infected and die if you don't go to the hospital." Of course, he got arrested when he went to the hospital. So what I was doing was deciding when it was heavy-duty enough to risk arrest versus when it wasn't serious and would heal.

Did all of that change the world? No. But you know, one thing led to another. You had to support the Panthers at that moment in history. It's not about the details of what I did or what anyone else did. There was the Movement, and the Panthers were symbolically in the forefront of that Movement, even though we didn't agree with a lot of what they said. They did some crazy things. But the Panthers were at the forefront of the Movement. It wasn't only a matter of the Panthers organizing an event and ten thousand people coming. That's not the point. In the Movement of those times, the Panthers occupied a key symbolic place. Today, it's the incarceration of masses of people of color that fuels racism. Racism was—and still is—the central issue we have to deal with.

# Rick Whaley

*We met at Rick's house in Milwaukee on a Saturday in March. Rick and his wife Ellen live on the second floor of a simple duplex in a working-class neighborhood, Black and white, with some Hmong. They chose to live here because they have African American grandchildren and children, whose pictures cover the walls of the living room. Although it's now just the two of them who live here, Rick and Ellen are in constant contact with their children and grandchildren. When we arrive, Ellen is off with their granddaughter Star doing errands; Star, who is thirteen, decided that she wanted to be with her grandma and grandpa for the weekend. Rick tries to pull us into the family goings-on by asking if we have time on Sunday to practice driving with one of his daughters, using our rental car. It's easy to imagine that this is a typical day in this family. That evening, we all go to a powwow at State Fair Park in Milwaukee, where Rick introduces us to friends and Ellen coaxes us to dance in the circle.*

*At fifty-one, Rick is eager to reflect on his life. A new edition of his book,* Walleye Warriors, *co-authored with his mentor and Anishinabe friend Walter Bresette, has just been published. It's the story of how the Anishinabe (Chippewa), supported by allies, asserted their rights to spearfish in northern Wisconsin in the face of intense hostility from sports fishermen, local residents, resort owners, and even the state government. His current job is as a teaching assistant in the Milwaukee public schools; for many years he was an at-home day care provider. He has been a political activist since the mid-1970s, working with groups like the National Organization for an American Revolution, a Black-led antiracist formation, and then cofounding the Witness for Nonviolence, the Midwest Treaty Network, and the Milwaukee Greens.*

• • •

I often wondered if I would ever have a straight job. I started in day care; next I did family day care; then I was a nanny for a while, watching my nieces. That's not the usual career ladder for men. I'm working now in public schools, and I suppose you could say that's a straight job. Finally I'm a working Joe with health insurance.

I got into day care work when I lived in Madison. I thought I'd go nuts if I had to sit in an office, plus I missed being around my younger brothers and sisters. I consciously aimed to be a feminist man—it was a political requirement of the times. I always felt welcome as a man in day care. It was powerful, intense but gratifying, to be in this wonderful world of young people. I also did family day care in Milwaukee, and I did feel some isolation then from not being around adults. At least in day care, you work with other adults, but to work all day just with kids and not get out into the world was hard. I needed politics to get out of the house and into the world.

For a while, sports were my sideline. I played basketball with my buddies until I was forty-five. My knees couldn't take it anymore, and if I got knocked to the floor, I'd be sore for days, and I wouldn't be patient with children or my family or anybody. [Radio host] Garrison Keillor said something like, "Guys need to get together periodically just to burp and fart and be politically incorrect for a few hours." That's what sports were for me. You get together after a hard week; you push each other around trying to get rebounds; you grunt and groan and swear. I think basketball and politics were my outlets, my relationship to a more traditionally masculine world.

I was doing house husbanding when we lived in Sherman Park in Milwaukee, and the neighbors were supportive of me. There were a lot of Black men living there who were getting laid off from factory jobs. They were home watching the kids, so they could relate to me and I to them. But there were a few Black women, nice people, some even political, who commented to me, "You've got an apron on?" or "You *let* your wife have a career and you're the one at home?" And here I thought I was cutting edge. I realized that the way white feminist women see the world is not the way that all women see the world.

My wife wanted a teaching career outside the home. She also wanted kids, and so she picked a day care teacher for a husband. I was comfortable moving from community-based day care to family day care. That way, we could raise kids, and even foster kids, on a shoestring budget because her income was good enough to cover us and, in most years, to provide health insurance. That worked out good for both of us. I couldn't have done the politics and the community work I did and survived on a day care salary. It had to be two politically committed people's income.

In the next twenty or thirty years, if I have that much time left in my life, I want to write about some of the incredible things that happened in the midst of political organizing that I didn't take time to sort out. We raised a family with foster kids during our strongest political years. I think about the skills I have from raising a family and how that's connected to building a political organization. Or skills I learned in building a marriage that are helpful when I'm facilitating a meeting. There's a whole emotional life that doesn't get told in the political stories we tell. I think that side is just as powerful and important.

My wife lived in Brazil before I knew her and adopted a daughter, Haydee, who is African Brazilian, now American. We thought about raising her in Madison, which is where we lived when we got together. One day her kindergarten teacher said to us, "She's such a nice kid, so clean and quiet, a credit to her race." That was sort of it for my wife and me in liberal Madison. We decided that we needed to move to Milwaukee so that even though our daughter would grow up with white parents, she'd live in an integrated community and grow up in the grace of Black culture. So in Milwaukee we enrolled her in the Harambee Community School and lived in Sherman Park, which had been integrated since the 1950s.[1] Haydee got a chance to have many Black friends, she learned to do her hair, and many Black women were her aunties or her other mom.

I was a draft resister during the Vietnam War, when I was a university student. But it wasn't until after 1978, when we moved to Milwaukee, that I began to do political organizing. Being an interracial family, we're almost political by definition. You're forced to deal with things even if you aren't political—your child's schooling is political.

Being an interracial family is connected to my getting involved up north with the Witness for Nonviolence for Treaty and Rural Rights in Northern Wisconsin. It was a way to pay back what I owed to the southern Civil Rights Movement for making it possible for interracial families like ours to live in relative safety. This is still a dangerous country, but there are more spaces of harbor and stability than there used to be in the 1950s, North or South. Our daughters and grandchildren haven't had to face the heavy-duty "n-word" stuff. There's room to maneuver, and still there are subtle situations that happen, like urban white teachers who don't "get" all they should about Black kids.

I feel some guilt for not having been involved in the southern Civil Rights Movement. People risked their lives just for things like eating in restaurants and going to school. Until I really started studying the Movement, I didn't realize how harrowing an experience it was for everyone who did it. I don't know if I would have had the courage to be there. Would I have been capable of being a supporter, let alone the father of a Black child in the 1960s? It's sobering to think about. It's humbling to know what other courageous political people did. So my work with the Witness was one small payment to that legacy.

• • •

The Witness began in 1987 as a response to the racial taunts, death threats, and violent protests at northern Wisconsin boat landings when Chippewa spearfishers tried to harvest resources on off-reservation public lakes after the federal courts had reaffirmed their treaty rights. I was ashamed and angry that white protesters would spit on and throw rocks at Indian people. Then the state of Wisconsin responded, basically saying, "Let's not upset white people. Let's back up a little on these Indian rights." It was a disgrace to hear state government and congressmen responding like they were a bunch of southern politicians saying, "These Indians are going too far too fast. We're not going to tolerate that. We won't listen to Indian militants." All the while, the violence and illegal behavior were coming from white protesters.

The Witness was a committed peace presence and documentation of what was happening. We did not do civil disobedience or counterdemonstrations. We did not carry signs or go to argue. We were doing what the spearers asked us to do as allies. We would speak the truth about the evil we saw. We were there to receive anger, to deflect it from Indian people at the landings and in the boats. We believed that if enough people witnessed it all, we could stop the bullets that hadn't been fired yet.

We were disciplined in nonviolence. The clarity of the strategy was so strong that it kept us focused. But as we practiced it, it became more than a strategy. It became a way to center us while we were fearful. It kept us from bringing our intellectual anger to the landings. We grew into the philosophy of the Witness. People saw how we behaved—we weren't carrying picket signs. We were there to figure out if there was some way that people could live together in northern Wisconsin.

I went to the landings to do antiracism work, but Walt Bresette always said to me, "This isn't a racism issue. It's just a fight between neighbors, Indian and white. This is an environmental issue. We've got to stop the poisoning of the fish due to acid rain and acid mine drainage." That was always an interesting tension between Walt and me. The racism was clear. He knew it and felt it, too. But he had a deeper vision: "If white people who are fighting us about fish really know what's coming down the pike with the mining companies, they're going to drop this stuff and be on our side." So we dialogued with as many people as possible away from the landings—and sometimes at the landings, too—in order to reconcile the common interests of spearers and sport fishers.

In planning the Witness, we had an inkling of the danger. But it wasn't until we were actually at boat landings, with big anti-Indian crowds on the other side, that I felt that sinking in my stomach and my adrenaline would flow. That's when it really hit us. There were police there, but they weren't sympathetic to Indian rights or even nonviolence—same as the police in the South. To actually see a howling mob, livid toward Indian people and theiir friends, and know that at any moment it could go out of control—that was terrifying.

The spearfishers were under more of a threat than the witnesses were. They wore headlamps to go look for the fish at night, so they were easy targets. There were people pissed off enough to try and shoot spearers out on the lakes. For the witnesses and Indian families, there was danger at the boat landings, too. You were never sure if someone would be off in the woods with a gun or if there might be some crazy driver on the road who would take people out just for being Indian or standing with them. We were lucky. It was only a two-week witness; most political witnessing goes on a lot longer, often in even more dangerous situations.

I was a coordinator, so I had to do more than just be on top of things and save my own ass if all hell broke loose! I had to get all these people home safely at the end of the night. There were some nights we were following cars driven by Indian people who knew the back roads, but we didn't have a clue where we were. We could easily have gotten lost or had rogue protesters pick off people out of the caravan.

*(We recall for Rick a passage he wrote in the chapter "Healing, Not Winning" in* Walleye Warriors*):*

> On the way home from the witness season, I stop and rest near a great pine tree. When I awake, the sun is behind the tree, its light broken apart by the branches, so that I think at first that I'm looking at a Christmas tree all lit up. . . . The edge of this hill is a border between designed spaces and forest wilderness. I walk other borders in my life: between white and Black culture, between Native and immigrant (four generations back) American culture, between urban and rural. These are borders that are more like different but interacting ecological communities than they are like political boundaries that can't be crossed except with great risk. I am grateful that what I learned from being on cultural borders has helped a little in northern Wisconsin. I pray that what we learned at boat landings might be of help with the daily violence and rising despair in the city. A soft wind blows across my face and reminds me it is time to go home.

For three springs in a row, I went to the boat landings and thought that I might not see my kids graduate from high school or go to college. I might not make it home to my wife. I was looking at my mortality and wondering,

"Are my politics strong enough to do this?" It really deepened my appreciation for what I had. It's not just the fact that you might die. I think the question is, "How do I cope with the fear?" You need something more than a belief that you can out-organize the racists. It was very clear that we could do that, but that didn't give me what I needed to survive and maintain my discipline at the landings.

It made me look toward people who were both political and had a sense of faith and spiritual center. Many Indian people have that. I remember one woman in particular. She wasn't one of the Chippewa families, but she was white Appalachian and Cherokee. She had spiritual gifts. She looked to me to know what was going on politically and strategically, and I looked to her to figure out how to get us through all the fear. On days after bad nights, she spent time working to heal the Indian and Witness women stung from the vilifications at boat landing confrontations.

The turmoil and frustrations of being a witness tested my relationship with my wife. I came back really needy, demanding attention, wanting all the things that make men happy! A lot of relationships broke up after a season of confrontations, though some new relationships formed and lasted. People were damaged and depressed from the confrontations. Or they had partners that weren't as political as they were, or people just weren't the same people anymore. My wife and I try to do political projects together now, so that we both have that experience, so that the excitement of doing Movement politics doesn't generate its own temptations. What really matters is where you begin and how you get through life-and-death crises.

. . .

I have not forgiven a few of the people who were against spearfishing and the Witness. I think of them as the embodiment of evil. The leaders were very self-conscious of their demagoguery and political agenda. I don't know if I've come to see their good points. There are many other people I was angry with for standing on that side for so long, but I could relate to them and see where they were coming from. Since I grew up in northern Wisconsin, I saw them as people I could have been if I had stayed in Wausau, if I had gone to the Naval Academy in Annapolis like my father wanted. I might have been a Vietnam vet with a lot of frustration to vent. Winters in northern Wisconsin are hard. It's a depressed economy. People are just trying to get by. There's a lot of displaced anger, and Indian people are an easy target.

There were other levels of racism to deal with in our solidarity work. One time, Walter was invited to speak on a television show in Milwaukee. The station flew him down from northern Wisconsin to have him talk about this hot issue, Indian spearfishing. I was the point person: I picked him up at the airport and took him to the studio and tried to prep him for the interview. He talked really well about the issues. It was done, and I was feeling good.

They followed him on the news hour with a credible liberal white activist from Madison and this conservative Marquette professor to talk about the treaty rights issue. I was in one of the control rooms watching these two talking heads. Somebody called the control room and said, "There's some crazy Indian yelling at the producers about these two guys talking about Indian issues." I thought, "Oh my God, what's happening? Did some tribal official show up and he's mad at Walt? Is there an AIM guy here we didn't know about?" It turns out it was Walt; he was pissed as hell at the producers. I tried to figure out what Walt might be mad about. Was it because the conservative professor didn't respect the constitutional issues around treaty rights, or was the liberal not doing a very good job of defending sovereignty rights?

I left the control room and went to talk with Walt. I tried to be supportive, and I asked him, "Walter, what happened?" He said, "Did you see what they did to me? They paid my way down here to speak, and then they put the white experts on after me, to put a frame around me, to explain what I was saying. Why did they do this to me?"

It should have been obvious to me, but I didn't catch it until Walt laid it out for me. White people shouldn't frame the politics of articulate activists in other communities. The public network didn't let Walt respond to what the "experts" on Indian rights were saying, and he had things to say to both the liberal and the conservative.

The other side of the coin of whites not framing the politics of others' struggles is this: what do you do when advice, both strategy and vision, is asked of you? After one of the heavy years at the boat landings and with the treaty fishing rights issue still unresolved, Walt asked me, "What would you think if tribal members were to go on public land and cut down trees in order to test Chippewa timber rights? We'd use the timber to build treaty schools so our kids wouldn't have to be terrorized on the off-reservation schools." I responded, something like, "We haven't even won over people on fishing rights yet. Let's do that one first." I was still processing the emotions and logistics of the political beating we took for supporting spearfishing.

That was a bad mistake. It's not the role of allies to throw practicalities in the way of vision. What we can do as allies is bring our skills toward making real the vision of movements in communities of color. What a wonderful opportunity it would have been to create the cultural, political, community schools American Indians need, and what a wonderful public angle for testing timber-gathering rights and bringing teachers into the cause.

Then there are the dynamics of communication styles in doing multicultural work. In an African American context, sometimes I get feedback on what I'm doing by being teased or kidded. If you're outside this culture looking at the situation, it might sound like they're really running somebody down. But it's a skill to be able to lay out all the things that are bugging you about someone and do it in a playful way.

Among upper–Midwest European descendents—us Irish, Swedes, Germans—we usually don't talk about such things. And in my experience, most Indian people are even more reserved. If you've offended someone on the reservation or an Indian person in your political work, you might not hear about it. The traditional teaching is that you don't point out mistakes. You do it indirectly through storytelling or modeling appropriate behavior. You don't confront people directly. It can even be disrespectful for a Native American or Asian child to make direct eye contact with an adult. That's so different from what often happens in Black culture, where, at home, parents lay out really clearly what kids should do and not do.

So the way that I would get feedback from Walter is that he would chuckle and make my mistake into a story. He would talk about how whites as a group didn't quite get it together. It would be a lesson for allies. It would be done in a tender way. Or he would tell me about what another white person was doing that pissed him off, and I'd have to go deal with it. If something in a situation or meeting didn't go quite right, I'd ask Native activists what that discomfort was I sensed, or I'd just have to figure it out myself. Being an organizer is like being a teacher after a bad day: you go back the next day, make amends if you need to, and focus on bringing the best to what's ahead.

. . .

Now—in the decade after my involvement in the treaty rights movement—I'm thinking that I'm not creating the path anymore. The path is coming to me. I'm being shown a different way. It's not just that I've reached my fifties and need full health coverage and a pension. Maybe the organizing work is for younger people, though I kind of miss the earlier work. The main thing I'm doing now is trying to figure out how spirituality relates to where I've come from in my life and how spirit and art can inform politics. I'm interested in the stories more than the analysis. Political organizing and analysis is important, but so is a sense of who you are and of your past.

I think my role for younger activists, including our son Teig, is to encourage them in their heart path. That's something I learned from my wife. Building trust and enlarging the circle are more important than whose position or strategy prevails or who has hegemony in an organization. That's the sensibility women bring to the movement, and it's something I learned from Walt, too. People have a reason for coming toward Indian and environmental issues. Now, what's the next level of serious politics?

I once heard Winona LaDuke say, "You need to know prayers in your own people's language."[2] I need to know prayers in Gaelic, the language of my ancestors, and the prayers for the place where I live. That's the combination I'm looking for now. You need a place to belong to and a place to be from. You need to know the stories and history and obligations of both places. So I've been exploring my Celtic Irish roots. There's something that I lost (that Indian people haven't completely lost) when my ancestors gave up their culture to become white, mobile Americans. I've found there's a rich, land-based heritage to reclaim: there is the Celtic lore of place (*dinnseanchais*), of how to live properly, of how to know the magic of life while you try to survive in nature and not destroy it. In the old Irish alphabet, every letter was a tree, so you couldn't write without acknowledging the power of nature. The Celts could be violent, but they were also extraordinary in sensing the spirit that emanates through the elements.

We've lost so much because of the racism of conquest and the ignorance of our own past. We've lost knowledge of how to live well in the natural world as well as how to live well with each other. This knowledge existed in cultures that were destroyed by everyone—from the white settlers who just wanted to survive against religious persecution, to the Manifest Destiny crowd, to modern-day developers. That wound is inside of us as well as outside of us. You can see air and water pollution; the pollution inside is our spiritual emptiness.

I didn't grow up thinking I was going to be an environmentalist. It just unfolded. I can't point to an epiphany. Maybe I became an environmentalist because it's in environmentalism where I feel the power of creation.

# Jim Murphy

*In addition to being a firefighter with the Boston Fire Department (BFD), Jim is a Vietnam vet. He is quick to point out that he was not in combat—he was a support troop—although he was there for over two years, and that was unusual. After returning from Vietnam in the early 1970s, Jim worked odd jobs, from driving trucks and cabs to manufacturing to dancing in a bar. He joined the BFD in 1979. When he first came into the department, he was assigned to various firehouses, including one of the biggest fire stations in Boston. In 1986, he was reassigned by choice to the administrative headquarters. In 1987, after coming out publicly as a gay man, he became what he believes was the first gay liaison for a fire department in the United States, and he held that position from the fall of 1988 to the spring of 1990. Currently, there is only one other member of the BFD who is out as either gay or lesbian—and she very recently came out—because there is such little support for being out.*

*From 1990 to 1998, Jim was a fire inspector and then did fire safety education. He returned to firefighting duty in 1998. Jim is fifty-four. He's one of a handful of white men assigned to what the African American firefighters in Boston call a "Black House." In 2001, he became the first white member of the Vulcan Society, the Black firefighters of Boston. (There is at least one biracial member of the Vulcans who is white and Native American.)*

• • •

The reality is that I work in a very patriarchal, male-dominated, tradition-based profession that vigorously and occasionally fanatically prides its old guard traditions. The culture in the firehouse is still fairly tradition-bound and very male. In my own fire station, I am fairly well accepted as a gay man. But the department at large is still fairly homophobic.

When it comes to women, the culture in the firehouse is generally un-friendly. That's true across the nation, not just in Boston. Women only represent 2 percent of urban fire service in the United States. It's a patriarchy. Women are really having a baptism of fire. What they've done to women in Boston is pissed in their bed, put nasty condoms under their pillows, sabotaged their gear, called them dykes and lesbians (even though the women are overwhelmingly straight), said some outrageously sexist things, and been verbally combative and insulting. They haven't extended a warm, human sense of goodwill. I know that they resent women more than gay men.

The fire service in the United States is still one of the very last vestiges of the old boys' club. It's a clubhouse, and the women are coming to the clubhouse and upsetting it. How dare they come in here! We can't read our porn as openly as we once did; we can't have our raucous bad boy behavior. I find that gay and bisexual and straight men get themselves involved in behavior that women find rude, crude, and lacking in understanding. And when men are told politely by women that they don't appreciate that behavior, some of them sulk and resent the women, saying, "How dare you, bitch!"

When it comes to African Americans, the fire station culture has significantly changed in twenty years, but the power structure and power dynamic is still invested in Charlestown and South Boston, traditional white, working-class communities in Boston. For African Americans, it's clearly changed for the better, and there's still a fair degree of racism. There was a presumption that when some African Americans rose up in the ranks and became lieutenants and captains, they would earn a greater degree of respect. From some white members of the department, they have. Yet there still is resentment. I clearly see it as culturally racist and a lack of appreciation of people's humanity. I don't get it. I don't get it.

. . .

Being in Vietnam gave me a clear view that the world at large was quite different than the world I had been raised in—a very traditionally Catholic, conservative world. What was a pronounced eye-opener for me was the reality of race relations between Caucasians and African Americans. I saw racial divisions and individuals segregating themselves. I chose to cross the barrier and was frequently criticized by Caucasians, and sometimes African Americans, for crossing the color line. I was informed that there would be a price to pay and things would happen to me. And for sure, it happened. I was questioned by army officers and my peers. They didn't understand why I was so friendly with Blacks, Hispanics, and Native Americans. Most of the U.S. Army officers and many of the troops were southern white boys who clearly didn't understand what I was doing. They were put off by, and sometimes hated, what I was doing and told me so.

A lot of the U.S. Army at the time was southerners, and I didn't identify with the southern white experience. I did not feel comfortable with the southern white boys. I didn't see much commonality. There was a lot of raucous behavior and excessive alcohol drinking, and that wasn't my choice in those days. I quickly became a pothead, and that was more identified with the Blacks and Hispanics and individuals who didn't fit in with the regular army culture.

After Vietnam, I came back to the U.S. and realized I was lonely and that I might be gay, although I was still a little confused about that. I decided to go on my own and try to find friends in the gay community. This was the early 1970s, so the community was mostly in the bars.

In 1971, I was raped horrifically by a Black man. I was kept captive in his apartment for three and a half days. It was a near-death experience. For about seven years after the rape, I was asexual. I found out many years later that that is not uncommon for rape survivors. I shut down, became very addicted to alcohol and marijuana. I was a very bad pothead, a daily smoker. I slowed down my marijuana usage by 1976 and stopped by 1980, but my alcohol usage picked up aggressively. I began to seek out recovery in 1982 or 1983 and became sober around 1986. I was dying from liquor.

I recovered from the rape by doing a hell of a lot of spiritual, intellectual, and social healing through many healing modalities. I had to proactively seek out healing venues when there weren't very many for men. And I had to address some racial stereotypes—I clearly had to. I had to address some issues of my own internalized homophobia, and I had to address issues of American violence and violence in general among and between men. By the mid-1980s, I saw the rape as probably an isolated incident of poor choice on my part. I picked the wrong person because I was drunk. The individual who was my perpetrator was an incredibly sick and twisted individual and probably was a perpetrator to other people. He was a psychopath. I realized that this person was wounded but also responsible for his own actions. Through my healing, I was able to unhook the rape from his being Black. I came to understand that it wasn't an issue of his race but an issue of his psychocriminal wounds and behavior.

• • •

Initially, I did not want to be a firefighter. A group of bar drinkers and friends I had at the time—they were straight white men—encouraged me to get steadier employment. I took the exam in 1978 and got hired in 1979, not thinking it would become a career. It was a job, and it paid the bills. Eventually it evolved into a career.

I wasn't out as a gay man at the time, although I clearly knew that I was gay by the late 1970s. While I was assigned to one of the biggest fire stations in the city, a firefighter presumed that I might be gay. Unbeknownst to me, he had seen me going in and out of some well-known gay bars. He started a slander campaign in the fire station, telling others that I might be a faggot. I was surprised because I thought I had a degree of camaraderie with him, but little did I know that he had a homophobic side to him. I was informed by two Black men—one of whom I remain friendly with to this day (the other died of AIDS)—that this guy was slandering me. I found out years later that he spent a lot of time in the Boston combat zone in the porn shops and bars.

Eventually, in 1986, it evolved into harassment. My gear was sabotaged, minimally, on a couple of occasions. This act was dangerous, but believe me, my gear wasn't sabotaged to the degree that a number of women had their gear sabotaged when they came into the department. I was gay, but I was still a man. By the winter of 1987, I had had a bellyfull of it.

There were also several homophobic events that occurred in Boston in the mid-1980s, including a notable gay bashing by several members of the BFD. Three individuals who were perceived to be gay were attacked and injured, and it turns out that only one was gay. They were hanging out, just being young people, and were set upon by a bunch of drunken firefighters. The firefighters got off because of an in-house game of politics. They knew what lawyers to hire, who were cousins and friends of the magistrates and clerks in the courts. They knew the inside track. The gay community did not know it and did not have the experience or the power to work the system. There was nothing the gay community could do about it. It really angered me that these guys got off. The reality was that they knew the system and had the cultural power to work the system.

Shortly after they got off, there was a fund-raising campaign in all the Boston firehouses for the "fag bashers." There were signs up everywhere: "We're raising money for the infamous fag bashers. Please help support us." I was so outraged. For the most part, they got away with that, too. I grabbed one of the announcements and brought it immediately to the attention of David Scondras, who was a Boston city councilor at that time and who knew I was gay. He encouraged me to come out. I was pretty much ready, so I came out under his guidance, although he wanted me to come out at a press conference and I didn't want to do that.

So in the spring of 1987, I came out in a private conversation with the commissioner of the BFD, Leo Stapleton. He asked me what I was going to do, and I said that I would come out in a step-by-step process, first with my captain and then the guys in my fire station. My captain flipped and was mortified. He advised me not to come out to the other firefighters; he was fearful for my personal safety. But I came out, and it was in the gay news-papers and *USA Today*.

Eventually I became the gay liaison for the fire department, but it became an untenable situation. The homophobia was raw. It was awful. I incurred outrageous, brash insults and commentary by senior fire department offi-cials. They told me that they didn't like me, they didn't like what I repre-sented, they found me morally deficient. I saw the writing on the wall and resigned from that position after eighteen months.

. . .

I've been involved with issues of racism in the department for at least the last ten years. I've chosen to devote my activities in the last ten years, and particularly in the last two years, to assisting the Vulcan Society in bringing the issue of the intolerable racial culture in the BFD to the forefront and addressing it once and for all. In 1990, I began writing letters to members of the Boston City Council about some racial incidents that occurred in the department. In the mid-1990s, I started a petition stating that the clear and disparate and horrific racist, homophobic, and gender-intolerance issues within the BFD weren't being addressed. I drafted the petition and got about 105 members of the BFD to sign it. I brought the petition to the chiefs. Oh boy, they wanted to bury that quick! Then I took it to a couple of members of the Boston City Council. They were very concerned, but not much happened.

Some of the incidents came to my attention through social affiliations with African American firefighters; some of the things that happened I had personally witnessed or knew about. The incidents included harassment and disparate disciplinary actions. For example, there was an infamous story in the mid- to late 1980s of a chief in the department who took pride in the fact that he was purposely targeting African Americans for heavy-handed disci-plinary action. And he bragged about it. I was astounded at his bald-faced racism, and it was never addressed. And a number of other Boston fire chiefs' racism was never addressed. That's what really has concerned me from 1990 to the present day: the outrageous actions of some senior chiefs have never been adequately addressed. They've never been disciplined for some obnox-ious behaviors.

I would speak to white officers about this, and they would say, "What the hell are you raising that issue for? They've got it coming because the Blacks are just troublemakers. And they took our jobs away from our family." Or some white officers would say to me, "Jim, you're going up against a system where the chiefs run the department. Yeah, there's a lot of racism, but you can't change it. Don't even try." A couple of times, when I raised the issues, I was told, "You're getting to be a troublemaker. You need to back off."

*Did you?*

No, I did not. I got frustrated with their responses, and so I brought the issues to members of the Boston City Council. That really pissed off some of the white members of the department, but the reality was that the white members of the Boston City Council didn't really want to hear what I had to say. And when I sent them letters, it really got them upset. At least some of the women on the council were more receptive, and Charles Yancey was always concerned and interested. But he told me, "Jim, there has to be a level of momentum before we can push this issue. It's not there yet." When he told me that a number of years ago, it really hurt me. You know what? Politically, he was right.

I was very much a loner as a white man fighting this. However, there were members of the Vulcan Society, all the way back to the late 1980s, who would raise the issue of racial incidents. But for the most part, they were not listened to, except for the most outrageous incidents. Some of the members of the Vulcan Society have said, "Jim's always been there for us. He's taken his lumps and bumps with it."

. . .

Once when I was in California doing some healing from the rape, I got talking to a gay male who was the son of a former ambassador to Cambodia. He regaled me with stories of sodomizing boys in Southeast Asia. I was appalled. I was a rape survivor. Then one night I was at a party in Boston, and a guy there, whom I had some respect for, told me about going to Sri Lanka and being able to fuck boys all night. This individual had a rather influential position in the U.S. Agency for International Development (USAID). I finally confronted him because I had had a lot of healing from my rape. I told him, "I don't find it endearing, enlightening, or spiritually enriching to sodomize youth. It's rape. That's what it is." He responded, "They just want fifty bucks to feed their family." "No, it's rape, and it always will be rape. Rape is rape. And you're a USAID official?" I was infuriated. I said to myself, "I'm going to do something."

One of my friends was in the State Department, and I told him about this. He told me, "Jimmy, it's unfortunate. We occasionally see cables about this. The child sex trade is an appalling reality. It's real and it's a major problem, and it's not just gay men who are doing this." And I just said, "I'm going to do something about it! That's it."

So beginning in 1991, I started going to Southeast Asia. It was a real eye-opener. At first, I just had inklings of the underground issue of child sex. When I went to Vietnam, I was rudely appraised of the ugliness of the child sex trade. It infuriated me and saddened me greatly. There was one young man I met. He was quintalingual—he spoke five languages. He had the nerve to think that my interest was simply in buggering some little boy or girl. I was infuriated by that. When I told him that I didn't want any sixteen- or seventeen-year-old kid, he told me, "Well, I'll get you an eight- or nine-year-old." Oh, it just infuriated me! Then I thought, "He's just a middleman." But why was he wasting his time in this when he speaks five languages? It was for the money.

Back in the United States, I talked with other people about what was going on in Indonesia and started reading about East Timor. I started learning about the mass murder of civilians by the military in the mid-1980s. Eventually I got involved in the East Timor Action Network (ETAN) and started going there every year. I was there when the Indonesian troops were killing teenagers. I was an eyewitness to that. In 1995, I was one of the first nonreligious Americans to document the violence directed at the youth. I wrote a report and faxed it out of the country to Congressman Joe Moakley. He called me as soon as I got back to the United States. He asked me, "Are you sure about this?" I told him, "Mr. Congressman, I have too much to lose if I don't write this report. You only live once, and these people are being killed left and right. I can't stand it." He eventually sat down with some activists from ETAN and told them, "One of the reasons I'm sitting down with you is because that firefighter over there has been writing me and contacting my office for several years about East Timor."

I'm very concerned about the tentacles of the child sex trade. On my trips to East Timor, I speak with religious activists, NGOs, women activists, community leaders. I've spoken to the Catholic bishop there about the child sex trade. They're very aware of it and are doing some interesting work with the orphans and street kids. They're the ones you really have to look out for. It's not as much of a problem there as it is in other countries in Asia, but I speak to them forthrightly. Being an activist there means hanging out with people, getting a sense of what's going on, what's the dynamic, and then writing some reports. When I return, I'll write a report for an organization called the International End Child Prostitution.

At one point, I was told by Indonesian friends, "Jim. We're warning you. We know you're involved in politics. People are talking. We like you. You're vivacious; you're full of love. We know that the military runs our country. They're not good. They're not about the right thing. Be careful." I've subsequently found out that a dossier was prepared about me by the military intelligence.

*Do people in the* BFD *know about your activism in East Timor?*

Yes. They're intrigued by it; they don't understand it. My former captain, who's a Vietnam vet, said to me, "Jimmy, what the fuck are you in East Timor for? They kill people there."

*Do you feel any sense of sadness or loss about not being understood by him and other guys in the* BFD?

I feel some sadness. I don't feel loss because the ties have not been completely cut. I'm still connected to them. I occasionally talk with some guys at the bar up the street. One guy is a former firefighter and is now a labor activist. I have a lot of conversations with him. We talk and kick it back and forth. I'm friendly with him, but he doesn't understand me. He tells me, "Jim, you're a likable guy. But I don't understand why you're involved in this human rights work." I can have arguments with people; they still like me, and I still like them. Most people, not all. But they don't understand me. That's the sadness.

The Next Generation

# Sean Cahill

*When the interview took place. Sean's paid job was the director of the Massachusetts Legal Services Coalition, a state government watchdog group that monitors policy on human services. Since then, Sean has become the director of the Policy Institute of the National Gay and Lesbian Task Force in New York City. Among the long-term projects he's working on are an initiative to place racial and economic justice issues on the agenda of the gay, lesbian, bisexual, and transgender movement. "One of the main reasons I left Boston to take the job of research director at the Policy Institute was so I could have the opportunity to work with Urvashi Vaid. At the Policy Institute, Urvashi and I were a team for nearly two years—she as director, me as research director. Together with other staff and community partners, we built the Policy Institute into a preeminent think tank on GLBT issues."*

*Sean's activism began when he was in high school in Massachusetts. He's been a member of ACT UP, an editor of the Dorchester Community News, and the chair of the Lesbian and Gay Political Alliance of Massachusetts. He is thirty-eight.*

• • •

I read an essay recently in GLQ, the *Gay and Lesbian Quarterly*. The author wants the word "gay" to be a verb more than a noun. That helped me to understand myself. I'm sort of like a shark. I'm always moving. For me, to be alive is to be involved, to be an agent of something.

I read the paper and hear things said, and I just get really angry. The only way I can deal with it—it's almost like therapy—is that I have to be an activist and challenge it. It's my passion; it's what motivates me. I don't know how else to deal with what I see going on in the world. When I open up the newspaper in the morning and see a story about gay people with all the stereotypes, I have this sense of being talked about, being stereotyped. For a lot of straight people, "gay" is about sex—not about teaching kids in school not to harass gay people or about the experiences of gay parents. It's always about sex. The *Boston Herald* is pretty bad; it's often explicitly antigay. The *Boston Globe* is more subtle in its failure to cover issues or the insensitive way that gay issues get written about and is less malicious than the *Herald*. But either way, I definitely feel that I'm being talked about. It gives me a sense of what it might be like to be Black, Latino, or Asian in this society and be frustrated at how people misunderstand, demonize, and highlight certain things about you. Gay people are sexualized; people of color are criminalized. Both groups are pathologized, albeit in different ways.

I definitely feel what that is like, but I also get frustrated with people in the gay community drawing too much of a parallel. A month ago I was at a protest after a Black transgendered woman was murdered. We were protesting the way that the *Globe* and the *Herald* portrayed her, including referring to her as "he." One of the speakers, a white gay guy, got up and said that calling her "he" was like calling a Black person "nigger." He went on and on and on. There was a Black Boston cop on duty at the protest with a scowl on his face. I was pretty annoyed, too. It's wrong to call her "he," but it's not the same as calling a Black person a "nigger." It's not the same.

When people are a little heavy-handed in the analogies between the gay rights movement and the Black Civil Rights Movement, I believe it plays right into the hands of people who want to set gay rights up as a threat to Black civil rights. Of course, gay rights isn't a threat, but I think we need to be sensitive to this. It's like comparing everything to the Holocaust—that's insulting to people who lost their families in the Holocaust. If there is mass murder somewhere, that's bad, but to compare it to the Holocaust is trivializing the Holocaust. So I try to avoid those comparisons.

All of what I do involves race, but it's not like its conscious. I don't tell myself, "I have to do this because of racism." But when I end up getting involved, I usually work on issues of race and racism. The most important mission I have is challenging racism within the gay community. And it's the thing I'm most proud of.

In the last election, there were two gay white men challenging the incumbent, Byron Rushing, in the race for state representative. Byron is a straight Black man who is a national leader and who has represented the South End and Roxbury since 1983. He was a sponsor of the gay rights bill—we were the second state in the country to have one—and he was the lead sponsor of the gay student rights law, which was the first of its kind in the country. He's led the way on domestic partner benefits. When these two guys ran against him, a lot of people assumed that the Lesbian and Gay Political Alliance of Massachusetts would support them because they're gay. At the time, I was chair of the alliance. We didn't support them. We decided to back Byron Rushing.

The guys running against Byron used the argument that he wasn't focusing on the needs of the district but was much more interested in international politics, as if there's no connection between what happens internationally and locally. From my perspective, the fact that Byron's great on gay rights, cares about equal access to housing and fights Northeastern University's expansion to Lower Roxbury, and then fights for human rights in Burma or Northern Ireland—it's really part of the same struggle. He's just making connections. And all of that is based on constituent requests.

When we endorsed Byron instead of the two gay white men, I looked at it this way: Byron is incredible on every issue. He's one of the best representatives in the state and in the country. He's also one of only 4 or 5 Blacks in the State House out of 160 people. I found it problematic that someone would want to knock off one of the few people of color in the legislature and replace him with a white person. There are not a lot of districts where it is easy for a person of color to get elected.

The two gay white men sought out our support, and I met with one of them. I asked him lots of questions about Lower Roxbury and the issue of Northeastern's expansion. He had some pretty ignorant things to say about people of color—something like, "People who don't vote are going to be treated badly, and it's their own fault that they don't vote." It was blaming the victim. I said to him, "Instead of saying that, why don't you ask yourself why this group of people feels so disempowered that they don't go to the polls? Why don't you work to change that instead of writing them off?" I knew he would be a disaster in terms of Black-white relations in the district.

One of the neighborhoods in Byron's district is the South End, which used to be a diverse neighborhood but has gotten gentrified and is very white now. And it's predominantly gay white men. The way I saw this was that gay white men were trying to gentrify this legislative seat. But I couldn't say that at the time. I thought it would polarize the situation in the short term and not necessarily lead to enlightenment on the part of the people who need to be enlightened. So instead I said, "Look. Byron was the sponsor of the gay rights bill in the 1980s. He's led the fight for us every step of the way. What kind of message does it send to straight politicians when we stab our best friends in the back?" That's how I dealt with it, and it worked. Byron won every precinct, including the heavily gay ones.

I can't imagine doing any of this work without the people of color that I work with. I can't imagine being without them. I know that the work would have gone in a different direction if they weren't there engaging me and wrestling with me over ideas. I don't think it would be as rich or fun or fulfilling as it is. I feel like I have a really good relationship with Representative Rushing and Senator Diane Wilkerson, Representative Gloria Fox, Charlotte Golar Richie, and so many other people of color.[1] I know that I can always count on them. We never have to worry about how they are going to vote. Why do white gay people not understand that? For these people of color, it is like a gut thing. I don't know if Gloria Fox has that many gay friends or constituents. For her, discrimination is simply wrong.

. . .

Since 1994, I've been working with Peace Watch Ireland, a multiracial group of activists based in the United States. The group includes people from many different communities in the United States—Native American, Latino, Black, Jewish, and other white people. What we've tried to do is build a community-to-community partnership with people who are oppressed by the current British and Protestant supremacist state structure in Northern Ireland, particularly Catholic communities and ethnic minority communities, like people of color who have immigrated there, and travelers, the nomadic people of Ireland.

I've now been to Northern Ireland seven or eight times with Peace Watch. We go over during marching season, in the summer, when the Orangemen march through the Catholic neighborhoods. For two hundred years, these marches have been accompanied by loyalist and police violence against Catholic civilians. In Portadown and many other places, the Catholics live in very segregated neighborhoods and risk their safety when they travel outside their neighborhoods. They suffer job discrimination, three times the poverty and unemployment, and police and loyalist brutality. That's the context that leads them to resist these marches and seek to have them rerouted.

Even though as an American I have privilege—I have a passport, I can come and go as I want to—I can really identify with what they're going through. I feel it in my gut because I am Irish Catholic. It's given me an opportunity to have a sense of what it's like to be a Black person in Boston and not feel safe going to the North End. Most white people think of the North End as a cute little neighborhood, nice restaurants. But a lot of Black people still don't feel safe going there. That's what Catholics in Portadown live with every day.

One of our goals in Peace Watch Ireland was to demonstrate that what's going on in Northern Ireland is really a human rights concern on the same level as Central America, South Africa, or the Middle East and not simply something that Irish Americans are concerned about or something to do with nostalgia or this innate anti-British sentiment that Irish people supposedly have. Instead, we've demonstrated that it's something that everyone is concerned about because basic human rights are being violated.

The parallels in that project have been so striking to me. For example, we work very closely with people who are trying to bring back the Gaelic language and teach their children this old and rich language that the British government deliberately and systematically wiped out. Just last year, for the first time, the British agreed to fund Irish language schools. This struggle over language is the same that Native Americans are going through, where only a few elders might know a language that is thousands of years old and where the U.S. government systematically tried to destroy the language by sending children to Indian boarding schools. Language helps you understand where you came from, and so if you're cut off from that, you really lose a lot.

Another parallel with race is that the people in Northern Ireland are really inspired by the Civil Rights Movement in the United States. You'll go into a Catholic home, and there will be pictures of John Kennedy, the Pope, and Martin Luther King. You'll even find pictures of Leonard Peltier. If you did a poll, you'd probably find more people there who know who Peltier is than in the United States because they've been involved in the struggle for so long and have looked to the United States as an inspiration, that we could reform our ways and work to dismantle the apartheid that existed here.

When we go to meet with a British government official, the fact that we have a Black or Native spokesperson for our group, that says so much to them. That sends the message that "You don't only have to worry about the Irish Catholic American community in the United States; you need to worry about a lot more people than that." That helps the struggle of the people over there. It raises the level of solidarity. This solidarity dates back two centuries, when Daniel O'Connell refused to step foot in America because of slavery and Frederick Douglass expressed shock at the poverty and oppression he witnessed on a trip to Ireland.

. . .

Challenging some of the simplistic understandings of why people are poor is one of the main roles that I've had at the Massachusetts Human Services Coalition. It's not directly challenging racism, but it's challenging this discourse that never quite gets around to focusing on race. The subtext, however, is always racial. When politicians and the newspaper editors talk about people on welfare, when they talk about cutting off services to immigrants, you know who they're talking about. The reality is that people of color are disproportionately represented on the welfare rolls; there are still more white people on welfare across the state and nationally, but if you're Black or Latino, you have 2–3 times the chance of being poor and in need of assistance.

With welfare policy, I know what's going on is racist. But it's really hard to prove it. A lot of people of color involved in welfare organizing want to highlight the fact that a big percentage of people on welfare are white because so many white people associate welfare with single Black women. So they don't want to reinforce that stereotype. But at the same time, in order to challenge the racism involved, you have to talk about how the policy is impacting Black women.

I believe that race is a part of everything. It's part of the way we talk about "safety": is this a "good" neighborhood or a "bad" neighborhood? There's all sorts of code language. Race really permeates so much of the way we live, but it's this eight-hundred-pound gorilla that never gets addressed head on.

One of the projects I've worked on is the Coalition against the Asphalt Plant. A close associate of the mayor was trying to put an asphalt plant into Roxbury's South Bay. It's environmental racism. It's also classism. It's right near South Boston and Dorchester, next to white working-class and Black neighborhoods. They're trying to dump the plant into this neighborhood because they don't think that people will rise up and resist. Instead, we did rise up and resist. The coalition brought together many people of all races and political persuasions. Two women from each neighborhood—one Black, one white—went to meet with the head of the Board of Health, who is a corporate lawyer, and told him that they didn't want the plant because of health reasons. We really made it difficult for them to put it there. It would be in operation today if it weren't for all that we did.

. . .

I need to tell you about Jennifer. She's nine years old. Her father and I were together for two years. She is his biological daughter, and he had just gotten custody of her when we met. She was one and a half then. So for two years, until she was three and a half, I was her papi and he was her daddy. He's Puerto Rican; Jennifer is Puerto Rican and Italian American. I see her as often as I can—I was with her yesterday. I'm really proud of her and the role that I've had in her life. I really love her. I can't explain how much I love her and what she does for me. And my family loves her—they buy her tons of Christmas presents.

It's always bittersweet. It's the closest I'll probably ever come to being a parent, but after being with her every day for two years, changing her diapers, feeding, etc., it ended. So I feel very lucky that I've got her in my life, but it's always a little painful when I see her. I thought that over time that would change, but it really hasn't. I love her in a way I love nobody else. Being her papi makes racism very personal for me, perhaps as personal as it can get for a white person.

# Tobin Miller Shearer

*Loretta Williams, an activist from Boston, sent us a flyer announcing Tobin's book,*
Enter the River, *and told us that she had met him and was impressed. Tobin is
thirty-six. He is a freelance writer and antiracism educator and organizer. He is the
cofounder of the Damascus Road Antiracism Project. The project is a Mennonite
Church initiative that is in its sixth full year of existence; it began by working with
Crossroads Ministry out of Chicago and now has its own process. It works with about
forty-five institutions in the Mennonite and Brethren of Christ family of churches. The
cofounder of the project is an African American woman, Regina Shands Stoltzfus.
Tobin and she have partnered together for about eight years now. Regina, Tobin, and
Iris deLeon Hartshorn have coauthored* Set Free: A Journey toward Solidarity
against Racism.*

Although he is no longer doing day-to-day administrative work with Damascus
Road, Tobin continues training and consulting for it. He recently helped found
an offshoot of Damascus Road, WiderStand, a white Anabaptist antiracism action
and reflection community. WiderStand is an Anglicized version of the German word
for "resistance," as well as a call for white people to take a wider stand against
racism.*

*We interviewed Tobin in a conference room at the Mennonite offices in Akron,
Pennsylvania. We began by asking him why he was so emphatic about something he
had said to us before the interview: that he is "trying" to be an antiracist white man.*

• • •

An antiracist and antisexist identity is one that I want to claim. There are
some personality elements and then some historical and cultural elements—
Germanic, Swiss, Mennonite roots—that cause me to be a bit humble and
understated about stuff. That's good and bad and everything in between.

My use of the word "trying" also comes from getting pushed to be
accountable by some very strong people of color. They always remind me of
how much I have yet to do and how my immediate response is resistance to
being held accountable. My individualism and need for control as a white

person and male come through in knee-jerk ways that I am always surprised by.

When Regina and I are talking about how we're doing antiracism work in our setting, I'm much more likely to use that white male style and say, "This is what we're going to do." Regina's much more likely to say, "There's a pastoral role we have to play here, holding some hands and walking with and paying attention to some people." I've got to find a way to enter some of the space that she's describing and challenge my own confrontational style.

One of the things I know—I don't know a lot, but one of the things I do know is that it's very hard for us white people, and I guess specifically for us as white males, to allow ourselves to take the guidance and leadership of people of color. That's a tough thing. We're socialized to do anything but that.

So the word "trying" is, for me, an image of journey, an image of working to attain something that I have not yet fully achieved. It's my cultural background that has taught me, from the time I was little, not to blow my own horn. I was actually uncomfortable about being interviewed for this project. But I'm also intrigued and also deeply moved to be with other white men who have made antiracist commitments. That feeds my soul.

In the last major three-and-a-half-day training Regina and I led in the Damascus Road Project, there were some real powerful representatives of our church structure attending. I was presenting information on white racism, and there were several white people making comments that had an edge to them. They were defensive, and my palms were sweating. Because I had spent time in prayer that morning and was conscious of a strength not my own, I was able to respond to them in a way that I would not have been able to otherwise. I didn't let them off the hook, but neither did I jump down their throats.

One of the things that I immediately key into after I've done a training is beating myself up. I read the evaluations: "Tobin was too intense; Tobin was too passionate"; I have the list memorized. As much as I have a handle on it, they're noticing that I totally believe what I'm saying. I've been around people who are passionate on other issues, and it's scared me at times, and I assume that that is going on for some people when I'm passionate. Maybe there is some stuff there about the fear of believing in themselves.

And then there are those that say, "Tobin wasn't passionate enough; he was disorganized." It will take me two or three days after having gone through the intensity of my response to trust myself to know that I'm doing good work, I'm a good trainer, I know what I'm talking about, I'm not doing this to harm people, I'm doing this out of love. It's because of the circle of other trainers I'm working with that I'm able to trust myself more. I know that that is connected to my ability and willingness to trust other white people.

Last weekend, we had a meeting of the accountability group and steering committee for the Damascus Road Project. It was a wonderful environment. There were fifteen people sitting around the table; four of them were white; the rest were Hispanic, African American, and Native American, all strong leaders in the church and very clear about issues of racism. At one point, the white people caucused; it was a very normal, natural, and helpful thing to do. Our spirituality was at the table.

At the meeting, with the steering committee surrounding us, Regina and I debriefed on some recent workshops that we had led where we both got wounded, shot down in some pretty hurtful ways. The group then spent time praying for us and blessing us, laying hands on us for the work that we were doing and for healing from a difficult setting. In all the embraces I received at the end of that time of prayer, the most meaningful and moving one for me was one I got from another white man. It was important to me because so many of my interactions with white males are full of conflict—even if there isn't overt conflict, there is at least mistrust.

. . .

I was talking with my wife Cheryl the other night about some comments our pastor had made. One of the things that I said to Cheryl—I don't know if I used the word "scary," but I think it connects with that affect—was, "People I've never met or with whom I've had very little interaction have opinions about me." I know that it comes with being a public persona in the church, and to a certain extent locally, as I say things about how I see racism in our community.

I had written an article in one of our church magazines, talking about the racism I saw implicitly and explicitly in our private church schools. I said that there was overt racism present in the student body and that the existence of these schools was only possible in the midst of desegregation and white parents looking for another "safe" venue to send their kids. Regina and I had been asked to come speak with some local Mennonite educators, and we were disinvited after the article came out. I found out through some friends and family members that their decision to disinvite us was because of the article.

I do not know what to do with this! I put my comments about racism out there with respect, trying to be gentle, and they disinvited us! I had that visceral fear. "Oh God, they might not like me." That's the biggest fear for me—that folks might not like me, they might not have a good opinion of me.

I'm always struck with being so young when I go out and work in church circles. Among my colleagues in antiracist work, I'm on the young end. Sometimes that gets reflected back to me, like when a Mennonite says to me, "I knew you when you were just two, before you were this agitator in the church. Don't get too smart!" I've heard this kind of comment from church leaders who know my parents as church leaders.

I don't know that I've done a whole lot of thinking about this, other than just knowing that I am young. And I'm always surprised when I have a college president or an executive secretary from my denomination call me up and ask me my opinion about something in the area of antiracism. I think, "What the hell are you asking me for? I just graduated from high school yesterday."

• • •

Historically, members of the Anabaptist community were martyred and persecuted because of their religious beliefs. That history has actually worked against some of our antiracist and antisexist efforts in a paradoxical way. Let me tell a story that illustrates this. We had just finished our first year of the Damascus Road Project, and the executive director of the Mennonite Central Committee was sitting in this same room we're now in. When we were discussing the Mennonite Church as a white institution, he said, "What do you mean? We're not white; we're Mennonite! Our headquarters had yellow paint thrown at it during World War II because of our opposition to the war, and before that, my relatives were tarred and feathered."

And so I said to the executive director, "But when you and I are walking down the street of Akron, Pennsylvania, we are white males. There's nothing that sets us apart from that lived reality. And when an African American colleague walks down the street, he is not seen as Mennonite. He gets responded to as an African American male, and we have all sorts of anecdotes about the disparities in our realities."

We are Mennonite in belief, but culturally we are white as a people. We do have an identity of being a persecuted people, but we haven't recognized the extent to which we have assimilated. There are nuances that we need to acknowledge, but we are white. That's a discussion I love to have when we're in a training because it's such a rich one for us to have as Mennonites.

So what we say in our workshops is that this experience of our oppression as Mennonites is an important thing to be remembered and that our history of resistance should be celebrated. That has opened a window for a lot of folks to explore some new realities about racism. Sometimes, the use of the term "antiracism" has gotten a lot of resistance in the church. Regina and I have said, "We have a history of being conscientious objectors—that's a 'negative' stance, and we embrace that—so why do you say that antiracism is too negative a term?"

. . .

I believe that race is a demonic force—that it is not only oppressing people of color daily but damaging us white folks in ways that we do not have a clue about. The image that I often think about is that it's cutting us up on the inside, and we don't know it. We're bleeding internally, and we don't know it. I believe it. I'm a true believer. My life experience has led me to believe that it is true.

One way I think about this is in terms of my kids. We've got two academically gifted children. Going to inner-city schools in Lancaster, Pennsylvania, where they are each one of the few white kids in their class, they are already set up to get a lot of attention. The teaching faculty and administration are almost all white, and since my kids are academic achievers in our Eurocentric patterns, the resources go their way.

The cutting that I feel sometimes is knowing how much I mute myself when I'm talking to my boys' teachers. In those settings, I don't really believe that it will be in my boys' benefit, and in the benefit of the other kids in their classes, to challenge the patterns of privilege that convey messages of superiority to my boys. It's racism to not challenge those patterns of privilege. This is where the rubber hits the road for me—we're talking about my sons, whom I love more than myself.

I said I was a true believer, and yet there are those places when I find myself not saying things that I would say in a workshop, not saying the things that I say when Regina is right there beside me. And I wonder then, "What's going on, Tobin? Why aren't you saying what you believe?"

That's one piece. There's another one that has to do with racial stereotyping. I run about three miles every morning. I've learned from experience that if I'm running up behind someone and they don't hear me, they often get startled. I even had someone pull a knife on me once. And so I've learned to shake the keys I have in my hand so that people can hear me coming. I've become aware that I am much more likely to do that if I'm coming up behind a person of color than if I'm running behind a white person. It's one of those startling awarenesses when I realize, "This stuff really is deep."

There's one last way I'll mention that racism cuts me on the inside. In this wonderful meeting of the steering committee we had about two weeks ago, where we don't follow white norms and it's a wonderful space to be in, even in that setting, I'm aware that I like to have the last word. I like to be the one who directs the discussion where I want it to go. I've learned the tricks so that I can look like I support what others are saying and still direct the decision to where I want it to go. And so issues of control are part of the cutting that I do to myself.

. . .

Cheryl and I have come through some rough waters in our relationship, working out our differences, our conflict styles, my intensity and need for control, and my being able to let her take more ownership and leadership. I took her middle name as my middle name. It was a deliberate choice of identity for me, as a way to recognize our life partnership.

My commitment to being antisexist is longer than my commitment to being antiracist, but it hasn't been as focused. My antisexism comes out in much more practical ways in relationship to Cheryl. I clean the bathrooms every week; I do most of the cooking right now because Cheryl works the evening shift; I do the stuff around the house. I believe that it's okay for my boys to see me cry, to not have all the nurturing and support come from Cheryl but from me as well. As I've spent more time with the boys, that shift has happened. They come to me if they're hurting, not just to Cheryl. That's work, to change the socialization they're getting as boys.

My son Zachary used to like to kiss me on the lips. And now I kiss him on the cheeks. Some of that's my sensitivity to intimacy and boundaries—could that lead to abuse? Some of it is how Cheryl and I talk about our expectations for them—are we expecting them to eventually go out with girls? And some of it's clearly my homophobia.

I haven't explored my own homophobia and how I've been acculturated in heterosexual patterns and all that that means. And one of the issues that has been painful in the Mennonite Church is sexual orientation. In one of our Damascus Road trainings, this pain was acute, when some participants suggested that heterosexism is another oppression that has to be visited in our church. The message coming from the leadership of people of color on our steering committee has been, "We don't want those parallels between racism and heterosexism made in our antiracism efforts." Regina and I had to go in front of the training group and say that this is not where we are personally. We think there are connections, that heterosexism is a very real oppression in the church and in society. Yet because of how we've set up our accountability structures right now, we can't give space to explore that in this setting.

We spent weeks and weeks processing that with our steering committee and connecting with the gay and lesbian group within the Mennonite

Church, who are, incidentally, in the midst of all kinds of struggles to stay alive. We made that compromise, and it was painful. Regina and I basically said, "We have to name where we are, but we'll live with the steering committee's position now." One of the most difficult phone calls I've had to make in a while was to call the leader of the Mennonite Lesbian and Gay Concerns Association and say to him, "We lost this one."

The other area that I haven't explored very much is class. In the Mennonite Church, or at least the white congregations in the Mennonite Church, we have some publicly stated and very subtle lived realities of wanting to do "simple living." It has some clear class overtones. The choice of not buying nice clothes, the choice to eat more grains and vegetable instead of meat, not really for reasons of health but to reduce consumption a little bit. All that's coming from a very middle-class mentality, in the sense that we can make choices to do that stepping down.

African Americans and Hispanic people in the Mennonite Church really push on this choice. "What do you mean, Tobin? What good is that doing for anybody? I want you to look nice like I look nice. When you're wearing wrinkly clothes, what good does that do for class oppression?" That's been a really good tension and dialogue for me. My wardrobe has changed! Instead of wearing T-shirts and jeans, I wear something that's a little more, I don't know, white, middle class, professional. And I feel fine about that.

. . .

I can't talk about doing this work without talking about my spirituality. I don't know how other folks do this work without having a spiritual core. I simply don't know how it's possible. Maybe they're stronger than I am; maybe spirituality comes in many different forms.

Obviously, we are very intentionally doing this work inside our ecclesiastical structures, working inside the church. That's a very deliberate choice on our part. We think that it's consistent with our theology of needing to work on ourselves and our own community before we can have a base of integrity to work outside.

My own journey in taking deliberate, proactive, public stances on antiracism in my own community has only been made possible out of my spiritual journey. Back in 1996, I'd been in this job for about three years and soaked up the stress of it. We had some very intense struggles here inside the organization, particularly with another white male in upper-level leadership who was trying to shut us down. He was disagreeing with our analysis, not ready to name racism in our institution.

My wife and I had just finished living with another couple—we shared a house together; they were leaving, and we were at a transitional point. Our congregation was recommending that I include my name in the pastor search. That was looking really attractive; I could set this other work aside and do something else. I had begun to experience some physical symptoms of stress like chest pains. Cheryl and I decided to just pray about this for a month, trying to determine where God wanted us to go. We finished that with no real indication of what to do next.

On the night of October 20, 1996, I had a vision. It was unlike anything I had ever had before. I was in bed, fell asleep, and at some point in the night found myself as conscious as I've ever been in a light and airy room in the presence of what I have come to call angels. I wanted to stay there, felt myself pushed backward, and heard the words, "It's not time for you to go yet." Then I heard the words, "You're doing the right thing." It was a reference to the work on antiracism. At that point, I felt this vision slipping away. And so I asked the question, "Should I put my name in to be pastor?" and heard, "No, the answer will come to you." As the vision slipped away further, I grabbed one of the angels and said, "You can't just do this to me. You can't leave me with a vision like this without giving me a sign." A hand reached out, touched me in the middle of my chest, and the pain I'd been feeling for weeks went away.

I immediately tried to disregard it as the result of a spoiled potato or rotten cabbage, to quote Scrooge, but I did write it down. I debated telling Cheryl but didn't quite have the gumption to do that. Finally I worked up the courage to call her from work the next day and tell her about this. I processed it with her, Regina, and other people, including people of color to whom I hold myself accountable in this work. I asked them if I was going off the deep end. This was way outside my experience. They said, "No, we think God's speaking to you."

I made plans to take a spiritual retreat ten days after that vision and on the first day got a real clear sense that I needed to continue in this work. I didn't know what that meant. On the beginning of the second day of the retreat, I woke up and knew that I'd been given a new name, Tobin. Again, I processed this with my church community and the people of color who hold me accountable, and they said, "This is for real; you have to take it seriously."

In January 1997, I had a naming ceremony and accepted this as a sign of recommitment, of putting my spirituality and my God at the center of my work, rather than some of the rage and anger that I was tapping into. Some folks here in the office didn't accept my name change and refused to call me "Tobin" for a while. That capsulizes in a most remarkable way for me the grounding in spirituality and the working out of that in community. Over the past couple of years, I've learned to let go my need for control and rely more on intuition, relying more on the strength that comes from my spirituality.

I hadn't articulated those connections until just now. I do know that the process of having taken the new name "Tobin" has opened up for me some new awareness of the importance and centrality of identity and the difficulty of shifting identity. It's been a metaphor for me, of moving from racist to antiracist, from sexist to antisexist. And that the shift is not something to be taken lightly. To have the identities of antiracist and antisexist applied to you by others and to claim those identities for yourself is a precious gift that has much of the sacred in it.

At the same time, I want to be more fully white and male, as a way to be more whole. The symbol of this for me, more than anything else, is that I wear a baseball cap, but it says "Dismantling Racism" on it! And I carry a pocketknife!

# Jason Wallach

*We met Jason in Chicago at a conference of the Radical Philosophy Association, where there was a workshop session on the work that he and others have done in Chiapas, Mexico. He spoke bluntly about oppression and the abuse of power and privilege and yet was self-effacing about his own abilities and understandings. The last half of the workshop was devoted to the comments of an activist Mexican woman; Jason translated from Spanish to English for forty-five minutes and then asked for help from the audience, saying that he was very tired and didn't believe he was translating very well. A member of the audience came forward and translated the rest of her comments. His willingness to openly admit what he couldn't do and then ask for help was both an expression of vulnerability and an act of faith.*

*The interview took place about three months later in Chicago on a Sunday morning in March. Jason wanted to go out to breakfast before the interview to check out a couple of concerns he had about the interview and this project. During the interview, he was again blunt yet often paused, reflected, and sometimes changed what he was saying in midsentence. He was both confident and very aware that he doesn't know what he doesn't know.*

*Jason is thirty-two. He currently works with the Chiapas Media Project and the Mexico Solidarity Network.*

•  •  •

A couple of days ago, I was reading an e-mail from some people in Mexico describing a march that's taking place from Chiapas to Mexico City. This march is a result of a political moment in Mexico. The president of Mexico doesn't really care about the interests of the indigenous people, but he's feeling pressure. The Zapatistas are saying, "You need to make a choice for us, because this is a democratic society and we represent the majority of popular sentiment." So the Zapatistas are on this march to demonstrate that.[1]

I cried while I was reading the e-mail. It mentioned a woman from an indigenous rights group. What she said was really beautiful. When the

Zapatistas arrived in her community, she told them, "Before 1994, we knew what we wanted. But we didn't know the path. You showed us the path, and now we walk with you." That night, when the Zapatistas left to move on to the next spot, she and some people from the community joined them.

I knew this woman, and so it was emotionally powerful for me. The woman who spoke those words spent a couple of nights at my house about a year and a half ago. She was on a speaking tour in the United States. She's a beautiful person. The first thing she did when she came to my house was to offer me *totopos*. They're basically chocolate tortillas, but the word "chocolate" doesn't do them justice because this is locally harvested cocoa. She gave me a stack of them that she had made herself and brought from Oaxaca as a gift for my hospitality, which I felt totally unworthy of.

I think the tears that welled up in me as I read her words had to do with the sense that this is a proud woman who refuses to give up her dignity in the face of a clearly oppressive and oppressing situation. Her words spoke of that human desire for liberation. And she was expressing her humility at the same moment that the strength of her actions and her being were expressed. She said, "We knew what we wanted, but we didn't know how to get there." In one sentence, you experience the humility, the humbleness, the dignity, the strength of spirit of struggle. There's something that's very core about all of that. And I think it exists in every human being but is very rarely tapped in one moment.

•  •  •

When I was a kid, the material needs in my life were met. I wasn't hungry. And I never really bought into what was around me. I didn't want to be the consumer that everyone wanted middle-class kids to be. I recognized that something was lacking, but I didn't know what it was. Something was clearly missing.

By the time I got to high school, I was a big dork. I didn't understand what kind of games people were playing, socially and stuff. I didn't understand why you had to be a certain way. I just didn't get it. I was like a deer caught in the headlights. I've never described it that way, but it makes a lot of sense now that I've said it.

I became involved in the punk community. That community embraced me; it had a space for me. It allowed me to just be who I was. I wasn't the kind of punk who dressed up in studded leather and got all bad ass; I didn't play around with my appearance. I just felt like it was an accepting space for whatever I was feeling. I'm still in that community; last night, I went to a punk rock show and spoke about the Zapatista movement.

Today, I'm in a different position. I feel more self-confident. I have a view of the world that I feel kind of centered in. I feel a responsibility to the punk community to help strengthen that because it provided a space for me. I think that punk is a subculture in the United States that provides a safe, creative space for young people to become politically active, to become creatively active in terms of music or art or video or web design. I want to encourage that.

Now, when I look back on it, [I see] that "something" I was missing was a spiritual connection between me and the rest of the world. The alienation that I felt—and it took me a long time to figure this out—was an alienation between me as a white male in the U.S. and the rest of humanity and the rest of the planet. Some people talk about a connection to earth and a connection to the land, and a lot of times when that's spoken about, it's very abstract and very kind of esoteric. It's a cliché to talk about a connection to the land. But I hear those words and get a deep sense of the spirituality that comes from a relationship with the earth.

Alienation is something that the punk community has always acknowledged, in many forms. Punk is many things to many people. But in a large sense, regardless of the race, class, and gender diversity within the punk movement, alienation is a common theme. I was talking to a guy last night after the punk rock show—this is like a straight-edged Latino punk from the South Side of Chicago. We had both been to a conference of young anarchists earlier in the day, and we were talking about the problem that most of the kids at the conference were middle class and weren't directly impacted by the issues brought up at the conference. The system is set up to support them, and they just didn't get what we were saying. What was evident in my friend's voice was this alienation between him and the rest of this anarchist movement that he really feels connected to in one way but feels so distant from in another. I really related to that. There was nothing I could say to make him feel better or whatever. All I did was hear him out. That understanding, right there, was enough for that moment.

This alienation thing is really key. When I was feeling like the deer caught in the headlights, I didn't understand what was going on around me. I knew something was wrong, but I didn't quite know what it was. Fortunately, I entered the punk rock community. That community allowed me to have access to a lot of information about the world.

When I was seventeen, we were doing punk percussion protests against apartheid at the South African Embassy in Washington, D.C. It was a concrete way for those of us doing antiracism work to get in the streets and manifest how we felt about stuff. We'd have free punk rock shows at an

African Methodist Episcopal church and then go en masse, four hundred punks marching up Massachusetts Avenue, to the embassy. Everyone was banging on pots; it was loud! You had to wear earplugs. It was just infernal noise. We'd get to the embassy, and when we first did these protests, there wasn't a gate. But they put one up, and then it was even better because it gave us this big iron instrument to play. Even if you didn't have a pot, you could make loud noise.

So through the punk community, I started to understand that there was more than suburban Maryland. I came to understand that there were people struggling all over the world. Somehow, the alienation that I felt and the struggle to reconcile the question I had about how I fit into all of this in itself paralleled struggles for liberation around the world. I've always paralleled my own struggle within myself and self-understanding with the ability of people around the world to struggle for their own liberation.

In spite of everything I just said, you know how they say that 85 percent of life is showing up? The whole theme of what I was just talking about is "being there," just "being there." I think you create the conditions that allow you to be in certain places. You don't know that you're going to be in a certain place, but all of a sudden you find yourself there and ask, "Wow, how did I get here?" You aim toward something, but you don't know what you're headed toward. You allow yourself to go in that direction.

One day in 1992, I was sitting in a bar in Washington State, drinking. I think I was bored. I had just gotten off work at a restaurant where I worked as a line cook. This guy walks in and says, "Earth First! just called from Portland, Oregon, and they need people at a site outside Rhododendron, Oregon, near Mt. Hood, where some trees are going to be cut." The four local indigenous tribes from that region—the Nez Perce, the Umatilla, the Yakima, and the Warm Springs—all those tribal councils had passed resolutions protecting that site because it was a sacred place. He said, "They need people. I'm going down there." I told him I'd go with him. We had to leave right away, so I didn't have time to go by my place and get my stuff. I just jumped in the van with him.

We got down there, I got a little sleep, and then I heard someone saying it was time to get up. Before I knew it—I had never made a conscious decision that this is what I was going to do; I just got in the van with the guy—I found myself on a mountainside in the middle of Oregon, putting dead wood in the middle of the road and digging up the road as a barricade to block the logging trucks. I remember it being pouring rain, with me having no rain gear, nothing but the clothes that I had brought on my back.

We did that until sunup, when the logging crew was coming in. They called the local cops and the forest police, who showed up with an amazing show of force—there were about seventy of us and fifty of them. We had this standoff, and the cops were saying, "You guys have to move. The loggers have a right to go in there." We said, "No they don't. This is Indian land."

I had never been in a situation like this. There's a line of Indian elders in front and a line of support activists from Earth First! behind them, blocking the road. They were saying, "You'll have to arrest us to get up the road." One of the Indian activists, Calvin—he's Northern Paiute—starts offering the pipe to one of the cops, as a way to show respect for the land. The cop just didn't understand what he was being offered and rejected it. Just after this happened, a Yakima woman who was standing in front of me said to some other cops, "I was a nurse in the Korean War. I healed your people. I watched them bleed, and I sewed up the wounds. And this is how you treat me and my land."

After a long battle like that, the women and elders moved out of the way. It was then just the cops facing us. They rushed us. Lots of people ran away and challenged the cops to chase them. I found myself in this surreal place. Twelve hours before this I was in a bar, and it wasn't luck and it wasn't coincidence that I was there; it was a very special thing that I was there. I had been in other protests and felt confident in being there, but it also was surreal because I hadn't planned on being there as I had in other actions. When everyone darted away, I walked forward. I didn't have any sense of conviction or any feeling in my gut; I just started walking forward. This cop puts his hand on my shoulder and another says, "Yeah, I want this one" because I had been provoking them and teasing them.

They slapped me on my knees and handcuffed me. Spontaneously, I dropped weight. It had been raining continuously for about six hours, and I was already soaked to the bone. So dropping weight meant that I got really muddy. They needed three cops to drag me through the mud, and they really enjoyed it. I was thinking to myself, "I should be the most miserable person on earth. I'm being arrested; I'm handcuffed; these guys are wrenching my arms behind my back; I'm freezing. But I feel like I'm exactly where I should be and want to be." Calvin, the guy who had offered them the pipe, was standing nearby. He looked down at me, I looked up at him, and he says to the cops, "That's the most beautiful man I've ever seen in my life." When he said that, this energy shot through me. It was electrifying. The cops threw me into their van, and I just lay there, shivering. Fortunately the next person they arrested was this big Indian woman, and I swear it was her body warmth that kept me from getting hypothermia.

That experience still has a huge impact on me. Just telling the story, I get shivers up my spine. I'm not so egotistical as to think that I'm the most beautiful man that Calvin's ever seen; the intent of his comment was to challenge power at that moment. But what I saw was that the powers that be in this country are willing to do anything and put anyone out of their way in defense of this racist, oppressive system that has really scourged this land for more than five hundred years now. At that moment, we were denying the ability of that system to continue to do what it is designed to do. I remain very committed to acting like that.

That moment continues to motivate me on a daily basis. I mean, I don't think about this story every single day, but I think about it often. When I do work in Chiapas and I'm in communities there and people ask me, "Why do you care about this? You're not Mexican. You're not indigenous," I tell them that I have a history of working with these communities, and I can confidently say that I understand the communities because I've spent the time there. I've been gifted with an intuitive sense; I don't know why, but it's there. Through that intuitive sense I've had the ability to really understand a lot of things that I think a lot of people don't understand. One of those things is the ways that oppressed communities survive oppressive conditions. At the same time, there's a lot that I don't know. I never assume that I know everything, or even a lot, or even some.

I don't come into a community and say, "This is what you want and need, and this is what I can help you get." For me, it's about respecting a community's struggles in their own context as they've defined it. The Zapatistas have always said, "Before you help me, go back to your own community, organize there, and do the work of liberation in your own community." If my liberation has been linked to my ability to "get real," my function with other white people is to help them achieve that, to "get real." Humility really does come in here because I'm not telling people, even in my own community, "Look, this is what you need to think."

One of the things I do in Chiapas is bring groups from the United States to learn about Chiapas and bring activists from Chiapas to the United States. It's promoting cross-cultural understanding, and it's connecting people with reality. And I realize that some people don't have the same perception of the importance of cross-cultural understanding that I do. Or they have other priorities.

I took a group of college students from the United States to Chiapas, and their professor really wanted to tell the community all about where they stood politically and why they felt it was important for them to come to Chiapas. I was thinking an hour from now, no one here is going to remember your name or the name of your college or why you came here. That doesn't hold much importance for the people here. What's important to them is that some people from far away came to visit and that they had the chance to express themselves to these visitors, who will then go back and use that information.

That's about the extent in Chiapas that you can hope for, especially for people who aren't going to be there to build long-term relationships. These groups come in for ten days, and they want to believe that they deeply understand the plight of the people in Chiapas. They believe that goodwill is going to translate into instant rapport. It doesn't work like that. Of course there's an acceptance and friendliness, but the rapport is built over time.

I take this work very seriously. If people don't take the trip seriously, we don't let them come with us. There was one incident where some people wanted to go see some old pyramids, but we had on the schedule some discussions with a group of Indian activists. We said to these people, "You'd rather see the dead remains of ancient cultures than talk with live human beings who are descendants of those cultures? If you think this is a tourist trip, you can go to the ruins, but you're not going to travel with us to meet people in the communities because it's obvious that you're not prepared to talk with people in the communities." They decided to stick with us.

I've worked to be both blunt and gentle. And there's a dichotomy in the work that we have to do. There's a battle for the resources of the earth, and there's a battle for the ideological control of how those resources are distributed. The people who are on the wrong side of that battle are spiteful and remorseless. They don't care who they have to knock off in their pursuit of what they want. The corporate capitalist mindset is voracious. It's devouring. It will eat anything in its path. For that reason we need to be tough, direct, clear, and blunt. We need to say that we're not going to take any shit. And it's not a nice thing. Sometimes we, as people who are defending the earth and supporting the struggles of targeted communities, need to do some things that are very difficult to do. That's one side of the dichotomy.

The other side—and this is where I think the white-dominated left goes awry—is if we don't have sensitivity and compassion and cultivate that in ourselves, then what kind of world are we creating? We need to know what we're fighting for and what we're fighting against. I'm fiercely antiracist, but that ferocity is expressed through sensitivity and caring for people. There are different ways of managing ferocity, and some of those can be surprisingly compassionate. This includes valuing and supporting the voices of people who recognize that white privilege is a cornerstone of white supremacy in the U.S. We should value voices that tell us we need to recognize this ugly privilege in our daily lives and personal relationships because by demasking the ways in which racism has dehumanized *white* people, we can take steps to become more fully human ourselves.

I really care about and respect white people who make concerted efforts to fight racism and look into themselves. That process is something I know personally and very much respect in other people, no matter what stage they're in, what level of understanding they're on in that journey. It is a journey that you commit to stumbling through. I know because I've made a few steps in it myself, and I've stumbled a lot, too! This journey has strengthened my sense of justice, clarified what I'm fighting for, and helped me become more fully human in the process.

# Bill Vandenberg

*Bill is a founder and the codirector of the Colorado Progressive Coalition (CPC), a statewide network of racial and economic justice supporters. The other codirector is Soyun Park, a Korean immigrant, and Bill's former girlfriend. In describing their relationship, he told us, "We have a great deal of respect for one another in the work we do. We know what we each do well and where we need a little support. And we give that support to one another."*

*In our initial conversation on the phone before the interview, Bill spoke about his sense of isolation as a young white man (he's thirty-one); we hoped that by interviewing him we might bring him into the circle of antiracist white men we'd already interviewed. He spends enormous amounts of time at work, and yet he readily carved out time for this interview. We met in his office in the Capital Hill section of Denver on a Sunday afternoon.*

• • •

When we formed the coalition, we decided that it wouldn't be the "usual suspects" kind of group—the usual suspects being older, white, well-educated, financially comfortable liberals who live in racially segregated communities. They are the traditional, self-identified progressive folks in this area. We thought if we want to be effective and have some power in Colorado on issues of racial and economic justice, we have to go beyond these usual suspects. We need to value their expertise and contributions but also put in significant resources, time, organizing, and relationship building with communities of color, with low-income communities, and with youth.

We took a look around the room at a meeting about a year and a half ago and said, "You know what? We're failing." It was a very hard realization because I think we all knew it but were afraid to talk about it. There were pockets of representation from communities of color, and people of color had come to meetings and wanted to participate and then didn't come back. We all knew it was going on; we didn't know how to address it. So we started a very long, difficult, drawn-out process of looking in the mirror, being frank, doing a strategic planning process around the state, and saying, "We've got to change if we want our organization to be truly relevant for the next decade." We started to change where we put our resources, who we had for volunteers, who we had for board members, who we had for staff, what communities we would organize in, what coalitions we would prioritize, and what issues we would take to the legislature. For the future of our organization, we would now look at all issues and structural matters through a race and class lens.

That produced some backlash. We lost about 10 percent of our progressive white membership, what I have sometimes called some of the more self-righteous folks on earth. People that give money to the United Farmworkers, march on Martin Luther King Day, support Affirmative Action, and think they're postracism. Meanwhile, they feel like they can walk into the room and exert their white skin privilege and be decision makers despite not having done any work. We realized that we had some kind of apartheid going on within our organization—not to trivialize that term, but it was a very segregated organization. People of color and younger folks and women were doing all the work, but the usual suspects—the old guard, if you will—would expect to be able to have power, critique, make decisions, and really not work to implement anything. So we started to talk really bluntly with folks. We said, "Your critique and criticism are really valuable, but if it's not going to be followed by any commitment to transforming this organization, then we don't want to hear it because it's easy to come into a meeting when you haven't done any work and say, 'Why is this the way it is?' "

We also had white people say that we were ageist and "reverse racists" in the way that we were doing things because we have quotas for racial representation on our board (what we call our coordinating committee). We now have about twenty people that work here, mostly part time. Seventeen out of the twenty are people of color, overwhelmingly twenty-five years old and under. The "reverse racism" and ageism stuff really rankles me. All these years, we've indulged older, wealthier white folks in these structures, and self-identified progressive movements are, by and large these days, very nondiverse. In some ways, these organizations are worse than corporate America, which we attack on a regular basis and challenge to be more racially inclusive. We're not willing to confront our own institutions on these things. If we want to transform society, how can we do it if our own institutions don't look anything like what we want this broader society to look like?

It's been very hard. Soyun and I have had e-mail campaigns behind our backs, and there has been lots of backstabbing. Unfortunately, I think it is more of a white trait than a person of color trait that white people would not talk directly with Soyun and me about this. So we heard whispers, then we would call people and ask them if they wanted to say something to us, and of course they'd say, "No."

For as difficult as it's been for me, for Soyun it's been intensely much more difficult. Every day for a period of six months or a year, she'd say to me, "I don't want to be here another day." She didn't feel that this organization was what it said it wanted to be. We always had the view that we had the right idea; we just needed to put some structures and systems in place and challenge things in order to get there. Through this process, we've gotten to that point. We did lose some membership, but we've built our membership incredibly since implementing this new plan. Soyun is enjoying working here and has found a niche where she is comfortable. And it's infinitely more valuable for me to come to work every day. My life is enriched more than I can even quantify by working in a multiracial setting.

We've started to identify a really solid core of white antiracist folks within our membership, people who share the same feelings and frustrations that I have with our movement. We're starting to talk more. We know one another. Change is slow to come, but having a group of antiracist white people makes it possible for me to come here in the morning and feel good about the work that I do. One of the things that used to make it difficult for me to be here was wondering if I was the only white person who cared about these things. So it's been good to get white people to come out of the woodwork and say, "I care about this, too."

This cadre of other white folks is very important to me. I don't think they know that, so I've started to talk about that. I've begun to thank white people not only for what they do here, but for being who they are and for being people I consider allies in this difficult process.

. . .

At CPC we try to chip away at classism, but our systemic analysis is pretty weak. We have some members of the organization who are socialists or who identify as communist. I've always seen it as a pipe dream. It's nice to theorize, but we're living in a hypercapitalist environment. How do we change it for the better while we're here?

I'm excited that our next training project for CPC is to develop a curriculum on classism for our membership. But I have some problems with the fact that a lot of our dues-paying members are from Boulder, a community with a very high per capita income. It's considered a liberal community, although I've not seen why exactly. It's clinging to a sense of '60s liberalism. I'd like to tell people what I think about class and race in Boulder and the whole retreating thing. Do people move there to get away from diversity? Yeah, it's a beautiful place, you have access to hiking trails, but what's your connection to the bigger world?

And we need to do something with folks in the wealthy subdivisions around Denver, and I have to believe that there are people there that would like to be a part of our movement. But I don't know how to reach them, and I don't know if I can. It's a struggle. You want to build something big and meaningful, but a lot of times I don't want to go to communities like Boulder, where 25 percent of our members live.

Sometimes I want to get back at people for how I was treated when I was a kid growing up in a small town in Maine. When I was a kid, I worked in the little supermarket there. One day, this woman who lived down the street from us—I remember this like it was a minute ago—came up to me at work and said loudly, "Are you and your brothers and sisters going to get the scholarship to the YMCA this year like you did last year?" That was the poor kids' scholarship, and I was ashamed. I'm still scarred by that.

When I'm trying to get back at people, I know at the time that I don't want to do that and that it's basically an immature, if human, reaction. But it just happens. I'm painfully aware of it, and I'm painfully aware that I'm not doing enough to address my own internal issues right now.

• • •

One of the things I'm most proud of is just being willing to admit what I don't know and recognizing that there are experts in our midst on these issues. Just being very honest about that. I'm willing to learn and fail occasionally and keep trying. I know that I fail. I catch myself often, Soyun catches me often, and I keep trying.

And I'm proud about being a codirector who is always asking, "What are we doing about the racism in our own institution? What are we doing to challenge white privilege in this supposedly progressive organization?" Bringing that up in every setting, at every meeting, and saying, "It's not going to go away if we don't talk about it."

I know I drive people crazy sometimes. Part of me really enjoys that. For example, prior to the World Trade Organization protest in Seattle, many of our members were very excited to go up there. I've done a lot of fair trade–related work in the past, but I definitely did not want to go to Seattle. CPC had done a similar "alternative summit" when the G7 had its summit in Denver in 1997. I really loathed the entire experience. It was dominated by the usual suspects, and they said, "Well, once we get things going, people of color, union members, low-income folks will all come to us." And of course, it didn't happen. Soyun and I and CPC were a significant minority voice in the discussions about the impact of our alternative summit. It was a bruising process.

When some of our members got back from the WTO demonstrations in Seattle, they were ecstatic, saying it was the greatest thing since the 1960s. I read stories where people said, "This is what democracy looks like." They were chanting that in the streets. I got an early copy of *Color Lines* magazine, where there was an article by Betita Martinez wondering about the lack of people of color at the demonstrations. A young woman of color was in jail with a group of white activists. They were saying, "This is what democracy looks like." She wrote, "I looked around the room, and no one here looked like me. If this is what democracy looks like, where everyone is white except for me, that isn't democracy."

I sent that article out to a lot of our members, including many self-identified progressives, especially those who had been to Seattle. I got a couple of nice comments back saying that it was good I was talking about this. But then I heard also that some folks were angry, like I was ruining their moment. They were happy about Seattle. In many regards, Seattle was a success in opening a new dialogue on globalization. But we can't overlook the racial issue. It's easy for progressive people to say, "We did a great job on this," and leave it at that. But if we don't challenge ourselves, we're never going to get any stronger. We're never going to be more relevant; we're never going to look like the society we say we want to have.

I don't think it's disrespectful at all to challenge other white people, but I certainly can see how other folks might feel that way. If you fight intensely for something, it feels good when there's a small victory. Working for progressive social change, there are very few clear-cut victories; most of them are incremental on a long road toward systemic change. But because of my commitment to being an organizer and doing something that I feel strongly about, if I don't challenge folks on issues of race and privilege, I don't feel like it can be considered a victory. That's my perspective, and that reflects my privilege and my ability to question folks in their time of happiness, saying to them, "You shut down the meetings in Seattle, and you started to reframe the debate. But what happens the day after this big victory?"

There was a white woman I confronted after a meeting about her white privilege. She was driving all of us crazy during the meeting, and I confronted her after the meeting. But I gave it a lot of thought afterward. Should I have confronted her? I think that it was the right thing to do. Could I have done it differently? Could I have acknowledged more where she was coming from? I tried to understand her response to the way I challenged her—she was very defensive—and her response since then, which is to not have any connection to our organization. I find myself saying, "That's okay. She's not the kind of person we want in our organization." I guess I don't have infinite faith in everyone. And I'm comfortable with our organization not being as large if we have a smaller group that is working together and is inclusive.

While I often feel isolated, I also derive validation and satisfaction from these efforts. In some regards, I get excited sending challenging letters and talking to people I know aren't going to "get it." That's a kind of passive-aggressive way of getting some sort of satisfaction for myself. I also get some personal strength from being an outsider and not liking the way our society is in many ways. I have complete confidence in my beliefs and the way I organize. I think that I'm right. I don't think that other folks are necessarily wrong, but they just haven't thought enough about things. That's a pretty cocky way of my getting some validation! I think that our organization is onto something, and we've heard that from enough people; I think that's a kind of validation.

I don't need a lot of external validation, but I do need to see people making an effort. I don't feel like most of my friends, most people in the progressive movement, or most people in the broader community are making an effort. I see people retreating. I've been giving a lot of thought lately to my friends from high school and college and other activists who work here in Colorado. I haven't been able to confront them yet on their lack of effort.

One of my best friends from college went to South Africa after school through World Teach, married a white South African, and moved back to Boston. They're both economically privileged. That's not at all my background, so I already have some issues I have to deal with. They bought a historic house in the Boston area. And where did they choose to live? Deep in the suburbs. Maybe I am reading too much into things or being overly harsh. I guess I just wish that my friends shared my commitment to challenging ourselves to live where it might not be so comfortable and white.

I really want to talk to people about retreating from diverse neighborhoods, from a multiracial society. I don't know how to talk to my friend about it. He's a very progressive, activist kind of guy. One of my closest friends from high school, it seems, moves every year to a smaller town in Maine. Maine is already 98 percent white and the second whitest state. When I go home now, there's a real void for me. I know there are certain amenities to country living or living in the suburbs. But from my living in the core city perspective, it pains me.

I want to be able to have respect and feel warmly toward my friends in an emotional way, but I'm having a real struggle with that right now. I keep trying, and I keep letting folks know where I'm coming from on things, but I'm not yet able to confront them directly about what I'm feeling. And every minute that goes by that I'm not able to do that, I feel a barrier going up even higher.

I think I have some antiwhite sentiments with regard to structures of oppression and systemic discrimination. I don't like the way that whiteness has manifested itself in our society. I am profoundly displeased with what my culture has perpetuated in the United States, and my own reactions at times to things just depress the hell out of me. And so I see my role as especially important in being what someone on a right wing talk show called me: a race traitor. I feel like I'm saying something that's not being said and that I have a particularly unique role as a white man to speak out on things that I see as being wrong. In some ways, I wear that as a badge of honor, that he thinks of me as a race traitor.

On the other hand, I use my privilege often. I'm aware of white privilege and all the different ways that I have that as I move through my life each day. A lot of time I'll confront it; a lot of times I'll check myself. But then other times, I'm in a hurry, and I want to get through a line quicker, or I want to be somewhere on time, and so I'm aware as I'm using my white privilege. I'm aware of it, but I don't confront it at every point in the day.

*How do you use your white privilege as codirector of* CPC?

That's a great question. It's something that we've struggled with. There's an interesting push and pull in the office. I'm more often perceived as the executive director, even though I'm codirector with Soyun. I am more likely to be the person who is more controlling about our budget—not in terms of allocation of money, but in terms of watching expenses. I will be a primary contact for many of the foundations with whom we deal, and I do most of the administrative work of CPC. I do a lot of the political liaison work for CPC, and so I know more politicians. The perception that I am more the executive director and that Soyun is more our community organizer or something like that—I haven't done nearly enough to challenge that perception. But on the other hand, there are places and meetings that Soyun or another staff do not want to go because they're white, privileged, and liberal settings. So I think I use my white privilege in some positive ways in that I will be the person who goes to meetings in Boulder or Ft. Collins. And I've also used my privilege to control some things. I need to chill out on that.

I think I'm kind of a dominant personality with regard to some parts of CPC. I like to be in control; I always like to be the driver in the car rather than the passenger. I like professional and college sports. I think that's more of a traditional guy thing. I probably have a fair amount of male chauvinism, but I'm not fully sure how I manifest it. But I don't think many of my emotional qualities are typically male. I cry often; I talk a lot about my feelings. I think I'm more of a gentle person with interpersonal relationships. I think I relate better to women than to men because there's more of an emotional connection.

Who I am doesn't seem to be very consistent with the men I grew up with and my male friends. They are more traditional in the way they don't typically express their feelings. I don't think men have less feelings than women; I think we just don't express our feelings. I grew up in a single-parent family. In some ways, my mom was strong, and in some ways, she was weak. Strong because she worked like hell for the four of us—I'm the oldest of four kids—and weak in that her emotional state can be like a roller coaster. Her father—my grandfather, who's ninety-two—has really beaten her down emotionally for many years. My dad is not present in my life. So in my family, I've not seen real positive male role models, especially with regard to emotions. In fact, I've seen unhealthy expressions of emotion.

*How are you about asking for support?*

Very stubborn. By asking, I'm admitting some vulnerability. That's hard for me to do. I'm starting to ask people a lot more. In the last year in particular, I've started to see how asking for support has made me feel much more comfortable being here at CPC.

I felt very isolated for a long time here in Colorado. Last night I went to several receptions for other progressive organizations. I felt like I didn't fit in. It's good that I have CPC, so that I have a place where I can fit in, because I didn't have that before. But I'm much more acutely aware of not fitting in when I go to other places. I think that factors in with my friends, my family, going home to New England. I grew up in a small town in Maine that has, I think, five people of color out of two thousand residents, and most of the people of color are Asian babies adopted by whites. I don't want to have to explain myself all the time. I just wish people would "get it," or at least understand where I'm coming from, saying, "Bill's an interesting one, and that's how he lives his life."

It was fun last night hanging out with people I hadn't been with in a while, from environmental, pro-choice, and GLBT communities, but it didn't feel comfortable to me. I could have had more conversations, but I didn't feel a connection with people. I've only started to feel that connection recently with the people of color and white antiracists in our organization. I don't feel that with my family and friends. That's the hard part.

# Matt Reese

Matt is twenty-six. He's involved with the Kentucky Alliance Against Racist and Political Oppression and the Braden Center. Matt is also a member of Citizens Against Police Abuse (CAPA), the Progressive Students' League (PSL), and the Strategic Planning and Leadership Committee (SPLC), a committee appointed by the mayor of Louisville to create community policing in Louisville. This is a family affair; his brother Nick, his girlfriend Kate, and her brother James are also members of CAPA, PSL, and SPLC and participate with Matt in many political actions.

Matt describes himself as an activist: "My life is about the Movement. That's number one to me. Angela Davis makes the comment that activism isn't a hobby; it isn't a one day thing; it isn't a one week thing; when you become an activist or, as she says, a revolutionary, it's a lifetime, and everything around you revolves around it. That's seriously how I feel. I went to college but never graduated. The only reason I'd go back would be if it bettered my ability to get a job in activism instead of basically spending eight hours a day in manual labor at a print shop and being angry and frustrated with the things I hear around me at work."

The interview took place on a Saturday in conjunction with a protest at a Klan rally in Elizabethtown, a small town about thirty miles from Louisville. It was also the week before the Kentucky Derby; Matt and others were busy planning a series of actions in conjunction with the derby. The actions included demonstrations at City Hall to support community-oriented policing, protests against police brutality and the unjust treatment of African Americans, and visibility campaigns at the airport and along the route to the derby to let visitors to the city know about police tactics. Matt and others planned to hand out flyers to visitors and hold signs saying things like, "Welcome to Louisville, the city where police brutality is allowed."

The morning of the interview, we met Matt at his apartment and then stopped by the Bardstown Road Youth Cultural Center (the BRYCC house) to meet up with some members of Anti-Racist Action (ARA). According to Matt, "ARA does direct action against the Klan all over the country. ARA and the Klan are sworn enemies. They're trying to stop the Klan from committing violence against people." After hanging out at the BRYCC house for about an hour, the twenty or so of us drove en *masse to Elizabethtown. At the rally, Matt and members of ARA confronted a half dozen members and supporters of the Klan while two hundred anti-Klan demonstrators looked on. Although there was no violence, local police stood near by, and local media videotaped the confrontation. We ended the day at the Harriet Tubman Cultural Center, where Matt introduced us to one of his mentors, Nailah Jumoke, the executive director of the center.*

*The interview begins with Matt talking about being at the Klan rally earlier in the day.*

• • •

I didn't want to engage in too much conversation with these guys because I felt like WAVE 3 (a local TV station) was gonna give them airtime. It seemed like the cameras were following them anyway. That's what I kept saying to everybody, "Quit engaging them in this conversation because they're just spouting their rhetoric. If the cameras are going to edit this, we don't know how they'll do that, and their rhetoric is gonna hit. It's not just gonna be in Elizabethtown; it's gonna be reaching Louisville also."

At the same time, I felt empowered when we got there. We walked up as a unified front, face-to-face with the Klan, and the crowd sitting there watching us. We were all wearing black shirts, and it looked like a crew that was coming in to directly confront the Klan. They knew who we were, and we knew who they were. They focused their rhetoric on us, and we pulled their shit away. They weren't spouting that rhetoric at anybody else, and then they left.

I'd never been face-to-face with Klan members like that. I've been at their rallies in Louisville, but there we were completely shielded so that we wouldn't be face-to-face like that. It's hard to engage them in real conversation. They're trying to spout rhetoric, and we're saying, "Where's this rhetoric coming from?" There's not much that I can say to them except to stand in front of them and show the other people there that we're not gonna back down from these guys and we're here to be as strong as they portray themselves to be. There's a definite rush to it because you're facing down something so openly bad, openly racist, everything that America's not supposed to be about.

We were timid going in. Not that we were going to be timid with the Klan, but timid in that we didn't know what was going to happen. We didn't want to get separated. If people were going to get arrested, if there was going to be violence—we know that's a possibility. With the Klan, you never know what you're dealing with. We're not going to start a fight with them, but with them, you never know. That's part of the rush of it. The excitement of it is that you don't know.

One of the first times I ever got involved in activism around the Klan was when I went to a meeting down at the YMCA to plan for a demonstration at a Klan rally. A man named Bob Cunningham was there, and I'll never forget what he told us: "You just have to remember that you're right. We're fighting for equality. We're fighting for justice." When we're at a demonstration against the Klan, we know who we are. And they know who they are. They see themselves as fighting for the white race, but they don't speak for me, and I'm part of the white race.

You carry everybody that you know with you when you're there. I speak for all these people when I go there—my mom, my dad, my family, my friends and their beliefs; I'm speaking for every organization I represent. I also know some liberal-minded people who say to me, "We need people like you in the world." I think they've got too much fear to be in a situation like the one we were in today. So what they're doing is giving me their energy so that I can face down the Klan for them. They want me to represent them. There's a rush to that because I know I have them behind me in spirit. People tell me that they're proud of me. And it's great to have some of my family coming to the rally with me: my brother Nick and my girlfriend Kate's brother James. You can also see the bond that's automatically there with all those twenty people from Anti-Racist Action. There's an energy; we care about each other.

At another Klan rally one time, I talked for a long time with one of the Klan members. I was there with a Black friend named Gary, who said "Hi" to a white guy who didn't respond to him. So immediately I turned to this guy and said, "My friend just said 'Hi' to you." He gave off a racist aura. I sat down and talked to him for about two hours. It turns out that he was one of the guys standing with the Klan at the rally. He was genuinely reaching out to me and telling me that this was how he was raised, that it was hard for him to fight this because his family believed in the Klan. I just told him that my friend Gary was no different to me than anyone else and that he needed to see that Gary was no threat to him in any way. Gary had just said "Hi" to him. I invited the kid over to my house, but he never came. I don't know where he ended up.

I was a racist at one point. I wasn't a skinhead or a Nazi. My mind was struggling. I was an angry white male. I could have easily been swayed to their way. Something inside me—my parents, the relationships I had with Blacks growing up—kept me from swaying that way. I don't know why I changed and why I am so passionate about this stuff now. It's something that Nick and James and Kate and I talk about all the time. We're trying to figure out what little steps in our lives put us in this direction.

I wrote a paper in 1994 or 1995, just after high school. I was searching at the time, so I wrote this paper to try to understand what was going on. I still have it. In the paper, I was saying, "Why do Blacks have to whine and cry all the time? The Rodney King thing happened, but why are they bitching about it? It's done." I read that proudly to my dad and my brother over the phone. They jumped my ass. For about two hours, they busted my ass. By the end of the conversation, I felt shame, I felt guilt, and my road went another way.

I became an activist when the Klan came to Louisville in April 1996. I knew the Klan was coming, and I thought all night about what I could do to challenge them. I had never done any organizing, had no contacts whatsoever, didn't know anything. The next day, I made phone calls to every church in Louisville. At the end of the day, I made a call to some group— maybe the Kentucky Alliance Against Racist and Political Oppression. I found out that the students at the University of Louisville were going to try to organize something against the Klan. They hadn't really gotten to the point of organizing anything but had planned a meeting about what to do. I'd already spent ten hours that day organizing this. I got in contact with the students and went into the meeting, and every single thing they brought up I'd already done. Right then is when I gained respect among the youth. I spoke publicly, even though I didn't have the rhetoric yet. What I did say was that we should have a moment of silence for all the fallen victims of the Civil Rights Movement.

On the day of the Klan rally, there were 150 students marching to the rally. That's when I felt the power of organizing, seeing all these kids marching and seeing Blacks come out and say, "We love you." I knew that there was something there. I saw that there's a truth to action. There's an energy to action. It's not just a bunch of kids sitting around a coffeehouse talking about politics, which we did all the time. I can say that that conversation with my dad and brother changed my mentality and that the Klan coming to Louisville made me see that this is serious stuff. I realized that people like me need to be organizers.

In the 1960s, kids thought they could change the world. Black kids in the South or the kids on the West Coast at Berkeley thought they could change the world. It didn't come from conversation. It came from direct action, whether it was protesting the universities or the police or the racist organizations. I'm the next generation of that. I'm the extension of that. I feel empowered. I know that I'm doing something. When I go to the Braden Center,

I'm accepted there because of what I've done. I have a line of actions behind me. I can say, "I've fought this and this and this." I'm not just talking.

I feel that I have to challenge racism. There's injustice and inequality. It's right in my face. I can't take the excesses that my color gives me when other people are oppressed. There's no gain in this for me. I'm not seeking anything; at least I don't think I am. Maybe subconsciously there's something in my head that I haven't figured out yet. For me, it's walking into a room and seeing people like Anne Braden, Anne Reynolds, and Alice Wade look at me with respect.[1] Maybe what I get out of this is the self-gratification of doing something right. Maybe I can sleep better at night. I've studied racism, I've learned it, and I feel that there is nothing else for me to do. I'm just a cog in the machine of the Movement.

. . .

People at work know I'm an organizer. It's hard when I get called "nigger lover," I get called "fag," I get called "Black wannabe." That's the hardest part for me. Just this past Friday I had a guy say to me, "Oh, you'll fight for the niggers, but you won't fight for me." I don't need that shit. I already know those thoughts are out there, and at my workplace, that shouldn't be going on.

Every place I've worked since I've been an organizer I get the same shit. I get treated differently because when someone says "nigger," I'm going to say something to them. I feel that in a workplace, if those comments are going to be made, then I have to counteract that for the people in the middle ground who don't believe that but somehow may sway that way because of this propaganda. In most of the places I've worked, I'm the only person who will stand up.

I once worked in a copy center that was a corporate franchise. I was twenty-one and a manager with no manager qualifications. They knew they could pay me $18,000 when normal rates were $30,000 for the position I was in. They hired some Bosnians at a cheap wage and wouldn't give them raises. Well, we hit our targets for profit, and we were getting busy, so I requested three more employees and was told to hire them. The only people I had apply were three Blacks. They all had experience, and so I hired them. My manager's exact words were, "When Blacks have experience in other companies, it's hard to train them how to do it our way." We weren't doing rocket science; we were making copies. I asked for someone from the corporation to come in and train the new employees, and they wouldn't send anyone. Finally, because of how they were treating the Bosnians and the Blacks and because they hadn't given me a raise in ten months, I accused the company of discrimination. I was fired within two weeks. It was a horrible experience. I can't tell you how many times I've been fired from jobs for my beliefs.

I've worked at my current job for two years—the longest job I've ever had. The good thing about this job is that my dad is my manager. He knows what I do. He allows me to take a long lunch when there's a protest, leave early, and take days off when I have meetings. My dad treats everybody this way; it's not just me. Everybody can leave when they want if we're not in a dire situation, and I wouldn't leave if we were in a dire situation. I wouldn't have these options with another company. So even though I put myself on the line at work, my dad definitely protects me. He knows what I'm saying and doing is right. If I go to another job, I'd have to start all over. At least at this job they know who I am, and it's not going to get any worse than it is now.

When I interact with other white people, I get so much shit all the time. If I'm sitting in a room full of whites that I don't know, I end up feeling very out of it. If Kate wants to go to a party, I have to sit there and listen to these mentalities. Either I'm going to cause a scene when I confront these people, or I can just sit there and be miserable and listen to these people bash other people that I fight for. That's a very hard thing for me. It's very hard to go somewhere and know that there will be comments made. It's inevitable. Once that first racist comment comes, it's on, personally. It's gonna be, "What did you just say?"

Here's a perfect example. James had some friends at his house. We were sitting around drinking beer and getting pretty drunk. Somebody made the comment that he didn't want Blacks in his community because they lower property values. It was like war. I flipped. I started out semicalm, but I definitely wanted him to know that I was offended by what he said. I wasn't expecting that comment from this person. He didn't say it in the way of, "That's the reality of the real estate business." It was a slam. By the end of it, we were yelling at each other. One of our other friends came in and told us to stop, but that friend thought I was in the wrong. He's not a politically active person either.

When I see people holding onto those beliefs, no matter what I'm showing them or what the people around me are showing them, it's hard to be content. I can't just be quiet and give them a hug when I leave and say, "Let's be friends." I can't do that. How can I give someone love when he doesn't love the people I love? When he is ruling out a whole segment of society for whatever reason, whether it be females or minorities? He's not a true American. He's not with the idea of what America is supposed to be based on. He's got his own set of rules. I just can't be content with that, sitting and smiling and feeling happy. So I feel responsible all the time. I can't let comments go. I feel that I have to give them statistics and a different perspective so that they can see something else.

I know that there are people out there who can switch. I changed the way I think. I've had people tell me, "The only reason I'm in the Movement is because of the passion I saw in your eyes." That's invigorating because I turned somebody. I got them away from that mentality.

There have been times when I thought I might burn out. When you're not doing action, when it's all talk and you're just getting mad and not putting your energy toward activism, you're gonna burn out. You can't live this stuff in your head. When we came onto the mayor's Strategic Planning and Leadership Committee, we had energy. We were disputing things and arguing and making points. We weren't being nice and polite; it was not a time to be nice and polite and hug and be happy. We're talking about creating community-oriented policing. This is an opportunity we have to change Louisville. We have that ability. We did it with the Civilian Police Review Board. The young people were so involved in that. We're now stepping up. We're making the progression to respected activists in the community.

I believe that I can change the world. Definitely. If I don't, then I can't be in this. That's what I think differentiates a liberal and an activist. Liberals talk about changing the world but don't have the empowerment to change the world. Activists truly believe it, or we wouldn't be activists. I'm not going out there meeting with police to just talk to them. I'm meeting with them so that I can change the culture.

I've really seen myself mature in the last five years. Kate, James, Nick, and I have all been talking lately about how proud we are of the maturity level we've got right now. We're about action, and people can count on us now. That's something they couldn't do in the past.

I've definitely been more angry than I am now. That's come through age and experience in this. I don't get as angry as I used to. I'm still passionate, but I realize that anger is just hurting the situation. If I'm talking like I am to you right now, there's a possibility that you might hear what I have to say, but if I'm sitting screaming at you, you're gonna close up right away. It took me a long time to realize that. I now have the education to be able to give someone facts and details and stories and examples and analogies; I know the stuff now.

I didn't learn this in school. It was me finding books and reading. I'd read something about the Panthers, and there would be another book mentioned, and I'd read that. Then there was a change in me when I read the *Autobiography of Malcolm X*. I understood that Malcolm X was an organizer; he was trying to organize people. And then, when I read some of the speeches of Martin Luther King, my anger kind of left. I didn't have to be as abrasive. I learned that you can deal with things peacefully.

• • •

*(We ask Matt about the role he plays as a "bridge" between the kids at* BRYCC *house and* ARA *and the elders in the Kentucky Alliance.)*

Sometimes, I feel the same way the elders do. But sometimes I feel that what the kids are saying is valid. Nick and James and I participate with the alliance. And we can go into the BRYCC house or attend a rally like today with ARA and gain their respect because they know us. So it's inevitable that we're kind of the in between.

I'm closer in age to these kids, and I was at the same mentality as they are. It's only five years since I was at the same place they are. I wanted to go screw with the Klan; I wanted to start a revolution, whatever it was. The members of the alliance used to be there, but they're forty or fifty years removed from that time period. I'm coming to a point of understanding where the alliance is. I don't know that I'd define myself as a bridge between the two; it's just what it is. When I've heard people criticize ARA or the BRYCC house crew, I've said, "They're kids! These are fifteen-year-old kids. You can't expect them to act like they're forty years old." At fifteen, I was playing soccer and going for girls and worrying about drinking beer. That was about it. The kids in ARA and at the BRYCC house are way farther ahead than I was at fifteen years old.

The kids from the BRYCC house deal with skinheads and Nazis directly on a daily basis. They see each other walking down the street. I live farther down the street; they are in constant interaction with each other. I can't very much tell these kids, "Don't say anything; don't get hostile with them," because that's their thing. I don't directly deal with the skinheads every day, so it's not my place to tell them, "Settle down, relax." There's a different kind of posturing that Nick and James and I did at the Klan rally today. It's more stand-back, realizing that the media's watching everything that's being said.

What I was fearing today was that some of the elders of the Movement would come and we would have to protect them. If the Kentucky Alliance had been there, it would have been a different situation. Here's a perfect example. When we went in a busload to protest Bush's inauguration in Washington earlier this year, it was a pretty diverse group in terms of elders and young people. There was a point where we could have gotten involved in the confrontations that were going on, but the elders said, "Let's move on to the protest because that's what we're here for." We listened to them and did what they said.

I wouldn't be where I am without the elders in the Movement. And they wouldn't have a future without us. Inevitably, everyone's going to die, and if we're not there to pick up the pieces, then the Movement is dead.

# Appendix:
## Interview Questions and Editing Guidelines

*Interview questions*

Although we never asked all of these questions, we used this list as a starting point for identifying the types of information we wanted to get from the interviews. The actual interview was much more fluid and circular than this set of questions suggests. We might begin by talking casually about each other's lives, or our first contact might be an activity together, like participating in a protest. And we frequently added questions that occurred to us during the interview.

- What work or activity do you do? With whom do you do it? What's the setting? What are you trying to accomplish? What are you most proud of in terms of what you've accomplished? How do you prepare yourself to do the work you do? For you, what's the connection between personal growth and institutional / political change?
- How did you come to challenge racism and sexism? Who and what influenced you? How does faith or spirit enter into your work? Why do you do this work?
- What does being a white man mean to you? What is your journey in identifying and understanding yourself as a white man? How did you learn about being white and male? Who taught you how to be white and male, overtly or covertly? How do you feel now about being white? About being male? For you, what's the meaning of white male privilege?
- In addition to being white and male, how else do you identify yourself? How (if at all) do other aspects of your cultural identity (e.g., religion, class) inform your beliefs, feelings, and actions about racism and sexism? Where are you in your journey of understanding these other identities? How (if at all) has your focus on racism or sexism led you to do work on other "isms"?
- How would you describe your relationships with people of color and

white women? Before starting your work? Now? What's hard / easy or exciting / difficult about these relationships? How have these relationships changed? How do you feel about these relationships?

- What have you felt, thought, or done when a person of color or white woman confronted you about a bias you had or for having done something racist or sexist or for exercising white male privilege? What do you feel, think, and do when others assume that you are a stereotypical white man or find out that you embody some traditional white male characteristics?

- How would you describe your relationships with white men before you began doing your work? Now? What's hard / easy or difficult / exciting about these relationships? How have these relationships changed? In general, what feelings come up for you when you are with other white men?

- What happens when family members or friends make what you believe are racist or sexist comments? What do you feel / think / do? As you experience or notice racism in other white people / white men, how do you respond? Do any examples come to mind?

- Where is your community? Where do you get the support to continue this work? Where do you turn when it feels hopeless? How do you celebrate your victories?

*Editing Guidelines*

Our primary goals in editing were to create an interesting and sometimes dramatic narrative, to preserve the interviewee's voice and develop a text that could be easily read, and to create narratives that would sound good if read aloud.

As it evolved, our process of creating a narrative from an audiotape of an interview involved several steps. We first listened to the interview and identified all the comments that we thought could be used in a narrative. The first draft would be created by transcribing those comments and simultaneously creating sentences and paragraphs. Next, the three of us read the draft, decided which parts were most useful, retained those and deleted the rest, and conducted follow-up phone interviews when we wanted to get more detail about something an interviewee had said. We created further drafts by rearranging text into comments and themes that in our perspective naturally flowed from one to another. In a few cases, this closely followed the actual interview; in most, it involved major revisions. Finally, we shared the narrative with the interviewee and invited his comments and edits and almost always incorporated these, particularly when he wanted to delete material from the narrative.

Although we didn't have any written guidelines for creating the narratives, we wrote the following list after the fact as a way to be more concrete about what we were intuitively doing.

- We used the inflection of the interviewee's voice on the tape, in addition to his comments, as a way to determine where we thought phrases, sentences, and paragraphs should begin and end. We used punctuation as best we could to show continuity, as well as pauses and breaks, in the flow of the conversation. Sometimes we collapsed into one written sentence what sounded like two or more sentences when spoken.
- We almost always used the actual words that were spoken, including "swear" words, colloquialisms, and made-up words to preserve the quality of the speaker's voice.
- We changed the order of words—or eliminated some words—when the phrasing seemed awkward or was confusing to read. For example, we would change "It's only probably some of the time that I . . . " to "Probably, some of the time I . . . " or even "Sometimes, I. . . . "
- We changed pronouns to nouns when the pronoun reference might be unclear. Sometimes we changed "you" to "I" when it was clear that the speaker was talking about his own experiences; on the other hand, if his use of "you" indicated that he was stating a value that he wished others had, we retained "you."
- We usually deleted a summary sentence like "That experience had a big impact on me" when it seemed obvious in context.
- Sometimes an interviewee would simultaneously provide commentary as he was describing an incident from his past. We usually separated the commentary from the description so that one followed the other.
- There were occasions when the interviewee switched from negative to positive statements several times in a row—for example, "I did X but didn't want to do Y, so I went ahead and did X but was thinking I should have done Y." When this happened, we usually eliminated the "back and forth" so that there was only one change in position: "I was thinking of doing Y but did X instead." Similarly, if there were double negatives, we usually changed those to a positive.
- Sometimes, we kept repetition in phrasing for dramatic effect—for example, "It's not a matter of A; it's not a matter of B; it's not a matter of C."

- With the encouragement of various people who reviewed early drafts of the narratives, we eliminated most of our questions and comments. This meant that we sometimes had to create a transition sentence or phrase so that the reader wouldn't be confused by a change in tone or content.
- We kept some questions in the narrative when we wanted to challenge the interviewee and felt that our question and his response gave a dramatic quality to the narrative.
- In creating paragraphs, we looked for a topic sentence and then tried to build each paragraph around that. We often moved sentences within and between paragraphs for flow and clarity. Sometimes we intentionally created shorter paragraphs for emphasis.
- As a way to create themes in the narrative, we sometimes grouped together comments related to a single theme, even though the comments might have appeared at different points in the interview.
- We usually changed the order in which comments were actually made in the interview for dramatic effect, particularly in the openings and closings of the narrative.

# Endnotes

*Foreword: Challenging Racism, Challenging History*

1   Five centuries earlier, the Norse lived on Newfoundland for two years before conflict with Native Americans caused them to give up their attempt at permanent settlement. Probably that conflict was prompted by inhumane acts by the Norse, especially since their word for the Natives was *skraelings,* a derogatory term in Norse, but we have little information about exactly what transpired across this earlier frontier.

2   *The Journal of Christopher Columbus,* translated by Cecil Jane (New York: Bonanza, 1960), 26.

3   Quoted in G. R. Crone, *The Discovery of America* (New York: Weybright and Talley, 1960), 182–3.

4   Bartolomé de Las Casas, *History of the Indies* (New York: Harper and Row, 1971), 289.

5   Las Casas quoted in Kirkpatrick Sale, *The Conquest of Paradise* (New York: Knopf, 1990), 159.

6   Las Casas in this and the following paragraphs quoted in Marcel Bataillon, "The Clerigo Casas," in *Bartolomé de las Casas in History,* ed. Juan Friede and Benjamin Keen (DeKalb: NIU Press, 1971), 415–6.

7   Las Casas, *History of the Indies* (New York: Harper and Row, 1971), 274–78.

8   J. H. Elliott, *The Old World and the New* (Cambridge: Cambridge University Press, 1970), 48. Oviedo quoted by Las Casas in *Ibid.,* 274. Of course, when Las Casas wrote, "peoples" and "men" were used as synonyms. Las Casas was *not* claiming that people are all one sex or that women cannot reason!

9   Quoted in Thomas Benjamin, "A Time of Reconquest: History, the Maya Revival, and the Zapatista Rebellion in Chiapas," *American Historical Review* 4 (2000): 424–27.

10  Lewis Nordan quoted in David K. Shipler, *A Country of Strangers* (New York: Knopf, 1997), 106–07.

11  Coles and Jefferson quoted in Robert P. Howard, *Mostly Good and Competent Men* (Springfield: Sangamon State University, 1988), 21–29.

12  In 1824, local political enemies would convict Coles of violating an Illinois law requiring that anyone bringing Blacks into the state post bond of $1000 for each. The legislature, however, pardoned him.

13 Dick Norrish, "Coles Kept Illinois Free State," *Edwardsville Intelligencer,* 5, 4 (1978).

14 This fact can be hard to remember, since the parties fundamentally reversed positions on racial matters during the 1960s.

15 Logan quoted in Mrs. John Logan, "A Thrilling Williamson County Incident of the Civil War," in *Souvenir of Williamson County, IL,* ed. J. F. Wilcox (Effingham: LeCrone Press, 1905); Carl D. Cottingham, P. M. Jones, and G. W. Kent, *Gen. John A. Logan: His Life and Times* (Carbondale: American Resources, 1989), 20.

16 Discussion of Matthews based on William Ivy Hair, *Carnival of Fury* (Baton Rouge: Louisiana State University Press, 1976), 17–35; "The Matthews Family Martyrizing," *Greenville (MS) Times,* January 3, 1891.

17 They were not "his youthful principles," of course. They were his principles.

18 James W. Loewen, *Lies Across America: What Our Historic Sites Get Wrong* (New York: The New Press, 1999), 394–404 and sources cited there; Michael W. Fitzgerald, *The Union League Movement in the Deep South* (Baton Rouge: Louisiana State University Press, 1989), 234–42.

19 The ability to do this with minimal personal cost is itself an aspect of white privilege.

20 Marshall Hyatt, *Franz Boas, Social Activist* (New York: Greenwood Press, 1990), 83–87, 135–37, 144–45, quoted on p. 151.

21 Ironically, Henry Ford was also a leader of anti-Semitism in the United States and helped develop Dearborn as a segregated white suburb of Detroit.

22 Discussion in this and the following paragraph draws on August Meier and Elliott Rudwick, *Black Detroit and the Rise of the UAW* (New York: Oxford University Press, 1979), 8, 109–33, 166–83.

23 Recent John Brown Day celebrations (May 8) in New York, Maryland, Kansas, and California exemplify what can be done.

*Herbert Aptheker*

1 "Jim Crow" refers to post-Emancipation legal and extralegal practices of racial discrimination against African Americans, ensuring their segregation, subordination, and dehumanization.

2 Debt peonage is a form of involuntary servitude that works through systematic indebtedness. After slavery was abolished in the South, debt peonage was a way for the planters to secure a cheap and stable workforce. For the recently freed slaves, who were given neither land nor capital and who needed work, it was hard to resist falling into contractual relations that led to debt peonage.

3 Angela Davis is a political activist, teacher, writer, and community organizer. She was involved in the Black Panthers and is a longtime member of the Communist Party.

4 Nat Turner was the leader of a slave insurrection in 1831 in Virginia; it can be seen as the culmination of a decade of slave unrest.

5 Carter Woodson, an African American educator and historian, devoted his life to

making "the world see the Negro as a participant rather than as a lay figure in history." He founded the *Journal of Negro History* and the Association for the Study of Negro Life and History and started a publishing firm in order to help young Black scholars get their work published.

6   W. E. B. Du Bois was one of America's preeminent intellectuals. As a young man at the opening of the twentieth century, he opposed Booker T. Washington's accommodationist strategies, urging racial unity and full participation of Blacks in American society. In 1909 he helped found the National Association for the Advancement of Colored People (NAACP) and for twenty-five years edited its journal, *The Crisis*. His campaign for the rights of African Americans dovetailed with his protests against racial oppression in the African colonies. He joined the Socialist Party in the United States in 1911 and late in his life became a communist and emigrated to Ghana.

7   "New Masses" was a cultural and political journal published in the 1930s by the U.S. Communist Party.

### Stetson Kennedy

1   As head of the Permanent Investigations Subcommittee of the Senate Committee on Government Operations, Joseph McCarthy engaged in a wide-ranging communist witch-hunt between 1950 and 1954, fueled by the public fear of communism and the government's desire to use this fear to decimate the left.

2   The novels of Richard Wright, an African American writer, deal with social class but center on racism and in particular internalized racism. *Native Son* is probably his best-known and most read novel.

3   David Duke, an ex-member of the Klan and present racist, ran for governor of Louisiana in 1992 and narrowly lost.

### Art Branscombe

1   For more about this realtor strategy, known as "blockbusting," see Chip Berlet's narrative.

2   Organized in California in 1966 by Bobby Seale and Huey Newton, the Black Panthers pushed to have control over their own communities and were dedicated to self-defense of the Black community in the face of racist aggression and police brutality. They were decimated in the 1970s by a systematic FBI campaign to exterminate them.

### Pat Cusick

1   Pacifist and five-time presidential candidate for the Socialist Party in the early part of the twentieth century, Eugene V. Debs was the founder of the American Railway Union and leader of the brutally repressed Pullman Strike of 1894.

2 The Dixiecrats were southern Democrats who split from the national party in 1948. Their unsuccessful presidential candidate was Strom Thurmond, later a senator from South Carolina.

3 The Progressive Party was comprised of a group of disaffected leftist Democrats who chose former vice-president Henry Wallace as their unsuccessful presidential candidate in 1948.

4 Students for a Democratic Society was a national student group organized in the 1960s. Members engaged in research on the military-industrial-university complex and organized protests against university complicity in the Vietnam War.

5 The War Resisters' League was a radical pacifist group with headquarters in New York City. Dorothy Day, a longtime peace activist and radical Catholic, cofounded the Catholic Worker Movement in 1933; today over 175 Catholic Worker communities continue to protest injustice, war, racism, and violence of all forms.

6 An activist in the Civil Rights Movement and at the forefront of the shift in the Movement from nonviolence and integration to self-defense and Black nationalism, Stokely Carmichael later changed his name to Kwame Ture. Carmichael first called for Black Power in June 1966 during a speech in Greenwood, Mississippi. He defined it as "a call for black people in this country to unite, to recognize their heritage, [and] to build a sense of community."

7 Bayard Rustin, an African American man who worked to integrate the peace movement and the Civil Rights Movement, was a conscientious objector during World War II; directed the War Resisters' League in the 1950s; and helped found the Congress of Racial Equality (CORE), guide the Montgomery bus boycott, set up the Southern Christian Leadership Council (SCLC), and organize the 1963 March on Washington. A gay man, he saw the gay rights movement as a logical extension of the Civil Rights Movement.

8 The March on Washington was the culmination of the pre–Black Power stage of the Civil Rights Movement. While largely comprised of Black Americans, there was a significant minority of white participants. The 1963 march is most remembered for Martin Luther King's "I Have a Dream" speech.

9 Mel King is a longtime community organizer, and Dianne Wilkerson is a Massachusetts state senator.

10 The Department of Housing and Urban Development (HUD) was created as a new Cabinet office in 1965 during the presidency of Lyndon Johnson as a response to Black activism. During the first 5–8 years of its existence, it oversaw well-financed programs for low-income housing construction but was "gutted" under the Reagan administration.

*Nat Yalowitz*

1 "Wobblies" was the nickname for the International Workers of the World (IWW), formed in 1905 by socialists, anarchists, and radical trade unionists. The

Wobblies believed that all workers in any industry should be organized into "one big union," undivided by sex, race, or skills, and that capitalism had to be overthrown by political and economic action.

2 Nine Black adolescents were arrested in 1931 and charged with raping two white girls. Two weeks later, eight of the "Scottsboro boys" were convicted and sentenced to death. They became a cause célèbre of several civil rights organizations. The ensuing court battles dragged on for the next nineteen years, at which time the last defendant won release.

3 The "little war going on in Spain" was the Spanish Civil War; in the United States, it was the center of left political discussion in the late 1930s.

4 The Student Nonviolent Coordinating Committee (SNCC) was set up in 1960 to coordinate the various student protests springing up after the sit-ins in Greensboro, N.C. It initially focused on voter registration drives and direct action campaigns and, along with the rest of the Civil Rights Movement, gradually shifted its focus over the years to embrace Black Power.

## Jesse Wimberley

1 Jesse Helms is a senator from North Carolina known for his reactionary and racist views and his longevity in the Senate. Pat Buchanan, a reactionary former talk show host and journalist, has been in and out of campaigns for political office for many years.

## Chip Berlet

1 Bernice Johnson Reagon is a founder and member of the all-female Black gospel group Sweet Honey in the Rock. She also composes music, is a professor of history, and has been active politically for decades, challenging racism, sexism, homophobia, classism, and other forms of oppression.

2 "Blockbusting" is a strategy used by realtors to profit from white racial fears: realtors target a white neighborhood, tell homeowners that Blacks are moving in, buy their homes at greatly reduced prices, sell them to Blacks at greatly inflated prices, and then profit on the turnover in ownership. (Art Branscombe talks about the history of blockbusting in his narrative.)

## Joe Fahey

1 John Carlos and Tommy Smith finished third and first respectively in the 200 meter dash at the 1968 Olympics. On the victory stand they raised their arms in unison with black gloves on their clenched fists in what became known as the "Black Power salute." The U.S. Olympic Committee stripped them of their medals because they had "injected politics" into sports.

*David Attyah*

1   An African American law professor and one of the most provocative intellectuals in American law, Patricia Williams is the author of *The Alchemy of Race and Rights*.

*Steve Bailey*

1   Bell hooks is the pseudonym of Gloria Jean Watkins, a prolific writer, scholar, lecturer, and cultural critic focusing on the intersections of race, class, and gender in contemporary culture.

*Billy Yalowitz*

1   In black-face minstrelsy, a U.S. tradition popular from the mid-nineteenth century to the mid-twentieth century, white performers darkened their faces and did stereotyped performances of African American song and dance.

*A. T. Miller*

1   The Stonewall Rebellion is generally considered to be the beginning of the modern lesbian and gay liberation movement. On June 27, 1969, some New York City police officers tried to shut down the Stonewall Inn, a gay bar on Christopher Street in Greenwich Village, and drag queens of color fought back by flinging bottles and rocks at police. The Harlem Renaissance was an unprecedented outburst of creative activity among African Americans in the 1920s. It spawned writers like Langston Hughes, Zora Neale Hurston, and Jean Toomer.
2   A poet, essayist, and activist, Audre Lorde was a major figure in the lesbian and feminist movements and a major proponent of viewing oppressions as interlocking and requiring simultaneous action. Many of her classic essays and speeches are in her collection, *Sister Outsider*. Barbara Smith, an activist and writer, was a founding member of the Combahee River Collective, a collective of Black feminists "committed to struggling against racial, sexual, heterosexual, and class oppression," and coeditor of *All the Women Are White, All the Blacks Are Men, But Some of Us Are Brave: Black Women's Studies*.

*Monte Piliawsky*

1   The Zulu Parade is an annual parade during Mardi Gras celebrations in New Orleans in which the participants are people of African descent.
2   A civil rights activist and advocate for children, Marion Wright Edelman was the first Black woman admitted to the bar in Mississippi and is the long-time director of the Children's Defense Fund.

*Nibs Stroupe*

1 An activist right wing Republican from Georgia, Newt Gingrich briefly led a congressional struggle to pass the Republican "Contract for America," which some progressives called the "Contract on America."

*Terry Kupers*

1 Michael Lerner is a white Jewish American author and progressive commentator.

*Rick Whaley*

1 The Harambee Community School is named for the Harambee schools in Kenya; after independence, the Kenyan government told villagers that if they built schools, the government would provide teachers for those schools.
2 A longtime Native American rights activist, Winona LaDuke lives on the White Earth Ojibwe (Chippewa) Reservation in Minnesota. She was the Green Party candidate for vice-president in 1996 and 2000.

*Sean Cahill*

1 Gloria Fox and Charlotte Golar Ritchie are Boston-based African American community activists.

*Jason Wallach*

1 The Zapatistas, the popular name for the Zapatista Army of National Liberation, are primarily indigenous people in the state of Chiapas in southern Mexico. The group, named after Emiliano Zapata, advocates for democracy and justice through constitutional reforms.

*Matt Reese*

1 Anne Braden, Anne Reynolds, and Alice Wade are longtime activists associated with the Kentucky Alliance Against Racist and Political Oppression.

# Suggestions for Further Reading

We have included in this reading list books by the white men we interviewed for this book, even if their narratives do not appear in the book; other books by and about antiracist white men; and some noteworthy books and articles by people of color and white women in the field of antiracism and social change.

Anzaldúa, Gloria, ed. *Making Face, Making Soul: Haciendas Caras. Creative and Critical Perspectives by Women of Color*. San Francisco: Aunt Lute Foundation Books, 1990.

Aptheker, Herbert. *Anti-Racism in U.S. History: The First Two Hundred Years*. Westport, Conn.: Praeger, 1993.

Baldwin, James. "On Being 'White' . . . and Other Lies." *Essence*, April 1984.

———. *The Price of the Ticket: Collected Nonfiction 1948–1985*. New York: St. Martin's / Marek, 1985.

Banks, Russell. *Cloudsplitter*. New York: Harper Perennial, 1998.

Barndt, Joseph. *Dismantling Racism: The Continuing Challenge to White America*. Minneapolis: Augsburg Fortress, 1991.

Berger, Maurice. *White Lies: Race and the Myths of Whiteness*. New York: Farrar Strauss and Giroux, 1999.

Berlet, Chip. *Eyes Right! Challenging the Right Wing Backlash*. Boston: South End Press, 1995.

Berry, Wendell. *The Hidden Wound*. San Francisco: North Point Press, 1989.

Blauner, Robert. *Black Lives, White Lives: Three Decades of Race Relations in America*. Berkeley and Los Angeles: University of California Press, 1989.

Bowser, Benjamin P., and Raymond Hunt, eds. *Impacts of Racism on White Americans*. Beverly Hills, Calif.: Sage Publications, 1981.

Bulkin, Elly, Minnie Bruce Pratt, and Barbara Smith. *Yours in Struggle: Three Feminist Perspectives on Anti-Semitism and Racism*. Brooklyn, N.Y.: Long Haul Press, 1984.

Campbell, Will D. *Brother to a Dragonfly*. New York: Continuum, 2000.

Chappell, David L. *Inside Agitators: White Southerners in the Civil Rights Movement*. Baltimore: Johns Hopkins University Press, 1994.

Chesler, Mark A., and James E. Crowfoot. "White Men in Multicultural Coalitions." Ann Arbor: Program on Conflict and Management Alternatives, University of Michigan, 1994. Working Paper No. 45.

Daloz, Laurent A. Parks, Cheryl H. Keen, James P. Keen, and Sharon Daloz Parks.

*Common Fire: Leading Lives of Commitment in a Complex World.* Boston: Beacon Press, 1996.

Davis, Angela Y. *Women, Race, and Class.* New York: Vintage, 1981.

Davis, Angela Y., and Bettina Aptheker, eds. *If They Come in the Morning: Voices of Resistance.* New York: Signet, 1971.

Dees, Morris, with Steve Fiffer. *A Season for Justice: The Life and Times of Civil Rights Lawyer Morris Dees.* New York: Scribners, 1991.

Du Bois, W. E. B. *John Brown.* Armonk, N.Y.: M. E. Sharpe, 1997.

Egerton, John. *Speak Now Against the Day: The Generation before the Civil Rights Movement in the South.* Chapel Hill, N.C.: University of North Carolina Press, 1994.

Frankenberg, Ruth. *White Women, Race Matters: The Social Construction of Whiteness.* Minneapolis: University of Minnesota Press, 1993.

Griffen, John Howard. *Black Like Me.* New York: Penguin, 1960.

hooks, bell. *Killing Rage: Ending Racism.* New York: Henry Holt, 1995.

Horton, Myles, with Judith Kohl and Herbert Kohl. *The Long Haul: The Autobiography of Myles Horton.* New York: Teachers College Press, 1998.

Hull, Gloria T., Patricia Bell Scott, and Barbara Smith, eds. *All the Women Are White, All the Blacks Are Men, but Some of Us Are Brave: Black Women's Studies.* Old Westbury, N.Y.: Feminist Press, 1982.

Ignatiev, Noel, and John Garvey, eds. *Race Traitor.* New York: Routledge, 1996.

Jacobson-Hardy, Michael. *Behind the Razor Wire: Portrait of a Contemporary American Prison System.* New York: New York University Press, 1999.

James, Joy, ed. *The Angela Y. Davis Reader.* Malden, Mass.: Blackwell Publishers, 1998.

Katz, Judith. *White Awareness: Handbook for Anti-Racism Training.* Norman, Okla.: University of Oklahoma Press, 1978.

Kennedy, Stetson. *Jim Crow Guide: The Way It Was.* Boca Raton, Fla.: Florida Atlantic University Press, 1959.

Kivel, Paul. *Uprooting Racism: How White People Can Work for Racial Justice.* Philadelphia: New Society Publishers, 1996.

Kupers, Terry. *Prison Madness: The Mental Health Crisis behind Bars and What We Must Do about It.* San Francisco: Jossey-Bass, 1999.

Lapchick, Richard. *Broken Promises: Racism in American Sports.* Lanham, Md.: Lexington Books, 1986.

Loewen, James W. *Lies My Teacher Told Me: Everything Your American History Textbooks Got Wrong.* New York: New Press, 1995.

Lorde, Audre. *Sister Outsider.* New York: Crossing Press, 1996.

McIntosh, Peggy. "White Privilege and Male Privilege: A Personal Account of Coming to See Correspondences through Work in Women's Studies." Wellesley, Mass.: Center for Research on Women, 1988. Working Paper No. 189.

Miller, Jerome G. *Search and Destroy: African American Males in the Criminal Justice System.* Cambridge and New York: Cambridge University Press, 1996.

Miller Shearer, Jody. *Enter the River: Healing Steps from White Privilege toward Racial Reconciliation.* Scottdale, Pa.: Herald Press, 1994.

Moraga, Cherríe, and Gloria Anzaldúa, eds. *This Bridge Called My Back: Writings by Radical Women of Color.* New York: Kitchen Table Press, 1983.

Novick, Michael. *White Lies, White Power: The Fight against White Supremacy and Reactionary Violence.* Monroe, Maine: Common Courage Press, 1995.

Piliawsky, Monte. *Exit 13: Oppression and Racism in Academia.* Boston: South End Press, 1982.

Reagon, Bernice Johnson. "Coalition Politics: Turning the Century." In *Home Girls: A Black Feminist Anthology,* ed. Barbara Smith. New York: Kitchen Table Press, 1983.

Roediger, David. *Towards the Abolition of Whiteness.* New York: Verso, 1994.

——. *The Wages of Whiteness. Race and the Making of the American Working Class.* New York: Verso, 1991.

——, ed. *Black on White: Black Writers on What It Means to Be White.* New York: Schocken, 1998.

Rothenberg, Paula S. *White Privilege: Essential Readings on the Other Side of Racism.* New York: Worth Publishers, 2002.

Segrest, Mab. *Memoir of a Race Traitor.* Boston: South End Press, 1994.

Seldon, Horace. *Convictions about Racism in the United States of America.* Boston: Community Change, 1992.

Smith, Lillian. *Killers of the Dream.* New York: Norton, 1994.

Stroupe, Nibs, and Inez Fleming. *While We Run This Race: Confronting the Power of Racism in a Southern Church.* Maryknoll, N.Y.: Orbis Books, 1995.

Terkel, Studs. *Race: How Blacks and Whites Think and Feel about the American Obsession.* New York: New Press, 1992.

Terry, Robert. *For Whites Only.* Grand Rapids, Mich.: William B. Eerdmans, 1970.

Thandeka. *Learning to Be White: Money, Race and God in America.* New York: Continuum, 1999.

Thompson, Becky. *A Promise and a Way of Life: White Antiracist Activism.* Minneapolis: University of Minnesota Press, 2001.

Thompson, Becky, and Sangeeta Tyagi, eds. *Names We Call Home: Autobiography on Racial Identity.* New York: Routledge, 1996.

Whaley, Rick, and Walt Bresette. *Walleye Warriors: The Chippewa Treaty Rights Story.* Philadelphia: New Society Publishers, 1994.

Williams, Patricia. *Seeing a Color-Blind Future: The Paradox of Race.* New York: Noonday Press, 1997.

Zinn, Howard. *A People's History of the United States.* New York: Harper Perennial, 1980.

——. *You Can't Be Neutral on a Moving Train.* Boston: Beacon Press, 1994.

# About the Authors

**Cooper Thompson** has been leading workshops, consulting, organizing, and writing about sexism, homophobia, and racism full time for over twenty years. He is the author of many essays and educational materials, including "A New Vision of Masculinity" (published originally in *Changing Men* magazine in 1987 and reprinted in dozens of anthologies and college readers); "White Men and the Denial of Racism" (in *Readings for Diversity and Social Justice;* Routledge, 2000); and "On Being Heterosexual in a Homophobic World" (in *Homophobia: How We All Pay the Price;* Beacon Press, 1992). He also coproduced a unique video on men and sexuality, *Finding Our Way* (New Day Films, 1990). He is Senior Consultant with VISIONS, Inc.

**Emmett Schaefer** first began teaching courses on social class, race relations, gender, and African studies at community colleges and universities twenty-five years ago and is currently Adjunct Professor of Sociology at the University of Massachusetts, Boston. As a result of his teaching and activism around issues of oppression, his support work for liberation struggles in southern Africa, and his personal relationships with Native people, Asians and Asian Americans, and Africans and African Americans, he has a strong working knowledge of white racism.

**Harry Brod** is a child of Holocaust survivors and a child of the '60s. Both heritages shape his commitments to justice, much of which he has expressed in twenty years of profeminist teaching, writing, and activism. He is Professor of Philosophy and Humanities at the University of Northern Iowa, where he also serves as Director of the University Honors Program. He is the editor of *The Making of Masculinities: The New Men's Studies* (Routledge, 1987) and *A Mensch among Men: Explorations in Jewish Masculinity* (Crossing Press, 1988); co-editor (with Michael Kaufman) of *Theorizing Masculinities* (Sage, 1994); and author of *Hegel's Philosophy of Politics: Idealism, Identity and Modernity* (Westview, 1992). He recently served as a member of the Iowa Governor's Task Force for Responsible Fatherhood, and is the father of two children.

Library of Congress Cataloging-in-Publication Data

Thompson, Cooper.

White men challenging racism: 35 personal stories

/ by Cooper Thompson, Emmett Schaefer, and Harry Brod;

with a foreword by James W. Loewen.

p. cm.

Includes bibliographical references and index.

ISBN 0-8223-3084-9 (cloth : alk. paper)

ISBN 0-8223-3096-2 (pbk. : alk. paper)

1. White men—United States—Interviews.  2. Civil rights workers—
United States—Interviews.  3. Political activists—United States—
Interviews.  4. United States—Race relations—Anecdotes.  5. United
States—Ethnic relations—Anecdotes.  6. Racism—United States—
Anecdotes.  7. Civil rights movements—United States—Anecdotes.
I. Title: White men challenging racism.  II. Schaefer, Emmett Robert
III. Brod, Harry  IV. Title.

E184.A1 T495 2003

323′.092′3034—dc21    2002014628